CATULLUS AND

A REAPPRAISA

CATULLUS AND HIS WORLD

A REAPPRAISAL

T. P. WISEMAN
Professor of Classics, University of Exeter

CAMBRIDGE
UNIVERSITY PRESS

CAMBRIDGE UNIVERSITY PRESS
Cambridge, New York, Melbourne, Madrid, Cape Town, Singapore, São Paulo

Cambridge University Press
The Edinburgh Building, Cambridge CB2 2RU, UK

Published in the United States of America by Cambridge University Press, New York

www.cambridge.org
Information on this title: www.cambridge.org/9780521266062

First published 1985
Reprinted 1986
First paperback edition 1987
Reprinted 1988, 1990, 1995, 1998, 2000, 2002

A catalogue record for this publication is available from the British Library

Library of Congress catalogue card number: 84–21342

ISBN-13 978-0-521-26606-2 hardback
ISBN-10 0-521-26606-8 hardback

ISBN-13 978-0-521-31968-3 paperback
ISBN-10 0-521-31968-4 paperback

Transferred to digital printing 2005

FOR CHRIS
hoc tibi quod potui

CONTENTS

vii

CONTENTS

PREFACE

The first three chapters of this book do not concern Catullus himself directly. After an introduction to warn the reader that the world of the first century B.C. is more alien than we sometimes think, the high society and political life of the Rome of that time are illustrated through the personalities of Clodia Metelli and M. Caelius Rufus. Traditionally (since 1862), those two individuals have been treated as part of Catullus' own story. I have quite deliberately kept them separate, preferring to emphasise the limits of our knowledge, which those who believe in the traditional view have not always recognised. But I hope that any reader who really *must* identify Clodia Metelli as Catullus' 'Lesbia', and Caelius Rufus as his successful rival for her favours, will be able, without too much mental effort, to make his own synthesis of chapters II, III and V. As the final chapter shows, he will be in good company.

I am very grateful to the University of Exeter for the study leave in 1983–4 during which most of this book was written, and to the British School at Rome for appointing me to the Balsdon Senior Fellowship for 1984 – not least because I hope it is the sort of book Dacre Balsdon himself might have enjoyed. The only part of it that was written earlier is chapter II, a version of which was given at the Classical Association Conference in Exeter in 1981.

Friends in both Rome and Exeter – Nicholas Horsfall, Andrew Lintott, my colleagues Susan and David Braund – have been kind enough to read some or all of the book in typescript. Their comments, and those made at various meetings and seminars in England and Italy where my heresies were tried out, have been very helpful to me. For particular points, besides those debts acknowledged in the notes, I owe thanks also to Nicholas Purcell (on the *carnifices*) and Roland Mayer (on Catullus in the 1930s); if I have used anybody else's ideas without acknowledgement, I apologise for the inadvertence. I must also express my particular gratitude to Professor G. P. Goold, who has generously allowed me to use his splendid translation (Duckworth 1983); all the English versions of Catullus are his, with adaptations, signalled in the footnotes, only where his text differs from the one I have used. (All other unattributed translations are mine.) Finally, I thank those authors and publishers who have allowed me to quote copyright material *in extenso* in chapter VII: William Hull ('In memoriam I: Catullus'); Jack Lindsay (dedication poem to *The Complete Poetry of Gaius Catullus*); David W. T. Vessey ('Lesbia in Orco'); the Thornton Wilder Estate (extracts from *The Ides of March*); Duckworth & Co. Ltd and Viking Penguin Inc. ('From a Letter to Lesbia' in *The Portable Dorothy Parker*, 1973); and Macmillan, London and Basingstoke ('To a Roman' in J. C. Squire, *Collected Poems*, 1959). The illustrations are reproduced by permission of the Deutsches archäologisches Institut, Rome (Plates 1 and 3); Bildarchiv Foto Marburg (Plate 2); and the Bibliothèque Nationale, Paris (Plate 4).

Forty-four is probably a good age to stop writing about Catullus, if not already a bit late. Thirty years ago at Manchester Grammar School, we read selections from Catullus, followed by the *pro Caelio*, under the sternly benevolent eye of R. T. Moore (a splendid teacher, whom all his ex-pupils must remember with affection); the imagination of one callow youth was caught, and that is what made me a classicist. I have been thinking about Catullus, on and off, ever since, and having now managed to do what I wanted to do even then, I feel I have paid a debt.

Exeter   T.P.W.
May 1984

CHAPTER I

A WORLD NOT OURS

I wondered, and I still wonder, what it was like to be there.

KEITH HOPKINS, *Death and Renewal* (1983) 203

I. EVIDENCE AND PRECONCEPTIONS

Of all the Latin poets, Catullus is the one who seems to speak most directly to us. And of all the periods of Roman history, the late Republic, in which he lived, is the one for which we have the best contemporary evidence. So Catullus and his world should be well known and unproblematical, hardly in need of substantial reinterpretation. But that is not the case: the familiar story of the poet's love for the wife of Metellus Celer, and his jealousy of Caelius Rufus, depends on a nineteenth-century reconstruction, learned and ingenious but essentially hypothetical,[1] while matters of more central interest, such as the poet's own background and the nature and circumstances of his literary output, have not been given the attention they deserve. I think we have been too easily satisfied with an illusory Catullus; to get to grips with the real one, we need to look hard at the evidence, and not take anything on trust.

It is true that we are comparatively well informed about the late Republic – but only comparatively. The information we have is very limited, very patchy, and needs careful interpretation. In particular, three common pitfalls in the use of evidence need to be recognised and avoided.

First, the tacit assumption that 'conspicuous' source material is somehow privileged. The works of Cicero and Catullus himself are of fundamental importance for understanding late-Republi-

[1] Schwabe 1862; see p. 217 below for the context.

can Rome, but what they tell us is not the only source of information. There is also what may be inferred from what they do *not* tell us, or allude to only in passing; and there is the humbler and more haphazard testimony of artefacts – coins, inscriptions, works of art – and of the 'fragments' of literary works now lost except for quotations in later authors. All that is just as important, if we can interpret it properly.

For instance, the identification of Piso in Catullus 28 and 47 is hindered rather than helped by concentrating on Cicero's brilliantly malicious portrait of L. Piso Caesoninus in the *in Pisonem*. That Piso was proconsul in Macedonia, Catullus' Piso evidently in Spain. But the glamour of the 'conspicuous source' seems to force the identification of the two, as if there were no other Pisones in Rome. In fact, a coin inscription allows us to infer the existence of a L. Piso Frugi of about the right age, who could well be the proconsul of Spain to whom Catullus refers.[2] Similarly, 'Lesbia' herself is commonly identified with Clodia Metelli rather than either of her sisters (despite the chronological problems involved) because her notoriety is more conspicuous for us than that of Clodia Luculli; but if, instead of Cicero's speech in defence of Caelius, we happened to possess the text of L. Lentulus' speech prosecuting Clodius in 61 B.C., precisely the reverse would be the case.[3]

This fallacy also has its effect on a grander scale. Much of what we know about the late Republic is about politics. That is inevitable, given the nature of our main sources. Politics was a subject of absorbing interest, at one particular social level. But it was not the only one, and for most of the population of Rome probably not the most interesting. What mainly obsessed the populace at large was *ludi*, entertainments – plays and shows in the theatre, chariot-racing and wild-beast hunts in the Circus, gladiators in the Forum. These things did not interest Cicero,

[2] Wiseman 1969, 38–40, *JRS* 69 (1979) 162f; Crawford 1974, 435 (C. Piso L. f. Frugi, implying an elder brother L.).
[3] Cic. *Mil.* 73, Plut. *Caes.* 10.5, *Cic.* 29.3f; Wiseman 1969, 52–5. Lentulus: Cic. *har. resp.* 37, Val. Max. IV 2.5, Schol. Bob. 85 and 89 St.

who mentions them only dismissively,[4] and for that reason, among others, the picture of late-Republican society that we see through his eyes is an untypical one. Suppose that instead of Caesar's *Commentaries* and the letters of Cicero, what had survived was Varro's *Menippean Satires* and the plays of Laberius.[5] We should have a very different picture in that case – and perhaps one which would be more helpful for understanding Catullus and the literary life of his time. We shall find, in fact, that theatrical shows and performances are relevant to Catullus and his world in various unexpected ways.

The second pitfall to be avoided is a chronological one – the assumption that everything changed with the end of the Republic. In political terms, of course, the existence of the *princeps* made a fundamental difference; for social history, however, the transition from Republic to Principate is much less significant. From the late second century B.C. to the late first century A.D. – that is, in the last two generations of the Republic and the first two of the Principate – there is a recognisable continuity in the *mores* of the Roman élite. The 'Julio-Claudians' were actually Iulii Caesares and Claudii Nerones, wealthy aristocrats who behaved as such; the only difference their 'imperial' status made was in the scale of resources they could deploy on what wealthy aristocrats liked to do. Their lifestyle was formed by the hellenisation of Roman society in the second century B.C., the results of which could be seen equally in the luxury and sophistication of their pleasures and in the respect – whether genuine or assumed – they paid to literary culture and the arts.[6]

[4] E.g. Cic. *Mur.* 38–40 ('populum ac vulgus imperitorum ludis magno opere delectari'), *fam.* II 8.1 (Cicero doesn't want to hear about *gladiatorum compositiones*); of the two passages where he discusses *ludi* at length, *Sest.* 115–27 is forensic special pleading (cf. the apology to the *iudices* at 115), and *fam.* VII 1 the response to a request by his correspondent.

[5] For the importance of drama (of various types) in Varro's *Satires*, see frr. 304B ('hic modus scaenatilis'), 348–69B (Ὄνος λύρας), and references passim to comedy, tragedy, music and dance.

[6] See now A. Wallace-Hadrill, *Suetonius* (London 1983) 186–8, cf. 156, 169, 178f, 181f. On the tastes and pleasures of the hellenised élite, see for instance Griffin 1976; A. F. Stewart, *JRS* 67 (1977) 76–90, esp. 78f; Lyne 1980, 8–17 and 192–8.

Here too we may be misled by the accident of what evidence survives. The 'Ciceronian' age would look very different through the eyes of Petronius or Martial. And just as Juvenal's sneer about bread and circuses would apply in much the same way to the Roman populace of the first century B.C., so too the glimpses we get from Suetonius of the tastes and habits of the early emperors can be used, with due caution, to illustrate the tastes and habits of the late-Republican aristocracy.[7] We learn an enormous amount from Cicero, but it is no use asking him for an authentic insight into the pleasures of the patrician Claudii. Yet that is what we need, if we are to understand an important part of Catullus' experience.

The third pitfall is the most important, and the most insidious. Because we find some parts of the late-Republican scene immediately intelligible and accessible (notably Cicero in his letters, Catullus in his love poems), it is easy to treat their world as if it were in general familiar to us, and to assume that their values were essentially similar to our own. I think we shall get closer to understanding the ancient world if we make the opposite assumption, always looking for, and trying to come to terms with, the alien and the unfamiliar. That is particularly important for Catullus: if his sentiments are indeed easily recognisable to us, that in itself may be something striking and unusual.

Studying ancient Rome should be like visiting some teeming capital in a dangerous and ill-governed foreign country; nothing can be relied on, most of what you see is squalid, sinister or unintelligible, and you are disproportionately grateful when you find something you can recognise as familiar.[8] Two particular examples of alien values are worth looking at in detail; and since they involve (in the clichés of our time) gratuitous

[7] As a crude example, compare Suet. *Gaius* 24.1 with Cic. *Sest.* 16, *har. resp.* 59, etc.: whether the allegations of incest were true or slanderous (and I see no reason to disbelieve them *a priori*), P. Clodius Pulcher and C. Caesar Augustus Germanicus were two of a kind – arrogant young patricians who did what they fancied.

[8] It was, after all, a city where a dog might pick up a human hand in the street (Suet. *Vesp.* 5.4).

violence and explicit sex, the rest of this chapter is not for the
squeamish.

2. CRUELTY

Catullus was a good hater. Those who offended him would
suffer for it – and the imagery of their suffering is vivid and
brutal. Aurelius will have radishes and mullets forced into his
fundament; Thallus will be branded with the stripes of the lash,
and writhe like a small boat in a rough sea; Cominius will be
lynched by the mob, his tongue and eyes torn out as food for
carrion birds.[9] What lies behind these sadistic imaginings is the
Roman idea of punishment, for that is what Catullus wants to
exact.[10]

It is striking that throughout Roman literature, from Plautus
to Prudentius, we find instruments of torture referred to as
something familiar.

> Verbera carnifices robur pix lammina taedae . . .

> Scourgings, executioners, the rack, pitch, the metal plate, torches . . .

Lucretius' list of the punishments of crime – which make men
think they will be tortured in the afterlife – can be paralleled in
many other authors, referring either to slaves or to condemned
prisoners or to the victims of tyranny.[11] From these passages a
grim typology may be drawn up, of floggings, rackings and
burnings.

The lash (*flagellum*) was more than just a whip; it was designed
to make deep wounds, so the thongs were armed with metal, like

---

[9] Cat. 15.18f, 25.10–14, 108; also 37.10, branding (cf. Sen. *de ira* III 3.6, Macr. *Sat.* I 11.19, Quint. VII 4.12); 97.10, put to the mill (cf. Cic. *de or.* I 46, Plaut. *Bacch.* 781, *Epid.* 121).

[10] Cat. 40.8 *longa poena* (cf. Plaut. *Mil.* 502f, Cyprian *de lapsis* 13), 116.8 *supplicium* (cf. pp. 198f below: crucifixion?). For all this section, see also the first chapter of Hopkins 1983, on the 'murderous games'.

[11] Lucr. III 1017 (trans. C. Bailey), cf. Ovid *Ibis* 183–8 for the Furies in Hades; Plaut. *Asin.* 548f, Cic. *Verr.* V 14, 163, Sen. *contr.* II 5.5–6, Val. Max. VI 8.1, Sen. *de ira* III 3.6, 19.1, *ep.* 14.5, 78.19, Cyprian *de lapsis* 13, Prudent. *Perist.* 5.61f, etc.

a goad or spur.[12] The victim could be hung up to receive it, his feet weighted, or made to stand with his outstretched arms fastened to a beam across his shoulders.[13] The 'little horse' (*eculeus*) and the 'lyre-strings' (*fidiculae*) were forms of rack, apparently vertical rather than horizontal but with the same purpose of disjointing the limbs;[14] painful distortion could also be achieved by confining the victim in a yoke for neck and feet (that was probably what Catullus had in mind for Aurelius).[15] As for burning, Lucretius' *pix lammina taedae* sums it up: boiling pitch, plates of red-hot metal, or simply flaming torches applied directly to the body.[16]

It is important to remember that all these things happened in public. The horrors that modern police states practise in secret cells were carried out openly, as an exemplary warning or a public entertainment. Rome was a city with a huge slave population; 'only by fear can you keep such scum under control'. So slaves were punished with the maximum publicity – flogged through the streets, or in the public *atrium* of the house, with the

[12] Hor. *Sat.* I 3.119 (distinguishing it from the *scutica*, a simple thong), Juv. VI 479; Plaut. *Most.* 56f, *Men.* 951, *Curc.* 131 (*fodere* or *forare stimulis*); Prudent. *Perist.* 10, 116f, 122 (loaded); Eusebius *HE* III 8.9, IV 15.4, VIII 6.3 etc (to the bone).

[13] *Pendens*: Plaut. *Asin.* 301–5 (weights), *Men.* 951, *Most.* 1167 etc.; Prop. IV 7.45 (by the hair); cf. Eusebius *HE* VIII 6.2, 10.5. *Patibulum*: Plaut. *Most.* 56f, *Mil.* 360, Dion. Hal. VII 69.2 (Val. Max. I 7.4 *sub furca*).

[14] *Eculeus*: Cic. *Mil.* 57, *Deiot.* 3, *de fin.* V 84, Sen. *contr.* IX 6.18, Sen. *ep.* 67.3, etc.; Prudent. *Perist.* 10.109f (*pendere*). *Fidiculae*: Quint. *decl.* 19.12, Isid. *Orig.* V 27.20, etc.; Sen. *Cons. Marc.* 20.3 (aggravated form of crucifixion?). *Talaria* (Sen. *ep.* 53.6, *de ira* III 19.1) were probably another variant.

[15] Non. 210L (*numellae*, wooden); Festus 162L, Plaut. *Curc.* 689f (*nervus*, metal); Cat. 15.18 ('attractis pedibus patente porta'); cf. also Festus (Paulus) 32L, Plaut. *Asin.* 549, Isid. *Orig.* V 27.12 (*boiae*, wooden or metal, details unknown). Eusebius refers to extendable stocks, similarly on the borderline between restraint and torture (*HE* V 1.27, VI 39.5, VIII 10.8).

[16] Cic. *Verr.* V 163, Val. Max. VI 8.1, Sen. *ep.* 78.19, Eusebius *HE* VI 1.21, etc. Variations: Prop. IV 7.38 (hot brick), *AE* 1971 88.II.12 (wax, candles), Prudent. *Perist.* 229f (hot fat), Eusebius *HE* VIII 12.6 (boiling lead). For the torch used in conjunction with flogging and pincers (cf. the *ungulae* so prominent in the Christian martyr-stories), see the Beldame Painter's playful satyrs: C. H. E. Haspels, *Attic Black-Figured Lekythoi* (Paris 1936) 170, plates 49–51.

doors open.[17] Judicial torture was also done in public: at the entrance to the Subura the bloody scourges hung ready for use, and any passer-by in the Forum might see, and hear, the dreadful *carnifices* in their red caps (to mark them out as men beyond the pale) inflicting agony on some criminal before his execution.[18] It was a spectacle to enjoy: the populace could 'feast their eyes and satisfy their souls' at the torture and death of a notorious malefactor. The fate of Vitellius gives us an idea of the scene:[19]

. . . having his hands pinioned fast at his back, a halter cast about his neck, and his apparel torn from his body, he was haled half-naked into the Forum. Among many scornful indignities offered unto him both in deed and word throughout the spacious street Sacra Via from one end to the other, whiles they drew his head backward by the bush of his hair (as condemned malefactors are wont to be served) and set a sword's point under his chin, and all to the end he might show his face and not hold it down, whiles some pelted him with dung and dirty mire, others called him with open mouth incendiary and patinarium [glutton], and some of the common sort twitted him also with faults and deformities of his body . . . At the last upon the stairs Gemoniae with many a small stroke all to-mangled he was and killed in the end, and so from thence drawn with a drag into the river Tiber.

The corpse might be maltreated (as Catullus imagines for Cominius) before the executioner's hook dragged it off amid the applause of the crowd.[20] The main work of the *carnifices* was 'outside the gate', for they were employed by funeral contractors for the burial or cremation of the dead. Just to the left as you emerged from the Esquiline Gate on the road to Tibur there was a noisome area, part

---

[17] Plaut. *Most.* 56 (*per vias*), Suet. *Aug.* 45.4 (*atrium*, also *per trina theatra*); Livy II 36.1, Dion. Hal. VII 69.1, Val. Max. I 7.4 (*medio circo*, Forum etc.). Quotation from Tac. *Ann.* XIV 44.5 (C. Cassius' speech).

[18] Mart. II 17.2 (Subura); *AE* 1971 88.II.3–14 (*carnifices*); Cic. *Verr.* V 163 (*in foro*, Messana), Prudent. *Perist.* 10.709 (*corona plebium*, Antioch). Public torture for evidence or a confession was normal in the late Empire (*JRS* 72 (1982) 105, an everyday sight for a schoolboy), but probably not in the first century B.C. (Cic. *Mil.* 60, slaves evidently not tortured in public).

[19] Suet. *Vit.* 17 (translation by Philemon Holland, 1606); quotation from Cic. *Verr.* V 65.

[20] E.g. Dio LVIII 11.5 (Sejanus); Ovid *Ibis* 165 (*populo plaudente*); Cat. 108 (*populi arbitrio*).

cemetery, part rubbish tip, where official notices vainly tried to limit the dumping of dung and carrion.[21] There they plied both parts of their trade; it was where the stake was unfastened from the shoulders of the beaten slave to be set upright for his crucifixion – or even more horribly, for his impalement – and where they flogged him at a charge to his master of 4 sesterces for the whole operation.[22]

Naturally, free citizens could not be treated in this way; but how strong was the protection of the law? The Roman citizen who witnessed the agony of slaves or criminals could imagine it inflicted on himself, and sometimes his fears came true. The emperors could torture whomever they liked ('let him feel he's dying', said Caligula), for there was no one who could invoke the law against them. In the Republic, the same applied in the provinces under a brutal governor, or anywhere, if one fell into the hands of a sufficiently powerful enemy.[23]

The law connived at summary vengeance exacted by the injured party (most notoriously on adulterers, who if caught in the act might be flogged, raped or even castrated), and this concession could all too easily be extended to the indulgence of private pique. A passing rustic makes an untimely joke? A humble neighbour's dog keeps you awake? Out with the whips, and have the culprit beaten – if he dies, too bad.[24] In a city without a police force, where self-help was basic to the operation of the law, the humble citizen needed a powerful friend for his

21 *CIL* VI 31577, 31615 (cf. also 31614 from outside the Porta Viminalis); Varro *LL* V 25, Festus 240–1L (rotting corpses); Hor. *Sat.* I 8.8–13 (whitened bones); R. Lanciani, *Ancient Rome in the Light of Recent Discoveries* (London 1888) 64–7; M. Albertoni, in *L'archeologia in Roma capitale tra sterro e scavo* (Venice 1983) 148f. *Extra portam*: Plaut. *Mil.* 359f (slave punishment), *Cas.* 354 (cremation), Festus 240L (*puticuli*).
22 *AE* 1971 88 and 89 (88.II.10 for the 4 *HS*). Impalement: Sen. *ep.* 101.11f, *Cons. Marc.* 20.3, Dio XLIX 12.5, etc.
23 Emperors: e.g. Suet. *Gaius* 27–33 (quotation from 30.1); P. A. Brunt, *ZSS* 97 (1980) 259f. Provincial governors: e.g. Cic. *Verr.* V 163f, *fam.* X 32.3. Private *inimicitiae*: Sall. *Hist.* I 44M, whence Val. Max. IX 2.1, Sen. *de ira* III 18.1 etc. (Sulla and M. Marius); Cic. *Phil.* XI 5–7 (Dolabella and Trebonius); Plut. *Cic.* 49.2 (Pomponia and Q. Tullius Philologus).
24 C. Gracchus *ap.* Gell. *NA* X 3.5, Juv. VI 413–18. *Deprensus adulter*: Ter. *Eun.* 955–7, Hor. *Sat.* I 2.41–6, Val. Max. VI 1.13, Juv. X 316f.

protection, and the great men of the time went about with armed escorts as a matter of course.[25] When Clodius and his men attacked him on the Sacra Via in November 57, Cicero was well equipped to resist; his escort, he says, could have killed Clodius, which clearly implies that the cudgels and swords were not all on one side.[26]

These violent scenes were the result of a value system that regarded honour (*fama, dignitas, existimatio*) as the supreme good, and pursued it competitively in feuds that could be savagely brutal. The inscription on Sulla's tomb in the Campus Martius boasted that no friend excelled him in doing good, no enemy in doing harm – and that harm included the most horrific physical torture.[27] If your enemy's honour required your total humiliation, you had better keep out of his way. The danger was real: Cicero would not risk going to Octavian to beg for mercy in 43, in case he should be tortured. When an Augustan rhetorician imagined a client of Clodius carrying out the triumvirs' sentence by torturing Cicero to death, that reflected a real situation; long after his enemy was dead, Cicero would not use the Via Aurelia that led past Clodius' estates.[28]

No doubt it was not yet as bad in the late Republic as it was for Seneca, who dwelt on the awful apparatus of the *carnifex* as one of the hazards of public life.[29] The political change had made that difference. But the novelty was not the cruelty itself, only the emperors' total freedom to indulge it.[30] The state of mind that

[25] Cic. *Mil.* 10 ('quid comitatus nostri, quid gladii volunt?'); late-Republican examples collected in Lintott 1968, 83–5. Self-help: Kelly 1966, esp. the first three chapters; Lintott 1968, 22–34. The *locus classicus* for the poor man's defencelessness is Juv. III 278–301.

[26] Cic. *Att.* IV 3.3: 'clamor, lapides, fustes, gladii . . . Qui erant mecum facile operas aditu prohibuerunt. Ipse occidi potuit.'

[27] Plut. *Sulla* 38.4; see n. 23 above for his treatment of M. Marius Gratidianus.

[28] Plut. *Cic.* 47.4, Sen. *contr.* VII 2.13 (Varius Geminus), Cic. *Phil.* XII 23f. L. Cestius Pius evidently dwelt with pleasure on the 'contumeliae insultantium Ciceroni et verbera et tormenta' (Sen. *suas.* 6.10, cf. 7.12f for his grudge).

[29] E.g. Sen. *ep.* 14.4–6, *de ira* III 19f.

[30] The invention of *tormenta* and other punishments was attributed to the archetypal tyrant Tarquinius Superbus: see Mommsen *Chronica Minora* I 145 (the 'Chronographer of A.D. 354'), Eusebius *Chron.* II 96 Schoene (ann. Abr. 1470), Isid. *Orig.* V 27.23,

made them want to do so was already a familiar part of the world of Catullus.

3. SEXUAL *MORES*

The question 'Was Catullus homosexual?' could not have been asked by his contemporaries, because their terminology – and therefore also, we assume, their conceptual framework – was quite different from that of the twentieth century. The words 'homosexual' and 'heterosexual' were unknown even in the English language before Krafft-Ebing and Havelock Ellis; their etymology is 'barbarously hybrid', as Ellis himself observed in 1897, and the concepts they express are neither Greek nor Roman.[31] The ancients evidently did not find it helpful to categorise sexual activity according to the sex of the person with whom it is performed. What mattered to them was the question of active or passive, of penetrating or being penetrated.

That distinction is basic to the understanding of Roman sexual vocabulary and sexual *mores*. The Latin verbs for sexual intercourse vary according to the three possible modes of penetration – *futuere* (vaginal), *pedicare* (anal), *irrumare* (oral). All three verbs are active, both grammatically and conceptually; their passive forms, of course, refer to being penetrated in each of those ways, and may be subsumed under the general phrase *muliebria pati*, roughly 'to submit to the woman's role'.[32] However, *irrumari* (passive) had a grammatically active metaphorical synonym, *fellare* ('to suck', properly of an infant at the breast), perhaps because that mode of intercourse seemed to require a greater degree of participation by the 'passive' partner.[33]

It was A. E. Housman who observed, in the elegant Latin he employed to discuss these matters, that those brought up in the

Lydus *de mens.* IV. 29, Suda s.v. Σούπερβος; Suetonius' *de regibus* (Auson. *ep.* 23, p. 267 Peiper) is a likely source.
[31] *OED* Supplement (1933) 460, 473, quoting Ellis' *Studies in the Psychology of Sex.*
[32] Sall. *Cat.* 13.3, Tac. *Ann.* XI 36.5, Petr. *Sat.* 9.6, Ulp. *Dig.* III 1.1.6.
[33] See Adams 1982, 130–4 on *fellare.*

Judaeo-Christian tradition do not find it easy to grasp the distinction that mattered crucially to the Romans, between the act of *pedicatio* or *irrumatio*, which was not in itself disgraceful, and submission to either form, which certainly was.[34] That is, a male who willingly allowed penetration by another was treated with contempt, and one who was compelled to allow it was thereby humiliated. But the penetrator himself was neither demeaned nor disgraced; on the contrary, he had demonstrated his superiority and his masculinity by making another serve his pleasure.

The question of degradation was most acute where the oral mode was involved; thus *fellator* – or *fellatrix*, of a woman – was the most contemptuous of insults, and *irrumare* came to have also the more general meaning of 'to get the better of someone regardless of his wishes'.[35] That is what Catullus means when he calls Memmius an *irrumator*: he is not literally complimenting him on his virility, but complaining about the thoroughness with which he cheated his staff (it was a very obscene way of saying it, which Catullus emphasised by his vivid development of the imagery).[36] But when he threatens Aurelius and Furius with *pedicatio* and *irrumatio* for imputing effeminacy to him (on the strength of the kiss poems), or Aurelius alone with *irrumatio* for making passes at a boy Catullus feels responsible for, he probably means it in the literal sense.

Sexual assault as a punishment was a familiar idea to the Romans; if you were caught on another man's property, or with his wife, it might well feature – at his hands or those of his slaves – among the summary vengeance he could inflict.[37] As with

[34] Housman 1931, 408 n.1 = *Classical Papers* (Cambridge 1972)III 1180 n.2: 'Scilicet non facile qui Pauli Tarsensis et Iudaeorum norma uti a pueris adsueverunt opinionem mentibus comprehendunt quae, ut Catullo et Martiali, ita nunc cuivis de plebe Siciliensi vel Neapolitana penitus a natura insita est, obscaenos fellatores et cinaedos, pedicones et irrumatores non obscaenos esse.'

[35] Baehrens 1885, 117; Housman 1931, 408f; Adams 1982, 129f; *TLL* VII 2.444.

[36] Cat. 10.12f, 28.9–13; Adams 1982, 130. Cf. Suet. *Jul.* 22.2 for the same play of metaphor (*insultare capitibus*).

[37] Trespassers: *Priapea* passim, esp. 52.6–8 (slaves), 56.5f (master). Adultery: Val. Max. VI 1.13 (slaves), Apul. *Met.* IX 28 (master), Hor. *Sat.* I 2.133 (cf. n.24 above).

flogging, so with rape – the 'legitimate' chastisement of a male-factor caught red-handed, who had thereby put himself into the power of the offended party, merged imperceptibly into private vengeance, a way for affronted dignity to get its own back or teach the insolent a lesson.[38] Again, the danger could be real: in a society with little effective control of casual violence, an aggrieved enemy and his clients might be as hard to resist as a gang of randy youths.[39]

The purpose of the exercise was humiliation, to express dominance and treat the victim like a slave (here too the parallel with corporal punishment is close). To submit to another's sexual demands was a disgrace in a freeborn citizen, but a slave had no choice in the matter, and even a freedman might find that obliging his ex-master in this way was one of his residual duties.[40]

That tripartite formulation – shame for the freeborn, necessity for the slave, duty for the freedman – was coined by an Augustan orator defending a freedman. But the epigram backfired:[41]

Res in iocos abiit: 'non facis mihi officium', et 'multum ille huic in officiis versatur'. Ex eo inpudici et obsceni aliquamdiu officiosi vocitati sunt.

The idea became a handle for jokes, like 'you aren't doing your duty by me' and 'he gets in a lot of duty for him'. As a result the unchaste and obscene got called 'dutiful' for some while afterwards.

The jokes warn us not to be too schematic. There is often a dissonance between the generally accepted values of a society, and what every one knows actually goes on. The 'unchaste and

---

38 E.g. Sen. *suas.* 7.13 (*flagra*), Cic. *Cael.* 71 (*stuprum*); cf. Diod. Sic. XVI 93.3–7 (Attalus' vengeance on Pausanias).

39 For *iuvenes petulantes*, see for instance Cic. *Planc.* 30 (mime-actress), Fest. 439L (boys and girls at fountain), Alciphron III 37 (young widow).

40 See Treggiari 1969, 68–81 on freedmen's duties in general. Slaves: Hor. *Sat.* 12.115–18, Petr. *Sat.* 75.11, etc.

41 Q. Haterius *ap.* Sen. *contr.* IV pref. 10 ('impudicitia in ingenuo crimen est, in servo necessitas, in liberto officium'); translation by M. Winterbottom.

obscene' might be persons of rank and fashion, who just enjoyed the passive role; the hellenisation of Roman society in the late Republic afforded them plenty of scope for their preferences, even if the traditional morality of Rome continued to condemn them.[42] So Catullus can abuse his enemies as *pathici* and *cinaedi*, but in another mood he and Calvus can play at being *delicati*, which means the same without the pejorative overtones.[43] The Juventius poems betray a similar ambiguity: Catullus pretends that his readers will shrink from touching them, but he clearly expects them to go on reading.[44]

Apologies to the reader can be revealing. Those in Martial's epigrams, for instance, show firstly that respectable women were not supposed to read poems on explicitly erotic themes, and secondly that they would if they got the chance. He uses the image of a well brought up girl putting her hand to her eyes as she passes Priapus' ithyphallic statue in the garden – but looking all the same.[45] Martial justifies his material by comparing it with the performances everyone saw in the theatre; women certainly enjoyed the mimes, licentious scenes and all, and according to the sardonic Juvenal sighed and squealed at the star pantomime-dancers as if in an erotic climax.[46] For his 'Saturnalia' book (XI), where the obscenities are most frequent, Martial openly admits his aim to be erotically stimulating, like a belly-dancer from Gades. What is interesting is that he hopes to excite female readers as well as males; in fact the girls from Gades performed

---

[42] See MacMullen 1982 on 'Greek love' and Roman attitudes to it. *Impudici* who affected an old-fashioned guise were a favourite target of satirists: Mart. II 36.5f, XII 42.1, Juv. II 11–13, 41.

[43] *Pathicus:* 16.2 (Aurelius), 57.2 (Caesar), 112.2 (Naso). *Cinaedus:* 16.2 (Furius), 25.1 (Thallus), 29.5 and 9 (Pompey?), 33.2 (Vibennius *filius*), 57.1 and 10 (Caesar and Mamurra). 'Ut convenerat esse delicatos': 50.3, cf. *TLL* v 444f.

[44] Cat. 14b; Wiseman 1969, 7. I assume that what they are expected to be shocked at is the citizen – and aristocratic – status of Juventius (cf. pp. 130f below).

[45] Mart. III 68, 86, XI 16.9f. Priapus: III 68.9f, cf. *Priapea* 66.1f.

[46] Mart. I pref., 4.5f, 35.8f, VIII pref. (*mimica licentia*); II 41.15–18, III 86.3f, Juv. VI 63–5.

not only for male audiences but in the presence of women too, though naturally it was not the women they aimed to arouse.[47]

Cultured Rome was full of erotic images, from Priapus' grotesque erection in the ornamental garden[48] to old-master paintings of mythological copulation on the walls inside.[49] Out in the streets, prostitutes plied for hire practically naked,[50] and every April at the Floralia the girls who played the mimes were stripped for the audience's enjoyment, to a flourish of trumpets.[51] Of course old-fashioned moralists disapproved, but what they had to shut their eyes to was ubiquitous at every level of society.

What makes one person blush may make another laugh. The world of Catullus was made up of individuals, and there is a limit to how far one can generalise about it. Male or female, slave or free, rich or poor, straight-laced or luxurious, cultured or ignorant – the permutations of those categories and others naturally resulted in a kaleidoscopic variety of values and attitudes. It is time to consider two or three of those individuals, in so far as we can get to know them. This introductory chapter has been merely a reminder not to imagine them in too familiar a world.

[47] Mart. XI 16.5–8; for *uda* in line 8, cf. Juv. X 318. Saturnalia: XI 2.5, 15.12. *Gaditanae*: XI 16.4, cf. V 78.26–8, VI 71.1f, XIV 203, Juv. XI 162–76 (wives watching at line 165), *Priapea* 27.
[48] Cf. *Priapea* 47, evidently an outdoor triclinium (cf. Varro *RR* III 13.2).
[49] Cf. Suet. *Tib.* 44.2, Parrhasius' painting 'in qua Meleagro Atalanta ore morigeratur'; no doubt she obliged him in this way (a very special favour, cf. Mart. IX 40) because he gave her the spoils of the Calydonian hunt (Ovid *Met.* VIII 425ff).
[50] Prop. II 22.8; Ovid *Trist.* II 309–12, Tac. *Ann.* XV 37.3; cf. Cat. 55.11f, an unsolicited display.
[51] Val. Max. II 10.8, Sen. *ep.* 97.8; cf. Mart. I pref., 35.8f etc. Trumpets: Juv. VI 250, cf. Pliny *ep.* II 7.1.

CHAPTER II

CLODIA: PLEASURE AND SWAY

In Men, we various Ruling Passions find,
In Women, two almost divide the kind;
Those, only fix'd, they first or last obey,
The Love of Pleasure, or the Love of Sway.

ALEXANDER POPE, *Epistle to a Lady:*
Of the Characters of Women (1735) 207–10

1. *MULIER NOBILIS*

In *I, Claudius* Robert Graves imagined a secret autobiography written by the emperor. If only we had an *I, Clodia* like that! The trouble with Clodia Metelli is that we see her only through the eyes of the man who detested her, and whose purpose in the speech for Caelius was deliberately to blacken her character so that the jury would not believe her evidence.[1] A proper first-hand account of her would indeed require the imagination of a novelist. In fact, several fictional portraits of her have been attempted, all more or less unsuccessful; despite the conspicuous excellence of women in this branch of fiction, the authors have all been men.[2] I have no intention of competing with them. But I shall try as far as possible to look at Clodia in her own terms, using the evidence of Cicero with the greatest circumspection.

Mulier nobilis, he calls her,[3] and it is from her nobility that we must start. Six generations of consuls back to Ap. Claudius Caecus, and another six before that to the first known Appius

---

[1] Cic. *Att.* II 1.5 ('sed ego illam odi'); *Cael.* 47–50, cf. 1, 38, 57 (pp. 85f below).
[2] See Wiseman 1975, and chapter VII below.
[3] Cic. *Cael.* 31, 36; cf. 33f on her family ('amplissimum genus'), 68 on her *cognati* ('nobilissimi et clarissimi').

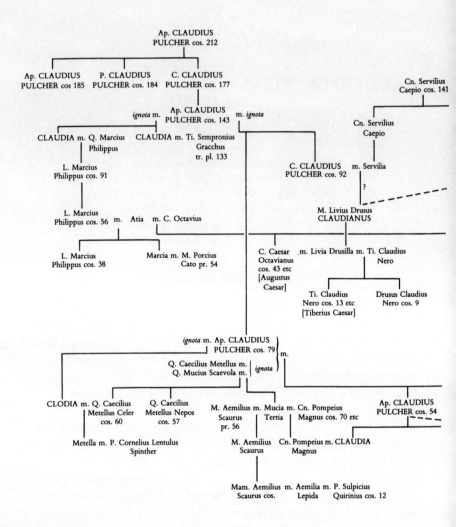

FIGURE I

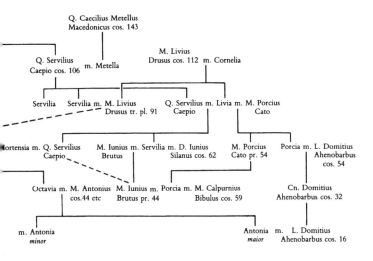

Q. Caecilius Metellus
Macedonicus cos. 143

Q. Servilius
Caepio cos. 106 m. Metella

M. Livius
Drusus cos. 112 m. Cornelia

Servilia Servilia m. M. Livius   Q. Servilius m. Livia m. M. Porcius
                  Drusus tr. pl. 91   Caepio   Cato

Hortensia m. Q. Servilius   M. Iunius m. Servilia m. D. Iunius   M. Porcius   Porcia m. L. Domitius
              Caepio   Brutus   Silanus cos. 62   Cato pr. 54   Ahenobarbus
                                                                                          cos. 54

Octavia m. M. Antonius M. Iunius m. Porcia m. M. Calpurnius   Cn. Domitius
          cos.44 etc   Brutus pr. 44   Bibulus cos. 59   Ahenobarbus cos. 32

m. Antonia   Antonia m. L. Domitius
minor   maior   Ahenobarbus cos. 16

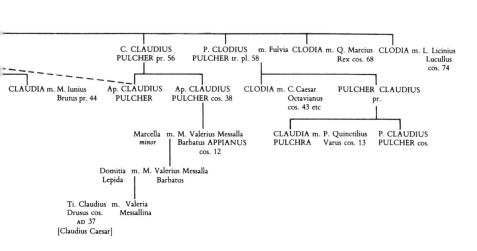

                  C. CLAUDIUS   P. CLODIUS   m. Fulvia CLODIA m. Q. Marcius CLODIA m. L. Licinius
                  PULCHER pr. 56   PULCHER tr. pl. 58   Rex cos. 68   Lucullus
                                                                                             cos. 74

CLAUDIA m. M. Iunius   Ap. CLAUDIUS   Ap. CLAUDIUS   CLODIA m. C.Caesar   PULCHER CLAUDIUS
          Brutus pr. 44 PULCHER   PULCHER cos. 38   Octavianus   pr.
                                                                cos. 43 etc

                       Marcella m. M. Valerius Messalla   CLAUDIA m. P. Quinctilius P. CLAUDIUS
                       minor | Barbatus APPIANUS   PULCHRA   Varus cos. 13   PULCHER cos.
                                  cos. 12

               Domitia m. M. Valerius Messalla
               Lepida | Barbatus

   Ti. Claudius m. Valeria
   Drusus cos.   Messallina
   AD 37
   [Claudius Caesar]

17

Claudius, consul in the fifteenth year of the Republic – her father's *atrium* must have been crowded like a museum with the portrait busts of consuls, censors, dictators and *triumphatores*. And beside the 'vertical' stemma of the great *maiores* there were also the 'horizontal' affinities that the patrician Claudii, like any other noble house, established with their peers. Since recent prosopographical research has revolutionised our knowledge of the Claudii and their *adfines*, it may be helpful to offer a diagram – inevitably speculative in places – illustrating the remarkable ramifications of Clodia's relatives (Fig. 1).

The main credit must go to Professor Shackleton Bailey, who in two misleadingly modest pages established the probable nature of the relationship between Clodia, her brothers and sisters, the Metelli Celer and Nepos, and Mucia.[4] Professor Sumner attached the Claudii to the Servilii, through Clodia's uncle (a powerful personage of whom we know too little),[5] and thus brought in the great complex of relationships established by Münzer and made familiar to English readers by the 'kinsmen of Cato' stemma in Syme's *Roman Revolution*.[6] My own contribution has been an attempt to sort out the Claudii of the triumviral, Augustan and Tiberian periods.[7]

Complex as it is, the stemma could easily have been extended. At several points it overlaps with two much more familiar family

---

[4] Shackleton Bailey 1977, 148–50, expanding on – and correcting – my note in *CQ* 21 (1971) 180–2. However, Dr T. W. Hillard points out to me that a different reconstruction would equally account for the data, if the father of Celer and Nepos had been by birth a Claudius – brother of Gaius *cos*. 92 and Appius *cos*. 79 – subsequently adopted as a Metellus.

[5] Sumner 1973, 162f on 'Cn. Caepio Serviliae Claudi pater' at Cic. *Att*. XII 22.2; for C. Claudius *cos*. 92 see especially Cic. *Brut*. 166 ('propter summam nobilitatem et singularem potentiam magnus erat'), *Verr*. IV 133 ('potentissimus homo').

[6] See Münzer 1920, 328–47, Syme 1939, stemma II; cf. Wiseman 1974, 181–7 on the Caepiones and the Metelli; I am not convinced by J. Geiger's reconstruction in *Ancient Society* 4 (1973), 143–56.

[7] Wiseman 1970; on pp. 219f, add the evidence of *PCol* 4701.6 (Augustus' funeral oration for Agrippa), which shows that in 13 B.C. Quinctilius Varus was still married to the daughter of Agrippa; his marriage to Claudia Pulchra took place before A.D. 2 (L. Koenen, *ZPE* 5 (1970) 266).

trees, those of the Metelli[8] and of the Julii and Claudii Nerones.[9] We should never forget that scholars draw up stemmata by using a *selection* of the available evidence. The neatness and comparative unity of the Metellan and Julio–Claudian family trees should not deceive us: their limits are essentially artificial, imposed to illustrate a particular historical point. The point I want to make is precisely the *absence* of realistic boundaries, the number and variety of families with whom the Claudii were connected. In particular, the danger of making stemmata look too self-contained is that they then give rise to loose talk about 'family groups' and 'factions'. There are no political conclusions to be drawn from this diagram. Clodia herself exemplifies the point perfectly. We might, in the absence of other evidence, be tempted to interpret her marriage as forming a political bond between her family and the Metelli; but Cicero's correspondence reveals her 'waging civil war' with her husband over Clodius' attempt to transfer himself to the *plebs*, which Metellus Celer was persistently opposing.[10] She was on Clodius' side: when the chips are down, it's the success of your *own* family that matters.

It is infuriating that we do not know the identity of Clodia's mother, nor of her stepmother, the thrice-married lady whose eight children included three consuls, P. Clodius, and the wives of Pompey and Lucullus. Ten years ago I thought I knew who Mucia's mother was, but Shackleton Bailey has made me think again.[11] One thing we *can* say: it is very likely that she was

---

[8] Cf. Syme 1939, stemma I; revised and extended version in Wiseman 1974, 182f, where the sister and suggested wife of Q. Metellus Celer *tr.pl.* 90 should be deleted as a result of Shackleton Bailey's arguments.

[9] Cf. Syme 1939, stemma III; see now B. Levick, *Tiberius the Politician* (London 1976) stemmata A, B. and C.

[10] Cic. *Att.* II 1.4–5, *Cael.* 60 (but cf. *Att.* I 18.5).

[11] *CQ* 21 (1971) 182: one of the daughters of Q. Caepio *cos.* 106? Shackleton Bailey (1977, 149) politely regards it as still possible, but I don't think it is: if Servilia Q.f. was married to Ap. Claudius, as his reconstruction would require, and Servilia Cn.f. was married to C. Claudius (n.5 above), Cicero's description of the latter lady as 'Servilia Claudi' would be impossibly ambiguous. However, this objection does not apply if Dr Hillard is right (n.4 above).

closely related to Cato.[12] What the stemma demonstrates above all is the closeness of Ap. Claudius and his children to many of the most powerful and influential Romans of the first century B.C., from Livius Drusus through Lucullus and Pompey to Cato, Brutus and Octavian. No less important, though it is not registered on the stemma, was the proximity of Sulla (via the Metellan connection)[13] and of Hortensius and Catulus (via the Servilii).[14] So *mulier nobilis* is putting it mildly: this daughter of the patrician Claudii was not merely a member of an ornamental social élite, but at the heart of the ruling class of the Roman Republic.

Let us leave the diagrammatic abstractions of the family tree, and take a walk in the streets of Rome. Throughout the city there were 'sermons in stone' reminding the passer-by of the great men of the past, and their achievements: temples, basilicas, arches, porticoes, each preserving (as Cicero put it) the *nominis aeterna memoria* of the man who built it, whether he were a consul or censor acting on the Senate's authority, or – more characteristically – a triumphant proconsul disposing of his booty in such a way as to make the glory of his triumph last as long as the inscription on the building.[15] The *monumenta* of the patrician Claudii were the Appian Way and the Appian Aqueduct[16] – but also, in the city itself, the temple of Bellona vowed by Ap. Claudius in his Etruscan campaign of 296 B.C. and dedicated by

[12] Plut. *Cato min.* 14.3 (Cato's συγγένεια with Mucia); was she a Porcia, or a Livia? It is natural to think of the Claudian connections of the Livii Drusi: Vell. Pat. II 75.3, 94.1, cf. Suet. *Tib.* 3.1 (M. Livius Drusus Claudianus); *AE* 1969–70 118 (Livia C.f. Pulchra).

[13] Plut. *Pomp.* 9.2, *Sulla* 33.4, cf. Cic. *Sest.* 101, Asc. 27C: Metella married first to M. Scaurus (father of Mucia's second husband), then to Sulla.

[14] Cic. *Verr.* II 24, *de or.* III 228 on Hortensius, son-in-law of Servilia and Q. Catulus *cos.* 102. (Hortensius' daughter evidently married a Q. Caepio: Münzer 1920, 342–5 on *Inscr. de Délos* 1622.) Sulla's fifth wife Valeria was the niece of Hortensius (Plut. *Sulla* 35.4); cf. Val. Max. V 9.2 for the connection with the Valerii Messallae, who show a link with the Claudii two generations later (Messalla Appianus, *cos.* 12).

[15] Festus (Paulus) 123L: 'monumentum est . . . quicquid ob memoriam alicuius factum est, ut fana, porticus . . .'; Cic. *Verr.* IV 69 (Catulus' *nominis aeterna gloria*, cf. *leg. agr.* II 61, *fam.* I 9.15, *Verr.* I 154, *dom.* 102 on the connection with *manubiae*; D. E. Strong, *BICS* 15 (1968) 99f, M. G. Morgan, *Klio* 55 (1973) 222–4.

[16] Cic. *Cael.* 34, *Mil.* 17 ('in monumentis maiorum suorum interfectus').

him a few years later (evidently at his own expense, since he did not hold a triumph).[17]

To be exact, it was not *in* the city but just outside, in the *prata flaminia* outside the Porta Carmentalis.[18] That was no accident: the Claudian burial-ground below the Capitol, supposedly granted to the first Appius by a grateful people when the Claudii migrated to Rome, was evidently at that very spot, just outside the gate.[19] The podium of the temple survives, but of the tomb only the alabaster urn, now in the Louvre, that had held the ashes of one of Clodia's nephews, and was discovered in the ruins in 1615.[20]

In the two centuries after its foundation, the Bellona temple acquired some very impressive neighbours, the magnificent temples and porticoes put up round the Circus Flaminius (a piazza, I think, rather than a race track) by M. Fulvius Nobilior, Q. Metellus Macedonicus, D. Brutus Callaicus and other *triumphatores*.[21] Perhaps it was a little overshadowed; at any rate, Clodia's father in his consulship in 79 B.C. decorated the temple with shield-portraits of all his ancestors, thus turning it explicitly into a *monumentum* of the family as a whole.[22] Of all the public places in Rome, it was there that his fellow-citizens, in pride or envy, could see visibly displayed the history and *res gestae* of the patrician Claudii.

---

[17] Livy x 19.17–21, Ovid *Fasti* vi 199–208.

[18] Site identified by Coarelli 1965–7, 37–72 (cf. *PBSR* 42 (1974) 14–17): next to the temple of Apollo *in circo Flaminio*. For the *prata flaminia* that preceded the *circus*, cf. Livy iii 54.15, 63.7.

[19] Suet. *Tib.* 1.1; Wiseman 1979, 59, cf. R. E. A. Palmer, *MEFR* 87 (1975) 653 nn. 3 and 5 on *CIL* vi 1282. For the connection of temple and tomb, see F. Coarelli, *Dial. arch.* 6 (1972) 71f on the Marcelli and the temple of Honos and Virtus outside the Porta Capena (Asc. 12C).

[20] *CIL* vi 1282, 'prope theatrum Marcelli sub Tarpeio'.

[21] Evidence summarised in *PBSR* 42 (1974) 5–7, with notes at 21f. For D. Brutus' Mars temple, see now F. Zevi in *L'Italie préromaine et le Rome républicaine* (Coll. de l'école fr. de Rome 27, 1978) ii 1052–62.

[22] Pliny *NH* xxxv 12, cf. Wiseman 1979, 60. The Aemilii did the same with the Basilica Aemilia (Pliny *NH* xxxv 13, 78 B.C.), and the Fabii with the *fornix Fabianus* (*ILLRP* 392, 57 B.C.); perhaps the Scipiones had led the way with the statues on their Capitoline arch (Livy xxxvii 3.7, with Coarelli, n.19 above).

He hoped to add to the glory of his house with a triumph from his proconsular province of Macedonia. But it was not to be: he died there in 76, and it was his successor who won the triumph.[23] His successor also collected the tribute Appius had demanded from the Thracian tribes;[24] there would be no spoils of empire coming back with Appius' ashes.

That must be the context of the first piece of specific evidence we have about Appius' children. His eldest son (also Appius), who became consul in 54 and censor in 50, appears as a character in Varro's third dialogue de re rustica. The discussion on bees is introduced by Q. Axius challenging him: What about honey? Just because Appius in his youth was too economical ever to drink honey-wine, is that any reason for not discussing it?

'He's right,' Appius told us; 'for I was left in poverty with two brothers and two sisters. I gave one of the sisters to Lucullus without a dowry; he relinquished a legacy in my favour, and it was only then for the very first time that I began to drink honey-wine at home myself – though it was served to all the dinner guests practically every night.'

The dialogue dates from the mid-thirties B.C., when there were Claudii alive and influential who could challenge any inaccuracy; in substance, the story must be true.[25] The poverty, of course, was only relative, and there were dinner parties nearly every night, even if the host himself had to drink cheap wine. Young Appius was nineteen when his father died, his brothers Gaius and Publius respectively eighteen and sixteen.[26] They had expensive political careers to finance, and husbands to find for their sisters. I think we should see those dinner-parties as an investment, with the young aristocrats using what assets they had – youth,

[23] Oros. v 23.19; Eutrop. VI 2.1–2.
[24] Sall. Hist. II 80M; cf. Livy per. 91, Florus I 39.6 on Appius' successful first campaigns.
[25] Varro RR III 16.1–2 ('cum pauper . . . essem relictus'), cf. I 1.1 for the date of RR (Varro's eightieth year); Wiseman 1970, 207ff on Ap. Claudius cos. 38 and his brother and cousins.
[26] Inferred from their senatorial careers: I accept the argument of Badian 1964, 140–56 = JRS 49 (1959) 81–9, that 'patricians had an advantage of two years over plebeians in the minimum ages required for the senior magistracies'; see also, however, Sumner 1973, 7–10, 134–7.

promise, and no doubt plenty of patrician glamour – to make up for the disadvantages of their father's untimely death.

It was later said of the youngest boy, Publius, that he sold himself for the sexual pleasure of 'wealthy playboys'.[27] We must remember the slanderous norms of Roman political invective; but it is likely enough that all five of the siblings made themselves agreeable to guests who could be of future value to their careers. Five, not six. We know from Plutarch (*Cic.* 29.4) that there were three sisters, but young Appius, *paterfamilias* at nineteen, had to provide for only two of them. One was already married, and Shackleton Bailey's reconstruction makes it practically certain that that one was our Clodia. It is not at all surprising that the first thing we know about her is her marriage, and even that is attested only indirectly. Children – even male children – are almost totally absent from our evidence on the Roman aristocracy of this period. A few implausibly hagiographical stories about the young M. Cato; Catullus' vision of a baby Torquatus in the wedding poem for Manlius and Vibia;[28] beyond that, nothing. Girls especially, in this as in so many historical periods, are wholly invisible between birth and betrothal. It is a reasonable guess that Clodia was born about 97 B.C., but we have no idea at all where, how, with whom or by whom she was brought up. Did her mother die in childbirth? Was that why Appius married again to get his sons?

Even without invoking the aid of psychohistory and the stepmother *topos*,[29] we can be sure that Clodia had a less than tranquil adolescence. Her father, praetor in 88, was left in charge of the siege of Nola by the departing Sulla. Summoned by a hostile tribune, he refused to obey; his command was legally terminated, and he went into voluntary exile. For the next four years, when Appius under normal circumstances would have held a consulship and governed a great province, the family had

---

[27] Cic. *har. resp.* 42, *Sest.* 39 ('scurrae locupletes'); cf. *dom.* 139, *har. resp.* 59, and p. 130 n.4 below.

[28] Plut. *Cato min.* 1–3, Cat. 61.216–30.

[29] See (e.g.) Sen. *contr.* IV 6, VI 7, IX 5; Quint. II 10.5, Virg. *Georg.* II 128, Jer. *ep.* 54.15.

to lie low, deprived of his support.[30] Clodia was probably in her early teens. Her father no doubt returned when Sulla did. It would be reasonable to date her betrothal to young Q. Metellus Celer in or about 82 B.C., when he was twenty and she was about fifteen, and their marriage, perhaps, to Appius' delayed consulship in 79.

A fragment of the first book of Sallust's *Histories*, which covered the years 78 and 77, reveals Metellus Celer in a position of military responsibility.[31] It would be natural to expect Appius to take his new son-in-law with him to Macedonia as a *praefectus* or military tribune. We know from the case of Caesar and Trebatius how profitable such service could be for a young man, and since Appius' first campaigns were evidently successful, it is likely that Metellus did well out of the province, despite the death of his father-in-law.[32]

Twenty years later, when Clodia, now widowed, was prosecution witness in the trial of M. Caelius, Cicero's closing speech for the defence included a superb passage prompted by the allegation that Caelius had tried out the efficacy of a quick-acting poison on a slave bought for the purpose:[33]

Ye immortal gods! Why do you sometimes close your eyes to the worst crimes of men, or put off until tomorrow the punishment of today's wrong-doing?

I imagine the court was puzzled: why all this thunderous indignation over a slave? But the real point was immediately revealed:

For I saw it – I saw it, and drained the bitterest sorrow of my whole life – when Quintus Metellus was being snatched away from the bosom and embrace of his native land . . .

After describing the deathbed scene and Metellus Celer's patriotic virtues in three long and magnificent periods, Cicero concludes:

[30] Cic. *dom.* 83–4, Livy *per.* 79.
[31] Sall. *Hist.* I 135M (Maurenbrecher suggests a context in the Macedonian campaigns).
[32] Caesar and Trebatius: Cic. *fam.* VII 5–18 (54–53 B.C.). Appius' successes: n.24 above.
[33] Cic. *Cael.* 63f; cf. *Pis.* 8 (on Celer), *Cael. ap.* Quint. VIII 6.52 (on the suggestion of Clodia's responsibility for Celer's death), p. 89 below.

And will that woman, coming from *this* house, dare to speak of quick-acting poison? Will she not be terrified that the house itself will find a voice, will she not shudder at the walls that know her secret, and tremble at the memory of that night of grief and death?

Ex hac domo progressa . . . It must have been common knowledge where Clodia lived, and from which house she had come down to the Forum that day; we can hardly dismiss this as 'mere rhetoric'. Clodia was evidently still living in the house where Metellus had died three years before. The conclusion is inevitable: it was her property, not his.

The house was on the Palatine, as were two others belonging to Clodia's youngest brother – one that he tried in 58 B.C. to extend into a palatial mansion with a 300-foot portico, and one evidently let as flats in which M. Caelius rented an apartment for an allegedly astronomical sum.[34] Clodia's house shared a party-wall with that of Q. Catulus (a point made much of in Cicero's purple passage); since Catulus' house had become part of the Augustan complex by about 10 B.C., and Augustus' property can be placed by its proximity to the temple of Apollo, we may assume that it was towards the western side of the hill.[35] Clodius' house, on the other hand, was next to Cicero's, which was close to the *domus publica*, which adjoined the house of the Vestals; the *domus publica* was large and rambling, but even so, it should mean that Clodius' house was towards the northern side of the hill.[36] It must have been a different sister whose house was next door to his, and whose access was cut off (according to Cicero's allegation in the *pro Milone*) when he extended a wall through her *vestibulum*.[37]

[34] Clodia: Cic. *Cael.* 18 ('Palatina Medea', pp. 8of below), Plut. *Cic.* 29.3 (neighbour of Cicero). Clodius: Cic. *dom.* 115f etc.

[35] Catulus' house: Cic. *Cael.* 59, cf. Pliny *NH* XVII 2 for its splendour. Augustan compl; suet. *gramm.* 17.2 (*domus Catulina*); Suet. *Aug.* 29.3, Dio XLIX 15.5, Vell. Pat. II 81.3 (Apollo temple); F. Castagnoli, *Arch. Class.* 16 (1964) 173–90, esp. 186f.

[36] Cic. *har. resp.* 33 (Cicero); Cic. *Att.* II 24.3 (end), Suet. *Caes.* 46, cf. Plut. *Cic.* 28.2 and *Caes.* 10.2 on the *domus publica* and its size; Dio LIV 27.3 (Vestals).

[37] Cic. *Mil.* 75, possibly referring to the 'house of Scaurus' bought by Clodius in 53 (Asc. 32C), though it would be an odd coincidence if his new house was next to his sister's

It is clear that the Claudii had several properties on the Palatine, one of which no doubt went with Clodia as part of her dowry, and stayed with her when her husband died.

2. NOBILIUM LUDI

Topographical detail can often be a help to social history, especially in the case of those ambiguous areas where different sorts of neighbourhood overlap. There was a famous Busby Berkeley musical, of which the title song celebrated a place in New York 'where the underworld can meet the élite – Forty-Second Street';[38] in late-Republican Rome, we can find the equivalent of a 42nd-Street speakeasy in the *salax taberna* of Catullus poem 37, frequented equally by the *boni ac beati* and by *omnes pusilli et semitarii moechi*. Tenney Frank even thought that the *salax taberna* was Clodia's house – an absurd idea, since the address Catullus carefully gives places it among the 'old shops' on the south-west side of the Forum, soon to be swept away by the building of the Basilica Julia.[39] In another sense, however, the property of Clodia and her family does show an intriguing juxtaposition, not with the underworld but with 'show business'.

Bellona's temple, the *monumentum* of the Claudian house, was next to the temple of Apollo, facing the south-eastern end of the Circus Flaminius where the *ludi Apollinares* were held each July, and where (no doubt for that very reason) the theatre of Marcellus was later built.[40] Clodia's house, if we may trust our inference from the house of Catulus and Augustus' property,

property. For the position of Scaurus' house, see Asc. 27C, with F. Coarelli, *Il foro romano: periodo arcaico* (Rome 1983) 24f.

[38] Harry Warren and Al Dubin, '42nd Street' (1932).

[39] T. Frank, *Catullus and Horace: Two Poets in their Environment* (Oxford 1928) 281. *Tabernae veteres*: Livy XLIV 16.10; cf. Prop. IV 2.6, Ovid *Fasti* VI 410, *CIL* VI 804 for the *signum Vortumni*. Basilica: Aug. *RG* 20.3. For the *pilae* of Cat. 37.2, cf. Hor. *Sat.* I 4.71, Mart. VII 61.5.

[40] Plut. *Cic.* 13, with Coarelli 1965–7, 67f; cf. also *PBSR* 42 (1974) 14–17, and J. A. Hanson, *Roman Theater-Temples* (Princeton 1959) 18–24.

must have been close to the temple of the Magna Mater in the precinct of Victoria, where the *ludi Megalenses* were held every April, and probably also Sulla's *ludi Victoriae* every October.[41] An appropriate proximity, even if fortuitous; for it is quite clear that in the minds of Cicero and his audience, at least, Clodia was naturally associated with the stage.

'Veniamus ad ludos.' In the *pro Sestio*, eager to prove the unpopularity of Clodius among the citizen body as a whole (as opposed to his own hired claques), Cicero makes much of his absence from the magnificent theatrical shows given by M. Scaurus as aedile in 58:[42]

> Ipse ille maxime ludius, non solum spectator sed actor et acroama, qui omnia sororis embolia novit, qui in coetum mulierum pro psaltria adducitur, nec tuos ludos aspexit in illo ardenti tribunatu suo . . .

> That arch-buffoon himself, not just a spectator but a performer and an entertainer, who knows all his sister's interludes, who is brought into a women's gathering in the guise of a lute-girl, he never saw your shows in that fiery tribunate of his . . .

Embolia were balletic interludes, performed between the acts or while the next play was being prepared, by dancing girls whose soft limbs haunted Lucretius' dreams.[43] Clodius is clearly imagined as a performer, but are we meant to think of his sister as dancer, or librettist? The scholiast assumes the former, citing unnamed early authors to the effect that Clodia was 'given to

---

[41] See n. 35 above. For the site of the temple of Victoria, see *AJ* 61 (1981) 35–52 on Dion. Hal. 1 32.3–33.1, *CIL* vi 3733, 31060, etc. For *ludi* in this precinct, see Cic. *har. resp.* 24 (with P. Pensabene, *Quaderni del centro di studio per l'arch. etrusco-italica* 4 (1980) 67–71) and Jos. *AJ* xix 75f (with *LCM* 5.10 (Dec. 1980) 231–8), on the *ludi Megalenses* and *Palatini* respectively; the site of the *ludi Victoriae* is inferred from that of the temple.

[42] Cic. *Sest.* 116; the passage 106–27 is subdivided into *contiones* (106–8), *comitia* (legislative 109–12, electoral 113–14), *ludi* (115–23) and gladiatorial *munera* (124–7).

[43] Schol. Bob. 136St ('pertinent ad gestus saltatorios'); Pliny *NH* vii 158 (Galeria Copiola, *emboliaria*), cf. *CIL* vi 10128 (Sophe, *arbitrix imboliarum*); Lucr. iv 788–93, 978–83. '[Mimi] olim non in suggestu scaenae sed in plano orchestrae positis instrumentis mimicis actitabant' (Diomedes *Gramm. Lat.* 1 490K); 'solebant ‹enim saltare› in o‹rc›hestra, dum ‹in scaena actus fa›bulae componeren‹tur, cum gestibus ob›scaenis' (Festus 436L, suppl. Mommsen, on *saltationes*). See Giancotti 1967, 23f on *embolia* and *exodia*.

CLODIA: PLEASURE AND SWAY

dancing more extravagantly and immoderately than befitted a *matrona*'. But Cicero probably meant the latter: a month or so later, attacking Clodia herself in the defence of Caelius, he calls her 'vetus et plurimarum fabularum poetria' – an experienced writer for the stage.[44]

In fact, the *pro Caelio* is full of theatrical references. We have the quotation from Ennius' *Medea* when Clodia is first referred to, the theatrical *prosopopoeia* of Appius Caecus when she is introduced as the power behind the prosecution, the trochaic septenarius put into her brother's mouth as Cicero ironically imagines him advising her, the stern and indulgent fathers quoted respectively from Caecilius and Terence when Caelius' involvement with her is being assessed, the Terentian 'hinc illae lacrimae nimirum' as Cicero attributes to her wounded vanity the origin of all the charges brought against his client.[45] Most explicit of all is the long and brilliant passage in the second half of the speech, in which Cicero tries to make nonsense of the prosecution's account of the attempt by Clodia's friends to catch Caelius' agent in the act of handing over poison to Clodia's slaves at an agreed meeting place. It is in that context that Cicero calls her *poetria*; the rendezvous at the Senian Baths, he suggests, is a mere *fabella*, just another scenario from her fertile imagination, but one with no coherent plot, no satisfying *dénouement*. The ending is so arbitrary it must be a mime, not even a straight play: someone gets away – the clappers sound – curtain![46]

Mention of the mime, of course, reduces the lady librettist's dignity still further. Moreover, a moment later Cicero drops a malicious allusion to the most popular of all mime plots, the

---

[44] Schol. Bob. 135St, where Stangl suggests a confused recollection of Sall. *Cat.* 25.2 (on Sempronia); but the report may be accurate (p. 47 below). Cic. *Cael.* 64.

[45] Cic. *Cael.* 19, 33–4, 36, 37, 38 (Ter. *Adelphi* 120f), 61 (Ter. *Andria* 126).

[46] Cic. *Cael.* 64–5: 'velut haec tota fabella veteris et plurimarum fabularum poetriae quam est sine argumento, quam nullum invenire exitum potest! . . . Mimi ergo iam exitus, non fabulae; in quo cum clausula non invenitur, fugit aliquis e manibus, dein scabilla concrepant, aulaeum tollitur.' Cf. Wiseman 1974, 133 and plate 2a for mime, *scabilla* and a dancing girl.

concealed adulterer. He is anticipating the evidence to be given by Clodia's friends:

Ex quibus requiram, quem ad modum latuerint aut ubi, alveusne ille an equus Troianus fuerit qui tot invictos viros muliebre bellum gerentes tulerit ac texerit.

I'm going to ask them how they were hidden, and where – whether it was the famous tub, or the Trojan horse that concealed all those heroes waging a woman's war . . .

'Alveus *ille*' must be an allusion, and I take it to be the same as *cista Latini* in Juvenal's sixth satire.[47] The lover Latinus played hid in a chest; amorous Falstaff hid in a laundry-basket; the hero of the Adultery Mime on the late-Republican stage must have hidden in a tub, like the lover of the baker's wife in Apuleius.[48] With that sort of plot in their minds, the jury and the audience were ready for the *obscaenissima fabula* about Clodia (whatever it was) with which Cicero closed his argument, satisfied that Clodia's reputation was in tatters and her lovers' testimony no longer to be feared.

Cicero's speech was given on the first day of the *ludi Megalenses*, and he may have felt that theatrical allusions would be appropriate for a holiday crowd. But it is at Clodia in particular that they are aimed. His brilliant and shameless innuendo leads his audience to think of her not just as a writer of mimes but as a character in one. The picture he builds up of her – the wealthy matron with the morals of a whore – was a familiar one in contemporary mime, as we know from the fragments of Laberius and Publilius Syrus.[49] The smooth young dandies he

[47] Cic. *Cael.* 67, cf. Juv. VI 44. Not recognising the allusion, C. M. Francken (*Mnem.* 8 (1880) 228) proposed to delete *an* in the Cicero passage; this suggestion has been rightly ignored, but commentators still do not explain *ille*.

[48] Apul. *Met.* IX 23, 26f, cf. 5 (*dolium*), Hor. *Sat.* II 7.59 (*arca*). For the 'adultery mime', see Reynolds 1946 and McKeown 1979, 74–6.

[49] Laberius *Compitalia* fr. 33R (Nonius 89L): 'quo quidem | me a matronali pudore prolubium meretricie | progredi coegit.' Petr. *Sat.* 55 (attributed to Publilius): 'quo margarita cara tibi, bacam Indicam, | an ut matrona ornata phaleris pelagiis | tollat pedes indomita in strato extraneo?'; see Giancotti 1967, 235–66. For the social background, cf. Lyne 1980, 13–17.

imagined hiding in the famous tub – Clodia's devoted lackeys –
are equally recognisable in the *cultus adulter* of the mimic stage.[50]
Not all mimes were crude, vulgar and subliterary; on the
contrary, at this very period there is plentiful evidence for mime
as sophisticated entertainment, appealing to the same audience
and exploiting the same subject matter as elegiac love poetry.[51] It
is no accident that Gallus' Lycoris was a mime actress: we now
know that he called her his *domina*, and the languishing attitude
attributed to him in the tenth *Eclogue* is what Cicero, in his
different mode, contemptuously attributes to the sophisticated
young men who made themselves Clodia's slaves.[52] The world
of mime is also the world of the *barbatuli iuvenes*.

It is a relief for the historian to turn from self-dramatising
poets and disingenuous barristers to the comparative security of
epigraphic evidence. The real background to all this – the
common ground of Roman high society and the popular stage –
may be elicited from a late-Republican funerary inscription from
Rome (Fig. 2).[53]

> Eucharis, freedwoman of Licinia.
> She lived fourteen years, a maid skilled and learned in all the arts.
> Ah, you who with casual eye look on the house of death,
> halt your step and read my epitaph to the end.
> My father's love gave it to his daughter
> where the remains of my body were to be laid down.
> Here, when my fresh youth was flowering in the arts
> and attaining glory as my age increased,
> the gloomy day of my fate came in haste
> and denied any further breath to my life.
> Skilled and taught almost by the Muses' hand,

---

[50] Cic. *Cael.* 67: 'lauti iuvenes . . . in conviviis faceti, dicaces, non numquam etiam ad
vinum diserti . . . vigeant apud istam mulierem venustate, dominentur sumptibus,
haereant, iaceant, deserviant.' Ovid *Trist.* ii 499, 505, with Reynolds 1946, 82; cf.
Apul. *Met.* ix 27f (*venustus, mollis*).

[51] McKeown 1979, 71f.

[52] *Domina*: P. J. Parsons and R. G. M. Nisbet, *JRS* 69 (1979) 140, 144; Cic. *Cael.* 67 (n. 50
above, *deserviant*). For the *servitium amoris* theme in general, see Lyne 1979.

[53] *CIL* vi 10096 = i² 1214 = *ILLRP* 803. On dance in the late Republic, see E. J. Jory,
BICS 28 (1981) 154f, 157; for the visual evidence for mimes, clowns, etc., see H.
Goldman, *AJA* 47 (1943) 22–34.

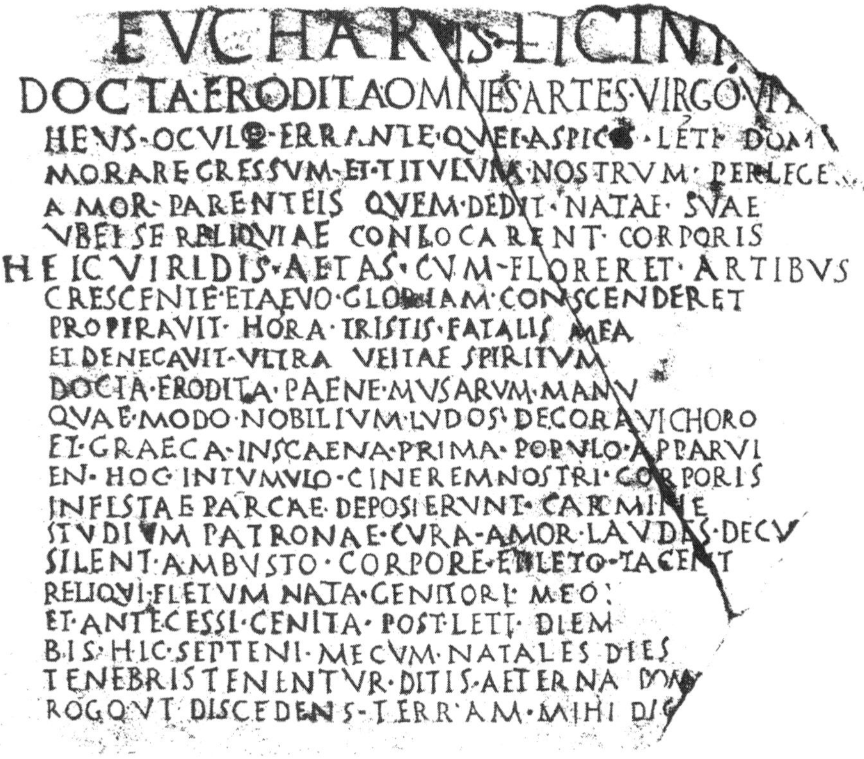

EVCHARIS·LICINI
DOCTA·ERODITA·OMNES·ARTES·VIRGO·V
HEVS·OCVLO·ERRANTE·QVEI·ASPICIS·LETI·DOM
MORARE·GRESSVM·ET·TITVLVM·NOSTRVM·PERLEGE
A·MOR·PARENTEIS·QVEM·DEDIT·NATAE·SVAE
VBEI·SE·RELIQVIAE·CONLOCARENT·CORPORIS
HEIC·VIRIDIS·AETAS·CVM·FLORERET·ARTIBVS
CRESCENTE·ET·AEVO·GLORIAM·CONSCENDERET
PROPERAVIT·HORA·TRISTIS·FATALIS·MEA
ET·DENEGAVIT·VLTRA·VEITAE·SPIRITVM
DOCTA·ERODITA·PAENE·MVSARVM·MANV
QVAE·MODO·NOBILIVM·LVDOS·DECORAVI·CHORO
ET·GRAECA·IN·SCAENA·PRIMA·POPVLO·APPARVI
EN·HOC·IN·TVMVLO·CINEREM·NOSTRI·CORPORIS
INFESTAE·PARCAE·DEPOSIERVNT·CARMINE
STVDIVM·PATRONAE·CVRA·AMOR·LAVDES·DECV
SILENT·AMBVSTO·CORPORE·ET·LETO·TACENT
RELIQVI·FLETVM·NATA·GENITORI·MEO
ET·ANTECESSI·GENITA·POST·LETI·DIEM
BIS·HIC·SEPTENI·MECVM·NATALES·DIES
TENEBRIS·TENENTVR·DITIS·AETERNA·DOM
ROGO·VT·DISCEDENS·TERRAM·MIHI·DIC

FIGURE 2

I who recently graced with my dancing the games of the nobles,
who was first to appear to the people on the Greek stage –
see how in the tomb the ashes of my body
the cruel Fates have laid down with a dirge.
The encouragement of my patroness, care, love, applause and honour
are mute at the body's cremation, are silent in death.
A daughter, I left grief to my father;
born later, I went before him to the day of death.
Twice seven birthdays are with me here,
held fast in the darkness in the eternal house of Dis.
As you leave, please pray that the earth may be light on me.

In death, as no doubt in life, Eucharis speaks in iambic senarii. A freed slave, like most mime-actresses, she quickly achieved the *gloria*, *laudes* and *decus* of popular applause, and but for her untimely death might have become a wealthy woman like Dionysia, a senator's mistress like Nicopolis or Tertia, a poet's inspiration like Volumnia Cytheris.[54] What she did do, even before her fifteenth birthday, was to dance in the *nobilium ludi*, and be the first to appear before the public on the *Graeca scaena*. Both those phrases need some explanation.

The great dramatic festivals of the Roman year were a show-piece for the magistrates who presided over them. For the curule aediles the *ludi Megalenses* and *Romani*, for the plebeian aediles the *ludi Florales* and *plebeii*, for the urban praetor the *ludi Apollinares* – all offered an unparalleled opportunity for conspicuous expenditure and the attraction of that popular approval and applause which was the life-blood of the Roman politician.[55] Those magistrates were prominent senators, often *nobiles*, but the regular public festivals cannot, I think, be the *ludi nobilium* referred to by the Eucharis inscription: on the contrary, they were *ludi deorum immortalium*.[56] We must think rather of two other sorts of *ludi* – funeral games and votive games – where the greatness of the presiding aristocrat and his family was even more directly advertised.

For *ludi funebres*, Polybius' famous description of a Roman aristocratic funeral provides a clear context: the ancestors were thought of as being physically present, the next generation was

[54] Dionysia: Cic. *Rosc. com.* 23, Hortensius *ap.* Gell. *NA* 1 5.3. Nicopolis: Plut. *Mor.* 318c, *Sull.* 2.4; C. Garton, *Phoenix* 18 (1964) 137–56 = *Personal Aspects of the Roman Theatre* (Toronto 1972) 141–67, on Sulla's theatrical interests. Tertia: Cic. *Verr.* III 77–83, V 31. Cytheris: Serv. *ecl.* 10.1, cf. *vir. ill.* 82.2, Cic. *Phil.* II 58, 69 etc.

[55] Expense: Pliny *NH* XIX 23, XXXVI 114–20, and passages cited in n.71 below. Applause: Cic. *Sest.* 115, *Att.* I 16.11, II 19.3, IV 15.6, *Phil.* I 37, etc. For Clodius at the Megalesia, on the second day of the Caelius trial, see Wiseman 1974, 159–69.

[56] Vitr. *Arch.* v 3.1, Cic. *Verr.* v 36, Livy VI 42.12f, Aug. *CD* VI 5, etc.; see J. A. Hanson, *Roman Theater–Temples* (Princeton 1959), passim.

expected to imitate their greatness, and in general the whole aim and purpose of the celebration was the glory of the *gens*.[57] As for *ludi votivi*, they were often given in association with triumphs – either directly, to give thanks for the victory, or indirectly, at the dedication of temples or other public buildings put up as *monumenta* from the spoils of war.[58] In either case, it was the triumphant general who paid for them, and his own *res gestae* that were being celebrated. Moreover, such games could be put on at any time, by anyone who could afford them. Remember Caelius, who borrowed money from Clodia to pay for staging *ludi* (or so he said); he was of very junior senatorial rank, with no reason to give games except mere self-advertisement.[59] Remember Milo, who spent three patrimonies on the most extravagant *ludi* Rome had ever seen; Cicero thought he was crazy, but Milo was preparing for a consular candidature the following year, and had powerful enemies.[60] As it happens, neither Caelius nor Milo was technically a *nobilis*, but if Eucharis performed for either, as she may well have done, she would hardly have let that worry her. The shows they put on were surely the sort of thing she meant by *nobilium ludi*.

What sort of plays were shown? We know of comedies by Terence being played at funerary *ludi*, and tragedies by Accius and Naevius at votive games. *Fabulae praetextae*, with Roman plots that could glorify the giver of the games directly, would also be particularly appropriate; the view expressed in the standard history of the Roman theatre, that the *praetexta* had become obsolete by the late Republic, is not only unlikely *a priori* (why ignore such a popular way of celebrating your ancestors' great

---

[57] Pol. VI 53f; cf. *didascaliae* to Ter. *Hecyra* and *Adelphi* for L. Paullus' funeral *ludi*.

[58] E.g. Pol. XXX 22, Livy XXXVI 36, XL 52.1–3, XLII 10.5. Pompey illustrates both types: the first in 70 (Cic. *Verr.* act. I 31), the second in 55 (Cic. *Pis.* 65, Asc. 1C, Dio XXXIX 38: dedication of the theatre). For *monumenta* see n. 15 above.

[59] Cic. *Cael.* 53 (pp. 73f below); whether he gave them or not, Clodia evidently believed he was going to. For Caelius' career (quaestor in 58?), see Sumner 1971, 247–9.

[60] Cic. *QF* III 6.6, Asc. 31C ('impensas ludorum scaenicorum ac gladiatorii muneris maximas'); cf. Cic. *fam.* II 6.3, *Mil.* 95 for the *munera*.

deeds?), it is also inconsistent with the evidence.[61] But comedies, tragedies and *praetextae* – in which the actors were all male – offered no role to Eucharis. She was a dancer, her medium was the mime. We know that *mimae* performed at votive games and in the regular annual festivals, and it is likely that they performed in the *ludi funebres* as well.[62]

That brings us, indirectly, to the *Graeca scaena*. Dionysius of Halicarnassus tells us that at wealthy funerals in the Augustan period, the dancers were dressed as satyrs and imitated the Greek dance called *sikinnis*. He takes it as an archaic Roman custom, evidence for his perpetual theme that the Romans were really Greek in origin themselves.[63] It is much more likely to be an innovation of the late-Republican period, one more aspect of that hellenisation of Roman culture that followed the disappearance of the courts of the Hellenistic kings. Rome became the centre of patronage for Greek artists and intellectuals,[64] and with them, ill-documented but no less important, came the theatre people. Our sources tell us about the scholars and the literary men – Archias, Parthenius, Philodemus, Athenodorus, Timagenes – but for every Roman aristocrat who appreciated *their* talents, there must have been ten who could find work for actors and dancing girls from the Greek East.

Already in the late second century B.C., Antipater of Sidon bade farewell to 'Aphrodite's chick', the dancer Antiodemis,

[61] Comedies: n.57 above. Tragedies: Cic. *fam.* VII 1.2. *Praetextae*: W. Beare, *The Roman Stage* (3rd ed. London 1964) 42–4. See Cic. *fam.* X 32.3 (Pollio) for L. Balbus' *praetexta* on his own deeds, performed in *ludi* at Gades; Beare is surely wrong to try to explain this away as untypical (p. 42) or a literary exercise (p. 44). See Shackleton Bailey 1977a, I 325 on Cic. *fam.* VII 1.2: Aesopus acting a *praetexta* at Pompey's games?
[62] Pliny *NH* VII 158 (*votivi*), Cic. *Att.* IV 15.6 (*Apollinares*), Val. Max. II 10.8 (*Florales*). *Mimi* at funeral processions: Dion. Hal VII 72.12 (referring to his own time), Suet. *Vesp.* 19.2.
[63] Dion. Hal. VII 72.10–12, cf. 70.2, I 90.2; J.P.V.D. Balsdon, *JRS* 61 (1971) 24f.
[64] Wiseman 1979, 154–61. Cf. also *History* 217 (1981) 380f; Griffin 1976, 89–96; G. Williams, *Change and Decline: Roman Literature in the Early Empire* (Berkeley 1978) ch. 3, esp. 112–16; Horsfall 1979, esp. 84–6.

setting out to captivate Rome with her melting eyes and her arms
that flowed like water. Perhaps she performed at Marius'
triumph in 101, when we know there were 'Greek shows' in the
theatre.[65] By the fifties B.C., Greek influence on the mimic stage
was all-pervading. 'We've *heard* about Alexandria before,' said
Cicero to the jury at Rabirius Postumus' trial in 54; 'now we
know about it – the source of all trickery and deceit, where the
plots of all the mimes come from.' Presumably it was Alexandrian performers that had brought the plots with them, and
Cicero's implication that they were a novelty fits in well with the
claim on Eucharis' gravestone that she was the first to act on the
'Greek stage' at Rome.[66]

The final point to notice in the Eucharis inscription is the name
of her patroness, Licinia. Was she related to the philhellene L.
Licinius Crassus? or to the Atticising orator C. Licinius Calvus?
or to L. Licinius Lucullus, patron of Archias and a Greek
historian in his own right? or to L. Licinius Murena, who
transformed the archaic temple of Juno in his native Lanuvium
with splendid Hellenistic sculptures?[67] Whichever of the
branches of the *gens Licinia* she belonged to, she was probably a
lady whose tastes and background were very much like those of
Clodia herself.

The patrician Claudii enjoyed widespread and long-standing
clientelae in the Hellenistic world. Clodia's brothers Appius and

[65] Antipater of Sidon 61 G–P (*Anth. Pal.* IX 567), Plut. *Mar.* 2.1. Antipater's description
Λύσιδος ἀλκυονίς suggests some connection with the *lysiodoi*, evidently female
impersonators (Athen. XIV 620e, 621c–d, Strabo XIV 648); Sulla loved the lysiode
Metrobios (Plut. *Sulla* 36.2).

[66] Cic. *Rab. Post.* 35; he cannot mean that all mime-plots had always been Alexandrian,
since *mimi* had been performing at Roman *ludi* since the third century B.C. (Festus 438L,
a veteran *mimus* in 211). Cf. Adams 1982, 31f, 93 on Greek sexual terms in mime
(Festus 410L, Laberius fr. 25, 139), and Helly 1983, 373 for a Roman organising mime
performances in Thessaly in the first century B.C.

[67] L. Crassus: Cic. *de or.* II 365, III 75, 194. C. Calvus: Cic. *Brut.* 284–91. L. Lucullus
(Clodia's sister's husband): Cic. *Arch.* 5, *Att.* I 16.15, 19.10, Plut. *Luc.* 1. L. Murena
(stepfather of Clodius' wife, Cic. *dom.* 118, 134): F. Coarelli in *L'art décoratif à Rome à la
fin de la république et au début du principat* (Coll. de l'école fr. de Rome 55, 1981) 229–84,
esp. 251f.

Publius had had long experience in the Greek East, and their households were full of *Graeculi comites*.[68] The third brother, Gaius, as proconsul of Asia from 55 to 53 B.C., was honoured at Pergamum for his ancestors' sake as well as his own, perhaps with reference to the transfer of the Magna Mater from Pergamum to Rome in 204; Quinta Claudia was the *matronarum castissima* chosen to receive her, and C. Claudius Nero one of the censors who let the contract for her temple.[69] The story of Q. Claudia was elaborated in a stage version known to Propertius and Ovid – perhaps a mime, perhaps a *fabula praetexta*[70] – and we may be sure that when Claudian aediles held the *ludi* of the Magna Mater, as Clodia's uncle Gaius and her brother Publius did on two memorably spectacular occasions,[71] that piece would have a prominent place in the programme.

Clodia's brother was, notoriously, a demagogue. In that context one is curious to know whether he exploited the theatre claque, those hired professionals whose applause and rhythmic chanting were brilliantly documented by Alan Cameron in his book on 'circus factions', and whose recorded history begins in the Ciceronian age. (They are, in fact, first attested in the *pro Sestio* passage we have already considered.[72]) Percennius, the leader of the mutineers in Pannonia in A.D. 14, had been prominent among the *operae theatrales*; Tacitus' description of him as 'procax lingua et miscere coetus doctus' is reminiscent of those other *operae* who worked for Clodius in the fifties B.C.. Certainly the

---

[68] *Clientelae*: evidence collected by Rawson 1973 and 1977. Clodius' *Graeculi comites*: Cic. *Mil.* 28, 55. Appius': Cic. *QF* II 11.4; cf. *fam.* III 1.1f and Treggiari 1969, 179f and 220 on his confidential agents Cilix and Phania.

[69] *Inschr. von Perg.* II 409, with Rawson 1973, 230 and 1977, 353; Cic. *har. resp.* 27, *Cael.* 34, with Wiseman 1979, 95–9 on the development of her legend; Livy XXIX 37.2; XXXVI 36.4.

[70] Ovid *Fasti* IV 326 ('mira sed et scaena testificata loquor'), cf. Prop. IV 11.51f. Mime suggested by McKeown 1979, 76.

[71] C. Claudius: Cic. *har. resp.* 26, Val. Max. II 4.6, Pliny *NH* XXI 6, XXXV 23; for other events in his *aedilitas magnificentissima*, see Cic. *Verr.* IV 6, 133, *de off.* II 57, Pliny *NH* VIII 19, Gran. Lic. 32F. P. Clodius: Cic. *har. resp.* 22–9, with Wiseman 1974, 161f, 166–8.

[72] Cameron 1976, 234f, cf. 158f on Cic. *Sest.* 115: 'theatrales gladiatoriique consessus dicuntur omnino solere levitate non nullorum emptos plausus exiles et raros excitare' (minimising their effect? cf. n.75 below); see also Tuplin 1979, 359f on *Sest.* 118.

skills of such *claqueurs* could be applied on any crowd, and not just theatre audiences. Professor Cameron cites examples from fourth-century Antioch and twentieth-century Vienna, and we can add Pliny's famous letter on the hired applause at the centumviral court, 'indecent even in the theatre'.[73]

I think we can see Percennius' predecessors in action in the scene in the Forum in February 56, when Clodius prosecuted Milo before the people. The chanting of Clodius' *operae*, irresistibly reminiscent to the modern reader of the chanting of football fans, was surely the work of theatre *factiones*, whose antiphonal technique is amply attested.[74] Not that all of them were on Clodius' side: Milo's supporters chanted obscene verses about Clodius and Clodia, though naturally Cicero is not so indignant about that.[75] It's worth noticing as well that among the insults chanted at Pompey were two that appear also in an epigram of Calvus[76] – further evidence for the common ground between the theatrical world and the literary élite, and for the association of both with Clodius and his sister.

This picture of the patrician Claudii, as hellenised aristocrats with a more than just aesthetic interest in the theatre, is heavily

Rhythmic applause was evidently an Alexandrian speciality (Suet. *Nero* 20.3); cf. n.66 above.

[73] Tac. *Ann.* I 16.3 on Percennius, cf. I 77.5 ('lascivia fautorum'), Pliny *ep.* VII 24.7 ('opera theatralis'), Suet. *Nero* 20.3 ('divisi in factiones'), 26.2 (*signifer*), *Tib.* 37.2 ('capita factionum'); Cameron 1976, 259f on *demarchoi* as cheer-leaders. Pliny *ep.* II 14.4–13; Cameron 1976, 240 and n.1.

[74] Cic. *QF* II 3.2, Dio XXXIX 19.1–2, Plut. *Pomp.* 48.7 (ὥσπερ χορὸς εἰς ἀμοιβαία συγκεκροτημένος); Cameron 1976, 246f on antiphony. In the spring of 1984, the Yorkshire miners' chants of support for the President of the N.U.M. at their strike rallies were the same as those of the football crowd at (for example) Elland Road: 'Arthur Scargill' and 'Leeds United' are metrically equivalent.

[75] Cic. *QF* II 3.2; the demonstrations recorded at *Sest.* 115–23 may have been the work of an anti-Clodian claque, interpreted by Cicero (of course) as the authentic voice of the people. For *populi versus*, see also Plut. *Sulla* 6.10, Cic. *Verr.* V 81, *Phil.* I 36; H. D. Jocelyn, *LCM* 7.10 (1981) 145f.

[76] Plut. *Pomp.* 48.7, with Calvus *ap.* Sen. *contr.* VII 4.7 and Schol. Luc. VII 726 (fr. 18M): 'Magnus, quem metuunt omnes, digito caput uno scalpit; quid credas hunc sibi velle? virum.' For obscene libel at a literary level, see Adams 1982, 11 n.3 on Suet. *Jul.* 49.1, Macr. *Sat.* II 4.21, Mart. XI 20.

dependent on arguments from probability. That is inevitable, given the fragmentary nature of our evidence. But there is at least one piece of direct testimony. Macrobius tells us that the mimographer D. Laberius turned down a request from Clodius that he should write a mime for him. What made the story worth telling was not that Clodius asked, but that Laberius dared to refuse.[77]

3. *MULIER POTENS*

The concept of *potentia* offers another approach to understanding Clodia. Laberius was a bold man to defy a Claudius. People who did that were likely to have disagreeable things happen to them.[78] Cicero begins his defence of Caelius with ironical sympathy for the prosecutor Atratinus: he has his orders, Clodia's *libido* and *odium* give him no choice. And when he hints at the Claudii behind the scenes, supplying the ammunition for the prosecutors to use, Cicero's formulation sums up the Roman aristocracy in general and the patrician Claudii in particular: 'they are doing what gallant gentlemen habitually do – when injured they resent it, when angered they lash out, when provoked they give battle'.[79]

'Periculosa potentia', he calls it – and Clodia herself is *mulier potens*, the *imperatrix* of those elegant and sophisticated young men, a *domina* who liked to have her lovers bound to her by her wealth and social position.[80] A young man called Vettius had offended her (probably by sending the purseful of coppers that

---

[77] Macr. *Sat.* II 6.6: 'cum iratus esse P. Clodius D. Laberio diceretur quod ei mimum petenti non dedisset, "quid amplius" inquit "mihi facturus es nisi ut Dyrrachium eam et redeam?", ludens ad Ciceronis exilium.'

[78] Cic. *Att.* IV 3.2–3 (attacks on Cicero, Quintus' house burnt down), *Cael.* 50 (Clodia's *crudelitas*); Cic. *dom.* 115, *Mil.* 74f for techniques of intimidation attributed to Clodius.

[79] Cic. *Cael.* 2 (Atratinus' *necessitas*), 21. For the latter passage as referring to the Claudii, see Heinze 1925, 215 and Wiseman 1979, 122f.

[80] Cic. *Cael.* 22 (*potentiae*), 62f (*mulier potens*), 67 (*imperatrix*, *deserviant*: nn.50 and 52 above). 'Vis nobilis mulier illum filium familias patre parco ac tenaci habere tuis copiis devinctum' (*Cael.* 36, cf. 38, 67 for her wealth).

gave rise to her nickname 'Quadrantaria'); she soothed her wounded pride, according to Cicero, by getting two of her hangers-on to assault him homosexually.[81] The picture is brilliantly built up of a wilful, domineering and impetuous character impatient of any restriction to her least desire, a character motivated, in Cicero's memorable phrase, by a headstrong and unbridled mentality – 'mente nescioqua effrenata atque praecipiti'.[82]

In general terms, I see no reason to doubt the essential accuracy of this portrait of Clodia. It fits in perfectly with the behaviour of her brothers in the fifties B.C., the arrogant assumption that they could do what they liked, however outrageous, and get away with it – behaviour for which the evidence is much more than just Ciceronian forensic allegation, and which I think may well have given rise to the recurring theme of *superbia Claudiana* in the pseudo-history of the early and middle Republic.[83] They were evidently a close-knit family, and we know that Clodia identified herself with Publius' career, at least.[84] But are we to consider her *potentia* in the same light as that of her brothers? Was she, in any sense, politically significant?

At first sight it might seem that she was. Cicero could allege, to an audience familiar with the events of only a few days before, that the trial of Clodius' right-hand man Sex. Cloelius had ended in an acquittal thanks to the influence (*gratia*) of Clodia.[85] In one sense, as the drafter of Clodius' legislation and

---

[81] Cic. *Cael.* 71; Plut. *Cic.* 29.4 (cf. *Cael. ap*. Quint. VIII 6.52) for 'Quadrantaria'.

[82] Cic. *Cael.* 35, cf. 2, 70, 78 (*libido*); 49, 55 (*temeraria, procax, irata*); 53 ('o immoderata mulier!').

[83] Wiseman 1979, part II (esp. 121–5). The theme is first detectable in the early forties B.C. (pp. 104–11); so is the work of Valerius Antias (pp. 117–21).

[84] Cic. *Att.* II 12.2, cf. 1.5; Cic. *Sest.* 81, *QF* II 12.2 for the *gens Clodia* considered as a political unit. Clodia and Publius: Cic. *Cael.* 32, 36, 78, *har. resp.* 9, 38f etc. Publius and Appius: Schol. Bob. 127St.

[85] Cic. *Cael.* 78, cf. *QF* II 5.4. See D. R. Shackleton Bailey, *CQ* 10 (1960) 41–3 for the name as Cloelius, not Clodius; there has been some resistance to this idea (see J.-M. Flambard, *MEFR* 90 (1978) 235–45, and bibliography cited there), but it seems to me that Shackleton Bailey's main arguments have not been refuted.

CLODIA: PLEASURE AND SWAY

the administrator of the *lex frumentaria*,[86] Cloelius was a
person of political importance – but his politics were those of
the street, not of the Forum or the Senate House; his importance was simply as Clodius' agent, handling the arson, intimidation and grievous bodily harm which Clodius disdained to
carry out in person.[87] He was a *scriba*, and a man of no social
position – a dependant of Clodius, or as he would no doubt
have put it himself, one of his *amici tenuiores*. The Claudii
looked after their own: he expected protection, and he got it.[88]
But why was it Clodia's influence in particular that got him
off?

We must be very careful here, for our only evidence is Cicero's
hostile rhetoric, with no corroboration from the letters or any
other more objective source. In all the invective Cicero devotes
to Cloelius, one item recurs constantly: the uncleanness of
Cloelius' mouth and tongue.[89] Ironically commenting in the *de
domo* on Cloelius' powers of logic, Cicero remarks 'You have a
taste for that *too*' – and the word he uses is *ligurrire*, 'to lick',
which, like its synonyms *lingere* and *lambere*, was also used in an

---

[86] *Scriptor legum*: Cic. *dom.* 47f, 83, 129, *Sest.* 133, *har. resp.* 11, cf. *Mil.* 33, *dom.* 50 (*auctor*),
Asc. 33C (*scriba*). *Res frumentaria*: Cic. *dom.* 25f; cf. *JRS* 59 (1969) 64 n.48 for the
probable relevance of the burning of the temple of the Nymphs (Cic. *Cael.* 78,
Mil. 73).

[87] Asc. 7C, 'familiarissimus Clodii et operarum Clodianarum dux'; cf. Cic. *Pis.* 23, *har.
resp.* 59 (*canis*), *Cael.* 78 ('minister aut dux seditionis'), *Mil.* 90 (*satelles*). See in
particular *Cael.* 78: 'qui aedis sacras . . . incendit (cf. *Mil.* 73), qui Catuli monumentum
adflixit (cf. *dom.* 102f, 114), meam domum diruit, mei fratris incendit (cf. *Att.* IV 3.2),
qui in Palatio et in urbis oculis servitia ad caedem et ad inflammandam urbem incitavit'.
Intimidation: *Mil.* 33. Violence: Asc. 47C (cf. *Mil.* 18, 37) on the death of M. Papirius.
For each outrage Cicero blames either Sex. Cloelius or Clodius himself, according to
the requirements of his argument at the time.

[88] 'Homo egentissimus' (Cic. *dom.* 25); 'sine re, sine spe, sine sede, sine fortunis'
(*Cael.* 78); 'iis dignissimus quibuscum vivit' (*Sest.* 133); Asc. 33C (*scriba*), cf. 7C
(not a freedman, *pace* Flambard, n.85 above). Cic. *Cael.* 21: 'funguntur officio,
defendunt suos'. *Tenuiores amici*: Cic. *Mur.* 70, with P. White, *JRS* 68 (1978)
80f.

[89] Cic. *dom.* 26 ('ore impurissimo'), 47 ('spurca lingua'), *har. resp.* 11 ('impuro ore'), *Cael.*
78 ('ore, lingua inquinatus'); cf. *dom.* 25 ('helluo spurcatissimus'), 48 ('omnium impu-
rissimus'), *Pis.* 8 ('homo impurus . . . osculo tuo dignissimus').

obscene sense.[90] Cicero's audience understood the innuendo perfectly well, since only a few minutes earlier, addressing Clodius, Cicero had described Cloelius as *praegustator libidinum tuarum* and as *socius tui sanguinis*. 'Go and look for him,' he urges Clodius later in the speech; 'you'll find him hiding at your sister's house – with his head down.'[91] What Cicero alleges – though not, of course, in so many words – is that Cloelius too was Clodia's lover, or at least the instrument of her pleasure. We cannot know what truth there was in the allegation, but the type of intercourse to which Cicero alludes would indeed be appropriate to their respective statuses – she the wilful and imperious mistress, he the dependant who must gratify her wish, whatever the humiliation to himself.[92]

It may be, then, that the story of her *gratia* getting Cloelius acquitted in 56 means no more than that the Claudii successfully protected a loyal servant, and that Cicero, for his own forensic purposes in the Caelius case, attributed it in particular to the influence of Clodia. Even if he was right (and I repeat that we cannot know), it hardly indicates *political* influence, in the true sense of the phrase. To see the nature – and the limits – of Clodia's political importance, we need to go back three years and look at Cicero's correspondence with Atticus in the spring of 59 B.C.

The dramatic first months of Caesar's consulship had already seen the agrarian law forced through (with uproar in the Forum) despite the furious opposition of Bibulus and Cato, and Pompey's settlement of the East at last ratified, to the public humiliation of Lucullus. Cicero had unsuccessfully defended his

---

[90] Cic. *dom.* 47; cf. *Verr.* III 177, *fam.* XI 21.5 for *ligurrire* as 'to be keen on'. Obscene sense: Suet. *Tib.* 45 (from a *fabula Atellana*), Mart. III 96.1 (*lingere*), Juv. II 49 (*lambere*), etc.; see Adams 1982, 140f. For the extent of obscenity permitted in oratory, cf. Adams 1982, 222f.

[91] Cic. *dom.* 25, 83, cf. Cat. 88.8 (*capite demisso*). Is the implication of *dom.* 25 that Clodius too was a *cunnilingus*? Cf. Cat. 79.4, with Cic. *Pis.* 8, Suet. *gramm.* 23, Mart. XII 59.10, 85.3.

[92] For the humiliation involved, see for instance Juv. IX 3–5, Sen. *quaest. nat.* I 16.4–7, Mart. VII 67.13–17, IX 67.5–8 (*mala condicio*), *Anth. Pal.* XI 219–21.

consular colleague C. Antonius, in a trial which had two unexpected consequences: the victorious prosecutor, young M.
Caelius, moved to the Palatine and made Clodia's acquaintance,
and a rash remark by Cicero caused Caesar and Pompey to agree
to Clodius' transfer to the *plebs*. Metellus Celer had died suddenly, leaving the consular province of Transalpine Gaul
without a governor; Pompey, equally suddenly, had married
Caesar's daughter Julia, to the chagrin of the Servilii Caepiones;
and Ptolemy Auletes had bought his title to the throne of
Alexandria for 144 million sesterces.[93] By the time of the senatorial recess in April, when the *principes civitatis* habitually retired
for a month or so to their villas and estates, the political atmo-
sphere was electric. Who would get Metellus Celer's place in the
college of augurs? Who would get the fat embassy to Alexandria?
Who would be picked for the new agrarian commission? What
was Clodius going to do now that he could look forward to
being tribune?[94]

It was the last question that mattered most to Cicero, as he left
on a tour of his country houses. His first stay was at Antium, on
the coast some forty miles south of Rome, where he disconten-
tedly counted the waves and tried not to think about politics.[95]
Clodia herself was only a few miles to the north, at her villa at
Solonium, where a family council was evidently taking place.
She and Cicero, of course, were not on visiting terms, but she
had promised to report to Atticus when she got back to Rome,
and Cicero looks forward to hearing all about it in Atticus'
letters.[96] That was on the 16th or 17th of April; a couple of days
later, en route to Formiae, Cicero's party came up from Antium

[93] Bibulus and Cato: Dio xxxviii 6.1–3, Plut. *Cato min.* 32, etc. Lucullus: Suet. *Jul.* 20.4,
cf. Plut. *Luc.* 42.6. Caelius: Cic. *Cael.* 18, 74f. Clodius: Cic. *dom.* 41. Metellus Celer:
Cic. *Att.* I 20.5, II 1.11 (60 B.C.), *Vat.* 19, *Cael.* 59. Julia: Cic. *Att.* II 17.1, VIII 3.3; Plut.
Caes. 14.4; *Pomp.* 47.6 etc.; see Wiseman 1974, 185. Ptolemy: Suet. *l.* 54.3, Caes. *BC*
III 107.2 etc. (pp. 55–8 below).

[94] Cic. *Att.* II 4.2, 5.1–3, 7.2f, 12.1f etc.

[95] Cic. *Att.* II 4.4, 5.2, 6.1f; 8.4 and 10 for his itinerary.

[96] Cic. *Att.* II 9.1; for the site of Solonium see Cic. *de div.* I 79 (*ager Lanuvinus*), Festus
296L (off the Via Ostiensis), Livy VIII 12.2.

on to the Via Appia at the staging post of Tres Tabernae. There they ran into young Curio, full of hot news about Clodius' plans, and a letter-carrier from Atticus. Cicero eagerly read the letters, and dashed off an immediate reply (*Att.* II 12.2):

So much for *viva voce*! I got a far better idea of what's going on from your letters than from talking to Curio – all about the daily rumours, Publius' plans, Lady Ox-Eyes sounding the charge, Athenio carrying the standard, the letter to Gnaeus [Pompey], what Theophanes and Memmius said. How you've whetted my appetite about that licentious party! I'm ravenous with curiosity, but I don't mind your not writing to me about that particular *symposion*: I'd rather hear it in person.

'Lady Ox-Eyes' is Clodia, the Homeric epithet βοῶπις referring to Hera, who was both sister and wife to Zeus. She had evidently returned from Solonium; Atticus, it seems, had been present at one of her sophisticated dinner-parties, but was saving up his account of it until he came to Formiae himself. Cicero looks forward to it eagerly: 'I'm all agog,' he writes a few days later, 'about your talk with Lady Ox-Eyes, and about that *delicatum convivium!*'[97]

Atticus was easy company – like Harold Nicolson at the dinner table of Sybil Colefax or Lady Cunard. Society hostesses provide an opportunity for political gossip to be disseminated, but they are not themselves political figures of any importance. Nor was Clodia, except as the sister and confidante of a politician momentarily at the very centre of the stage. In any case, it is clear enough from Cicero's language that what he was dying to hear was not so much the political outlook as what went on at the sort of party he never got invited to himself. Remember his letter to Paetus thirteen years later, written from the dining-room of Volumnius Eutrapelus, where Cytheris was reclining on the couch of the host. 'What?' he imagines Paetus saying: 'the exemplary Cicero at that sort of *convivium*?'[98] Cicero reassures him: 'even as a

---

[97] Cic. *Att.* II 14.1; for Atticus' contacts, and his familiarity with Clodia, cf. *Att.* II 22.5 and Shackleton Bailey 1965–8, I 6–9.
[98] Cic. *fam.* IX 26.2, cf. Suet. *Gaius* 24.1 for the significance of *infra cubare*.

young man I wasn't interested in all that, and much less now I'm old'. But the correspondence in 59 shows that he was at least curious about the habits of the *beau monde*.

Inevitably, our investigation has brought us back from the Forum to the Palatine, and into the dining-room of Clodia's house. 'In triclinio Coa', Caelius called her, apparently alluding both to the transparency of her dress and to her sexually encouraging manner.[99] Cicero, in a different style, preferred to speak darkly of *inusitatae libidines* and *omnia inaudita vitia*.[100] In non-forensic contexts, fortunately, he was less portentous, and more helpful to the social historian.

Here he is in the *de finibus* (II 23), arguing against the Epicurean position:

Mundos, elegantes, optimis cocis, pistoribus, piscatu, aucupio, venatione, his omnibus exquisitis, vitantes cruditatem, quibus 'vinum defusum e pleno sit †hirsizon (ut ait Lucilius) cui nihil dum sit vis et sacculus abstulerit', adhibentes ludos et quae sequuntur, illa quibus detractis clamat Epicurus se nescire quid sit bonum; adsint etiam formosi pueri qui ministrent; respondeat his vestis, argentum, Corinthium, locus ipse, aedificium; hos ergo asotos bene quidem vivere aut beate numquam dixerim.

Look at the smart and fashionable – people with the best chefs and confectioners, the choicest of fish, fowl, game and all that. They avoid overeating, they have their wine, as Lucilius puts it, 'decanted from a full cask, with nothing caught in the strainer'. They go in for shows, and what follows shows, the things without which Epicurus announces he doesn't know what the Good is. Throw in beautiful boys to wait on them, and clothes, silver, Corinthian bronzes, the dining place itself and the house, all in keeping. Well, I would never admit that profligates like that live a good or happy life.

'Shows, and what follows shows' – here we are back with the stage-folk again, and in an explicitly erotic context. For what Epicurus declared inseparable from the Good was *obscaenae*

---

[99] Cael. *ap*. Quint. VIII 6.52: 'in triclinio coam, in cubiculo nolam' (p. 76 below); for *Coae vestes* (Hor. *Sat.* I 2.101 etc.), see J.-M. Poinsotte, *MEFR* 91 (1979) 455f. See Lyne 1980, 192–8 for the social background.

[100] Cic. *Cael.* 57, emphasising the participation of Clodia's servants.

voluptates, to use Cicero's own unlovely translation of αἱ δι᾽ Ἀφροδισίων ἡδοναί.[101] Perhaps the best commentary on Cicero's *ludi et quae sequuntur*, in the context of banqueting, is the last scene of Xenophon's *Symposion*. At the end of Callias' dinner-party in honour of Autolycus, a mime-scene of Dionysus and Ariadne is performed to music; so convincingly do the young dancers mime their love, that as the party breaks up the unmarried guests swear to marry, and the married ones gallop off to enjoy their wives.[102] At a less decorous Greek *symposion*, there would probably be *hetairae* or complaisant flute-girls ready to hand.[103] More significant for our purposes, the Roman tradition was for wives to dine with their husbands; and though they were supposed to sit up rather than recline, in fashionable circles that distinction was already being ignored in the late Republic.[104] It is the combination of Roman dining customs with Greek theatrical entertainments[105] – often, of course, erotic – that lies behind Cicero's phrase and the lifestyle of ladies like Clodia.

Whether or not they should be included among the *nobilium ludi* at which young Eucharis starred, such 'private engagements' must have been an important part of the mime-actor's work.

The first regular stage entertainments of the year were at the *ludi compitalicii* on or about 1 January, reintroduced by Clodius in

---

[101] Epicurus περὶ τέλους 67 Usener (Athen. VII 278f, 280a, XII 546e, Diog. Laert. X 6): οὐ γὰρ ἔγωγε δύναμαι νοῆσαι τἀγαθὸν ἀφαιρῶν μὲν τὰς διὰ χυλῶν ἡδονάς, ἀφαιρῶν δὲ τὰς δι᾽ ἀφροδισίων, ἀφαιρῶν δὲ τὰς δι᾽ ἀκροαμάτων, ἀφαιρῶν δὲ καὶ τὰς διὰ μορφῆς κατ᾽ ὄψιν ἡδείας κινήσεις. The last phrases show that the *ludi* themselves are included, as well as *quae sequuntur*. Cicero's version: *ND* I 111, *de fin.* II 7, *Pis.* 69, cf. *Tusc.* III 41, 46.

[102] Xen. *Symp.* 9.2–7, cf. 3.1 (erotic effect of dancers), 7.5 (θεάματα).

[103] See (e.g.) Aristoph. *Wasps* 1346, Athen. XIII 607d–e, Machon 253 Gow, Alciphron IV 13.14–16; cf. K. J. Dover, *Arethusa* 6 (1973) 63.

[104] Val. Max. II 1.2; n.98 above.

[105] See Livy XXXIX 6.8 on the Hellenistic luxury brought back by Manlius Vulso's army in 187 ('psaltriae sambucistriaeque et convivalia alia ludorum oblectamenta addita epulis'); Sall. *Hist.* II 70M on the dinner for Q. Metellus Pius in 74 ('scaenis ad ostentationem histrionum fabricatis'); Vitr. *Arch.* VI 7.3f on *oeci* for *virilia convivia* in Greek mansions ('ministrationum ludorumque operis locus'); Sall. *BJ* 85.39 on *histriones* in the context of aristocratic dinner parties.

58 after a period of suspension and presided over with suitable pomp in that year by Sex. Cloelius himself as one of the *magistri vicorum*.[106] Although these *ludi* lasted only one day in the late Republic, performances were evidently held simultaneously at crossroad stages throughout the city,[107] offering plenty of work for actors and actresses. The main theatrical festivals provided six 'theatre days' at the Megalesia (4–9 April), seven at the Cerealia (12–18 April), five at the Floralia (28 April–2 May), seven at the *ludi Apollinares* (6–12 July), nine at the *ludi Romani* (4–12 September), six at the *ludi Victoriae* (26–31 October), and nine at the *ludi plebeii* (4–12 November). With the Compitalia, that amounts to a total of fifty days in the year. Some of the minor annual *feriae*, such as the Liberalia and the Quinquatrus, may have involved stage performances; trade-guilds and religious associations may also have provided regular engagements; but it is hard to imagine that more than about one third of the actor's year was booked up, and one-off public shows for triumphs and funerals would certainly not fill the rest.[108] It is clear that if they were not reduced to competing with the cheapjacks and fortune-tellers in the booths of the Circus Maximus,[109] what actors did most of the time was perform for private parties.

We see Pylades performing at Augustus' dinner-parties, and Paris at Nero's; Trimalchio had bought a troupe of *comoedi*, while Ummidia Quadratilla had her own *pantomimi*, who were also to be seen in the theatre when they were not entertaining their mistress and her guests.[110] Cicero's casual reference to *ludi et quae*

---

[106] Cic. *Pis.* 8, Asc. 7C; Livy XXXIV 7.2, Dion. Hal. IV 14.3–4, *ILLRP* 702–4 on *magistri vicorum*; cf. Wiseman 1979, 127. Date: Cic. *Pis.* 8, cf. *Att.* VII 7.3, Varro *LL* VI 25.

[107] Macr. *Sat.* I 7.34, cf. Suet. *Aug.* 43.1; Prop. II 22.3–6, with W. A. Camps, *Propertius Elegies Book II* (Cambridge 1967) 151f.

[108] Major *ludi*: evidence summarised in A. Degrassi, *Inscr. Ital.* XIII.2 (Rome 1963). Liberalia: Ovid *Fasti* III 783, Tert. *de spect.* 5.4. Quinquatrus: Tac. *Ann.* XIV 12.1, cf. Suet. *Dom.* 4.4. Collegia: Asc. 7C, with Treggiari 1969, 170 n.8, 198f. Religious associations: *ILLRP* 701, cf. Wiseman 1974, 131–4. Triumphs and funerals: p. 33 above.

[109] Suet. *Aug.* 74 ('triviales ex circo ludii'), with *PBSR* 48 (1980) 13.

[110] Macr. *Sat.* II 17.6, Tac. *Ann.* XIII 20.1; Petr. *Sat.* 53.13, cf. G. N. Sandy, *TAPA* 104 (1974) 329–46; Pliny *ep.* VII 24.4–6, cf. Syme 1979, 662 = *Historia* 17 (1968) 75f. *Dig.*

sequuntur makes it clear that much the same applied to the sybaritic banquets of his own contemporaries.

Moreover, the guests themselves might choose to perform. Cicero paints a splendid picture of Gabinius' house echoing with music and song as the consul himself dances naked *in convivio*; the exquisitely sophisticated young men who hung about Catiline in 63 did that too, and it is no surprise to find it recorded of M. Caelius, who like Gabinius had been one of that number, that he was proud of his dancing skill.[111] Velleius shows us the sort of performance that was involved: L. Plancus, he reports, danced the role of the sea-god Glaucus at a banquet, naked except for a fish-tail, with reeds around his head and his body painted blue.[112] When admiration of the professional's art came to mean more than the dignity of his own status, at a private party the sophisticated Roman could let his hair down and act as a *mimus* himself.

Similarly, the Roman lady could act as a *mima*. Transpose Xenophon's scene to Clodia's dining-room, and imagine the impact if the Ariadne role were danced by the hostess herself. Our only evidence for Clodia as a dancer comes from a scholiast who may have misunderstood Cicero's reference to her *embolia*; but it seems more likely than not that we may say of her what Sallust said of D. Brutus' wife Sempronia:[113]

Litteris Graecis et Latinis docta, psallere saltare elegantius quam necesse est probae, multa alia quae instrumenta luxuriae sunt.

Well read in Greek and Latin literature, she could play the lyre and dance more elegantly than an honest woman needs to; and she had many other gifts which are the stock-in-trade of *luxuria*.

XXXVIII 1.27 (Julian): a freedman *pantomimus* must offer his services free to his patron's friends. Cf. also Tac. *Ann.* 1 77.5 (a ban on private engagements in A.D. 15): 'ne alibi quam in theatro spectarentur'.

[111] Cic. *Pis.* 22, cf. 19, *red. sen.* 13, *dom.* 60, *Planc.* 87 (*saltator*); *Cat.* II 23, Macr. *Sat.* III 14.15; Cic. *Mur.* 13, with Endnote 1 below (Murena and Gabinius were probably two of a kind, though Cicero's treatment of each disguises the likeness).

[112] Vell. Pat. II 83.2; cf. Suet. *Aug.* 70.1, on the 'banquet of the twelve gods' with Octavian as *choragos*.

[113] Schol. Bob. 135St on Cic. *Sest.* 116 (p. 27 above); Sall. *Cat.* 25.2. For *matronae* being taught to dance by Greek professionals, see Hor. *Odes* III 6.21f, Juv. VI 0.19; for boys and girls, already in the second century B.C., Scipio Aemilianus *ap.* Macr. *Sat.* III 14.6

Remembering 'what follows' in Cicero's phrase, and the association in the Roman mind of *mimae* with *meretrices*,[114] we can see how easy it was for Cicero to blacken Clodia's moral reputation in the eyes of the jury in Caelius' trial.

Horti, domus, Baiae – those are the scenes of Clodia's *vita meretricia*.[115] Baiae, of course, with its beach parties and boat parties, was notorious for luxurious living;[116] the Palatine house we have looked at already; but what of the *horti*, Clodia's park on the Tiber bank? There if anywhere her lifestyle is likely to have been on more or less public view.

The site, Cicero maliciously suggests, was carefully chosen as a pick-up place, where the young men went to swim. We may recall another phrase Sallust used of Sempronia: 'so ardent were her appetites that she sought men out more often than they sought her'.[117] An episode in Petronius offers a commentary on these allegations. Circe, a wealthy lady of the city of Croton, takes a fancy to Encolpius, the anti-hero of the *Satyricon*, who is pretending to be a slave. She sends her fastidious servant-girl Chrysis to bring him to her park. Beneath the shade of the plane trees, on the grass among the flowers, she invites him to take her, if he wishes. But the anger of Priapus renders Encolpius impotent. Summoned again, this time by contemptuous letter, and with his manhood apparently restored, he is brought back to the same idyllic spot. Circe, reclining on a golden cushion, dismisses her servants and calls him to her embrace. But when it comes to the point, he fails again.

Stung by this public insult, bent on revenge she ran off calling for her grooms and ordered them to flog me. Not content even with this

---

(fr. 30 Malc.); for the social problem caused by well-born amateurs (of both sexes) appearing on the stage, see *AE* 1978 145, with B. Levick, *JRS* 73 (1983) 105–10.

[114] E.g. Cic. *Verr.* III 83 (Tertia), Hor. *Sat.* 1 2.58 (Origo).

[115] Cic. *Cael.* 38, 49.

[116] Varro *Men.* 44B (Non. 226L), Cic. *Att.* 1 16.10, II 8.2, *fam.* IX 12.1, Sen. *ep.* 51; D'Arms 1970, 39–72, esp. 42f. *Actae, navigationes*: Cic. *Cael.* 35, 49, *Verr.* V 31, 40, 63, 94, Sen. *ep.* 51.4, Suet. *Gaius* 37.2, *Nero* 27.3, Alciphron 1 15, etc.

[117] Cic. *Cael.* 36, cf. Hor. *Sat.* II 1.8, *Odes* 1 8.8, III 7.28, 12.7; Sall. *Cat.* 25.3.

savage punishment, she sent for her spinning-women and the very dregs of her household, and told them to spit on me . . .

And then he is thrown out bodily through the gates. That, it seems to me, is the true Clodia style, the real meaning of her *potentia*, as she exercised it, for instance, on the unfortunate Vettius.[118]

If a fictional parallel is thought unsatisfactory, sober history may redress the balance. Another patrician lady (great-great-great-niece of Clodia herself) held a party in another park in the year A.D. 48, dressed as a Maenad, with a *procax chorus* of guests revelling in Bacchic guise, and her bigamous husband – the consul designate – wearing buskins and crowned with ivy. She was Valeria Messallina, another *mulier potens* whose fancies it was dangerous to refuse. One of her lovers was an actor, Mnester, who like Encolpius had suffered flogging at the order of his imperious mistress.[119]

Tacitus was afraid his readers would find the episode of Messallina and Silius incredible. Carrying on so openly, how did she think she could get away with it? He himself knew the answer: she just didn't care. Marrying Silius, as he points out with a fine psychological insight, appealed to her because of its very enormity; she took active pleasure in her reputation for outrageous behaviour.[120] Clodia didn't care either. Recklessly determined to pay back Caelius, with that 'headstrong and unbridled mentality' of which Cicero speaks, she laid herself wide open to the character-assassination so effectively carried out by Caelius and by Cicero himself.[121]

4. *IMMODERATA MULIER*

Before taking leave of Clodia, we ought to remember the man she was married to for twenty years, Q. Metellus Celer. In at

[118] Petr. *Sat.* 126–32 (trans. from 132); Cic. *Cael.* 71 (p. 39 above).

[119] Tac. *Ann.* XI 31, cf. 12.2 for the danger, 36.1 on Mnester; Dio LXI 31.4, συμποσιόν τε περιβόητον καὶ κῶμον ἀσελγέστατον (cf. Cicero on Clodia at *Att.* II 12.2).

[120] Tac. *Ann.* XI 26.3: 'ob magnitudinem infamiae, cuius apud prodigos novissima voluptas est'. Cf. 12.3 ('non furtim sed multo comitatu'); 27 for the reader's incredulity.

[121] Cic. *Cael.* 35; n.82 above.

CLODIA: PLEASURE AND SWAY

least one respect – his arrogance – Metellus was worthy of her.
His surviving letter to Cicero in 62 is a cold and high-handed
rebuke; and as consul two years later he is said to have told
Clodius in the Senate that he would kill him with his own hands if
he didn't behave.[122] He could probably have done it, too, for he
knew how to handle arms. As his whole career reveals, Metellus
was a *vir militaris*.

We have seen that his first appearance is as a junior officer in the
early seventies, perhaps serving under his new father-in-law in
Macedonia.[123] How long he was away we do not know, nor
whether he fought in his quaestorship against Spartacus or Mithridates or the Sertorians; there was plenty of opportunity for an
ambitious young soldier to see some action. The year after his
tribunate he was away again, as legate, perhaps with his brother-
in-law Pompey in the campaign against the pirates.[124] He certainly served in the Mithridatic War; late in 66 he fought off a
dangerous attack on his winter camp near the Caspian Sea, and he
probably saw through the rest of Pompey's campaign in the lands
of the Caucasus before returning to stand for the praetorship in
the summer of 64. Before his year of office as praetor was over he
was in arms again, leaving early for his province of Cisalpine
Gaul to counter the forces of Catiline; as he pointedly remarked to
Cicero in January 62, he was in charge of an army and waging a
war.[125] Back again to stand for the consulship in 61, he was duly
elected, and given Transalpine Gaul by senatorial decree when
the news of the migration of the Helvetii reached Rome in March
60. He had high hopes of a triumph, and might even have cheated
Caesar of his fame if he had not died so suddenly in 59.[126]

122 Cic. *fam.* v 1, *Cael.* 60; cf. Dio xxxvii 50.3 for his notorious φρόνημα.
123 Sall. *Hist.* 1 135M, p. 24 above.
124 Cic. *leg. Man.* 58, with Syme 1979, 557–65 = *JRS* 53 (1963) 55–60; cf. also Sumner
  1973, 132f and Gruen 1974, 182 n.72, against the suggestion made in *CQ* 14 (1964)
  122f. Or Celer could have been *legatus* to his cousin Q. Creticus in Crete.
125 Dio xxxvi 54.2–3; Cic. *Cat.* ii 5, 26, *fam.* v 1.2 ('qui exercitui praesum, qui bellum
  gero'), Sall. *Cat.* 30.5, 42.3, 57.2 (three legions); E. Badian, *Mélanges André Piganiol*
  (Paris 1966) 914–16.
126 Cic. *Att.* 1 19.2 (Helvetii), 20.5 (triumph).

No doubt it suited Clodia that her husband was away so long with the legions, though we have no way of telling whether all his periods at home were marked by the state of civil war between the two of them that Cicero reveals in the year 60. She bore him one child, so far as we know – a daughter, who grew up like her mother.[127] Roman marriage was explicitly 'for the begetting of children' (the wedding formula), and we can be sure that Metellus wanted a son. Two generations earlier, his family had been proverbially prolific: two generations later, it was extinct.[128] One of the reasons, no doubt, was the lifestyle of ladies like Clodia. Somebody once asked an heiress of the noble Popillii Laenates why it is that animals have sexual intercourse only when they want to conceive: 'because they're animals', said Popillia – and her family too is not heard of in subsequent generations.[129]

With marriage *sine manu*, a woman did not come under the legal control of her husband. She remained her father's responsibility, or, if her father was dead (as Clodia's was), the responsibility of her relatives; if they did not choose to exert their authority, she could do pretty much as she liked.[130] It is unlikely that Clodia's brothers Appius, Gaius and Publius, whose own behaviour was extravagant enough, would have bothered to do anything serious to control Clodia's. The Claudian 'family council' approved Clodia's manumission of the slaves who had betrayed Caelius' poison plot to her: 'At last!' says Cicero ironically, 'we've found something she's done which her relatives approve of!'[131] Whether as wife or widow, it is clear that Clodia went her own way.

---

[127] Civil war: Cic. *Att.* II 1.5. Daughter Metella: Shackleton Bailey 1965–8, v 412f on *Att.* XII 40.4, 52.2, XIII 7; Wiseman 1974, 111f, 188–90 on Ovid *Trist.* II 437f, Hor. *Sat.* II 2.239, etc.

[128] Cic. *de fin.* v 82, Pliny *NH* VII 59; Vell. Pat. II 11.3; Wiseman 1974, 176–91. Wedding formula: Tac. *Ann.* XI 27.1 and p. 113 n.73 below.

[129] Macr. *Sat.* II 5.10 ('Populia' M.f.). On contraception and abortion, see S. B. Pomeroy, *Goddesses, Whores, Wives, and Slaves* (London 1975) 166–8, and Hopkins 1983, 94–7.

[130] S. B. Pomeroy, *Ancient Society* 7 (1976) 215–27; on the obsolescence of *manus*, see A. Watson, *Law-Making in the Later Roman Republic* (Oxford 1974) 99, 115, and in *ANRW* I.2 (1972) 219f.

[131] Cic. *Cael.* 68. For the brothers and their habits, see Wiseman 1979, 124f and 134f.

But independence has its price. To do without restrictions is also to do without protection. Clodia was vulnerable – to rude songs chanted about her in the Forum,[132] to well-publicised gifts like the purseful of coppers or the perfume-jar filled with something unmentionable,[133] and above all to the sort of treatment meted out to her at the trial of Caelius.[134] She could fight back, of course, using her bully-boys to pay out the impudent Vettius and to keep on hounding Caelius even after his acquittal.[135] But that must have been little consolation for the public ridicule to which the brilliant oratory of Caelius and Cicero had exposed her in April 56. Maybe she didn't care, *praeceps* and *effrenata* to the last. But her brothers were coming up to their praetorships and consulships, and were perhaps more sensitive about bad publicity. At any rate, for whatever reason, she drops completely out of the limelight, reappearing in our sources only eleven years later, when Cicero was actually thinking of buying the once notorious *horti* himself.[136]

Where was Clodia, for instance, when her brother Publius was murdered on the Appian Way in 52? The tears of bereaved noblewomen made a great impact at his killer's trial, but they were those of his wife and his mother-in-law, not his beloved sister.[137] My guess is that after 56 she spent much more of her time not in her town house but at Baiae or Solonium or in her

---

[132] Cic. *QF* II 3.2 (Feb. 56); cf. n.75 above, and Tac. *Ann.* XI 13.1 on *populi lascivia* at the theatre (prominent ladies insulted).

[133] *Quadrantes*: Plut. *Cic.* 29.4, cf. Cic. *Cael.* 62, Cael. *ap.* Quint. VIII 6.52 ('Quadrantaria'). *Pyxis*: Cic. *Cael.* 69 ('audita et percelebrata sermonibus'), Quint. VI 3.25 ('quod neque oratori neque ulli viro gravi conveniat'); cf. Wiseman 1974, 170–5.

[134] See esp. Cic. *Cael.* 31f (explanation to the presiding magistrate); p. 83 below.

[135] Cic. *Cael.* 71 (Camurtius and Caesernius), *QF* II 12.2, cf. *fam.* VIII 12.2f (Servius Pola).

[136] Cic. *Att.* XII 38a.2–XIII 29.2 (May 45); Shackleton Bailey 1965–8, V 412f for the identification. The Clodia of *Att.* IX 6.3 (49 B.C.) was probably the ex-wife of Lucullus: see Wiseman 1974, 113f on *IG* III² 4233.

[137] Asc. 40C, cf. also 32C for Fulvia. Was Clodia in Asia or Cilicia with Gaius or Appius? Unlikely: in the Republic, proconsuls' women-folk did not accompany them to the province as they did later under the Principate (A. J. Marshall, *Ancient Society* 6 (1975) 118f).

riverside *horti*, enjoying the life of luxury as always, but away from her eloquent ill-wishers in the city.[138]

In May 45 B.C., when Clodia was about fifty-two and the limelight of notoriety was now on her daughter Metella,[139] she received an approach from her old acquaintance Atticus about the possibility of her selling her riverside gardens.[140] Cicero was looking for somewhere to live in retirement, at Rome but not in the centre of things – and he wanted a place where he could build a shrine to his beloved daughter. What Clodia thought of that proposal we are not told. At any rate, she didn't want to sell. Why should she? 'She likes the place, and she's not short of money.'[141]

And that is where we leave her, pleasing herself to the last, sumptuous in her park like a dowager duchess. To our age, with its egalitarian and essentially puritanical preconceptions, she is a figure fascinating but scarcely comprehensible. It takes the eighteenth century to do her justice. Alexander Pope would have understood her perfectly, for she exemplified both the ruling passions by which he maliciously defined 'the characters of women'. Everything we know about Clodia suggests a woman motivated by the love of pleasure and the love of sway.

---

138 She was out of Rome in May 45 (Cic. *Att.* XII 42.1, 47.2, 52.2), though that need not be significant. For the comparative seclusion of *horti*, cf. Cic. *Att.* XII 29.2 ('nec enim esse in urbe possum nec a vobis abesse').

139 See n. 127 above.

140 See n. 136 above. Atticus: n.97 above, with Cic. *Att.* X 8.3 (Sex. Cloelius his *cliens*, 49 B.C.), XIV 8.1 (will know what Clodia is doing, April 44).

141 Cic. *Att.* XII 42.2, 'delectatur enim et copiosa est' (n.80 above for her wealth).

CHAPTER III

THE TRIAL OF MARCUS CAELIUS

Dic aliquid contra, ut duo simus!

CAELIUS, quoted in Seneca *de ira* III 8.6

I. THE CRIMES

The greatest city in the world was Alexandria. Rome was the centre of power, about to transform herself into a capital architecturally worthy of her empire, but still in the mid-first century B.C. no city could rival Alexandria 'in elegance and extent and riches and luxury'. Indeed, it was Alexandria that served as the model for the new Rome of Caesar and Augustus.[1]

Politically, however, the Ptolemies' capital was a disaster area: 'from the death of Philometer [145 B.C.] it is a grim picture of king and populace involved in murderous and irresponsible hostility'. Philometer's brother and eventual successor, Euergetes II, earned himself such hatred by his brutal massacres that the populace rose against him and threw him out; they did the same in the next generation to his elder son Soter II (in 107) and his younger son Alexander I (in 88).[2] In the constant wars between Soter and Alexander, whoever was losing would retire to Cyprus; meanwhile a third son, Apion, ruled over Cyrene. Cyprus and Cyrene were valuable kingdoms, but Alexandria was the real prize: it was worth the hostility of the mob to be able to control the unparalleled fertility of Egypt, an emporium 'like a

---

[1] Diod. Sic. XVII 52.5f (eyewitness account); Fraser 1972, passim. For the architectural inadequacy of Rome, cf. Cic. *leg. agr.* II 96, Suet. *Aug.* 28.3; for Alexandria as the model see F. Castagnoli, *RFIC* 109 (1981) 414–23.
[2] Diod. Sic. XXXIII 6, 12, Justin XXXVIII 8.5–11, Paus. I 9.2, Porph. *FGrH* 260F2.8, etc.; Fraser 1972, I 121–3 (quotation from 120), cf. 81f and 86f on the mob.

meeting-place of the whole world', and revenues of 6,000 talents per year.[3]

When Apion died in 96, he bequeathed Cyrene to the Romans. They did nothing with it (at first); but the last such bequest, by Attalus of Pergamum in 133, had been immediately exploited to provide regular tribute for a Roman treasury now responsible for supplying the citizens of Rome with subsidised corn supplies. The principle that the empire should pay for the benefits of the Roman citizen body was a dangerous one for wealthy kingdoms like those of the Ptolemies.[4] How long could they stay independent if the Romans decided they needed more money?

Ptolemy Alexander died in 88, Soter in 80. The only male heir was at Rome – Alexander's son Alexander II, who had escaped from the hands of Mithridates and entrusted himself to those of Sulla. Armed with Roman diplomatic backing and funds borrowed from Roman bankers, Alexander II entered on his inheritance, married the queen (his aunt), murdered her, and was in his turn murdered by the infuriated multitude – all within nineteen days.[5] It may be that their fury was not only for the death of a popular queen but also because of increased taxation to pay off the king's Roman creditors.[6]

How the next succession was effected we do not know, but two illegitimate sons of Soter were found who were to divide the remaining inheritance between them: one was to have Cyprus, the other Alexandria and Egypt.[7] But there was a problem. The murdered king had allegedly made a will bequeathing his realm to Rome.[8]

Neither brother could feel safe until that will had been discre-

[3] Strabo XVII 798, Dio Chrys. *Orat.* 32.36 (trade centre); Diod. Sic. XVII 52.6 (revenues); on Egypt as a corn growing land, see Rickman 1980, 114–16.
[4] Badian 1968, 45–9 for the principle; for royal bequests in general, see Braund 1983 (23f on Apion).
[5] App. *BC* I 102, Porph. *FGrH* 260F2.11, Cic. *de rege Alex.* fr. 9 (Schol. Bob. 93St, calling her his sister).
[6] Braund 1983, 27f on Cic. *leg. agr.* II 41.
[7] Pomp. Trog. *Prol.* 40, cf. Cic. *de rege Alex.* fr. 8 (Schol. Bob. 93St).
[8] Cic. *leg. agr.* I 1, II 41–4, *de rege Alex.* (Schol. Bob. 91–3St); Braund 1983, 24–8 (*contra* Badian 1967, who attributes the will to Alexander I).

dited or superseded. The king in Alexandria (we do not know the titles of his brother of Cyprus) was Ptolemaios Theos Philopatoɪ Philadelphos Neos Dionysos, nicknamed 'Auletes' from his talent on the pipe; his enemies said that was all he could do, but for twenty years he was clever enough, or lucky enough, to hang on to his precarious throne.[9] The first danger came in 75 B.C., when a crisis in Rome's public expenses, and an acute corn shortage that caused riots in the streets, led to the belated exploitation of the royal territories in Cyrene, followed in due course by the organisation of Apion's bequest as a regular province.[10] It may have been in this context that the Senate resolved to accept the will of Alexander II; certainly two Syrian princes who came to Rome to claim the disputed throne of Alexandria for themselves found the Senate unresponsive, despite the magnificent gift they had brought for the new temple of Iuppiter Capitolinus. But the Senate's resolution was vetoed, and Ptolemy could breathe again.[11] Evidently his support in Rome was well organised, and the fact that the will could not be produced must have been a strong point in his favour.[12] Nevertheless, senior senators remembered, and the question of whether or not to recognise Ptolemy as king was a serious political issue in 70 B.C.[13]

The consuls in that year were Cn. Pompeius and M. Crassus, life-long rivals in the pursuit of glory.[14] Pompey, with two triumphs already to his credit, went on to hold special commands against the pirates and against Mithridates; he was the Roman Alexander, setting wholly new standards of achievement

---

[9] Diod. Sic. I 44.1 (Neos Dionysos); Strabo XVII 796, Athen. v 206d (Auletes), cf. Cic. *leg. agr.* II 42 'neque genere neque animo regio'.

[10] Sall. *Hist.* III 43, 45, 47.6M, with Badian 1965, 119f; province first attested in about 63 (Cic. *Planc.* 63).

[11] Cic. *leg. agr.* II 41, with Braund 1983, 26f (*contra* Badian 1967, 181f). For the two princes, see Cic. *Verr.* IV 61–71, esp. 61 ('temporibus rei publicae'), 64 (alleged reason for not dedicating gift).

[12] Deduced from Cic. *leg. agr.* II 42.

[13] Cic. *Verr.* II 76, cf. *leg. agr.* II 42 (L. Philippus); for the recognition (*appellatio*) of friendly kings, see Braund 1984, 23–9.

[14] Plut. *Crass.* 6.4, 7.1–3, 12.2–4 etc.

for his competitors to aspire to. Few of them even came close, but one of those few was Crassus. As censor in 65 B.C. (in itself a splendid honour by normal standards), he hoped to trump Pompey's ace by declaring Alexandria and Egypt a tributary province of Rome.[15]

Crassus' colleague Q. Catulus was able to frustrate this scheme, but the danger for Ptolemy was still acute. For the Romans were now very used to the idea of bringing down kingdoms. Bithynia had been willed to Rome by its king in 74 but immediately occupied by Mithridates; Pompey now recovered it as a Roman province, along with Mithridates' own kingdom of Pontus, and took over as well the remains of the once great Seleucid empire in Syria. In little over ten years, Cyrene, Bithynia, Pontus and Syria had been added to Macedonia and Pergamum as the eastern empire of Rome, with direct and spectacular benefit for the Roman treasury and the welfare of the Roman citizen body.[16] Of all the hellenistic kingdoms that had grown out of Alexander's empire, only two were left, the realms of Ptolemy and his brother.

Knowing that he kept his throne only because the Romans let him, Ptolemy was assiduous in cultivating their favour. But he lost thereby the favour of the Alexandrian populace, who feared and hated the Romans. When the news reached Alexandria in 63 B.C. that a tribune had presented a bill proposing the sale of the royal estates of Egypt to finance land distributions in Italy, serious rioting broke out. He invited Pompey, then in Syria, to bring his army to help suppress the disturbances.[17] Pompey declined, but the incident illustrates the realities of the 'Egyptian question' – the precariousness of Ptolemy's throne (because of the alleged will), the people's dissatisfaction with their king (as

15 Plut. *Crass.* 13.1, Suet. *Jul.* 11.1 (with details wrongly imported from later events); cf. Cic. *leg. agr.* II 44. The Roman Alexander: Plut. *Pomp.* 2.2 etc.

16 Plut. *Pomp.* 45.3, Pliny *NH* XXXVII 16 etc.; cf. Plut. *Cato min.* 26.1, *Caes.* 8.4 (7.5m denarii on corn distribution).

17 Cic. *leg. agr.* II 41–3, App. *Mith.* 114 (the connection between the two events is hypothetical). For the Alexandrians' attitude to Romans at this time, cf. Diod. Sic. I 83.8f.

often in previous reigns), and Ptolemy's anxiety to please the man who now controlled the Greek East, the arbiter of the fate of princes.[18]

Back in Rome after his third triumph, Pompey found his ill-wishers in the Senate well able to block the ratification of his eastern settlement. So, with his old rival Crassus (who had his own reasons), he entered into the notorious political alliance with C. Caesar, consul in 59. Now was the moment for Ptolemy to get Roman recognition of his title. Not for nothing, of course: the tribune's bill in 63 had been defeated, but now the consul himself was pushing through an expensive land-distribution programme (of which Pompey's veterans would be among the beneficiaries). If the king was to keep his crown lands, he had better make a generous cash contribution instead. Say, one year's taxes, 35 million denarii in Roman money – and to be paid not to the Roman treasury but directly to Caesar and Pompey themselves, for distribution as necessary to any senators who might need special persuasion.[19]

Early in 59 the Senate duly voted – and the popular assembly confirmed by a law – that Ptolemy be formally recognised as king of Alexandria and Egypt and enjoy the status of Friend and Ally of the Roman People.[20] An embassy of distinguished senators was sent to convey the good news officially to the king, and to get the money out of him, half now and half when he could raise it.[21]

There was a long-standing Roman business community in

[18] Diod. Sic. XL 4 (Pompey's own *res gestae* inscription), App. *BC* II 9, Dio XXXVII 20.2, etc.

[19] Suet. *Jul.* 54.3 ('prope sex milia talentorum'), cf. Diod. Sic. XVII 52.6; the 17.5m still owing in 47 (Plut. *Caes.* 48.4f) was presumably half. The money went τισι τῶν 'Ρωμαίων (Dio XXXIX 12.1) – i.e. presumably not just to Caesar and Pompey themselves. Expense of Caesar's land-distributions (on which see in general Brunt 1971, 312–19): Dio XXXVIII 1.4f, to be taken from the booty of Pompey's conquests.

[20] Caes. *BC* III 107.2, Cic. *Vat.* 29 (*lex Vatinia*), *Att.* II 9.1, 16.2 (Pompey's backing), *fam.* I 9.7, *Rab. Post.* 6 (formal treaty).

[21] Cic. *Att.* II 5.1, 7.3 ('illa opima ad exigendas pecunias [legatio]'), Diod. Sic. I 83.8. Money: Dio XXXIX 12.1, cf. Plut. *Caes.* 48.4f (n.19 above); Braund (1984, 59) assumes that no cash was paid in 59.

Alexandria made rich by commercial profits at 'the meeting-place of the whole world';[22] they could help him find the ready cash immediately, and if Caesar and Pompey wanted it in Roman money, their funds would be the only source.[23] So Ptolemy had to pay their interest charges, as well as finding the second half of the total sum, and all he could do was to pass on the burden to his subjects. They were already disaffected; increased taxation made the situation worse; and when in 58 the Romans coolly expropriated the kingdom of Cyprus to fund free corn rations for their citizen body (the king, Ptolemy's brother, killed himself),[24] the full fury of the Alexandrian populace was unleashed on him.[25]

To avoid suffering the fate of his predecessor, Ptolemy left his capital in secret, and sailed first to Rhodes (where he got nothing out of Cato, the Roman commissioner for Cyprus, except unhelpful good advice) and then to Italy. He was a Friend and Ally of the Roman People – there on the Capitol, in front of the temple of Public Faith, was the inscription that proved it[26] – and he had come to invoke the Roman's treaty obligations. He wanted a Roman army to restore him to his throne.

The money that had bought him his recognition didn't extend to this as well. Caesar was far away in Gaul, Pompey had lost much of his influence; to persuade sceptical senators that it was not just an internal affair between the king and his subjects, more money would be needed. Ptolemy borrowed heavily, making his financial arrangements in Pompey's villa at Alba, where he was staying in suitably regal style.[27] The lenders knew they

[22] *Inscr. de Délos* 1526 = *OGIS* 135 (late second century B.C.), *ILLRP* 343, Cic. *Verr.* v 157, *Rab. Post.* 4 (*iam ante*); Fraser 1972, I 155f, II 169f, 270–2.

[23] Public revenue might be paid in local coin, treated by the Roman treasury as bullion (cf. Crawford 1977, 52), but that would not be helpful for this transaction.

[24] See Badian 1965, 112f and 116–18 for the interdependence of the two *leges Clodiae*: 7,000 talents were confiscated (Plut. *Cato min.* 38.1) to fill the treasury emptied by the *lex frumentaria* (Cic. *dom.* 25). Suicide of king: Plut. *Cato min.* 36.1. Braund 1983, 28 points out that Cyprus was part of what Alexander II had willed to Rome.

[25] Dio XXXIX 12.1f, Plut. *Cato min.* 35.2, Dio Chrys. *Orat.* 32.70.

[26] Cic. *Rab. Post.* 6; cf. *ILLRP* 174–81b, with E. Badian, *JRS* 58 (1968) 247–9. Temple: Val. Max. III 2.17, Cic. *ND* II 61, *de off.* III 104.

[27] Cic. *Rab. Post.* 6. Loans: ibid. 4f, *fam.* I 1.1, *QF* II 2.3.

would only make a profit if Ptolemy were successful, and that depended not only on the vote in the Senate but also on the military operation itself. The crucial question was, who would get the command? It mattered as much to the financiers as to the potential commanders themselves.[28]

As soon as the Alexandrians realised where Ptolemy had gone, they sent an impressive deputation of 100 citizens, headed by Dio, a distinguished philosopher of the Academic school, to argue their case against the king. When they arrived at the port of Puteoli, they would naturally stay with friends and well-wishers in the neighbourhood, no doubt mainly at the Greek city of Naples, where they would feel most at home.[29] But Ptolemy was ready for them. He had plenty of men at his disposal,[30] and no scruples about protecting his investment. Some of the Alexandrians were beaten up in Puteoli itself, while at Naples a mob of local citizens may have been mobilised against them. None of them was safe: several were murdered on the way to Rome; more died in the city itself; those who survived were bribed or terrorised into silence.[31]

So brutal a display of force was what might be expected in the murderous politics of Alexandria, but this was Rome. Public opinion was scandalised, and even the Senate (Ptolemy's bribes notwithstanding) could not ignore it. A junior senator forced the House to invite Dio to come and give evidence before it; but he never came, and there was no debate about the murders – much to the relief of those members who had received presents from the king.[32]

---

[28] See Shatzman 1971, 365–9 on Cic. *fam.* I 1.1f, 5a.3f, 7.6 (creditors for and against Lentulus Spinther).

[29] Cf. Suet. *Nero* 20.3, *IG* XIV 747; for the persistence of Greek culture at Naples, see Strabo V 246, Cic. *Rab. Post.* 26, *Balb.* 21, Tac. *Ann.* XV 33.2. On Alexandrian commercial relations with Campania (especially Puteoli), see N. Purcell in M. W. Frederiksen, *Campania* (London 1984) 326f and 330.

[30] Cf. Cic. *QF* II 9.2 for the hundred swordsmen that went with the litter he lent to Asicius.

[31] Cic. *Cael.* 23, with Ciaceri 1929–30, 12 on the *seditio Neapolitana*; Dio XXXIX 13.

[32] Dio XXXIX 14.1f: M. Favonius, the friend of Cato (Cic. *Att.* I 14.5, Plut. *Cato min.* 32.6, etc.). On 'client kings' and their influence at Rome, see Braund 1984, 55–73.

Dio was lying low. He had first stayed at the house of L. Lucceius, a senior senator and a cultured philhellene.[33] But Lucceius was a close friend of Pompey, and Pompey was a friend of the king.[34] After an attempt was made to bribe Lucceius' slaves to poison him, Dio moved to the house of T. Coponius, whom he had known in Alexandria.[35]

Late in 57, Ptolemy got half of what he wanted. The Senate decreed that he should be restored, and that the proconsul in Cilicia should do it. Ptolemy wanted Pompey to have the job, and had leaflets to that effect scattered round the Forum and Senate-house.[36] Then came a thunderbolt. A tribune hostile to Pompey announced that the *decemviri* in charge of the Sibylline Books had found therein an oracular warning not to 'assist the king of Egypt with any multitude'.[37] The Senate cancelled its decree, and resolved not to use an army to restore Ptolemy. Since Pompey and his rivals still wanted the great command, and the financiers funding the king still needed it, the manoeuvring went on. But Ptolemy had had enough; leaving his agent Hammonius (and his Roman supporters) to agitate on his behalf, he retired to Ephesus to await events.[38]

His absence freed the conscience of the Senate. The murders of the Alexandrian ambassadors could now be debated, and the question became acute when their leader Dio, who had so far managed to survive, was murdered while staying at the house of Coponius.[39] Public indignation flared up again, and there was a

---

33 Cic. *Cael.* 54 (*in urbe*) – had he gone there from Lucceius' villa at Puteoli (Cic. *fam.* v 15.2, D'Arms 1981, 64)? For Lucceius, cf. *Att.* 1 17.11, *fam.* v 12, etc.

34 Lucceius and Pompey: Caes. *BC* III 18.3, Cic. *Att.* IX 1.3, etc. Pompey and Ptolemy: Cic. *Rab. Post.* 6, Dio XXXIX 14.3, Strabo XVII 796 (from Timagenes? cf. Plut. *Pomp.* 49.7).

35 Cic. *Cael.* 24, 51–4.

36 Cic. *fam.* 1 1.3, Dio XXXIX 12.3 (P. Lentulus Spinther); Plut. *Pomp.* 49.6 (leaflets).

37 Dio XXXIX 15.1–16.2, cf. Cic. *Rab. Post.* 4 ('ut dixit Sibylla').

38 Dio XXXIX 16.3, Cic. *fam.* 1 1.1 (Hammonius). Political manoeuvres: *fam.* 1 1–6, *QF* II 2.3, 3.2 (Crassus); see Shatzman 1971, 366f.

39 Dio XXXIX 14.3f, Cic. *Cael.* 24. *Pace* Heinze 1925, 198 n.1 (followed by Austin 1952, 74), Dio's narrative makes it clear that the murder occurred after Ptolemy's departure, therefore early in 56.

succession of prosecutions in the first few months of 56. Various members of the king's entourage were put on trial, and a few even convicted. Of the Roman citizens who had been involved with Ptolemy's machinations, and whose cases naturally drew more attention, we know only two. One was P. Asicius, prosecuted by C. Licinius Calvus (Catullus' friend) and successfully defended by Cicero.[40] The other was M. Caelius Rufus.

2. THE ACCUSED

Caelius was born about 88 or 87 B.C.,[41] at 'Praetuttian Interamnia' in the eastern foothills of the Appenines between Asculum and Hadria.[42] He was of equestrian rank; his father had overseas financial interests which included estates in the province of Africa, possibly (though this is guesswork) growing corn for export to the city of Rome.[43] It is likely that Caelius senior spent more time at Rome than in his home town away beyond the mountains,[44] and certain that he had ambitions for his son in the public life of the capital.

As soon as Caelius came of age – say about 72 B.C. – he began his 'apprenticeship' (*tirocinium fori*) with M. Crassus and with Cicero. Crassus was the senior man, *nobilis* and with a formidable military reputation; Cicero was still only an ex-quaestor, but his brilliance as an orator was already recognised.[45]

---

[40] Dio XXXIX 14.4 (Alexandrians); Cic. *Cael.* 24 (Asicius, cf. n.30 above), Tac. *dial.* 21.2 (Calvus' speech).

[41] Inferred from his senatorial career: Sumner 1971, 247f, cf. A. E. Douglas, *M. Tulli Ciceronis Brutus* (Oxford 1966) 199; Pliny (*NH* VII 165) must be mistaken in dating his birth to 82 B.C., on the same day as Calvus'.

[42] Cic. *Cael.* 5, with Austin 1952, 146f; for the Praetuttii and their territory, see Pliny *NH* III 110–12, with N. Alfieri in *Plinio il vecchio sotto il profilo storico e letterario* (Como 1982) 199–219, esp. 216f.

[43] Cic. *Cael.* 73, cf. Rickman 1980, 110f. The *vicus* of Horrea Caelia, on the coast north of Hadrumetum, was in a corn-growing area (Rickman 1980, 109), though the name is attested only in late antiquity (Mommsen, *CIL* VIII.1 p.18).

[44] Cic. *Cael.* 3 implies that in his younger days he was a familiar figure in Roman public life. Communication with Interamnia was probably by the Via Caecilia across the northern shoulder of the Gran Sasso: *PBSR* 38 (1970) 135f.

[45] Cic. *Cael.* 9 (cf. *de am.* 1, Tac. *dial.* 34); *Brut.* 318 for Cicero's oratorical maturity.

It was a very intelligent choice of mentors, and Caelius must have learned a great deal in the next few years if he saw at first hand the defeat and punishment of Spartacus' gladiators, Crassus' *ovatio* and subsequent consulship with Pompey, the Verres trial, the tribunates of Cornelius, Gabinius and Manilius, Cicero as praetor (and the speech for Pompey's command), Crassus as censor (and the attempt to take over Egypt). As one perceptive critic suggests, it may be that he learned too much.[46]

Caelius is about the best known minor character in Roman history, but most of what we know of him we know from Cicero (or from his own letters written to Cicero), and our picture may well be one-sided. Cicero naturally emphasises his own part in Caelius' training[47] – reasonably enough, in so far as oratory in particular was concerned – but we may well suspect that Crassus was more important as a political influence. 'Watch out, he has hay on his horns'; Crassus' reputation as a formidable operator who should not be crossed, and the patient, self-effacing accumulation of political credit on which it was based, are both clearly attested in our sources, though inevitably over-shadowed by the more glamorous doings of Pompey and Caesar.[48] (Not that Crassus was any stranger to the grand gesture when it suited his purpose,[49] and his ambition for a glory as great as Pompey's lasted till the end of his life; but his normal style was less obtrusive.) To be in his confidence would be a political education in itself.

Caelius was at Cicero's side during the consular candidature of 64 B.C., but left him in the following year to support his enemy Catiline.[50] That was perhaps because Crassus was

[46] G. Boissier, *Cicéron et ses amis* (Paris 1865): 'cette éducation . . . lui apprenait trop vite des choses qu'il vaut mieux ignorer longtemps'.

[47] Cic. *Cael.* 9f, cf. 72.

[48] Plut. *Crass.* 7.9 (Sicinius in 76 B.C.), cf. *TLL* VI 167.32–9; Sall. *Cat.* 48.5 (*summa potentia*, cf. Cic. *de fin.* II 57 *praepotens*), Cic. *Brut.* 233, Plut. *Crass.* 3.1–3, 7.2–4 etc.; Gruen 1974, 66–70.

[49] Plut. *Crass.* 2.2, 12.2, *comp. Nic. Crass.* 1.4.

[50] Cic. *Cael.* 10–12.

encouraging Catiline, and hoped to see him consul in 62.[51] But when Catiline failed to get elected, and then threw in his lot with an armed rising in Etruria, his former friends abandoned him. In 62, Crassus took a well-publicised trip to Asia to avoid Pompey's triumphant return; his protégé Caelius went to Africa, to get provincial experience and to look after the family business there.[52]

On his return, Caelius entered the arena in his own right. He prosecuted C. Antonius, Cicero's colleague as consul in 63, and got him convicted of extortion against a defence led by Cicero himself. Antonius had been in charge of the army that defeated Catiline; he had sent Catiline's head to Rome, and received public honours for his exploit. When he was convicted, Catiline's tomb was decorated with flowers. Caelius could hardly have made a more spectacular entry into public life, or one less welcome to his former patron Cicero.[53]

The execution without trial of the 'Catilinarian conspirators' in 63 made Cicero politically vulnerable, and his personal enemy P. Clodius, a young patrician a few years older than Caelius, was using this issue against him with great effect. At just this moment in the spring of 59 – as a result of what Cicero said at the trial of Antonius – Caesar and Pompey allowed Clodius to transfer to the *plebs* and so become eligible for the tribunate. That was very bad news for Cicero; and at just this moment also, Caelius moved into a Palatine apartment owned by Clodius, and became the lover of Clodius' sister, the recent widow of Q. Metellus Celer.[54]

---

[51] Asc. 83C – from Cicero's *expositio consiliorum suorum*, but not therefore necessarily untrue (E. Rawson, *LCM* 7.8 (Oct. 1982) 121–4). For his attitude in 63, cf. Sall. *Cat.* 48.4–9, Plut. *Crass.* 13.2f, *Cic.* 15.1f.

[52] Plut. *Pomp.* 43.1, Cic. *Flacc.* 32 (Crassus); Cic. *Cael.* 73 (Caelius, on proconsul's staff). Cf. Gruen 1973, 305 on Crassus and Caelius.

[53] Cic. *Cael.* 73f, cf. 15; *Flacc.* 95 (flowers); Dio XXXVII 40.2, cf. Obs. 61a (Antonius' honours in 63). Full details and discussion in Gruen 1973 (cf. 1974, 287–9).

[54] Cic. *Cael.* 17f, 75 (see chapter II for Clodia Metelli). Clodius: Cic. *dom.* 41, Suet. *Jul.* 20.4, Dio XXXIX 10.4; Gruen 1973, 306f, Rundell 1979, 304–7. Caelius' fellow-prosecutor was Q. Fabius Maximus (Schol. Bob. 149 St); a Fabius was a friend or lover

The move marked Caelius' arrival as a serious politician, to be cultivated by well-wishers who would not wish to go out to his father's house in the suburbs. He was about twenty-nine (not much younger than Cicero had been when he took Caelius as a pupil), and no doubt already collecting that entourage of friends and clients who surrounded him in later years.[55] At this turning point in his life, as Cicero later called it,[56] it is worth looking more closely at this formidable young man.

He was tall, strikingly handsome, a dandy in his dress, and with a taste for extravagant social life.[57] He loved laughter, and his wit was cruel: there was no better joke than the expression on the face of an enemy he had done down.[58] Quarrelsome, violent, generous, passionate, in a later crisis he defined his own motives as good intentions overcome by anger and affection; what counted with him was resentment and exasperation.[59] He could sum up other men's failings as ruthlessly as his own, and his insight into character and motive made him a brilliant interpreter of the politics of his day.[60] It is revealing that one of his favourite authors was Cleitarchus on Alexander, conquest and immortal glory in sensational and melodramatic narrative.[61] Caelius too

of Clodia in 60 (Cic. *Att.* II 1.5), and Q. Fabius Vergilianus later served under her brother Appius in Cilicia (Cic. *fam.* III 3.1, 4.1).

[55] Cic. *Cael.* 18 ('quo facilius et nostras domus obire et ipse a suis coli posset'); cf. 1, 74 (*inter suos gratia*), 77 (*catervae amicorum*); Sen. *de ira* III 8.6 (client). See especially Cic. *fam.* II 14, to Caelius in 50: 'novi ego vos magnos patronos; hominem occidat oportet qui vestra opera uti velit.'

[56] Cic. *Cael.* 75, with Austin 1952, 135.

[57] Cic. *Cael.* 6, 36 (*candor, proceritas*); 77 (*purpura, splendor, nitor*); 27 (*convivia, horti, unguenta*).

[58] Cic. *fam.* VIII 3.1, 4.1, 8.1, 9.1. Laughter is the *Leitmotiv* of his whole correspondence with Cicero: *fam.* II 12.1, 13.3, 16.7, VIII 14.1 and 4.

[59] Cic. *fam.* VIII 17.1 and 2 (48 B.C.): 'nam mihi sentio bonam mentem iracundia et amore sublatam . . . hoc nullius praemi spe faciam sed, quod apud me plurimum solet valere, doloris atque indignitatis causa.' Cf. *Cael.* 76 (*violentia*), 77 (*vis, ferocitas*). Quarrelsome: Sen. *de ira* III 8.6, Quint. VI 3.69; Cic. *fam.* VIII 8.1, 12.1–3, 14.1. Generous: Val. Max. IV 2.7.

[60] Cic. *fam.* VIII 1.1 (Cicero), 1.3 (Pompey), 4.2 (Curio), 6.2 (Dolabella), 10.2f (consuls of 51); II 8.1, 10.4 (Cicero on his foresight), 12.1, VIII 14.3.

[61] Cic. *fam.* II 10.3; for Cleitarchus (cf. Cic. *Brut.* 42), see N. G. L. Hammond, *Three Historians of Alexander the Great* (Cambridge 1983), esp. 17–20, 23f, 82f.

was a born winner in pursuit of glory – and he saw the political scene as a spectacle, a drama to watch for amusement or to act in for the pleasure of applause.[62]

For a young man of such ability and such ambition, the murderous power game of Ptolemy's threatened kingdom must have been irresistibly attractive.[63] With stakes so high, it was not for the diffident or the scrupulous. Caelius was neither; and if, as is likely, he had been in Crassus' confidence in 65, he had inside knowledge to help him too.

His new friendship with Clodius also kept him involved with foreign affairs. Clodius' family now enjoyed a marriage-alliance with Pompey, the organiser of the eastern empire.[64] And it was Clodius as tribune in 58 who gave the Roman populace free corn rations, and confiscated the Ptolemaic kingdom of Cyprus to pay for them. Caelius was probably quaestor in that year, administering public revenues either at Rome or in a province; Cicero's silence on the subject in his account of Caelius' career in the *pro Caelio* suggests that he may have been directly involved with Clodius' schemes.[65]

Clodius' alliance with Pompey had served to get him transferred to the *plebs* (and thus eligible for the tribunate), but was ruthlessly abandoned immediately afterwards.[66] In March 58 he got Cicero exiled, whose protection Pompey had guaranteed; and for most of that year he hounded Pompey in the most

[62] Cic. *Cael.* 76, 'de impetu animi loquor, de cupiditate vincendi, de ardore mentis ad gloriam' (cf. 18, 47, 72, 74); *fam.* VIII 3.3, 15.1 for the pursuit of fame. *Spectaculum: fam.* VIII 4.1, 14.1, 14.4, cf. 11.3 (*scaena*).

[63] His background in overseas business may be relevant: see n.43 above, and D'Arms 1981, 49–55 on Cic. *fam.* VIII 8.1 (Puteoli businessmen); *fam.* VIII 4.5 may indicate that he was one of Ptolemy's creditors (Shackleton Bailey 1977a, I 393).

[64] See T. W. Hillard, *PBSR* 50 (1982) 34–44 on Cic. *har. resp.* 45 and Plut. *Cato min.* 31.2: the betrothal of Appius' daughter to Cn. Pompeius *filius*?

[65] See Sumner 1971, 248 n.11 for the suggestion; contrast Cic. *Cael.* 74–7 with *Sest.* 68–71, *Planc.* 99 etc., on Cicero's supporters in 58. The *cursus honorum* makes 58 and 57 the most likely years for Caelius' quaestorship, and 57 is unlikely *e silentio*, since at least two of the crimes he was charged with took place in that year.

[66] Cic. *Att.* II 7.2f, 9.1, 12.1f (April 59); 22.1f (August); Rundell 1979, 309. The break seems to date from his non-selection for the Alexandria embassy.

humiliating manner.[67] Caelius was always quick to see where the advantage lay, and will surely have given aid and support to his mistress' beloved brother, especially as Crassus was edging that way too.[68] But the triumphant return of Cicero in September 57, followed immediately by Pompey's five-year proconsular *imperium* to control the corn supply, drastically changed the political balance.[69] Pompey's command had no geographical limit; with fifteen deputy commanders, he could operate wherever he chose. And this was just at the time when Ptolemy, in flight from Alexandria, came to look for Roman help to restore him to his throne, and was offered hospitality at Pompey's villa (p. 59 above).

Caelius' activities in the period from September 57 to March 56 are best understood on the following hypothesis: that he was working secretly for Ptolemy (therefore, in effect, in Pompey's interests), and that when this became known to Clodius and his sister it caused a sudden violent breaking-off of relations at both the political and the personal level.

Late in 57 Caelius was supporting L. Calpurnius Bestia for election to the praetorship;[70] in January 56 he was prosecuting Bestia for electoral bribery.[71] Bestia was acquitted (Cicero defending), and Caelius promptly initiated another prosecution on the same charge, presumably for alleged bribery in the campaign for the *next* praetorian elections.[72] This *volte-face* may reflect Caelius' break with the Claudii, though the personal obligations involved were clearly complex;[73] a clearer piece of

---

[67] Cicero: Cic. *Att.* II 21.6, 22.2, Plut. *Cic.* 31.2f, etc. Campaign against Pompey: Asc. 46–7C; Cic. *har. resp.* 48f, *Sest.* 69, *Pis.* 28, *Mil.* 39; Plut. *Cic.* 33.1, *Pomp.* 49.1; Rundell 1979, 318f.

[68] Dio XXXVIII 17.3 (March 58), Cic. *fam.* XIV 2.2 (October 58), 19.20 (*gravissimae iniuriae*, undated).

[69] Cic. *Att.* IV 1.5–7, cf. 2.4 for Clodius in a minority of one.

[70] Cic. *Cael.* 26 (no real argument against the prosecution's allegation), cf. *fam.* IV 3.3f for the postponed elections.

[71] Cic. *Cael.* 76, *QF* II 3.6 (the trial took place on 11 February).

[72] Cic. *Cael.* 1, 76, 78; cf. *Phil.* XI 11 for Bestia's eventual conviction.

[73] Bestia had rescued one of Cicero's supporters from Clodius' strong-arm men in 58 (Cic. *QF* II 3.6), and Cicero emphasises friendly relations with him at *Cael.* 26 and 76.

evidence is his hostility at the pontifical elections to a candidate friendly to Clodius.[74] At any rate, when Bestia's son L. Sempronius Atratinus fought back on his father's behalf by prosecuting Caelius himself, the Claudii gave every help and support.

The charge was *vis*, political violence.[75] Caelius was accused of beating up the Alexandrian envoys at Puteoli, of causing the riot at Naples, and of murdering Dio. A fourth charge, 'on the property of Palla',[76] may also have had to do with the terrorising of the embassy, but we have no details.[77] Atratinus' assistant prosecutors were P. Clodius and L. Herennius Balbus – the former not Clodius himself, but probably a freedman or non-citizen enfranchised by him.[78]

Caelius had to organise his defence very quickly. The patrician Claudii were formidable enemies, and he would need all the help he could get. He turned to his two mentors of long ago, Cicero and Crassus. After the events of 63–57, it must have taken all his charm to convince Cicero that his days of friendship with men

On the other hand, Bestia's son Atratinus could be represented as under Clodian influence (*Cael.* 2, *necessitas*); his step-daughter Atratina married L. Gellius Poblicola (*IG* II² 4230–1, *Hermes* 30 (1895) 630; cf. *ILS* 9461 and Münzer 1909, 135f), who had been the lover of one of Clodia's sisters (Cat. 91.6) and was probably nephew of one of Clodius' henchmen (Cic. *Vat.* 4, *Sest.* 112, *Att.* IV 3.2); see Wiseman 1974, 119–29 for the relationships of the Gellii (with one reservation, n.76 below).

[74] Cic. *Cael.* 19, 'de teste Fufio' – i.e. Q. Fufius Calenus *tr.pl.* 61, for whom see *Att.* I 14.1 and 5. Clodius needed reliable *pontifices* in the dispute over Cicero's house (Cic. *dom.*, esp. 118f).

[75] Cic. *Cael.* 1, 70; Lintott 1968, 109–24.

[76] Palla is probably a *cognomen*: I. Kajanto, *The Latin Cognomina* (Helsinki 1965) 345. Austin (1952, 74) refers to Dio XLVII 24.6 on the mother of L. Gellius Poblicola and M. Messalla Corvinus, but the name is not plausible for a Roman lady: read Πώλλα, as in Boissevain's edition, and amend Wiseman 1974, 119–29 accordingly (esp. 120 and n.7).

[77] Cic. *Cael.* 23 (p. 60 above), cf. Quint. IV 2.27, 'de bonis Pallae totamque de vi causam'. Ciaceri 1929–30, 12 makes the ingenious suggestion that Caelius had organised an attack on a country house where one or more of the deputation were staying (cf. Cic. *Rosc. Am.* 21f for *bona* as estates); in that case Cicero's phrase would be euphemistic, as at *Cael.* 30, 51 ('crimen de auro' for a charge of attempted murder).

[78] Cic. *Cael.* 27; D. R. Shackleton Bailey, *Ciceroniana* I (1973) 4, points out that a freedman would be referred to by his *cognomen*, but Cicero here was being studiously mock-polite. For *peregrini*, cf. 'A. Licinius' (Cic. *Arch.* 1), 'Cn. Pompeius' (Caes. *BG* v 36.1), and p. 36 n. 68 above on Clodius' *comites*.

like Catiline and Clodius were over, and that if he saved him now, Cicero could rely on his good behaviour in the future.[79] Even Crassus may have been hard to persuade: machinations in Pompey's interest would not please *him*, and he had been openly supporting Clodius in recent weeks.[80] But in the end, it was an offer neither could refuse. Caelius was too valuable as an ally, and too dangerous as an enemy, for either man to miss the chance of tying him down with a compelling obligation.[81]

So the lines were drawn up, and the trial fixed for 3–4 April, overlapping with the start of the Megalesia.[82] Trials for *vis* were regarded as so important that the court sat even during public holidays. Indeed, this trial would itself be a public spectacle as dramatic as anything to be seen in the theatre or the Circus. Great issues were at stake, and great performers would be in action. What was involved was not just murder and political terrorism, but scandal in high society as well. For it must soon have become known that one of the prosecution's witnesses would be a patrician lady with damning testimony to deliver against her former lover.

3. THE PROSECUTION

Trials in the Roman Republic were not held in a sober court-room, but outside in the sunshine, with the Forum crowd jostling around. The *corona*, or ring of bystanders, enclosed the space like an arena, and what went on within might well be, in effect, a mortal combat.[83] Within the space were the presiding magistrate on his tribunal, the three *decuriae* of judges on their

---

[79] Cf. Cic. *Cael.* 77–80.

[80] Cic. *QF* II 3.2 (6 February 56), implying Crassus had his own plans about the Alexandria command.

[81] For this aspect of defence speeches, and for the formal agreements that could be involved, cf. Q. Cic. *comm. pet.* 19.

[82] Cic. *Cael.* I, with Austin 1952, 149.

[83] Cic. *Cael.* 67 (sun), 21 (forum crowd), 47 (combat). *Corona*: Cat. 53 (shouts, gestures), Cic. *Brut.* 290 etc. (*TLL* IV 986). *Vitae dimicatio*: Cic. *Planc.* 77, *Balb.* 23, *Arch.* 14 etc. (*TLL* V 1201).

benches (usually 25 men in each *decuria*, but there may have been more in the Caelius case, with no other courts in session), and confronting each other from opposite sides, the benches of the prosecution and defence. On one side, young Atratinus and his two assistant prosecutors, with their friends and supporters and the witnesses they intended to call, including Clodia; on the other, Caelius, his two *patroni*, his sorrowing parents, and a greater crowd of friends, well-wishers and character witnesses.[84]

Once the judges had been sworn in, the main speeches would be given, prosecution first, then defence. After that, witnesses would be called.[85] This postponement of testimony till the end is important for understanding the tactics of each side, particularly in trying to neutralise in advance the effect of the opposition's witnesses. It also represents the accepted priorities: 'With me, as with a good judge', said Cicero in quite another context, 'arguments count for more than witnesses' – and by *argumenta* he meant the *a priori* arguments deduced by the orator from within the case itself.[86] It was more persuasive to be able to say 'it stands to reason' than to depend on the assertion of an individual, even under oath. And persuasion was the orator's business – to sway or 'turn' the judges to accept his view of the case.[87]

That elementary fact must be constantly borne in mind as we try to reconstruct the prosecution's case from Cicero's speech for the defence. It was in his interests *not* to present it as they did, but to spend time and emphasis on minor points where he had a plausible answer, and to skate quickly over the telling arguments, or break them up and deal with them in a garbled,

---

[84] Cic. *Vat.* 34 (tribunal), *Cael.* 67 (benches), 77 (Caelius' friends), cf. *Rosc. Am.* 104, *Flacc.* 22, 42, *fam.* VIII 8.1 etc. Parents: *Cael.* 4, 79; Caelius himself was not in conventional *squalor* (cf. Val. Max. VI 4.4, Plut. *Cic.* 35.4), but his father made up for it. *Decuriae* numbers: Cic. *Pis.* 56, *Att.* IV 16.9, *QF* III 4.1, Asc. 28C.

[85] Cic. *Rosc. Am.* 82, 84, 102, *Cluent.* 18, *Verr.* act. I 55; Quint. V 7.25.

[86] Austin 1952, 115 (whose phrase I have borrowed) on *Cael.* 54; Cicero quotation from *de rep.* I 59.

[87] Cic. *orator* 69 ('probare necessitatis est . . . flectere victoriae'), *Brut.* 142, *de or.* II 205, 211 for *flectere*.

piecemeal way in order to damage their overall impact.[88] What follows is therefore inevitably speculative, especially in the distribution of arguments between the three prosecution speakers.

Their two great tactical advantages were the nature of the crimes and the lifestyle of the defendant. Ptolemy's attack on the Alexandrian embassy had been so openly brutal that even Roman public opinion had been shocked (ambassadors were sacrosanct under the *lex gentium*);[89] and Caelius' conspicuous dissipation and extravagance did not endear him to conservative Romans of conventionally straight-laced moral views. 'Caelius was full of show and swagger': the sumptuous purple of his tunic stripe, the loudness of his voice and the expansiveness of his gestures, the crowds of eager hangers-on who clustered round him, his whole glamorous and histrionic style would be enough to affront the middle-aged knights and senators on the judges' benches even before the proceedings began.[90]

It is clear that the prosecutors set out to exploit this advantage from the start. Atratinus led off with an attack on Caelius' morals, no doubt drawing an implicit contrast with his own virtues, according to good rhetorical practice.[91] His tone was deliberately modest as he inferred effeminacy and sexual licence from Caelius' luxurious ways, promised witnesses who would prove Caelius' indecent assaults on respectable married women, and dwelt on Caelius' intimacy with the depraved revolutionary Catiline.[92] Like all Catiline's followers, Caelius was heavily in debt: his extravagant expenses, like the rent of his Palatine

[88] See Drexler 1944, 24 (cf. 6, 17f, 20) on 'Beiseiteschieben und Bagatellieren'. The best analyses of Cicero's tactics in the *pro Caelio* are in Heinze 1925, Reitzenstein 1925, Drexler 1944 and Classen 1973; my account owes more to them than individual citations can acknowledge.

[89] Dio XXXIX 14.1; cf. Caes. *BG* III 9.3, Cic. *Verr.* I 85, Livy I 14.1 etc. (*TLL* VI 1861).

[90] Austin 1952, 137, on *Cael.* 77 and Quint. XI 1.51 ('vox immoderatior . . . iactantior gestus', etc.).

[91] *Rhet. Her.* I 8; e.g. on *pietas* (*Cael.* 3f, 18, contrasting with Atratinus' defence of his father against his persecutor)?

[92] *Cael.* 6–8 (*impudicitia*: 7 for Atratinus' *pudor*); 19 (*matronae*); 10, 15 (Catiline), cf. *Cat.* I 13, II 22f etc. on the *pueri lepidi ac delicati* in Catiline's train.

apartment, could not be met from what his father allowed him. If he denied it, let him show the court his account-books.[93]

It was probably in this context that Atratinus introduced a theme that was to keep recurring throughout the trial. Caelius, he said, was *pulchellus Iason* – a 'pretty-boy Jason' who would need to find a golden fleece to pay for such a life of luxury.[94]

It is not known whether Atratinus went into any detail about the charges themselves; he may have left that to his *subscriptores*. But he would not have failed to point out the circumstantial evidence that pointed to Caelius' guilt. Caelius was used to beating people up – Fufius, for instance, at the pontifical elections, who would give evidence to prove it – and his pursuit of disgraceful pleasures often took him to the bay of Naples, where two of the crimes (at least) had been committed.[95] Quite apart from his extravagant personal tastes, Caelius had squandered large sums in electoral bribery;[96] it was obvious that he needed money badly, so Ptolemy's Egyptian gold provided a perfect motive.

The second prosecution speaker was P. Clodius, whom Cicero mentions only to dismiss with an ironical jest. But it is likely that his speech was the one that dealt in most detail with the crimes themselves. If we are right to infer that he was a client of the patrician Claudii, with no independent political position to jeopardise, then it would be natural to let him loose on the story of Ptolemy and the embassy, with all its damaging revelations of the involvement of Pompey and the king's Roman creditors. His speech was characterised by anger and indignation; on such a subject, it could hardly have been otherwise.[97]

---

[93] *Cael.* 17, 38; cf. 3, 36 (father *parcus ac tenax*).

[94] Fortunatianus *ars rhet.* III 7 (*Rhet. Lat. min.* 124H) on *nomina translata*: 'cum Atratinus Caelium pulchellum Iasonem appellat et Cicero Clodiam Palatinam Medeam'. Cf. Münzer 1909, 136 n.3, Classen 1973, 73; Serv. *Aen.* III 119 for the overtones of *pulcher*.

[95] *Cael.* 19 (Fufius); 35, 38 (Baiae); cf. *Rhet. Her.* II 5 on circumstantial evidence.

[96] *Cael.* 16, 'isto infinito ambitu' (a quote from the prosecution?), perhaps at his quaestorian elections. Cf. *Cael.* 38 ('at fuit fama') on Caelius' bankruptcy, with *Rhet. Her.* II 12 on the exploitation of rumour.

[97] *Cael.* 27, cf. n.78 above.

After the fracas at Puteoli and the Naples riot, the king's agents had pursued Dio to Rome. When he stayed at the house of Pompey's friend L. Lucceius, an attempt had been made to poison him. That was Caelius' doing: a noble lady would testify that he had borrowed gold from her, on a trumped-up excuse, to bribe Lucceius' slaves, and that when she discovered the truth he had tried to bribe her own slaves to poison *her*. Dio then moved to the house of T. Coponius, and now the king's agents succeeded in killing him. The guilty men were Caelius and P. Asicius. Asicius had been acquitted in a corrupt trial, which did him more good than harm – there must be no such scandalous acquittal in *this* court![98]

L. Herennius Balbus wound up for the prosecution. He returned to the subject of moral depravity, emphasising Caelius' treachery towards Bestia, once his close friend (as witnesses would prove), whom he was now hounding through the bribery courts. It was for Bestia's sake that Balbus was involved with this case, supporting Bestia's son.[99]

Balbus' style was quiet, reasonable and compelling. The judges nodded in silent agreement as his description of the goings-on of the younger generation – licentious parties, adultery, extravagance and debt – confirmed their initial prejudice against Caelius and his way of life.[100] A man like that was capable of anything.

Elaborating on one part of the indictment, the abortive first attempt on Dio's life, Balbus explained how Caelius' guilt had come to light. Clodia had been on good terms with Caelius, as a friend of her brother,[101] so when he asked her to help him finance a public show (*ludi*), she lent him some gold ornaments

---

[98] *Cael.* 23f (*praevaricatio* at Asicius' trial); 30f, 51f, 55f (Clodia's evidence). Cf. Ciaceri 1929–30, 16: did the prosecution allege Lucceius' connivance in the first attempt?

[99] *Cael.* 26, 56: otherwise, as a fellow-*sodalis* of Caelius', he would not have prosecuted him.

[100] *Cael.* 25, 27, 29 (silence), 30 (*invidia*), 35 (details of parties); Austin 1952, 82 on the text at §27.

[101] A relationship ignored by 'Appius' at *Cael.* 34 ('cognatus, adfinis, viri tui familiaris?'); cf. 53, Balbus on their *familiaritas*, no doubt quoted out of context.

without any suspicion.[102] She later discovered that he had used the gold to bribe Lucceius' slaves, and threatened to denounce him.[103] Shortly afterwards her slaves reported that Caelius was trying to get them to murder her: he had some poison ready, and his friend P. Licinius would hand it over to them at the Senian Baths.[104] Clodia told them to play along with him, and arranged for some of her friends to be in hiding at the baths at the stated time to catch Licinius red-handed. The plan worked: the friends jumped out just as Licinius was handing over the container, but in the confusion he escaped. Clodia rewarded her faithful slaves by giving them their freedom, with the approval of the family council of the patrician Claudii. Naturally Balbus emphasised the nobility and distinction of those gentlemen, on whose authority Clodia had acted.[105] The lady herself would give evidence (as would the friends who helped her), but Balbus could assure the judges that he had her full approval for everything he had told them.[106]

Atratinus and his colleagues could not afford to reveal that Clodia had been Caelius' mistress.[107] Their strategy was to focus all the odium of moral delinquency on to the defence benches, and it would weaken their case if anything but unsullied virtue sat on their side. It was a risk based on the calculation that the defence could hardly mention the affair without branding Caelius himself as an adulterer,[108] and thus making his character even less sympathetic to the judges.

[102] *Cael.* 52f; the *ludi* were perhaps at Interamnia, where Caelius was co-opted on to the local council *in absentia* (*Cael.* 5).

[103] Inferred from *causa* at the end of §56.

[104] *Cael.* 57f, 61f; presumably in the *apodyterium* of the baths (as is suggested *e silentio* in §62).

[105] *Cael.* 62–6 (ambush), 68 (manumission).

[106] *Cael.* 35 (quoted out of context); 50, 66f (testimony).

[107] This crucial point is recognised by Heinze (1925, 228f and 245–8) and Drexler (1944, 25); Reitzenstein (1925, 29 n.1 and 32), Austin (1952, 86) and Classen (1973, 76 n.74 and 82), arguing that the prosecution must have mentioned the affair or Cicero would not have done so himself, seem to me to misinterpret both sides' tactics.

[108] Or more exactly a *stuprator*, since Clodia was a widow; but 'lex stuprum et adulterium promiscue et καταχρηστικώτερον appellat' (Papin. *Dig.* XLVIII 5.6.1, on the *lex Iulia de adulteriis*).

4. THE DEFENCE

The main qualities of Caelius' oratory, as of his personality, were wit, verve and merciless aggression. He fought better with the sword than with the shield, and would certainly defend himself by attacking.[109] But first he had to put in some work with the judges, to counter the bad impression they had of him.

He began with a modest deprecation that later won the approval of Quintilian:[110]

> Ne cui vestrum atque etiam omnium, qui ad rem agendam adsunt, meus aut vultus molestior aut vox immoderatior aliqua aut denique, quod minimum est, iactantior gestus fuisse videatur.

> I trust that none of you, gentlemen, and none of all those present at this trial, will find my expression too offensive, or any word of mine too unrestrained, or even – if it comes to trivialities – my gestures too expansive.

The prosecution claimed to stand for old-fashioned virtues – frugality, for instance, as against extravagance. Well, Caelius had that virtue, if one understood the word aright; he was a valuable citizen, of service to the Republic, which would harvest the fruits (*fruges*) of his abilities as an orator and a politician.[111]

And he *was* an orator, unlike the boy Atratinus, whose speech was the work of his rhetoric-master, that barley-blown, sordid old windbag.[112] On to the attack already, Caelius picked up the mythological allusion in Atratinus' speech. 'Pretty-boy Jason', was he? In that case Atratinus himself was Pelias in ringlets, effeminate and corrupt;[113] for the prosecution was a put-up job, and Atratinus was trying to destroy him just as Pelias hoped to send Jason to his death.

---

[109] Cic. *ap.* Quint. VI 3.69, *Brut.* 273; cf. Tac. *dial.* 25.4 (*amaritudo*), Quint. X 2.25 (*asperitas*), X 1.115 (*urbanitas*). Examples in Quint. IV 2.123 (*in Antonium*), Pliny *NH* XXVII 4 (*in Bestiam*).

[110] Quint. XI 1.51 (fr. 23 Malc.); cf. Cic. *Arch.* 3, *de fin.* II 3 etc. for *rem agere*.

[111] Quint. I 6.29 (fr. 28 Malc.); cf. Cic. *Cael.* 28 (*ad frugem bonam*), 76 (*fruges industriae*), 80 (*fructus uberes*).

[112] Suet. *rhet.* 2 (fr. 24 Malc.), on L. Plotius Gallus.

[113] Quint. I 5.61 (fr. 37 Malc.); Münzer 1909, 136 n.3. Cf. Cic. *red. sen.* 12, *Sest.* 26 for the overtones of *cincinnatus*.

As for the prosecution's star witness, remember how suddenly her husband died. She may be a great lady, but so was Clytemnestra. You know the story of the purse full of coppers – that's all her lovers think she's worth. Remember the perfume-jar and what was in it? (Here Caelius waved the jar, like the one the alleged poison was contained in; his allusion – unworthy of a gentleman, sniffed Quintilian – was to an obscene practical joke supposedly played on Clodia by one of her lovers.) Do they really expect us to believe this cut-price Clytemnestra when she takes the oath?[114]

Whether Caelius admitted having enjoyed Clodia's favours himself is far from clear. It would certainly undermine her testimony to suggest that it was motivated by personal pique against a lover who now rejected her. On the other hand, one of the *bons mots* he threw out about her implies that an inviting wantonness at dinner was followed by a haughty refusal in the bedroom;[115] and that makes better tactical sense. Probably he did *not* refer explicitly to the affair, but concentrated on denouncing Clodia's morals without making any admissions about his own.

Amid these fireworks of invective, we know that Caelius dealt with the main charges themselves. So too did Crassus in his very different style – thorough, painstaking, rather pedestrian – in the second defence speech.[116] The division of labour would allow two quite different political lines to be taken; Caelius could attack Clodius, and win over judges who were sympathetic to Pompey, while Crassus could criticise his old rival Pompey, and thus divide the loyalties of Clodius' friends.[117] What grounds

---

[114] Quint. VIII 6.52 (fr. 26 Malc.), 'quadrantaria Clytaemestra'; Plut. *Cic.* 29.4 (p. 39 above) for the purse full of *quadrantes*. Quint. VI 3.25 ('in illa pyxide Caeliana'), Cic. *Cael.* 69; Wiseman 1974, 170–5.

[115] Quint. VIII 6.52 (fr. 27 Malc.), 'in triclinio Coa, in cubiculo Nola'; Hillard 1981, 149–51.

[116] Quint. IV 2.27 (Caelius), Cic. *Cael.* 23 (Crassus); *Brut.* 233 on Crassus' style.

[117] For Crassus supporting Clodius against Pompey in February 56, see Cic. *QF* II 3.2 and 4. (There is no evidence for any earlier alliance between Crassus and Clodius: see T. W. Hillard, *LCM* 6.5 (May 1981) 127–30 on Cic. *Att.* I 16.5.)

they had for denying Caelius' involvement in Ptolemy's terrorist crimes, we do not know.

What we do know is that Crassus carried on the play of allusions to the Jason story, by applying the first lines of Ennius' *Medea* to Ptolemy's voyage to Italy: 'Would that the trees that made the ship had never been cut down . . .' The parallel with the *Argo* was not particularly close, but the quotation offered Cicero a beautiful opening later on.[118]

When Cicero got up, the judges had sat through five long speeches already. It was the second day of the trial, and a public holiday (the first day of the *ludi Megalenses*) for everybody but them. Some of them may have been feeling irritably uncertain – what had looked like an open-and-shut case, a scandalously dissolute young man to be found guilty of notorious crimes, was turning out to be something more complicated. They had to be soothed, flattered, put into a good humour, and somehow persuaded to think kindly enough of Caelius to be able to acquit him with a good conscience.[119]

Cicero's opening was masterly. In three elegant formal periods he sympathised with the judges, dismissed the crimes as imaginary, alleged improper influence on the prosecution side, and at the turning point of his third sentence let fall a word which must have caused gasps of astonishment around the court.[120]

Si quis, iudices, forte nunc adsit ignarus legum iudiciorum consuetudinisque nostrae, miretur profecto quae sit tanta atrocitas huiusce causae, quod diebus festis ludisque publicis, omnibus forensibus negotiis intermissis, unum hoc iudicium exerceatur, nec dubitet quin tanti facinoris reus arguatur ut eo neglecto civitas stare non possit. Idem cum audiat esse legem quae de seditiosis consceleratisque civibus qui armati senatum obsederint, magistratibus vim attulerint, rem publicam oppugnarint cotidie quaeri iubeat, legem non improbet, crimen quod versetur in iudicio requirat. Cum audiat nullum facinus, nullam audaciam, nullam vim in iudicium vocari, sed adulescentem inlustri ingenio, industria,

---

[118] Cic. *Cael.* 18; Enn. *trag. fr.* 103J (*Rhet. Her.* II 34). Cf. Cic. *leg. Man.* 22: Mithridates as Medea.

[119] And thus get the future benefit of his goodwill; cf. *Cael.* 80, with nn. 81 and 111 above.

[120] *Cael.* 1; cf. Quint. IV 1.39 ('ut res exspectatione minor videretur'), IX 2.39.

gratia accusari ab eius filio quem ipse in iudicium et vocet et vocarit, oppugnari autem opibus meretriciis, illius pietatem non reprehendat, libidinem muliebrem comprimendam putet, vos laboriosis existimet quibus otiosis ne in communi quidem otio liceat esse.

If by chance, gentlemen, there should be someone present here who is unfamiliar with our laws and courts and procedures, I am sure he would wonder what the specially heinous nature of this case might be, that this one trial is being held when all legal business is suspended for the holidays and public festivals, and he would be in no doubt that the defendant's crime must be so serious that the state would be in jeopardy if it were neglected. When informed that there is a law requiring cases to be heard every single day that involve seditious criminals who have laid armed siege to the Senate-house, attacked the magistrates and made war on the Republic, he would approve, and ask what charge is being brought in the present trial. When further informed that no crime, no outrage, no deed of violence is before the court, but that a brilliant, hard-working and influential young man is being prosecuted by the son of the man accused in two prosecutions of his own, and attacked by the resources of a prostitute, he would find no fault with the prosecutor's filial loyalty, he would take the view that women's passions should be kept in check, and he would consider you overworked, since you are not allowed to be at leisure even when everyone else is.

What the prosecution's case rested on, as the judges would realise, was 'somebody's insufferable passion and excessive malice'.[121]

One imagines there was some anxious conferring on the prosecution benches as Cicero went blandly on. He hated Clodia, who had persecuted his family after her brother had sent him into exile; and just at the moment he was feeling very confident politically.[122] How far would he dare to go in blackening her character?

Having dropped his opening bombshell, Cicero moved on to more predictable matters, countering some minor points used by the prosecution to put Caelius in a bad light; he embarrassed Atratinus with patronising praise, and scolded him gently for

[121] *Cael.* 2, cf. 19 and 25 for *nitor*.
[122] Hatred: Cic. *Att.* II 1.5 (60 B.C.), *Cael.* 50. Confidence: QF II 5.2, *fam.* I 7.7; D. Stockton, *TAPA* 93 (1962) 487f.

descending to scurrilous slander (not surprising that the young man had got the same in return); and he contrived to suggest that Caelius was like himself, an honest man from an equestrian background with all the industrious virtues of municipal Italy.[123] One tricky point was Caelius' friendship with Catiline. That was undeniable, and damaging; but Cicero was equal to the challenge, moving back into his most splendid periodic style with a purple passage on Catiline himself, whose chameleon-like personality had deceived many others besides Caelius. 'Why, I myself, gentlemen, even I was once almost taken in . . .' After the antitheses, the rhetorical questions and the wonderful rhythmic *cola*, Cicero concluded with a rueful little joke against himself, smoothly varying his tone and manner to keep the attention of his difficult audience.[124]

Not that he wanted them *too* attentive, as he airily dismissed the allegation that Caelius had been involved with Catiline's conspiracy. Was he so mad, so depraved, so bankrupt?[125] No doubt the prosecutors shouted 'Yes!', but Cicero went on unperturbed:

Nimium multa de re minime dubia loquor; hoc tamen dico. Non modo si socius coniurationis, sed nisi inimicissimus istius sceleris fuisset, numquam coniurationis accusatione adulescentiam suam potissimum commendare voluisset.

I'm wasting words on a matter that admits of no doubt at all. Nonetheless, I say this: not only if he had himself been privy to the plot, but even if he had been anything less than totally opposed to it, he would never have chosen to make his mark as a young politician by prosecuting a man for complicity in it.

To the careful reader, the *non sequitur* is obvious,[126] but the jury had no time to think as Cicero moved plausibly on, using the same argument to prove Caelius' innocence of bribery ('or he would never have accused Bestia of it').[127]

---

[123] *Cael.* 2–9. Atratinus: §§2, 7f. Cicero: §§4, 6, 9 (cf. Wiseman 1971, 107–13).

[124] *Cael.* 10–15, esp. 12f. Joke at end of 14: 'non numquam . . . erroris mei paenitet'.

[125] *Cael.* 15; cf. *Sest.* 97 and 99 for these three criteria.

[126] In any case, Antonius was *not* prosecuted for complicity with Catiline: see Austin 1952, 156f and n. 53 above.

[127] *Cael.* 16; cf. Drexler 1944, 12f, Classen 1973, 72 on Cicero's sleight of hand.

Then quickly to the next point, where the damaging charge was dismissed even more shamelessly:[128]

Nam quod aes alienum obiectum est, sumptus reprehensi, tabulae flagitatae, videte quam pauca respondeam. Tabulas qui in patris potestate est nullas conficit. Versuram numquam omnino fecit ullam.

As for the charge of debt, the complaints of extravagance, the demands for account books, see how briefly I reply. A man in his father's legal authority does not keep accounts. He has simply never borrowed at all.

All right, so the money he spent and borrowed was technically in his father's name – but how much of *that* does he owe? and why don't you produce his *father's* account books? Are you telling us that no one can get into debt before his father is dead? Before such questions could be asked, or thought, Cicero put them out of the judges' minds with another joke. 'Thirty thousand sesterces for rent? Ah, I see – Clodius is selling the apartment block and wants to attract a buyer.'[129]

Imperceptibly, Cicero had guided his succession of arguments on the various allegations about Caelius' morals and behaviour to the point where he could naturally refer to Clodia. Yes, Caelius left his father's house and went to live in the apartment on the Palatine. And here Cicero reminded the judges of the first line of Ennius' *Medea*, quoted earlier by Crassus with reference to Ptolemy:[130]

Ac longius mihi quidem contexere hoc carmen liceret: 'Nam numquam era errans' hanc molestiam nobis exhiberet 'Medea animo aegro, amore saevo saucia.' Sic enim, iudices, reperietis quod, cum ad id loci venero, ostendam, hanc Palatinam Medeam migrationemque hanc adulescenti causa sive malorum omnium sive potius sermonum fuisse.

For my part, I might extend the quotation a little further: 'For then never would straying mistress' have caused us all this trouble, 'Medea, sick at heart, wounded by cruel love.' For that, gentlemen, is what you will find when I get

---

128 *Cael.* 17, the last 'nam quod . . .' in the series beginning at §4. On *patria potestas* see J. A. Crook, *Law and the Life of Rome* (London 1967) 107–13.
129 *Cael.* 17, alleging both lies and Clodian influence on the prosecution side.
130 *Cael.* 18, cf. n.118 above.

to that point; I shall show that it was this Palatine Medea, and his change of lodging, that caused all the young man's troubles – or rather, all the talk.

Now the prosecution's fears were confirmed. The game of allusions showed that 'when he got to that point' (ominous phrase) Cicero would exploit Caelius' affair with Clodia in order to make out that her evidence was just the malice of a woman spurned. If Caelius was Jason, as Atratinus had first suggested, then Clodia was Medea, queen, witch and murderess, whose fury against Jason was because he left her.

For that reason,[131] Cicero isn't afraid of the witnesses the prosecution will bring; as the judges will surely realise, they have all been suborned by powerful influences in the background (no names, but the allusion to the patrician Claudii was clear enough).[132] *He* will have no witnesses, but demonstrate the truth by logical proofs, indications clearer than the light of day: 'fact against fact, motive against motive, reason against reason'.[133]

Now, it seemed, Cicero had got his introductory arguments out of the way, and could address himself to the charges themselves. Crassus had dealt fully with the Naples riot, the fracas at Puteoli, and the business of Palla's property. All that was left was the murder of Dio – but what could he say about that? Everyone knew who had done it; it was the king, he didn't even deny it. The man who was prosecuted for it, P. Asicius, had been acquitted. By collusion? Nonsense – Cicero himself had been defence counsel, and he ought to know. Anyway, it was nothing to do with Caelius, and the gentleman Dio was staying with at the time would no doubt testify to that effect if he was called. They could forget all that; it was time to get down to the *real* issues in the case.[134]

As a confidence trick, it was breathtaking. Did the prosecutors protest? Did the judges laugh, or frown, or mutter? No matter if

---

131 See Heinze 1925, 215 n.1 on *quam ob rem* at §19.
132 *Cael.* 19–22, with Heinze 1925, 215 and Drexler 1944, 16. Note the contrast between *accusare* and *oppugnare* at §20f (as in §1).
133 *Cael.* 22, cf. n.86 above for *argumenta*.
134 *Cael.* 23–5.

they did: already Cicero had changed his tempo to distract them. 'I noticed, gentlemen, how attentively you listened to my friend Herennius yesterday . . .'

For Cicero, Herennius Balbus' strictures on the behaviour of modern youth were precisely the real issues in the case. He could not afford to deal seriously with the question of Caelius' guilt until he had countered the effect they had made. The first stage of his campaign was a long address to the judges, seriously argued but lightened with delicate irony against Herennius,[135] on the injustice of imputing the shortcomings of a whole age-group to one particular member of it. Plenty of men have been dissolute in their youth and then become sober and respectable citizens; it is accepted that young men's natural appetites are harmless if indulged in the proper way; but Cicero will not avail himself of that excuse. All he asks is that prejudice against the younger generation in general should not be directed at Caelius in particular. 'Naturally I shall answer in meticulous detail the charges which are properly brought against my client himself.'[136]

Now at last he came to the charges. But he defined them in his own way, not as they appeared on the document before the court.[137]

Sunt autem duo crimina, auri et veneni; in quibus una atque eadem persona versatur. Aurum sumptum a Clodia, venenum quaesitum quod Clodiae daretur, ut dicitur. Omnia sunt alia non crimina sed maledicta, iurgi petulantis magis quam publicae quaestionis.

Now, there are two charges, one about gold, one about poison, and the very same person is involved in both. It is said that the gold was taken from Clodia, and the poison procured to give to Clodia. All the other matters are not charges but slanders, more for a slanging-match than a court of law.

It was clear enough by now what Cicero's aim was – to concentrate all attention on the comparatively minor matter where

---

[135] E.g. *Cael.* 26 (on the Luperci), 27 (*precario* . . .).

[136] *Cael.* 28–30.

[137] Heinze 1925, 222 and 248, Drexler 1944, 17f, Lintott 1968, 111f; I think Austin (1952, 150f) was wrong to include 'de veneno in Clodiam parato' among the formal charges. For the *inscriptio*, cf. Paul. *Dig.* XLVIII 2.3.

Clodia's testimony was directly involved. The main charges of riot and murder had been waved away (already answered by Crassus, or not worth answering anyway), and Cicero proceeded as if all that mattered to the court were the details of the unsuccessful attempt on Dio's life while he was staying with Lucceius, and its consequence, the abortive plan to poison Clodia. Both were based on her evidence, and so her credibility must be destroyed in advance.[138]

It was a dangerous strategy, but Cicero was bold and clever. A little innocent innuendo first (how intimate she must have been with Caelius if she lent him the gold, how cruel the rupture if he planned to kill her), followed by a disingenuous appeal to the president of the court, apologising for the necessity of bringing a lady's name into the proceedings. But what else could he do, when the case against his client was wholly dependent on her resources?[139] He was hampered in his defence by his personal enmity with the lady's husband – sorry, her brother, he always made that mistake – and he would say no more than his responsibility to the case required. 'I never thought I should have to be unfriendly towards a woman, especially one with the reputation of being friendly with everyone.'

This is the point at which we must remember the audience. By mixing his disclaimer of impropriety with malicious asides at which the Forum crowd would laugh and applaud, Cicero made it very difficult for the president of the court to bring him to order. Cn. Domitius would not want to risk whistles and catcalls by putting a stop to what everyone (except the prosecutors) was enjoying so much; Cicero had given him enough of an excuse to allow it to continue, though one imagines that Clodia's famous eyes were blazing at him from the prosecution benches.[140]

Having got away with it, Cicero settled down to exploit his success with a display of oratorical virtuosity. To avoid the odium of attacking Clodia himself, he impersonated her famous

138 See Reitzenstein 1925; Quint. v 7.6 on *reprehensio testis*.
139 *Cael.* 32, 'opes ad oppugnandum' (cf. 1, and n.132 above).
140 *Cael.* 49, *har. resp.* 38 (eyes); *Att.* 1 16.11, *Sest.* 115, *Pis.* 65 (whistles).

ancestor Appius Claudius as a spokesman for the old Roman virtues she had flouted. A great orator had to be a great actor (Cicero himself had studied Roscius' technique),[141] and Appius' tirade must have been a histrionic *tour de force* more than compensating the Forum crowd for the performances they were missing in the theatre that day. But it was not just for entertainment. Cicero's Appius would sweep his audience off their feet, *make* them believe in the standards of the good old days.[142]

For Caelius' counsel, that was a two-edged weapon. No sooner had Appius ceased to thunder than Cicero turned to the judges with a candid admission:

Sed quid ego, iudices, ita gravem personam induxi ut verear ne se idem Appius repente convertat et Caelium incipiat accusare illa sua gravitate censoria? Sed videro hoc posterius atque ita, iudices, ut vel severissimis disceptatoribus M. Caeli vitam me probaturum esse confidam.

But gentlemen, why have I brought on stage a character so puritanical that I'm afraid this same Appius might turn round and start accusing Caelius with that famous censor's severity of his? I shall attend to that later on, gentlemen, and in such a way that I am confident I shall justify Marcus Caelius' way of life to even the strictest critics.

Then straight back to the attack:[143]

Tu vero, mulier – iam enim ipse tecum nulla persona introducta loquor – si ea quae facis, quae dicis, quae insimulas, quae moliris, quae arguis probare cogitas, rationem tantae familiaritatis, tantae consuetudinis, tantae coniunctionis reddas atque exponas necesse est. Accusatores quidem libidines, amores, adulteria, Baias, actas, convivia, comissationes, cantus, symphonias, navigia iactant, idemque significant nihil se te invita dicere. Quae tu quoniam mente nescio qua effrenata atque praecipiti in forum deferri iudiciumque voluisti, aut diluas oportet ac

---

[141] Plut. *Cic.* 5.3, cf. Cic. *de or.* 1 128 etc.; Austin 1952, 141–3.
[142] Quint. XII 10.61; cf. Plato *Ion* 535c (Walbank 1960, 230) for how audiences could be moved.
[143] *Cael.* 35, putting the responsibility for Clodia's discomfiture on the prosecutors (cf. n.106 above).

falsa esse doceas aut nihil neque crimini tuo neque testimonio creden-dum esse fateare.

As for you, madam – for now I address you in person, with no imaginary character in between – if you intend to justify *your* actions, statements, allegations, plots, charges, then you will have to give an account and explanation of a relationship so familiar, a connection so intimate. The prosecutors go on about debauchery, love-affairs, adulteries, the beach at Baiae, banquets and parties, songs and music, revelry on shipboard – and they also suggest that they have your approval for everything they say. And since in some uncontrolled and reckless mood you have decided to bring all this into the Forum and the court, you must either disprove it and show it to be false, or else admit that neither your charge nor your testimony is to be believed.

This was much more damaging for Clodia. What lay behind it was the ill-defined legal concept of *infamia*, which could impose various disqualifications on persons engaged in activities that were considered degrading. One of these was prostitution; the testimony of a prostitute might not be accepted in court, and if it was, it would certainly carry very little weight.[144] It was becoming clear what Cicero had meant by that startling use of the word in his opening remarks. He was proposing to define Clodia's sophisticated lifestyle as morally equivalent to prostitution, and destroy her credit as a witness that way.

However, he still had some way to go. Before spelling out the implications of the dilemma he had just imposed on Clodia, he softened up the audience with another dramatic monologue. Not Appius this time, but still within the family – Clodia's youngest brother, who always slept with his sister when he was little because he was afraid of the dark . . . Roars of laughter (the Forum crowd liked chanting rude songs about Clodia and her brother)[145] – but again, it was more than just comedy. Cicero's impersonation of Clodius and his casual morals was even more damning than the ranting of Appius. 'What's the fuss about? You pick up some good-looking boy, you give him presents to keep

---

[144] Cf. *Dig.* xxii 5.3.5 (not allowed to testify under the *lex Iulia de vi*); on *infamia* in general, see now B. Levick, *JRS* 73 (1983) 108–10.

[145] Cic. *QF* ii 3.2 (Feb. 56); Wiseman 1969, 53–5 for the rest of the evidence.

him, but now he wants to get away. So pick up another – after all, that's why you've got your gardens just where the boys go to swim.'[146]

After the applause died down, Cicero turned to Caelius with a pretence of severity to lecture him on his part in these goings-on.[147] More play-acting: the strict father from Caecilius' comedy is imagined as demanding why Caelius moved into a prostitute's neighbourhood, instead of fleeing from the temptation; and the easy-going father from Terence's *Adelphoe* has nothing to complain of anyway, as Cicero explains with a transparent pretence of protecting Clodia's good name:

Nihil iam in istam mulierem dico; sed, si esset aliqua dissimilis istius quae se omnibus pervolgaret, quae haberet palam decretum semper aliquem, cuius in hortos, domum, Baias iure suo libidines omnium commearent, quae etiam alerent adulescentis et parsimoniam patrum suis sumptibus sustineret, si vidua libere, proterva petulanter, dives effuse, libidinosa meretricio more viveret, adulterum ego putarem si quis hanc paulo liberius salutasset?

I am saying nothing now against that woman. But if there were someone not like her, who made herself available to everyone, always had some man openly marked out as her lover, owned gardens, a town house and a villa at Baiae where every lecher had the right of entry, kept young men and subsidised their pocket money at her own expense – if there were a widowed lady living permissively, a saucy lady living wantonly, a wealthy lady living extravagantly, a lusty lady living like a whore – should I call it adultery if some man were a little free in his attentions to her?

With this magnificent rhetorical flourish, Cicero at last made clear the full implications of his case. Clodia was a rejected mistress, attacking her ex-lover out of pique; she was a woman of bad moral reputation, whose testimony should not be credited; and she was a whore, whose favours any man could enjoy without damage to his own good name.[148]

Cicero was nearly home and dry. All he had to do now was to

---

[146] Cf. Classen 1973, 80: no other known example of *prosopopoeia* of a living person.
[147] As promised in §35.
[148] *Cael.* 37–8; the word *meretricius*, not used since §1, appears twice in this passage.

prove that relations with prostitutes were indeed compatible with conventional Roman moral standards. At this point he used the argument he had denied himself earlier: natural appetites must be catered for, superhuman self-denial could not be expected, sexual relations that did no harm to honour, status or the family had always been acceptable. At length, and in a properly serious tone with just a few brief smiles, the distinguished senior senator discussed moral behaviour with his peers.[149] Yes, Caelius had sown his wild oats, as many other distinguished gentlemen had done in their time. But sexual indulgence had never obsessed him; the proof was in his prowess as an orator, a calling which demanded dedication, hard work and strict training. If he were really abandoned to a life of dissipation, he could never have become the formidable adversary they knew he was.[150]

But what about the Palatine, Baiae, all that fevered gossip? Surely that must mean something? Yes – it meant that *her* depravity was so shameless that she didn't even hide it. It meant that like a true professional she loved publicity.[151] But it didn't do *his* reputation any harm.

Somehow, Cicero had succeeded in proving, not only that Clodia was morally disreputable, but that Caelius was not. The prosecution's gamble had failed spectacularly. Caelius himself, who loved to see his enemies squirm, must have enjoyed the spectacle as Cicero harangued first Balbus and then Clodia, nagging them to admit the logic of his case – is it really so dreadful for a young man to go with a woman like that?[152]

It had taken Cicero about an hour to get to the point where he could allow the judges to think about the facts of Caelius' alleged

---

[149] *Cael.* 39–44 (cf. 28, 30), cf. Lyne 1980, 12 on the social background. Light relief: deserted lecture-halls at §41, the pleasures of the table appealing to older men at §44.

[150] *Cael.* 45–7, ending at *dimicaret?* (Heinze 1925, 238f).

[151] For the significance of the argument cf. *Dig.* XXIII 2.43.1–3 (Classen 1973, 81 n.96); Cicero can therefore go on immediately to refer to *meretricii amores* at §48.

[152] *Cael.* 48–50, still preserving the decencies with the fiction that he doesn't mean Clodia herself, and that it was the prosecutors who made out that she lived an immoral life (n.143 above).

murder attempts on Dio and Clodia. Twice already he had seemed to be on the point of discussing the charges; each time it had been a feint.[153] But now that he had neutralised their prejudice against the defendant, and drastically undermined the credit of the chief prosecution witness, he could afford to get down to business at last:[154]

Sed quoniam emersisse iam e vadis et scopulos praetervecta videtur esse oratio mea, perfacilis mihi reliquus cursus ostenditur. Duo sunt enim crimina una in muliere summorum facinorum, auri quod sumptum a Clodia dicitur, et veneni quod eiusdem Clodiae necandae causa parasse Caelium criminantur.

But since my speech seems to have emerged from the shallows and got past the rocks, it looks like plain sailing from now on. For there are two charges of very serious crimes, both involving one woman: one about gold supposedly taken from Clodia, and one about poison which they allege Caelius procured in order to murder the same Clodia.

'The charge about gold' was the defence euphemism for the attempt on Dio's life while he was staying with L. Lucceius. Cicero's answer depended entirely on a written statement by Lucceius himself. Why not a proper testimony that could be cross-examined? Wouldn't he naturally deny all knowledge of a murder attempt under his roof? Hadn't Cicero himself said that witnesses were worthless compared with logical arguments? But the judges were given no time to think of all that; Cicero was posing specious dilemmas, booming indignantly at Clodia, lavishing all his rhetorical ornament on the build-up to the reading of Lucceius' statement, and finally clinching his case with the argument that all his previous hard work had enabled him to use:[155]

. . . ut res minime dubitanda in contentione ponatur, utrum temeraria, procax, irata mulier finxisse crimen, an gravis, sapiens moderatusque vir religiose testimonium dixisse videatur.

[153] *Cael.* 22f, 30.
[154] *Cael.* 51, cf. n.137 above on Cicero's definition of the 'charges'.
[155] *Cael.* 51–5 (cf. 22 on witnesses); Heinze 1925, 251f and Classen 1973, 88f on the weakness of the arguments.

So the point at issue admits of no doubt – whether you think a wayward, capricious and angry woman has fabricated the charge, or a serious, sensible and moderate man has given his evidence conscientiously.

For 'the poison charge' – that is, the plan to murder Clodia – Cicero had no defence at all except what he could conjure up from the facts themselves. After some routine arguments from probability, with innuendo in passing about Clodia's relations with her slaves, he came to the allegation that Caelius had tried out the poison on a slave he had bought. Suddenly he launched into a tremendous display of righteous indignation. He had seen Clodia's husband, that great patriot Q. Metellus Celer, on his deathbed. Metellus had checked Clodius' political excesses, and had died with suspicious suddenness – would that woman, coming from that house, dare to speak of quick-acting poisons? It was a great performance, dramatic, powerful, and totally irrelevant. He thundered at Clodia, and then stopped and turned aside as if unable to go on: 'the reference I have made to that gallant and distinguished gentleman has made my voice weak with tears, my mind clouded with sorrow'.[156]

A moment to recover, and then away again with another change of tempo as he tried to prove the inherent implausibility of the story of Licinius' rendezvous with Clodia's slaves at the Senian Baths. Now his tone was light-hearted and ironical, though it hardened when he came to the friends of Clodia who would testify to the facts. No doubt they were fashionable young men about town, but this wasn't a party: 'we'll shake out all their fancy ways and foolishness if they come forward to give evidence'. After what they had seen Clodia suffer, the young men beside her on the prosecution benches might well be frightened off from giving their evidence at all. And he had another turn of the knife for her as well, as he concluded with a reminder of the perfume jar; whatever the story was (he was careful not to be too explicit), it left Clodia feeling foolish and defiled, and the audience grinning cruelly at her discomfiture.[157]

---

[156] *Cael.* 56–60 (cf. pp. 24f above): Classen 1973, 89.
[157] *Cael.* 61–9 (66f on the witnesses); Classen 1973, 90f; Wiseman 1974, 170–5.

That completed the case for the defence.[158] In his peroration Cicero returned to the theme he had started with, the abuse of the *quaestio de vi* to gratify a woman's private animosities. Two indignant attacks on Clodia's improper influence framed a lengthy and expurgated account of Caelius' career;[159] then came the appeal to pity (Caelius' heart-broken father), and at the very end a reminder to the judges that they might need Caelius' gratitude one day. Acquit him, and they would reap the fruits of his talent.[160]

5. THE AFTERMATH

Caelius was indeed acquitted, by what majority we do not know. The following day he was faced with a difficult political choice between his two defenders. At a noisy Senate meeting, Cicero attacked the legality of Caesar's agrarian legislation in 59 B.C., which Crassus had helped to force through.[161] In the resulting political crisis, Clodius unexpectedly changed sides to support Pompey, and Pompey and Crassus renewed their alliance of three years earlier.[162] They would hold the consulship together in 55, after which Crassus would have the province of Syria; he was planning to conquer Parthia, to equal the glory that Pompey had won against Mithridates and Caesar was now winning in Gaul.

It was during the consulship of Pompey and Crassus that the then proconsul of Syria, Pompey's friend A. Gabinius, was diverted from his own Parthian campaign by an offer of ten thousand talents from Ptolemy if he would turn his army south to Alexandria. Gabinius hesitated, knowing he would be tried for it when he got home; but in the end he marched south, defeated the Alexandrians and left a substantial garrison, including 500 Gallic and German auxiliaries, to protect the hated king

[158] *Cael.* 70: 'dicta est a me causa, iudices, et perorata'.
[159] *Cael.* 70 (*lex de vi, mulieris libidines*, as in §1f), 71 (assault on Vettius, p. 39 above), 72–8 (Caelius' career), 78 (acquittal of Sex. Cloelius, pp. 39–41 above).
[160] *Cael.* 80, cf. n.111 above.
[161] Cic. *QF* II 6.1, *fam.* I 9.8, cf. Dio XXXVIII 5.5, App. *BC* II 10 on Crassus in 59.
[162] Wiseman 1974, 162–5 for the chronology.

against his subjects. Ptolemy, wanting both money and revenge, murdered the richest and most distinguished citizens and imposed a Roman administrator to tax the rest.[163] The new debt, like the original one, was to be paid in instalments; in fact, half the original sum was still outstanding at Ptolemy's death four years later.[164] The much-disputed throne survived for another twenty years, until the young Caesar took it for Rome after the suicide of Ptolemy's daughter, Cleopatra.

By then, most of the protagonists in the Caelius case were spectacularly dead. On 9 June 53 B.C., Crassus died on the field of Carrhae with twenty thousand of his men; his head was used as a stage-prop in a scene from the *Bacchae* performed at a banquet for the Parthian king. On 18 January 52, Clodius was murdered on the Via Appia by the armed escort of a political rival; the following day the Roman populace burned down the Senate-house as his funeral pyre. On 28 September 48, Pompey was stabbed in the back by a renegade centurion as he landed in Egypt to beg help from Ptolemy's son; his head was embalmed and presented to his conqueror, Caesar. On 7 December 43, Cicero was killed in the grounds of his villa at Caieta by a triumviral execution squad; his head and hands were nailed up on the Rostra at Antony's orders.[165]

As for Caelius himself, he went on winning – tribune in 52, curule aedile in 50, praetor in 48 – until his quarrelsome ambition took him too far. Affronted at not getting the senior praetorship, and bitterly opposed to his successful colleague over the question of debt relief, he raised a riot in the Forum, was banned from public business by an emergency decree of the Senate, and finally left Rome in a fury. At Thurii in southern Italy he tried to bribe the Gallic and Spanish cavalry Caesar had posted there as a garrison, and they killed him.[166] He was about forty years old.

---

[163] Dio XXXIX 55–63, Plut. *Ant.* 3.2, Cic. *Pis.* 49, Caes. *BC* III 4.4 (Gauls and Germans), Cic. *Rab. Post.* 22, 28, 39f (C. Rabirius Postumus); Braund 1984, 60.

[164] Dio XXXIX 56.3, cf. n.19 above; Cic. *fam.* VIII 4.5 (Fraser 1972, II 226f) on the date of Ptolemy's death.

[165] Crassus: Plut. *Crass.* 31.7, 33.1–4; Ovid *Fasti* VI 465 (date). Clodius: Asc. 31–3C. Pompey: Plut. *Pomp.* 77–80; Vell. Pat. II 53.3 (date). Cicero: Plut. *Cic.* 48–49.1; Tiro *ap.* Tac. *dial.* 17.2 (date).

[166] Caes. *BC* III 20–2, Dio XLII 22–5, Vell. Pat. II 68.2–3.

CHAPTER IV

CATULLUS IN CONTEXT

We hear a good deal from Catullus about his joys, griefs and passions, but in the end we have hardly any idea of what he was really like.

RICHARD JENKYNS, Three Classical Poets (1982) 84

I. DELOS

I begin with two contrasting images. On the one hand, a Roman portrait head, characteristically unflattering with its jowls, bulging cranium and projecting ears (Plate 1a). On the other, the body of a Greek athlete, idealised and heroic in its muscular perfection (Plate 1b). In fact, they belong to the same statue, of a hellenised Roman in Delos in the middle of the first century B.C. (Plate 2).[1] We do not know his name, but he was a contemporary of Catullus – perhaps even an acquaintance, for we shall see that Catullus probably knew Delos in the fifties. Catullus too was a hellenised Roman, and if we are to understand that phenomenon Delos is a good place to start.

An Athenian colony since 166 B.C., Delos had been declared by the Romans a free port. She rapidly became an unrivalled centre of commerce (and in particular of the slave trade), with a substantial cosmopolitan population of traders and businessmen, among whom the most conspicuous were the Italians.[2] Great profits turned them into great men, who wished to be honoured and flattered in the same way as the quaestors, legates and

---

[1] C. Michalowski, *Les portraits hellénistiques et romains* (Expl. arch. de Délos 13, Paris 1932) 17–22 and plates XIV–XIX.

[2] Strabo X 486, XIV 668 (slave trade), Pol. XXX 31.9–13, etc.; *ILLRP* 343, 359, 362, 369, 747–62. P. Roussel, *Délos colonie athénienne* (Paris 1916); A. J. N. Wilson, *Emigration from Italy in the Republican Age of Rome* (Manchester 1966) 99–119.

proconsuls of Rome, and the various arts of Greek culture were applied to gratify them.

The best known example is C. Ofellius Ferus, whose statue happens to survive in the slave market; the Athenian sculptors Dionysius and Timarchides rendered this Italian *negotiator* in the style of Praxiteles' Hermes.[3] Literary men, in prose and verse, were active too, though the evidence is less conspicuous. Hellenistic historians were used to finding heroic genealogies for Roman aristocrats, whether in Greek mythology (like Anton the son of Herakles, whence the Antonii) or in hellenised versions of the Roman foundation legend (like the Aimylia who bore Romulus to Ares, whence the Aemilii); in the second century B.C. Zenodotus of Troizen invented a son of Romulus called Aollius, whence the Avillii, a commercial family from the Latin city of Lanuvium who we know were active in Delos.[4] Similarly, Hellenistic poets were used to writing up the glories of Roman military conquest, briefly in flattering epigram or at length in heroic epic; we happen to know from a later literary critic, discussing genres specially invented by the poets, that there existed a category called *emporika*, 'poems of commerce', for which I think the only plausible context is the need to provide a place in poetry, as well as in sculpture and historiography, for the businessmen whose wealth and aspirations now made them patrons of the arts of Greece.[5]

[3] E. Lapalus, *L'agora des italiens* (Expl. arch. de Délos 19, Paris 1939) 54–7 and plate xix. Cf. A. Stewart, *Attika* (London 1979) 142–6; R. R. R. Smith, *JRS* 71 (1981) 36–8; P. Zanker in *Les 'bourgeoisies' municipales italiennes aux IIe et Ier siècles av. J.-C.* (Paris & Naples 1983) 252–7, cf. 258f for other late-Republican Romans portrayed in heroic nudity (esp. plates xxvii and xxviii, Formiae). For the 'agora of the Italians' as a slave market, see Coarelli 1982, 119–45.

[4] Plut. *Rom.* 14.8 (Zenodotus *FGrH* 821f2), cf. *ILLRP* 961; *CQ* 33 (1983) 450–2. Plut. *Ant.* 4.2 (Anton), *Rom.* 2.3 (Aimylia). See in general *GR* 21 (1974) 153–64; on the commercial Cossutii (ibid. 156), perhaps 'descended from Bellerophon', see now E. Rawson, *PBSR* 43 (1975) 36–47, and M. Torelli in *Roman Seaborne Commerce* (Mem. Amer. Acad. Rome 36, Rome 1980) 313–21.

[5] Proclus gramm. *ap.* Photius *Bibl.* 320a8 (ed. Henry, vol. 5, p. 159), cf. D. A. Russell, *Criticism in Antiquity* (London 1981) 155, 201; this patronage of Greek poets by Roman *negotiatores* (as well as by military and senatorial grandees) should be added to the

At home, too, they were patrons of Hellenistic culture. Ambitious building programmes were being undertaken by the cities and communities of southern Italy in the late second century B.C. – the main theatre at Pompeii, the temple and theatre at Pietrabbondante in northern Samnium, the huge Fortuna Primigenia complex at Praeneste, and many others. It has been convincingly suggested that the resources necessary for these spectacular projects came from the purses of local aristocrats enriched by the commercial exploitation of the Greek East.[6] Moreover, the buildings themselves attest a desire to create in Italy the physical milieu of Hellenistic culture – theatres and porticoes where poets, rhetoricians and the 'artists of Dionysus' could find an audience on their accustomed circuit of festivals and invited performances.[7] By the end of the second century B.C., as Cicero put it with only a little exaggeration, Italy was full of the arts and literature of Greece.[8]

Patronage led to participation. We know of Italians resident in Greece who won prizes for poetry at the great festivals, set up honorific inscriptions in elegant Greek verse, and devoted themselves totally to the culture of their adopted land. Again, the same phenomenon was reflected at home: the local aristocracies of Italian cities such as Sora and Lanuvium included men with a profound knowledge of Greek literature and learning.[9]

After the War of the Allies, and the extension of the Roman citizenship to the Italian communities in 89 B.C., these hellenised

excellent account in Hardie 1983, 39–41. For poems in honour of a financial magnate at Delos, see G. Mancinetti Santamaria in Coarelli et al. 1982, 79–89.

[6] F. Coarelli in *Hellenismus in Mittelitalien* (ed. P. Zanker, Göttingen 1976) 337–9, and in *Les 'bourgeoisies' municipales* (n.3 above), 217–40.

[7] Wiseman 1983, 300; cf. Hardie 1983, 15–36 for Hellenistic poets on the circuit.

[8] Cic. *Arch.* 5: 'erat Italia tum plena Graecarum artium ac disciplinarum'. Cf. *de or.* III 43 (dramatic date 91 B.C.): 'nostri minus student litteris quam Latini'.

[9] Italians in Greece: e.g. Helly 1983, esp. 364 (Thessaly); L. Robert, *Études épigraphiques et philologiques* (Paris 1938) 7f on Πόπλιος at Delphi; *BCH* 16 (1892) 130f on Πόπλιος at Delos; *Mnem.* 47 (1919) 252–4 on Λεύκιος Λευκίου and Δημήτριος Ῥωμαῖος at Argos; *REG* 6 (1893) 181 on A. Mussius Aper at Miletus; Nep. *Att.* 2.3–4.3 (esp. 4.1) on T. Pomponius at Athens. Sora: Cic. *de or.* III 43, *Brut.* 169 on Q. Valerius, 'literatissimus togatorum omnium' and his brother Decimus. Lanuvium: Cic. *Brut.* 205, Varro *LL* VII 2, Gell. *NA* I 18.2 on L. Aelius, 'eruditissimus Graecis litteris'; cf. *CQ* 33 (1983) 451f.

and munificent local aristocrats – or at least, those of them who had been on the right side in the war and avoided ruin in the proscriptions – became Roman citizens of equestrian or even senatorial rank. We know them from Cicero's letters, recommended to friendly proconsuls for their provincial business interests and their devotion to literary studies.[10] We know them from Catullus too: bad poets like Aquinus and Volusius, bad prose writers like Sestius, whose families are known to have been active in commercial life.[11] With some, like the Rubellii of Tibur and the Caecinae of Etruscan Volaterrae, we can see a striking progression, in two or three generations, from provincial *negotia* and Hellenistic literary culture (now of course expressed in Latin) to power and prestige at the highest and most dangerous level in the first century A.D.[12]

Delos itself was sacked by Mithridates' forces in 87 B.C.. After the war the businessmen returned and the 'agora of the Italians' was restored, but in 69 the island was sacked again, this time by pirates. Yet again, commerce revived. It was at a much less prosperous level, since Pompey's defeat of the pirates in 67 deprived Delos of its profits from the slave trade. But slaves, important as they were, were not the only commodity bought and sold on the island. There was also grain, corn grown in the province of Asia and other neighbouring territories and shipped to Rome via Delos. In 58 B.C., the year when Rome's corn supply was reorganised under the *lex Clodia*, Delos was freed from

10 Cic. *fam.* XIII 12.2 (Q. Fufidius), 22.1 (T. Manlius), 28.2 (L. Mescinius), 29.1 (L. Munatius Plancus).

11 Aquinus: Cat. 14.18; cf. T. R. S. Broughton in *Polis and Imperium: Studies in Honor of E. T. Salmon* (ed. J. A. S. Evans, Toronto 1974) 15f on Aquini and Spanish lead mines. Volusius: Cat. 36, 95.7f; cf. D'Arms 1981, 69f on Volusii and speculations in Cilicia (Cic. *fam.* V 20.3f). Sestius: Cat. 44.10f; cf. D'Arms 1981, 55–62 on Sestii and wine exports to Gaul. We may add L. Lucceius the Hellenistic historian (Cic. *fam.* V 12); cf. D'Arms 1981, 64 on the various commercial activities of the Lucceii.

12 Rubellii: Cic. *fam.* XII 26.1 (*negotiator*), Sen. *contr.* II pref.5 (*rhetor*), Serv. *Georg.* I 103 (historian), Tac. *Ann.* VI 27 (husband of Tiberius' granddaughter); Syme 1982. Caecinae: Cic. *fam.* VI 6.3, 9.1 (*doctrinae studium*), VI 6.2, 8.2, XIII 66.2 (*negotia*), Tac. *Ann.* XI 33f (Caecina Largus and the Messallina crisis); R. Syme, *JRS* 56 (1966) 58f; P. Hohti in *Studies in the Romanization of Etruria* (Acta inst. Rom. Finl. 5, Rome 1975) 405–33; E. Rawson, *JRS* 68 (1978) 137f.

taxation by a law of the consuls Gabinius and Piso; and the inscription officially recording this event refers to *custodia publici frumenti* on the island. So there were still significant commercial interests on Delos, and still Romans with a taste for Hellenistic culture involved in them.[13]

The text of the *lex Gabinia Calpurnia* of 58 makes great play with the fame and sanctity of Delos as the birthplace of Apollo and Diana (Artemis).[14] This combination of the legendary significance of the island and its present importance for the corn supply of the Roman people is worth bearing in mind when we turn to Catullus' hymn to Diana (poem 34), which must be very nearly contemporary with the law:

> Dianae sumus in fide
> puellae et pueri integri:
> Dianam pueri integri
> puellaeque canamus.
>
> O Latonia, maximi
> magna progenies Iovis,
> quam mater prope Deliam
> deposivit olivam,
>
> montium domina ut fores
> silvarumque virentium
> saltuumque reconditorum
> amniumque sonantum:
>
> tu Lucina dolentibus
> Iuno dicta puerperis,
> tu potens Trivia et notho es

---

[13] Strabo x 486 (87 B.C.), Phleg. Trall. *FGrH* 257F12.13 (69 B.C.); M. H. Crawford, *JRS* 67 (1977) 121f on the slave trade and the effect of Pompey's campaign. Delos as a centre of commerce: see G. Mancinetti Santamaria in Coarelli et al. 1982, 85–8. *Lex Gabinia Calpurnia*: Nicolet 1980, revised text at 149f; ibid. 98f on the *frumentum publicum* clause, 37–44 for an important discussion of Delos in the fifties B.C. (by J.-L. Ferrary).

[14] '. . . in quo numero fanum [Apollinis in insula Delo antiquissum]um ac religiosissumum sit constitutu[m. Propter eius fani religion]em et sanctitatem caerimoniasq. pr[. . . illam] insulam, in qua insula Apollinem et Dianam n[atos esse homines putent] vecteigalibus leiberari . . .' etc.

dicta lumine Luna.

Tu cursu, dea, menstruo
metiens iter annuum,
rustica agricolae bonis
tecta frugibus exples.

Sis quocumque tibi placet
sancta nomine, Romulique,
antique ut solita es, bona
sospites ope gentem.

Under Diana's care are we, girls and boys unmarried. Of Diana let us sing,
unmarried boys and girls. Child of Latona, mighty offspring of mightiest Jove,
whom your mother brought forth by the Delian olive, to be mistress of the hills
and leafy woods and sequestered glens and splashing streams: you are invoked
as Juno Lucina by women in the pangs of childbirth, you as the magic Lady of
the Crossways and as Moon of borrowed light. You, goddess, with monthly
course measuring the journey of the year, fill full with goodly harvest the
farmer's rustic home. Be hallowed under whatever name it please you; and, as
you were wont in days of yore, succour with goodly aid the race of Romulus.

Artemis was the goddess of the wild; agriculture was not her
domain.[15] Yet here we have a whole stanza devoted to her filling
the farmer's barns with grain, followed immediately by the final
prayer for her good help to the race of Romulus. The combination of Delos, corn and the Roman people – just as in the *lex
Gabinia Calpurnia* inscription – is striking and suggestive.

For Diana as the bringer of the harvest the only parallel is in
Horace, who perhaps had Catullus' hymn in mind; he bids the
choir practising the Secular Hymn to sing her as Noctiluca, who
prospers the crops by speeding the months in their course.[16]
Scaliger in 1577 thought that Catullus' poem was itself a Secular
Hymn, a chronologically impossible idea which nevertheless

[15] Commentators cite Call. *Hymn* 3.130; but there the good harvest is part of a
description of the general prosperity enjoyed by those whom the goddess favours. For
Cato, the gods who mattered to the farmer were Mars, Jupiter, Janus and Ceres (*de agr.*
83, 134, 141).
[16] Hor. *Odes* IV 6.39f, 'prosperam frugum celeremque pronos volvere menses'. But in the
carmen saeculare itself (29–32) the harvest is predictably in the care of Tellus, Ceres and
Jupiter.

survived as late as Doering's edition of 1822. Other scholars offered more plausible contexts for the performance of the hymn – either when the Sibylline Books were consulted after a prodigy (so Marcilius in 1604),[17] or at the annual festival of the temple of Diana on the Aventine (so Bentley in 1711) – and those still held the field when Baehrens and Ellis produced their great commentaries in 1885 and 1889 respectively. But the twentieth century turned its back on the whole idea of a particular religious occasion: for three generations, dogmatically or with merely formal hesitation, commentator after commentator has treated Catullus 34 as a poem to be read, not a hymn to be sung.[18]

Now at last there are signs of a welcome reaction. The latest commentator, G. P. Goold, is tempted by the possibility ('but speculation it must remain') that the hymn was written for performance. Gordon Williams goes further, insisting that it is what it purports to be, and not a mere literary exercise – rightly, I think, though his suggestion for the occasion of the hymn is not a convincing one.[19] If it is a real hymn for a real choir, with an emphasis on Delos, the harvest, and the welfare of the Roman people, and written in the fifties B.C.[20] when we know that Delos was a centre for the transmission of corn supplies to Rome, then the occasion for its performance is not difficult to imagine.

Homer himself, 'the blind bard from rocky Chios', attested

---

[17] Cf. Livy XXII 1.16, Macr. Sat. 16.14 (217 B.C.); Livy XXVII 37.7, Festus 446L (207); Livy XXXI 12.9 (200); Obs. 27a (133), 34 (119), 36 (117), 43 (104), 46 (99), 48 (97), 53 (92). But the ritual regularly involved a choir of 27 *virgines* only, and there is no sign of any particular concentration on Diana; Iuno Regina is the divinity named most often in this context.

[18] E.g. Merrill 1893, Friedrich 1908, Kroll 1929, Fordyce 1961, Quinn 1970. For Goold 1983, see n.19.

[19] Goold 1983, 18; but in his note on the poem (242, my italics) 'a choir of boys and girls *is imagined as* performing this poem'. G. W. Williams in *Literary and Artistic Patronage in Ancient Rome* (ed. B. K. Gold, Austin 1982) 11f; he goes back to Marcilius' 'Sibylline books' idea (but see n.17 above), and suggests that 'Catullus was persuaded by the adherents of Caesar to compose this hymn after the news of the Parthian disaster' in 53 B.C. On the general issue of poems written for performance, Cairns 1984, 149–51 is fundamental.

[20] All the dateable poems of Catullus belong to the years 57–54 B.C.: see *JRS* 69 (1979) 162f, 167.

the antiquity of the Delian festival of music and poetry in honour of Apollo, which was revived by imperial Athens in 426–5 B.C. In the Hellenistic age, too, Delos attracted poets who 'hymned the patron gods of the island'.[21] Now that it was a centre of Roman commerce, its culture and its documents bilingual in Latin and Greek, a Roman poet passing through might well be asked to provide a hymn for the festival of Apollo's sister, with appropriate allusion to the present preoccupation of the Romans in business there.[22] A Roman hymn in Greek lyric metre, celebrating a Greek myth but invoking in archaic Latin the goddess' help to the Roman people, as of old, Catullus 34 is a bicultural document as striking in its way as that heroic statue of the anonymous Roman businessman with the jowls (who may, indeed, have heard it performed).

Delos was still, in the fifties, a natural port of call for Romans crossing the Aegean. Cicero stopped several days in 51 on his way to his province, and noticed Atticus' financial interests there.[23] We don't know whether Catullus did the same on his way to Bithynia in 57, but he probably did on his way back. Poem 4 recounts the voyage of a yacht from Pontic Amastris up the Adriatic to retirement in a clear lake; the poem itself does not say what the occasion of the voyage was, but in the context of the Catullan collection the reader soon infers it from poems 10, 31 and 46 – the return of the poet from his province to Sirmio, via Rhodes and the Cyclades.[24] Delos is the most likely harbour in the Cyclades for him to have called at, not only for its intrinsic interest and associations but also because Catullus may himself have had business there.

It is noticeable that when he says farewell to Bithynia in poem 46, it is the *fertility* of the place that Catullus emphasises. Indeed, whenever he mentions faraway places (and he does it quite a lot)

21 *Hom. Hymn Apollo* 146–78 (172 for choirs, cf. Cic. *Arch.* 19); Thuc. III 104; *SIG*³ 382 (Demoteles of Andros), 622 (Amphicles of Delos), *BCH* 13 (1889) 250 (Ariston of Phocaea) – all second century B.C.
22 *IG* XI 1150 for choric competitions, 133.81 for ῾Ρωμαϊσταί (second century B.C.).
23 Cic. *Att.* V 12, IX 9.4.
24 Cat. 4.6–9; cf. Wiseman 1969, 12f, *JRS* 69 (1979) 162.

his instinct is to allude as much to their produce as to their mythological associations – silphium from Cyrene, oysters from Lampsacus, boxwood from Cytorus, grain (probably) from Africa, rabbits, dyed linen and gold from Spain.[25] What we know of the later history of the poet's family, with its commercial interests in Spain and its marriage connection with tax-farmers in Asia Minor,[26] suggests that the association of ideas in Catullus' mind could be that of a Roman *negotiator*, interested as much in profits as in learned poetry.

As we have seen, there is no inconsistency between Hellenistic literary studies and the wealth and status that could be won by financial exploitation of the empire. The Valerii Catulli of Verona were a family just like the Rubellii of Tibur and the Caecinae of Volaterrae (p. 95 above), rising in three or four generations from equestrian rank in the late Republic to the highest levels of metropolitan society under the Julio-Claudians – a rise marked in their case by the building of the great palatial villa at Sirmio.[27] When Catullus was in Bithynia on Memmius' staff, and his brother in the province of Asia (where he died untimely), they were probably helping to found, or to consolidate, the financial fortunes of their house.[28] The family may have owned corn-lands in 'hot Nicaea's fertile plain', just as the cultured Atticus did in Epirus, or that excellent poet L. Julius Calidus did in Africa.[29] So when in poem 46 his itchy feet set out

[25] Cat. 46.5, 'Nicaeaeque ager uber aestuosae' (cf. Strabo XII 564); 7.4 (cf. Pliny *NH* XIX 38); frag. 1.4 (cf. Pliny *NH* XXXII 62); 4.13 (cf. Strabo XII 544); 37.18 (cf. Varro *RR* III 12 for commercial exploitation); 48.5 (reading *Africi* with Markland and Goold: cf. Hor. *Odes* I 1.9f, *Sat.* II 3.87); 64.227 (cf. Pol. III 114.4); 29.19 (cf. Pliny *NH* IV 115).

[26] *CIL* XV 4756 (Spanish *garum* amphora, between 30 B.C. and A.D. 60); *IG* II² 4159, L. Valerius Catullus married to a Terentia Hispulla (Augustan?), cf. Cic. *fam.* XIII 6.5, *Att.* XI 10.1 on P. Terentius Hispo. For the full argument, see Wiseman 1986, ch. 3.

[27] See Wiseman 1986, chs. 4 and 5: the Catulli were of senatorial rank under Augustus (the moneyer L. Valerius Catullus), consular under Tiberius (Sex. Teidius Valerius Catullus *cos. suff.* A.D. 31), and in the intimate company of the emperor under Gaius (Suet. *Gaius* 36.1) and Domitian (Pliny *ep.* IV 22.5, Tac. *Agr.* 45.1, Juv. IV 113–22, on L. Valerius Catullus Messalinus *cos. II* A.D. 85).

[28] The same applies to Veranius in Spain: see Endnote 3 below.

[29] Atticus: Nep. *Att.* 11.1–2, 14.3, Varro *RR* II 2.1f, 2.20, 5.1, 5.10–12. Calidus: Nep. *Att.* 12.4 ('quem post Lucretii Catullique mortem multo elegantissimum poetam

for the famous cities of Asia, Catullus may not just have been sightseeing. Perhaps there were also agents and financial partners to consult in Cyzicus, Pergamum, Ephesus, Miletus – and Delos too, as he headed back.

2. FINANCIAL ATTITUDES

Roman citizens in business in the provinces were not universally popular. Cicero was hard put to it in 66 to convince the Roman people that protecting the fortunes of *publicani* and *negotiatores* in Asia was a good reason for them to give Pompey the command against Mithridates;[30] similarly in 63, defending L. Murena before a jury, he passed very quickly over the defendant's recent proconsulship in Narbonese Gaul, where his main achievement had evidently been to enforce repayment of debts to Roman financiers.[31] The clearest evidence, though it needs careful interpretation, comes in the semi-public letter of advice to his brother Quintus, about to enter his third year as proconsul of Asia in 59.[32] Whom should he trust as a friend? Not a *negotiator*:

I don't say many residents in the provinces are not honest men; but this is something which it is allowable to hope but dangerous to decide . . . These people out of desire for money go without all those amenities from which we cannot bear to be parted. Are you likely to find any man among them to love you, a stranger, sincerely, not just pretending it for his own advantage? That would be most extraordinary in my opinion, especially if these same persons love hardly anybody in a private station but are always fond of every governor . . . There is no class of men with

nostram tulisse aetatem vere videor posse contendere'). Cf. p. 62 above on Caelius' father's *possessiones* in Africa, and Helly 1983 (esp. 378f) on Romans in Thessaly; in general, see M. H. Crawford, *Econ. Hist. Rev.* 30 (1977) 48f.

[30] Cic. *leg. Man.* 17f; he put greater emphasis on the *populi Romani gloria* (7–12) and the *salus sociorum atque amicorum* (12–16) – see §6 for the *divisio*.

[31] Cic. *Mur.* 42; cf. Sall. *Cat.* 40.1–3 on the Allobroges, driven to the point of rebellion by debt, both *publice* and *privatim*; one of the profiteers was probably the young P. Clodius (Cic. *har. resp.* 42).

[32] Cic. *QF* 1 1.15 (Shackleton Bailey's translation); cf. ibid. 2 'impudentia nonnullorum negotiatorum', 7 'improbus negotiator, paulo cupidior publicanus', 19 (and *QF* 1 2.6) on Tuscenius, a notorious example.

whom as intimates you should be more on your guard. They know all the paths that lead to money, everything they do is for money's sake, and they are not concerned to guard the reputation of someone who will not be with them indefinitely.

It is important to understand the values Cicero is applying here. He and his brother were first-generation senators, from a small-town family of local importance which may well have made its money by commerce. But by 59 B.C. they had come a long way from the Arpinum cloth business.[33] Since the great consulship, Cicero was a *princeps civitatis*: as this very letter eloquently reveals, his standards now were those of the Roman ruling oligarchy.[34] He owed it to his *dignitas* to have a ruinously expensive house on the Palatine, four or five country villas full of Greek statues, and status-symbol furniture at astronomical prices.[35]

What mattered was magnificence – spending money, not getting it. 'Only the vulgar and niggardly keep note of their expenses; gentlemen of true magnificence spend and squander.' That formulation was by Nero Caesar Augustus, but the principle itself had been familiar to the great men of Rome ever since the time of Scipio Africanus. An anecdote about one particularly open-handed senator shows it in practice. He ordered one million sesterces to be given as a present to one of his friends; his steward, horrified, set it out in piles of silver to show how huge a sum it was. 'Is that all?' said the senator when he saw it; 'I thought it would be more. You'd better double it.'[36] The steward, of

---

[33] Dio XLVI 4.2 ('son of a fuller'), *CIL* x 5678 (slave of a L. Tullius in the Arpinum woolworkers' guild); F. Coarelli, *Lazio* (Guide arch. Laterza, Bari 1982) 236.

[34] See esp. *QF* I 1.38 and 41: 'in eam rationem vitae nos non tam cupiditas quaedam gloriae quam res ipsa ac fortuna deduxit ut sempiternus sermo hominum de nobis futurus sit . . . propter earum rerum in quibus versati sumus splendorem et magnitudinem'; ibid. 2, 3, 44f (*gloria*), 43 (*amplissimum nomen*), etc.

[35] House: Cic. *fam.* v 6.2, *Att.* I 13.6, Gell. *NA* XII 12.2f. Villas: *Att.* I 4.3 (Tusculum, Formiae, Caieta; statues); I 20.1, *Acad.* II 9 (Pompeii); *Att.* II 4–9 (Antium); the Cumae villa was bought in 57 or 56 (*QF* II 5.4). Furniture: Pliny *NH* XIII 91f, 102 (citrus-wood table, a novelty at 500,000 *HS*).

[36] Suet. *Nero* 30.1 on 'praelauti vereque magnifici'; Plut. *Cato maior* 3.5 on Africanus' habitual πολυτέλεια; Plut. *Ant.* 4.3f on Antony (and cf. 28.4–7 on his son). See Cic. *Phil.* I 29 on the true aristocrat's contempt for money.

course, had the vulgar and niggardly job of keeping the accounts. Businessmen in the provinces would take his view, not his master's, and that is the point of Cicero's sneer.

Remember that Cicero was writing to his brother. He would have expressed himself differently to Atticus, who had spent over twenty years abroad going without all those amenities from which the Ciceros could not bear to be parted – the pursuit of honours and a life of splendour at Rome.[37] Though no one could call him vulgar or niggardly, Atticus shared the steward's attitude: he kept careful accounts, and his outgoings were modest. He was a man of wealth and taste, and he could be generous, but he did not throw his money about. Magnificence was not his style.[38]

Where is Catullus in this scene? The poems offer a consistent portrait of a man concerned more with economy than extravagance – not easy to borrow from, irritated by petty theft, alleging cobwebs in his purse, contemptuous of those who have run through their funds, explicitly assessing his provincial experience in terms of profit and loss. When he rashly tries to act the big spender, his sophisticated friends embarrassingly call his bluff.[39] As for magnificence, that's for the detestable Mamurra, *superbus et superfluens*, running through one fortune after another; though he has huge and fertile estates, the income from them (as the poet carefully specifies) is less than his expenses. One aspect of Mamurra's magnificence we know from other sources – a spectacularly luxurious house, the first in Rome to have marble-panelled walls.[40]

---

[37] Cic. *Att.* I 17.5 (*honorum studium*), cf. *Cluent.* 154 (*domi splendor*, etc.); Nep. *Att.* 2.2–4.5.

[38] Nep. *Att.* 13.5: 'elegans non magnificus, splendidus non sumptuosus; omnisque diligentia munditiam, non affluentiam affectabat'. Ibid. 13.6 on his accounts; 2.6, 4.4, 7.1, 8.6, 9.5, 11.3–6 on his generosity.

[39] Borrowers: Cat. 23 (Furius, 100,000 *HS*), 41 ('Ameana', 10,000 *HS*), 103 (Silo, 10,000 *HS*). Theft: 12 (Asinius, napkins), 25 (Thallus, napkins), 42 (unnamed girl, writing tablets). Cobwebs: 13.8. Contempt: 21.9–11 (Aurelius), 24.4–6 (Furius), 26 (mortgage), 41.4 = 43.5 (bankrupt). Bithynia: 28.6–8 (*in tabulis*), cf. 10.8. Bluff: 10.14ff.

[40] Cat. 29 (quote from line 6), cf. 41.4 = 43.5; 114–15 (114.4 'fructus sumptibus exsuperat'). House: Pliny *NH* XXXVI 48. Cf. Cic. *Att.* VII 7.6 on his notorious enrichment by Caesar.

At the moment of his greatest joy and confidence in love, Catullus reckons up the kisses on a calculator; each line is like a strip on the abacus, as he flicks the thousands to the left, the hundreds to the right –

> da mi basia *mille*, deinde *centum*,
> dein *mille* altera, dein secunda *centum*,
> deinde usque altera *mille*, deinde *centum* –

and then jumbles them up again with a verb from the language of accountancy.[41] Love and friendship are an investment, and the capital is easily lost. 'I trusted you, at great expense to myself'; 'I love you now at even greater cost, but you are cheaper and of less account'; 'it's all lost, entrusted to a thankless heart'. And when, against all expectation, love comes again, that is more precious than gold itself.[42]

It would be unjust to see in this a merely mercenary outlook – to apply to Catullus what Cicero said of provincial businessmen, 'everything they do is for money's sake'. A similar phrase was used by a Greek contemporary, Diodorus Siculus, commenting on the Celtic peoples' taste for alcohol:[43]

Many Italian merchants, because of their characteristic love of money, regard this love of wine on the part of the Gauls as a godsend. They transport the wine on boats along the navigable rivers, and on waggons over the level plain, and get an incredible price for it. A slave is what they get for a jar of wine – yes, a servant for a drink.

Nobody likes a profiteer. But trading in Gaul was a very dangerous business,[44] and if both parties were satisfied with the market

---

[41] Cat. 5.7–11. For the abacus, see H. L. Levy, *AJP* 62 (1941) 222–4; for *conturbare*, *TLL* IV 808.6–20; for *aestimatio* (5.3), cf. 12.12.

[42] Investment: Cat. 77.2 ('magno cum pretio'), 72.5f ('impensius . . . vilior'), 76.9 ('ingratae credita menti'). Cf. 8.2, 75.2, 91.2 (*perdita*); 77.4 ('omnia nostra bona'); 73.3, 76.6 (ingratitude). *Carius auro*: 107.3.

[43] Diod. Sic. V 26.3; cf. Caes. *BG* I 1.3, II 15.4, IV 2.6 (for *mercatores* in general, ibid. I 39.1, III 1.2, IV 2.1, 3.3, 5.2, 20.4, 21.5). Archaeological evidence vividly illustrates the Roman export of wine to Gaul (for metals as well as slaves): see A. Tchernia in *Trade in the Ancient Economy* (ed. Garnsey, Hopkins and Whittaker, London 1983) 87–104.

[44] Caes. *BG* VI 37.2, VII 3.1, 42.5, 55.5.

price, the man who had taken the risks to deliver the goods might reasonably feel that he had earned his profit in a fair transaction.

Nothing is more certain about the persona Catullus presented in his poems than that he cared deeply about fair transactions. Even at the lowest level, with Aufillena the dishonest tart, he uses the language of contract and obligation; even in the casual imagery of occasional poems, he alludes to the legal terminology of security and property rights.[45] And when it comes to the issues of friendship and love that really matter to him, then honest dealing and the proper repayment of obligations become almost obsessively dominant. *Fides* and *foedus* are the themes he dwells on – personal relations expressed as a contract, with Catullus the honest partner callously defrauded.[46] Here are the values of the *negotiator* as seen from the inside, and from that angle they seem less deserving of Cicero's offensive phrase.

Cicero himself knew as well as anybody that the greatest profiteers in the Roman provinces were those who professed to care least about money – the senatorial proconsuls, legates and quaestors themselves. Careless big spenders financed themselves by careless big plunder. Great men didn't care about contracts or legal niceties. Magnificence could regard itself as above the law.[47] Hence Catullus' distaste for Mamurra, rich from the loot of successive campaigns and lording it through all the bedrooms of Rome. Oh yes, Mamurra was great all right – a great prick![48]

The habit of magnificence meant spending big money on extravagant self-indulgence and display, and getting it back by

---

45 Aufillena: Cat. 110.7 ('fraudando officiis'). Legal imagery: 35.9f (*manus iniectio*), cf. A. Watson, *Roman Private Law around 200 B.C.* (Edinburgh 1971) 163f; 44.4 (*pignus*), cf. Watson pp. 88f; 42 (*flagitatio*), cf. Kelly 1966, 22f.

46 See especially poems 30, 73, 76, 87, 91, 102; also 72.5 (*iniuria*), 75.2 (*officium*), 109.6 ('aeternum sanctae foedus amicitiae'). Cf. Henry 1950–51, and Lyne 1980, 24–6.

47 Cic. *QF* I 1.7–9, 18f (Quintus' *integritas*, *continentia* etc. contrast with the norm); *leg. Man.* 13, 38f; 65f; *Verr.* passim; *Orac. Sib.* III 350–5, 642, etc. See Badian 1968, 81–91. Note the contrast between M. Brutus' disdain for financial business (Plut. *Brut.* 3.3) and the brutality of his agents in enforcing payment of his extortionate interest (Cic. *Att.* V 21.10–13, VI 1.3–7); and Brutus passed for a man of honour and scruple.

48 Cat. 29.13, 115.8.

the ruthless exploitation of empire. Sallust defined it as *luxuria atque avaritia*, the twin vices which had corrupted the moral strength of Roman society.[49] The historian was well placed to judge, and though his chronology of the corruption process is unacceptably schematic, his analysis of its causes is credible enough. So it had seemed to M. Cato the censor, whose determination to preserve the traditional Roman virtues took the form of an attack on the luxury and extravagance of men like Scipio Africanus; 250 years and a dozen ineffective sumptuary laws later, Vespasian was fighting the same battle, trying to impose the frugality of his Sabine ancestors on a society used to the reckless prodigality of Nero.[50] Both Cato and Vespasian were accused of vulgar niggardliness – the attitude of the senator's steward (pp. 102f above) – and both Cato and Vespasian were familiar with the profit and loss of commercial enterprise.[51] Perhaps, after all, the despised *negotiator* was the true representative of traditional Roman standards, his concern for his account-books a laudably old-fashioned and scrupulous attitude.[52]

Here too a Catullan pattern of thought is recognisable. The Delian hymn to Diana concludes 'Romulique, *antique* ut solita es, bona sospites ope gentem'. That may be conventional, a requirement of the genre. But in poems where his personal involvement

---

[49] Sall. *Cat.* 5.8, 12.2, 52.7 and 22, *Hist.* 116M; D. C. Earl, *The Political Thought of Sallust* (Cambridge 1961) 13–16. Cf. also *Cat.* 3.3 (*largitio* and *avaritia*), 5.4 (Catiline 'aliena appetens sui profusus'), 11.4 (looting and luxury of Sulla's veterans), 13.5 (*quaestus* and *sumptus*). Exploitation of empire: *Cat.* 12.5. Conspicuous expenditure: *Cat.* 12.3–13.5, 20.11f (Catiline's speech), *BJ* 3.7, 85.40–3 (Marius' speech). For Roman morals before the corruption set in, cf. *Cat.* 7.6, 9.2, 52.21.

[50] Cato: A. E. Astin, *Cato the Censor* (Oxford 1978) 91–103. Vespasian: Tac. *Ann.* III 55, Suet. *Vesp.* 11, Philostr. *vit. Apoll.* V 36 (Teubner p. 197); cf. the sketch in *Pegasus: Classical Essays from the University of Exeter* (ed. H. W. Stubbs, Exeter 1981) 3–15. Sumptuary laws: nine listed in Gell. *NA* II 24 and Macr. *Sat.* III 17; add *vir. ill.* 72.5 (Scaurus, 115 B.C.), Suet. *Jul.* 43.2 (Caesar), Tac. *Ann.* III 52–4 (Tiberius); see G. Clemente in *Società romana e produzione schiavistica* III (Bari 1981) 1–14.

[51] Plut. *Cato maior* 5.1 (μικρολογία, cf. *comp. Cato Arist.* 4.4f), 20.1 (χρηματιστής), 21.5–8 (his *negotia*). Suet. *Vesp.* 4.3 (mule trade), 16 (*pecuniae cupiditas*, cf. 23.2f, Tac. *Hist.* II 5.1).

[52] Plut. *Cato maior* 21.8, Pol. VI 56.1–3, XXXI 27.11; D'Arms 1981, 20f.

is unmistakable, the same traditionalist note is struck. In 68b, blessing Allius for his help in the Lesbia affair:

> huc addent divi quam plurima, quae Themis *olim*
> *antiquis* solita est munera ferre piis.

Thereto the gods will add all those many boons with which Justice once used to reward devotion in a bygone age.

And in poem 101, on his dead brother: 'haec *prisco* quae *more parentum* tradita sunt'. It mattered deeply to him that his brother was buried far from the family tombs and 'the ashes of his kin'. Behind the poet's obsessive insistence on *pietas* and *fides*, ancestral voices can be clearly heard.[53]

3. THE TRANSPADANE BACKGROUND

Catullus was a *Transpadanus*, and proud of it. But it is highly unlikely that his ancestors were born, as he was, in the territory of Verona.[54] In his father's youth, Verona (if it yet bore that name) was a hill fort in the march-lands of the Veneti, the Euganei and the Gallic Cenomani. It stood directly in the path of Boiorix and the Cimbric horde as they poured down the Adige valley late in 102 B.C. Its inhabitants fled, and for a whole winter and spring the Cimbri occupied the land between the Alps and the Po, plundering at their leisure. When the Romans destroyed the horde at the great battle of the Raudian Fields in July 101, they must have divided up the empty lands for settlement, the veterans of Marius' and Catulus' victorious legions no doubt getting the pick of the best sites. In 89, the settlements were organised as Latin colonies, and set about turning their administrative centres into real cities – a process surely reflected in Catullus' poem 17 on the *colonia* hoping for a smart new bridge.

---

[53] Cat. 34.22–4, 68b.154, 101.7f (ashes, 68b.97f); cf. *Hommages à M. Renard* 1 (Coll. Latomus 101, Brussels 1969) 778–84.
[54] Jer. *Chron.* 150H (p. 247 below); Cat. 39.13 ('aut Transpadanus, ut meos quoque attingam'), 67.34 ('Brixia Veronae mater amata meae').

(Strabo remarks, writing two generations after Catullus, that Milan had once been a village but was now a substantial city: its development must have been something like that of the mid-western cities of the United States in the nineteenth century.) It was those settlers, prosperous, confident, and perhaps more than a little brash, who now called themselves *Transpadani*.[55]

What was their prosperity and confidence based on? First, the land itself, proverbially fertile and extensive enough to give the new colonial centres *territoria* far larger than those of the towns of central Italy.[56] Second, the circumstances of its settlement, in the wake of the defeat and extermination of an entire people. Since the Cimbri had had twenty years of successful plundering, and nowhere to store their treasure except in their waggons, it must have been an unusually profitable victory for the legionaries. Then there were the 60,000 prisoners, presumably sold on the spot (to judge by Caesar's practice forty years later), and benefit-ting not just the professional dealers but the veterans themselves, or at least those who knew that their service was over. They could get land, and slaves to work it, as an almost immediate result of their hard-earned victory.[57]

In the broad acres of the Transpadane territory, there was far more land than individual settlement of legionary veterans could ever fill. Perhaps some of the previous Gallic occupiers were allowed back; much more significant was the influx of settlers from south of the Apennines. The epigraphic evidence reveals Transpadanes originating from Umbria, Picenum, Latium and other parts of Italy, now men of rank and substance in their new

---

[55] Plut. *Mar.* 23.6 (plundering the empty lands), Asc. 3C (Latin colonies), Strabo v 213 (Verona a πόλις μεγάλη); for the full argument, see Wiseman 1986. For cities as a secondary, and in a sense peripheral, aspect of colonial settlement, see M. W. Frederik-sen in *Hellenismus in Mittelitalien* (n.6 above) 342f, and P. D. A. Garnsey, *PCPS* 25 (1979) 10–26.

[56] Fertility: Pol. II 15.1–6, Strabo v 218; Brunt 1971, 172–84. Cf. Catullus' contempt for Pisaurum, 'moribunda sedes' (81.3); it was a citizen colony only a century older than Verona, but with a much smaller *territorium* and correspondingly less prosperous inhabitants.

[57] Livy *per.* 68, Plut. *Mar.* 27.3 (cf. Caes. *BG* II 33.6f). For soldiers with money to spend after a victory, cf. Livy XXXIII 29.4.

towns.[58] The process had begun very early, as we may infer from the case of the Sasernae, father and son: evidently Etruscan by origin, they were Transpadane landowners (already of two generations' standing?) when they produced their standard work on large-scale agriculture in the time of Varro.[59]

Though the evidence is largely circumstantial, it is very likely that the first-generation *Transpadani* – progenitors of that vigorous and self-confident provincial society whose influence and aspirations are so well attested from the sixties onwards[60] – were veterans from Marius' and Catulus' armies and enterprising settlers from Italy, to whom the newly divided land was allotted by Roman commissioners. (One of them, perhaps with a soldier's eye for a defensible site, was the Valerius who built his homestead on the peninsula of Sirmio in the territory of Verona. It is a reasonable guess that he was Catullus' grandfather.) The two categories should not be too sharply differentiated, since the legionaries too came largely from the rural areas of Italy; and since loyal allies were traditionally eligible to benefit from Roman land distributions, some of the veterans may well have come from areas of Italy which did not yet have the Roman citizenship. It is no accident that in the opening poem of his collection Catullus addresses his fellow-Transpadane Cornelius Nepos as 'unus Italorum'.[61]

In various ways, this Italian background had its effect on the

58 *CIL* v 564 (Tergeste, from Fanum Fortunae), 968 (Aquileia, from Interamna – local benefactor), 976 (Aquileia, *aedilis Sorae, publicanus Romae*), 2559 (Ateste, from Picenum?), 4348 (Brixia, from Paeligni – Augustan senator), 5442 (*ager Comensis*, from Sora – dedication to Mercury). Cf. Cic. *fam.* XIII 7.1 (Atella), 11.1 (Arpinum) for Transpadane estates owned or leased by Italian *municipia*.

59 Varro *RR* I 2.22–8 (*patris et filii*, cf. Pliny *NH* x ind., XVII 14), 16.5, 18.2–6 (*fundus in Gallia*), 19.1, II 9.6; E. Rawson, *JRS* 68 (1978) 151 for the Etruscan origin, emphasising *RR* I 2.27. The importance of emigration to the Transpadane lands is rightly stressed by K. Hopkins, *Conquerors and Slaves* (Cambridge 1978) 67, 95, 105; cf. Brunt 1971, 190–8, though with reference to the second century B.C. only.

60 Cic. *Att.* I 1.2 (65 B.C.): 'videtur in suffragiis multum posse Gallia'. Suet. *Jul.* 8, 9.3, Dio XXXVII 9.3–5, XLI 36.3, Cic. *Att.* V 2.3, *fam.* VIII 1.2 (demand for full citizenship).

61 Cat. 1.5. Cf. Wiseman 1986, ch. 2 (commissioners, e.g. *ILS* 48?; allied settlers, cf. Livy XXXIII 24.8f), ch. 3 (defensible Sirmio); on recruiting areas for Roman legions, see P. A. Brunt, *JRS* 52 (1962) 73–5, 85f.

energetic new society of the Transpadana. Three aspects of it, all relevant to themes already touched on above, are worth emphasising.

First, many of the communities of central Italy were at this time more hellenised than Rome itself (p. 94 above). It is clear enough that they exported their Greek learning to the lands they helped to settle. The new colonies equipped themselves with a legendary past – hence 'Brixia, mother of my Verona', and the 'Lydian lake' Benacus, evidence not for real prehistory but for the aspirations of settlers with a pride in their new country.[62] It is also clear enough that teachers and scholars were welcome there. Catullus got a first-rate grounding in Greek, and the extraordinary contribution of the Transpadanes to Roman literature in its most Hellenistically allusive period shows that his case was not a rare exception.[63]

Second, the local aristocrats of many of the towns of Italy, free from the anti-commercial prejudices of the Roman *nobilitas*, were much involved with trade and finance in the provinces (p. 95 above). This interest too was carried to the Transpadane territory, with its great natural traffic artery flowing eastwards to the Adriatic and the Greek East, and the Alpine passes leading directly to the Celtic peoples of the Rhône and the Danube.[64] It is probably not accidental that both Catullus and Cinna refer to sailing from Bithynia, and that Cornelius Nepos evidently made a speciality of the geography of northern Europe.[65] The *Transpadani* had wide horizons.

Third, the rural communities of Italy were where traditional morality lived on most strongly. Here too the continuity is clear from the elder Cato to Vespasian (p. 106 above): we have Cato's

[62] Cat. 67.34, 31.13; Wiseman 1986, ch.2.
[63] Helvius Cinna of Brixia(?), Cornelius Nepos of Mediolanum(?), Caecilius of Novum Comum (Cat. 35), P. Vergilius Maro of Mantua, etc. For the first two, see Wiseman 1974, 46f and 1979, 161 n.48; for Catullus' bilingual culture, Wiseman 1979, 167–71, Horsfall 1979, esp. 84, 92.
[64] See C. Peyre, *La Cisalpine gauloise du IIIe au Ier siècle avant J.-C.* (Paris 1979) 90–9; cf. n.43 above.
[65] Cat. 4, Cinna *ap.* Isid. *Orig.* VI 12.1 (fr. 1M); Wiseman 1979, 161–6 on Nepos.

own word for the *parsimonia* and *industria* of his youth as a farmer in the Sabine country, while Tacitus named Vespasian as the prime example of the *domestica parsimonia* characteristic of the Italian municipalities.[66] It is the picture familiar from Horace ('rusticorum mascula militum proles') and from Virgil ('Romana potens Itala virtute propago') – an idealised picture, frequently belied by the enthusiasm with which some of the hardy sons of Italy embraced the vices of the metropolis, but not wholly imaginary.[67] Tacitus' evidence guarantees its essential validity.

For Tacitus' friend Pliny, it was precisely the Transpadane communities which kept most faithfully the old-fashioned virtues of *verecundia* and *frugalitas*. Conspicuous exceptions notwithstanding, and making due allowance for Pliny's pride in his native region, we must accept his general picture – and if it was true in his day, then *a fortiori* it is likely to have been true in Catullus'.[68] The poet grew up in a hard-working, straight-laced, traditional society that knew and valued Greek culture, was not inhibited about commercial profit, but took seriously the responsibilities of honest dealing. It was an upbringing that left its mark on his poetry.

In poem 62, an antiphonal marriage song in lyric hexameters, with a specifically hellenised setting and clear allusions to Sappho, the legalistic Roman attitude to marriage is spelt out with disconcerting clarity: what matters is the contract between the bride's parents and the groom, and the bride's virginity is an asset in which she herself holds only a minority share.[69] There is

---

[66] Cato *or.* fr. 128 Malc. (Fest. 350L, from the speech *de suis virtutibus*); cf. *Orig.* fr. 51P, 76P, Plut. *Cato maior* 1.4, 2.1f, 3.1, *comp. Cato Arist.* 1.3. Tac. *Ann.* III 55.4f, explicitly in contrast with aristocratic *luxus, sumptus* and *magnificentia* (55.1f), cf. XVI 5.1.

[67] Hor. *Odes* III 6.37f, cf. *Epodes* 2.41f; Virg. *Aen.* XII 827, cf. *Georg.* II 167–70; see in general Wiseman 1971, 108–16 (also for those who fell short of the ideal). Augustus' funeral *elogium* for Agrippa referred to his *propriae virtutes*: E. Malcovati, *Ath.* 50 (1972) 143f.

[68] Pliny *ep.* I 14.4 (on Brixia), cf. 14.6 (on Patavium, 'nosti loci mores'). Exceptions: e.g. Cat. 67 (also Brixia).

[69] Cat. 62.28 and 62–5 (cf. 58 on the parents' attitude), and see further p. 119 below; Sappho 104–5 L-P, with Bowra 1961, 214–23 and Jenkyns 1982, 49–53. For the Greek flavour of *Olympo, Oetaeus, Eous* etc., in a poem which presupposes a Roman *deductio* of the

---

a similar contrast in poem 61, a choric hymn in Greek lyric stanzas (glyconic and pherecratean, like poem 34 to Delian Diana) for the marriage of Vibia Aurunculeia to the young patrician Manlius Torquatus.[70] A Callimachean ὕμνος κλητικός summons the god of marriage from his home on Mt Helicon, but the choir of girls sings his praises in traditional Roman terms:

> Nil potest sine te Venus,
> fama quod bona comprobet,
> commodi capere: at potest
> te volente. Quis huic deo
> compararier ausit?

> Nulla quit sine te domus
> liberos dare, nec parens
> stirpe nitier: at potest
> te volente. Quis huic deo
> compararier ausit?

> Quae tuis careat sacris,
> non queat dare praesides
> terra finibus: at queat
> te volente. Quis huic deo
> compararier ausit?

Without you Venus can take no pleasure that honourable report may approve: but with your consent she can. With such a god who dares compare? Without you no house can provide children, no one become a father supported by an heir: but with your consent he can. With such a god who dares compare?

---

bride, see E. Fraenkel, *JRS* 45 (1955) 6–8. On the bride's consent in Roman marriages, see S. Treggiari, *Echos du monde classique/Classical Views* 26 (1982) 34–44.

[70] 61.16, 82f, 209. At 61.16 the reading of *O*, *G* and *R*, the three witnesses to the lost *Veronensis*, is variously reported as Vinia (Baehrens, Schuster) and Iunia (Ellis, Mynors, Thomson), neither of which can be right unless we suppose a double *gentilicium* unparalleled at this date. Syme, in C. L. Neudling, *A Prosopography of Catullus* (Oxford 1955) 185, brilliantly suggested Vibia, a rare example of a feminine *praenomen* (cf. *Latomus* 22 (1963) 87f for a [Vibi]a Teidia a generation later). In that case, the bride was probably of non-Roman origin – like her mother-in-law, if the bridegroom is correctly identified as the son of L. Torquatus *cos.* 65, who married a lady from Asculum (Cic. *Sull.* 25).

Without your rites no land can provide guards to defend its boundaries: but with your consent it can. With such a god who dares compare?

There is no Greek precedent for this patriotic motif. We are in the world of *proles* and *propago*, where the importance of marriage is to provide citizens to defend the Republic.[71] The attitudes that lie behind Catullus' marriage poems are those that a generation later inspired the Augustan legislation *de maritandis ordinibus*.[72] Augustus believed that traditional morality – including marriage 'for the begetting of children' – had to be enforced against the self-indulgent permissiveness of metropolitan luxury. Cicero thought so too, in his advice to Caesar in 46 B.C.:[73]

comprimendae libidines, propaganda suboles, omnia quae dilapsa iam diffluxerunt severis legibus vincienda sunt.

Licentiousness must be held in check, the increase in population must be encouraged, everything that is now in a state of collapse and disintegration must be bound together by rigorous legislation.

It was part of the wider opposition in social *mores*, of which the financial aspect (traditional economy versus aristocratic magnificence) was discussed in the previous section. Sallust, though he does not mention marriage, identifies sexual self-indulgence among the symptoms of *luxuria* in his analysis of the corruption of Roman life; another was gluttony; and if we add the craze for gambling which Cicero emphasises among the *vitia* and *libidines* of contemporary sophistication, we have precisely the three

---

71 Cat. 61.61–75; cf. Gell. *NA* 16, Suet. *Aug.* 89.2 (Metellus' *de prole augenda*), Cic. *de off.* 1 54 (marriage as 'principium urbis et quasi seminarium rei publicae'). P. Fedeli, *Il carme 61 di Catullo* (Freiburg 1972) 50f: 'principi fondamentali dell'etica romana'. Ibid. 13f on Callimachus' influence: in particular, Hymen as the son of Urania (61.2) is now known to be Callimachean (fr. 2a.42f; R. Pfeiffer, *Callimachus* II (Oxford 1953) 104).

72 Suet. *Aug.* 34.1, with Brunt 1971, 558–66 and J. M. Carter, *Suetonius Divus Augustus* (Bristol 1982) 141–4. For the value-system that informed the legislation, K. Galinsky, *Phil.* 125 (1981) 126–44 is basic (esp. 131f on marriage).

73 Cic. *Marc.* 23. 'Liberorum procreandorum causa' in marriage contracts: Wiseman 1974, 114 n.56 (to which add Tac. *Ann.* XI 27.1), and D. Daube, *PCA* 74 (1977) 17–19 on 'the duty of procreation'.

types contemptuously singled out by Catullus as characteristic of
the rottenness of the age – *impudicus et vorax et aleo*.[74]

It was acutely observed by Karl Galinsky that Augustus'
programme of legislation presupposed moral excellence as a
condition and justification of empire. Nature herself grants
dominion to *optimus quisque*; it is right to obey those who are
meliores.[75] That idea, and the importance of begetting sons to
grow up as *praesides finibus*, would certainly appeal to new
settlers in a frontier land taken from Gauls and Germans.

It was an idea expressed in the simplest term of moral description, the basic adjective *bonus*, 'good'. For those who held this
view, the definition of that deceptively innocent word was
self-evident. So it was for Catullus, who makes it a conspicuous
recurring motif in the wedding poem for Torquatus and Aurunculeia, emphasising it by studied duplication: '*bona* cum *bona*
nubet alite virgo . . . dux *bonae* Veneris, *boni* coniugator amoris
. . . vos *bonae* senibus viris cognitae *bene* feminae . . . at *boni*
coniuges, *bene* vivite.'[76] The opposite is equally uncomplicated
(61.97–101):

> non tuus levis in *mala*
> deditus vir adultera,
> *probra turpia* persequens,
> a tuis teneris volet
> secubare papillis.

Not lightly given to some evil paramour or following shameful paths of
dishonour will your husband wish to lie apart from your tender bosom.

Marriage is good, adultery bad – a simple attitude appropriate in
the celebration of a wedding, but one which a true son of

---

[74] Cat. 29.2 and 10. Sall. *Cat.* 13.3 (sex and food), 14.2 ('quicunque inpudicus adulter
ganeo manu ventre pene bona patria laceraverat'), cf. Cic. *Cael.* 44. Gambling: Cic.
Verr. v 33, *Cat.* II 23, *Phil.* II 67 etc.

[75] Galinsky (n.72 above) 135f: Cic. *de rep.* III 37, Livy XXII 13.11, Tac. *Ann.* XIII 56.1, Sen.
ep. 90.5 (Posidonius); add Sall. *Cat.* 2.6.

[76] Cat. 61.19f, 44f, 179f, 225f; also 195–7, 219–21, and (without the duplication) 62, 159.
Cf. Sallust on *bonae* and *malae artes*: *Cat.* 2.9, 3.4, 10.4, 11.2, *BJ* 1.3, 4.7, 28.5, etc.; see
especially *Cat.* 3.3 and 54.6 (Cato) for *pudor, abstinentia, virtus*.

Transpadana who cared about *fides* and *pietas* might in any case express without either cynicism or irony.

4. THE BEAUTY OF INNOCENCE

Virtue, as represented by the tender breasts of Vibia Aurunculeia, is an attractive proposition. Not surprisingly, Catullus seems to have liked breasts (he draws attention more than once to the act of baring them),[77] but it is not eroticism alone which makes this glimpse into the marital bedroom so attractive. It belongs with the other vivid and affectionate vignettes of family life offered by Catullus in this poem – baby Torquatus' toothless smile at his father (61.209–13), Aurunculeia as a white-haired old lady nodding her head to all and sundry (61.154–6).

I think it is legitimate to use these passages as evidence for the poet's own sensibilities. To attribute them solely to the generic conventions of the marriage poem is merely to put the question back one stage. Why did he choose to write a marriage poem in the first place? It certainly was not expected of him: we have the best possible evidence – from a contemporary poet and literary theorist – that in Catullus' time the lyric *epithalamium* was long obsolete.[78] We don't know whether it was he or Calvus or Ticida who first made it fashionable again, but Catullus' admiration for Sappho, with whom the genre was particularly associated, makes it more likely than not that he was the innovator.[79] What made Sappho unique among the poets of the ancient world was her treatment of personal affection – delicate but intense, and with a vivid sense of the pleasures and commitments of the

[77] 55.11f (girl in colonnade), 64.18 (Nereids), 64.65 (Ariadne), 66.81 (brides), on which see J. Granarolo, *L'oeuvre de Catulle* (Paris 1967) 128–31 – perhaps added to Callimachus' original (cf. also Wiseman 1969, 21f).

[78] Philodemus *de mus.* 68K, referring of course to Greek poetry; there was no native Latin tradition of wedding poems, and both the metre and the opening lines show that Cat. 61 belongs in the Greek genre.

[79] Prisc. 1 170, 189H ('Calvus in epithalamio . . . Ticidas in hymenaeo'). Cat. 35.16f ('Sapphica Musa'), 51; for Sappho's *epithalamia* (Serv. *Georg.* 1 31), cf. Dioscorides 18.5f G–P (*Anth. Pal.* VII 407), Dion. Hal. *ars rhet.* 4.1, Himerius 9.4 (pp. 75f Colonna); Bowra 1961, 214.

emotional life. It is reasonable to infer that that appealed to something in Catullus' own psychological make-up, something that appears not only in the marriage poems but elsewhere in his work as well.[80]

Two generations ago, that observation would have been too obvious to be worth making. Catullus was the 'tenderest of Roman poets', and the smiling infant and nodding old lady represented the essence of his poetic nature. Our generation has concentrated instead on the allusive artistry of the *doctus poeta*, and shut its eyes to Catullus' 'sentimentality' as the Victorians shut theirs to his obscenity.[81] We have missed something, just as they did.

Catullus portrays the marriage of Torquatus and Aurunculeia as a love match. Both of them, groom as well as bride, have the duty of fidelity; both of them, bride as well as groom, have the reward of gratified desire.[82] For them, Hymenaeus is a god of mutual love (61.46f): 'quis deus magis est *amatis* petendus *amantibus*?' The ideal behind that play of participles was more to Catullus than just the generic requirement of a poem for a wedding. He expands on it in a poem for another couple, where marriage is clearly not involved (poem 45):

> Acmen Septimius suos amores
> tenens in gremio 'mea' inquit 'Acme,
> ni te perdite amo atque amare porro
> omnes sum assidue paratus annos,
> quantum qui pote plurimum perire,
> solus in Libya Indiaque tosta
> caesio veniam obvius leoni.'
> Hoc ut dixit, Amor, sinistra ut ante,
> dextra sternuit approbationem.

[80] Lafaye 1894, 63–77; D. Braga, *Catullo e i poeti greci* (Messina 1950) 45–79; Jenkyns 1982, 47–53, 72f, 80f.
[81] For an unusually explicit example, see Francis Cairns on poem 31, in *Quality and Pleasure in Latin Poetry* (ed. T. Woodman and D. West, Cambridge 1974) 2. The attitude he reacts against was perhaps last expressed (in English, at least) by E. M. Blaiklock, *The Romanticism of Catullus* (University of Auckland 1959), esp. 15f.
[82] Fidelity: 61.134–41 (groom); 214–23 (bride). Desire: 61.32, 169 (bride); 109–12, 164–6, 195–8 (groom); 199–203 (both).

At Acme leviter caput reflectens   10
et dulcis pueri ebrios ocellos
illo purpureo ore saviata,
'sic,' inquit 'mea vita Septimille,
huic uni domino usque serviamus,
ut multo mihi maior acriorque
ignis mollibus ardet in medullis.'
Hoc ut dixit, Amor, sinistra ut ante,
dextra sternuit approbationem.

Nunc ab auspicio bono profecti
mutuis animis amant amantur: 20
unam Septimius misellus Acmen
mavult quam Syrias Britanniasque;
uno in Septimio fidelis Acme
facit delicias libidinesque.
Quis ullos homines beatiores
vidit, quis Venerem auspicatiorem?

Septimius, holding his darling Acme in his arms, said 'Acme mine, unless I love you to desperation and am ready to go on loving you constantly for all time to come, as desperately as the most desperate of lovers, may I on my own in Libya or parched India come face to face with a green-eyed lion.' As he said this, Love first on the left and then on the right sneezed approval.

But Acme, gently bending back her head and kissing the dear boy's drunken eyes with those rosy lips of hers, said 'Dear Septimius, all my life's desire, so may we ever serve this master alone, as surely as a much greater and fiercer flame burns in my soft marrow.' As she said this, Love first on the left and then on the right sneezed approval.

Now setting out from this happy omen they love and are loved with mutual affection: love-lorn Septimius prefers Acme alone to any Syria or Britain; in Septimius alone does faithful Acme take all her pleasure and delight. Who ever saw more blessed mortals, who a more auspicious love?

The point is made with elegant dexterity in the first line (where the text says that Septimius embraces Acme, the word-order shows Acme embracing Septimius); it is emphasised by the conspicuous symmetry of the first two stanzas, and the central passage of the third;[83] and it is made explicit in line 20 with the same juxtaposition of active and passive as in the wedding song. This mutual love, with its equal commitment on both sides, is what earns the approval of the god. The omens are good: Venus could not be more auspicious.[84]

One would love to know from where Catullus derived this candid and comradely ideal. How were young women wooed and won in the frontier settlements of the Transpadana? Perhaps it was more natural there than it was in Rome to approximate love to friendship, equating the emotional rewards and responsibilities of each, as Catullus certainly did.[85] We can do no more than speculate about that. What does lie within our knowledge, however, is an area of society which shared his ingenuous ideal – the readership of Greek romantic novels, a new and popular genre in Catullus' time. As we have seen, the Transpadane élite was well read in Greek, and the Valerii Catulli knew their way about the cities of Asia Minor. Chariton of Aphrodisias, clerk to the *rhetor* Athenagoras at a date highly controversial but now thought to be the first century B.C., wrote the love story of Chaereas and Callirhoe, in which he sums up his readers' expectations in the final book as 'sanctioned love and legitimate marriage'.[86] In all the surviving Greek novels, the vicissitudes and obligations of the separated lovers apply equally to hero and heroine; he too has to be faithful, he too has to be pure to the end.[87]

For the heroine of such novels, every episode brings new and more horrid threats to her chastity – which she nevertheless miraculously manages to keep intact for the final reunion. Here too we touch a Catullan obsession.

---

[83] Septimius: desire (*misellus*) and commitment (line 22). Acme: commitment (*fidelis*) and desire (line 24).

[84] 45.19 and 26; 61.19f, 159, cf. 44, 195 (*bona Venus*).

[85] For this aspect of Catullus, see Adler 1981, 60ff. The crucial texts are poems 30, 50, 77, 96 and 109.

[86] Chariton VIII 1.4: ἔρωτες δίκαιοι καὶ νόμμοι γάμοι. On his date, see now Hägg 1983, 5f; for marriage and romantic love in the ancient world, N. Rudd, *Ramus* 10 (1981) 150–4.

[87] E.g. Xen. Eph. V 14.4: Habrocomes swears he is still καθαρός.

Again the key texts come from a marriage poem. Poem 61 for Torquatus and Aurunculeia contained within it, as part of the ceremonies represented or presupposed in the poem, a song by a choir of girls (celebration of Hymenaeus) and one by a choir of boys (Fescennine mockery and advice to bride and groom).[88] Poem 62, a choral hymn in Sapphic hexameters, is devoted entirely to the two choirs, singing in competition as the bride's arrival is awaited. This is marriage in general, not a particular wedding; the setting is deliberately unspecific, a mixture of Greek and Roman, and the bride is just an anonymous *virgo*. What is at issue is virginity itself, and its claims against those of marriage. Of course the boys, who defend marriage, have to win the contest, but Catullus makes them do so by appeal to parental authority and the force of law: the bride's parents give her legal rights to their son-in-law along with the dowry.[89] No equality of emotional commitment here – and it is the girls' case *against* marriage that stays in the reader's mind.

Hesperus, the evening star, brings the wedding night:

> Hespere, quis caelo fertur crudelior ignis?
> Qui natam possis complexu avellere matris,
> complexu matris retinentem avellere natam,
> et iuveni ardenti castam donare puellam.
> Quid faciunt hostes capta crudelius urbe?

Hesperus, what crueller star than you rides the sky? For you can tear a daughter from her mother's embrace, from her mother's embrace tear clinging daughter and give the chaste girl to an ardent youth. What crueller deed does the foe commit when a city falls?

The last line is shocking, and meant to be. The ancient world lived closer than we do to the reality of sacked cities and raping soldiers,[90] and some parts of Italy had suffered that reality only thirty years before. The boys' choir, with characteristic male

---

[88] 61.46–75 and 124–83, introduced by the parallel passages 36–45 ('in modum . . . ut') and 114–23 ('in modum . . . ne').

[89] 62.65; see n.69 above.

[90] Sall. *Cat.* 51.9, *Rhet. Her.* IV 51, *Orac. Sib.* III 529; e.g. Livy XXIX 17.15, Diod. Sic. XXIV–V 2.12, Tac. *Hist.* III 33.1.

indifference to the fear of physical violation, counters with its legal argument: Hesperus and the wedding night confirm the contract that has already been signed.[91] At the emotional level, that is no answer at all.

I think this emphasis on the arguments against marriage is part of the 'progress of pessimism' in the second volume of Catullus' collection, as the bright cheerfulness of Torquatus' wedding in poem 61 darkens to the betrayal of Ariadne and the ominously ambivalent marriage of Thetis and Peleus in poem 64.[92] What concerns us here, however, is Catullus' attitude to virginity. The next surviving part of the girls' case (after a stanza of which only one line remains) is one of the most famous passages in all his work:

> Ut flos in saeptis secretus nascitur hortis,
> ignotus pecori, nullo convulsus aratro,
> quem mulcent aurae, firmat sol, educat imber;
> multi illum pueri, multae optavere puellae:
> idem cum tenui carptus defloruit ungui,
> nulli illum pueri, nullae optavere puellae:
> sic virgo, dum intacta manet, dum cara suis est;
> cum castum amisit polluto corpore florem,
> nec pueris iucunda manet, nec cara puellis.

As in a garden close a flower grows in a nook, unknown to the flock, unscathed by any plough, which winds caress, sun strengthens, rain draws forth; it have many boys, it have many girls desired: but when nipped by the keen-edged nail it has shed its bloom, it have no boys, it have no girls desired. Thus a maiden, while untouched, the while is dear to her kin; when, her body sullied, she loses the flower of maidenhood, no longer to boys is she lovely, nor is she dear to girls.

This time the boys are given a worthy answer (the simile of the vine and the elm), but not even that can cancel out the 'union of verbal beauty, perceptiveness and tenderness of feeling' with

---

[91] 62.26–30, esp. 27f: 'desponsa conubia . . . quae pepigere viri, pepigerunt ante parentes'.

[92] See below, Endnote 2 on the structure of the collection, pp. 176f on poem 64.

which Catullus, drawing freely on Sappho, celebrates the fragile beauty of innocence.[93]

Catullus has an unusual imaginative sympathy for women's love, and for the delicate question of virginity and its surrender.[94] In a sense, he seems even to have understood it at first hand. At the very beginning of his collection, after the dedication and the first of the love poems, there stood a poem of which now only three lines survive:[95]

> tam gratum est mihi quam ferunt puellae
> pernici aureolum fuisse malum,
> quod zonam soluit diu ligatam.

It is as welcome to me as they say was to the swift-footed girl that golden apple which loosed her long-tied girdle.

Whatever it was that the poet was glad of, he expresses it as though he were a girl – in this case a heroine – about to become a bride.[96] And he closes another conspicuous poem, the first of the elegiac sequence, in very much the same way; Hortalus mustn't think that his request has slipped out of Catullus' mind like an apple out of the dress of an innocent girl:[97]

> ut missum sponsi furtivo munere malum
>   procurrit casto virginis e gremio,
> quod miserae oblitae molli sub veste locatum,
>   dum adventu matris prosilit, excutitur;
> atque illud prono praeceps agitur decursu,
>   huic manat tristi conscius ore rubor.

As an apple, stealthily sent as a gift from her lover, rolls out from a chaste maiden's bosom (for she forgets, poor thing, that it is hidden beneath her soft gown) and is shaken out when she starts up at her mother's coming; and is flung

---

93 Quotation from Jenkyns 1982, 50 (q.v. also for Sappho's influence).

94 See Adler 1981, ch. 6 (esp. 120, 122ff).

95 For the separation of the lines from poem 2, see Fordyce 1961, 91; cf. 14b, 78b for similarly fragmentary survivals.

96 Note the parallels with poem 61: *aureolum* (61.167), *zonam solvere* (61.52f).

97 65.19–24; *sponsi* at 19 brings in expected marriages again. Cf. Wiseman 1969, 17–20 (marriage may be alluded to elsewhere in the poem).

headlong it tumbles to the ground, while over her sorry face spreads a guilty blush.

Elsewhere too, even in his love poetry, we shall find Catullus thinking of himself in feminine terms. It is no surprise that the ideals his poems imply are most closely paralleled in a genre that appealed mainly to women.[98]

It was a dangerously vulnerable set of attitudes to take into the corrupt and cynical world of Roman high society. The effect on him of what he saw there is clear enough in his poetry. Not only in the invective epigrams, but also in the final passage of his most ambitious and self-consciously artistic work, the phrases of moral condemnation are explicit: *facinus, scelus, culpa, impia facta*.[99] Sometimes we can see it in personal terms – with Aufillena, the good-time girl who didn't play straight, always taking and never giving; or with Juventius, the spoilt young aristocrat who made his admirers beg for kisses and played the field with a casual heartlessness.[100] (Catullus' morality was not so old-fashioned as to prevent him taking part in the fashionable pursuit of beautiful boys; but he applied to it his own standards of fidelity and responsibility, as if the pampered minion were a virgin bride.[101]) Above all, we see it with Alfenus in poem 30:

> Alfene immemor atque unanimis false sodalibus,
> iam te nil miseret, dure, tui dulcis amiculi?
> iam me prodere, iam non dubitas fallere, perfide?

[98] See Hägg 1983, 95f on the Greek novel.

[99] 88.4–6, 89.5, 90.1, 91.4 and 10 (Gellius' incest, cf. Wiseman 1974, 117f and 119–29); 64.397–408. Jenkyns (1982, 148f) convincingly detects a slackening of the artistic tension in the final passage of 64; I suggest it is because Catullus *believed* his 'easy clichés about degeneracy', the seriousness of art giving way to a (less successful) seriousness of morality. 'He ought to have had the self-knowledge to say with Ovid "haec aetas moribus apta meis"' – but perhaps in the end the present age was *not* quite right for Catullus' morals.

[100] Aufillena: 110.4, 'quod nec das et fers saepe, *facis facinus*'. Juventius: 81.6, 'quem tu praeponere nobis audes, et nescis quod *facinus facias*'; 24.1–3 for his good birth, 24.6, 48.2, 99 and Adler 1981, ch. 4 for his character.

[101] On 'Greek love' and Roman attitudes to it, see MacMullen 1982. Responsibility: poems 15 and 21 against Aurelius, esp. 15.4 ('castum et integellum'), 15.18f (punishment for *adultery*); 15.15 (*culpa*), 21.7 (*insidiae*).

Nec facta impia fallacum hominum caelicolis placent.
Quae tu neglegis ac me miserum deseris in malis.
Eheu quid faciant, dic, homines cuive habeant fidem?
Certe tute iubebas animam tradere, inique, me
inducens in amorem, quasi tuta omnia mi forent.
Idem nunc retrahis te ac tua dicta omnia factaque
ventos irrita ferre ac nebulas aerias sinis.
Si tu oblitus es, at di meminerunt, meminit Fides,
quae te ut paeniteat postmodo facti faciet tui.

Alfenus, treacherous and false to loyal comrades, do you not now pity, cruel one, your cherished friend? Do you not now hesitate to deceive and betray me, traitor? But the sins of betrayers do not please the gods above. You ignore that and abandon me in my sorry plight. Ah, tell me, what is the world to do, whom is it to trust? Surely, villain, you kept asking me to hand over my soul, leading me on into love as though I had nothing to fear? Yet now you pull back and let the winds and airy clouds sweep all your words and deeds away to nothingness. Though you forget, the gods remember, Honour remembers too: she will one day make you repent of what you have done.

Alfenus had led him unsuspecting into love – with whom? Lesbia? Juventius? Alfenus himself? He doesn't tell us, so there is no point in asking. What he does tell us is that honest dealing is required in the investment of emotional capital; the gods of good faith do not approve of those who lead you on and then cynically back out of the deal.

Poem 30 is a very revealing document, but too uncomfortably self-pitying to be an artistic success. Catullus was not usually so nakedly vulnerable; he could hit back when he chose, and hold his own with those who held his moral standards in contempt. Take for instance poem 16, against the lean and lecherous pederasts Aurelius and Furius. They derided him for writing love-poems in which nothing beyond kissing was involved; that sort of thing, they said, wouldn't excite anyone but beardless boys. Writing such soft stuff, Catullus must be soft himself, and sexually effeminate. Catullus threatens to prove his masculinity on them in person, and argues that 'soft' poems that play on the emotions can be as stimulating as sexually explicit descriptions.[102] 'Pedicabo ego vos et irrumabo . . .': the very obscenity betrays the underlying conflict of attitudes; only thus could Catullus get his message through to sensibilities so much cruder than his own. What Aurelius saw as a high-class bit of tail was to Catullus something chaste and innocent, to be cherished and protected.[103]

5. THE POET AND HIS AUDIENCE

Aurelius and Furius had *read* the kiss poems (16.13, *legistis*). Of course; Catullus was a poet, and wrote to be read. But though that sounds obvious to us, it would be a gross anachronism to assume that it was equally obvious in the ancient world. As Kenneth Quinn rightly emphasises,[104]

the Romans even as late as the first century A.D. still felt that performance was the real thing . . . Until at least the Augustan age, at any rate where poetry was concerned, the written text played very much the role which the printed score of a musical composition plays today: it recorded the final text as passed for publication by the author.

What mattered artistically was the oral performance. It was taken for granted among the literary scholars of Catullus' day that the first stage in the art of criticism was reading the passage aloud, thus revealing its quality by the reader's delivery (*hypocrisis*), its craftsmanship by his attention to the metre, and the thought behind it by the modulation of his voice.[105] That was how poetry was taught in schools – first the *praelectio*, then the

---

[102] I summarise the argument in *LCM* 1 (1976) 14–17; cf. also Griffin 1976, 97. See now D. Lateiner, *Ramus* 6 (1977) 15f, and Skinner 1981, 53–5, both of whom (wrongly, in my view) take the poem as a general statement on the distinction between art and experience.

[103] See n.101 above. He and Furius are denounced as being too poor for Juventius (21.9–11, 24, cf. 81.3f).

[104] Quinn 1982, 90; the whole discussion (pp. 76–93) is fundamental.

[105] Dion. Thrax *ars gramm.* 2 (*Gramm. Graec.* 1 6): ἐκ μὲν γὰρ τῆς ὑποκρίσεως τὴν ἀρετήν, ἐκ δὲ τῆς προσῳδίας τὴν τέχνην, ἐκ δὲ τῆς διαστολῆς τὸν περιεχόμενον νοῦν ὁρῶμεν. Cf. Varro fr. 236 Funaioli (*GRF* 266f): 'lectio est varia cuiusque scripti enuntiatio serviens dignitati personarum exprimensque animi habitum cuiusque'. Quinn 1982, 102–4.

explication – but the *grammatici*, whose technique it was, applied it at more exalted intellectual levels as well. For instance, the author of the tripartite formulation I have just paraphrased was Dionysius Thrax of Alexandria, pupil of Aristarchus and a recognised expert on lyric poetry, whose school at Rhodes formed the intellectual background of the leading scholars of late-Republican Rome.[106] Besides, some of the *grammatici* were poets themselves (Catullus' contemporary Valerius Cato is a good example), and we can be quite sure that their order of priorities was not merely pedagogical. For poets too, the reading came first.

Cicero tells us that poets in his day liked to try their work out on the populace before putting the final touches to it; Horace refers to poets giving performances in the Forum, the baths, the theatres (unlike his own practice – but he too gave recitals, if only to friends); the epic poet Julius Montanus remarked that stealing material from Virgil was only possible if you could steal his face, his voice and his delivery (*hypocrisis*) at the same time; Petronius' Eumolpus performed in a public portico, with the theatre and the baths as alternative sites; and Juvenal complained of the constant recitations of poets as one of the hazards of Roman city life.[107] The continuity is clear. Far from being an innovation of the Augustan age, as is usually thought, the performance of poetry was familiar enough in the late Republic for Varro, documenting the cultural life of his time, to write three volumes *de lectionibus*.[108] It was inherited from the

---

106 *Praelectio*: S. F. Bonner, *Education in Ancient Rome* (London 1977) 220–6. Dionysius: Pfeiffer 1968, 266–72; Varro fr. 282 Funaioli (*GRF* 301), 'lyricorum poetarum longe studiosissimus'; he taught Tyrannio, the friend of Cicero and Lucullus (Suda *s.v.* Τυραννίων), and possibly L. Aelius Stilo as well (Pfeiffer 1968, 266).

107 Cic. *de off.* I 147; Hor. *Sat.* I 4.73–6, *Epist.* I 19.41–5; Sen. *ap.* Donat. *vit. Verg.* 29; Petr. *Sat.* 90–1; Juv. I 1–14, III 9. Cf. Wiseman 1982, 36–8, and (for late-Republican *acroaseis* in general) *Latin Teaching* 36.2 (1982) 33–7.

108 Funaioli 1907, 182 for Jerome's list of Varro's works (also three volumes *de bibliothecis*: for libraries, see Quinn 1982, 125–8). The 'Augustan innovation' idea is based on a misunderstanding of Sen. *contr.* IV pref. 2, on Pollio as the first to hold recitations by invitation at his house: see *History* 217 (1981) 384–7.

Hellenistic world, where poetry was above all something you heard in the theatre.[109]

Catullus has plenty to say about poetry, his own and that of his friends and enemies. It is striking that he never refers to public performance or an audience of listeners, but only to poems written down on writing-tablets, to be read.[110] Part of the reason is the informality of Catullus' short poems, but that cannot be the whole story. Archias and Philodemus read their ephemeral poems in recital, and Martial hoped that his would resound in the Forum, temples, colonnades and piazzas.[111] The difference lay not so much in the type of poetry as in the social status of the poet. Archias, Philodemus and Martial, in their various ways, wanted to turn their poetry into material benefits, and therefore needed a big audience.[112] Catullus was a man of substance, far from the necessity of earning patronage by his pen; he wrote for a cultured élite, and despised the popular taste (95.10).

But we should not rush to the conclusion that for Catullus and his fellow neoterics poetry was a matter of silent reading only. Much of what they wrote was concise enough for a poem to be written on a single wax tablet; and the fact that so many of Catullus' short poems have a named addressee suggests that they were sent, like informal correspondence (again, the suggestive parallel comes from Quinn) as 'notes' on *codicilli*.[113] What did the recipient do with it? As with correspondence in the proper sense, he might well share it with others, by reading it (or having it read) aloud to friends and acquaintances, individually or in an

[109] See for instance Athen. XIV 620b–d, quoting Clearchus, Chamaeleon, Poseidonius etc. Cf. also Gell. *NA* XVIII 5.2–4 (Puteoli, second century A.D.), and Tuplin 1979 (on the implications of 'cantores Euphorionis', Cic. *TD* III 45).

[110] Cat. 42 (*pugillaria, codicilli*), 50 (*tabellae, scribere*), 16.13, 35.13 (*legere*). For *volumina, libelli* and their *lectores*, see poems 1, 14, 14b, 22, 36, 44, 95.

[111] Cic. *Arch.* 18 (*vidi*), *Pis.* 71 (Philodemus' poems 'et lecta et audita'); Mart. VII 97.11f, on which see Wiseman 1982, 37f.

[112] Wiseman 1982, 31–4 (Archias), 38–42 (Catullus); R. Saller, *CQ* 33 (1983) 246–57, esp. 248f (Martial).

[113] Quinn 1982, 88f. *Codicilli*: Cat. 42, cf. Cic. *QF* II 9.1, *fam.* IV 12.2, VI 18.1, IX 26.1, Suet. *gramm.* 14.1.

audience.[114] We have no reason to think that in an oral culture a poem written on a wax tablet to a friend would have to wait for the *volumen* of collected works before it could be considered 'published'.

And what of the poems that have no addressee? A rueful joke against himself (poem 10), invectives against the great men of the day (29, 57), celebrations of Calvus' oratory or Cinna's poetry (53, 95), malice at Egnatius' expense or good-humoured wit at Arrius' (39, 84) – the rhetorical brilliance of the poems makes it natural to think that they were written to be read aloud to an appreciative audience, not of course in public, but *in ioco atque vino* among those whose social sophistication met the exacting standards of Catullus and his friends.[115]

Even with the short poems, for which evidence of a sort exists, we are quickly reduced to guesswork. With the long poems, we must admit total ignorance at the outset. It is highly likely that poem 64 was composed as a conscious masterpiece, and that as the *chef d'oeuvre* it occupied the central position in his 'collected works'.[116] But what of the stage between composition and collection? How was the great work first transmitted to the connoisseurs of literary culture who could be expected to appreciate it? We have no idea, and what follows is speculation – though not, I hope, without some basis in the realities of late-Republican literary and social life.

It would, I think, be very surprising if a poem organised round two rhetorical *tours de force* (Ariadne's complaint and the song of the Fates), and with very conspicuous rhetorical effects constantly deployed in the narrative,[117] were not intended in the first instance to be performed aloud. Perhaps by the poet himself, as with some of the short poems? It would test his voice, and his virtuosity in delivery; but if Virgil could read three books of the

---

[114] Cic. *Att.* 1 16.8 ('nolo aliis legi'), xv 17.2 ('in acroasi legere'). Naturally, some poems, like some letters, may have been private and meant for the recipient's eyes only.

[115] Cat. 12.2 (cf. 50.6); on *venustas, lepor, sal* etc., see R. Seager, *Latomus* 33 (1974) 891–4.

[116] See above all Jenkyns 1982, 85–150, on 'Catullus and the idea of a masterpiece'; for the position of 64 in the collection, see Most 1981, 111–20.

[117] E.g. lines 19–30, 60–70, 96–102, 254–64, 387–96.

Aeneid to Augustus and Octavia,[118] presumably Catullus could read the *Peleus and Thetis* to his privileged friends. An alternative possibility, however, is suggested by poem 67, the dialogue with the door. Where two voices are needed to read the poem effectively, we are moving from recitation proper towards dramatic performance – if indeed any such clear distinction was ever made in the ancient world.[119] The Peleus and Thetis epyllion would provide a superb script for six performers:[120] 256 lines for the narrator, 70 for Ariadne, 23 for Aegeus, and 59 for the three Fates.

There is no shortage of evidence for such performances: Cytheris the mime-actress starred in Virgil's *Eclogues* on at least one occasion, and Ovid's poems – we don't know which ones – were frequently performed in the theatre.[121] That was in public, at the *ludi scaenici*,[122] where the highly-wrought preciosity of Catullus' epyllion might not have found a sympathetic hearing.[123] But actors and performers were available for private parties as well as for public festivals, and it was surely not just for arbitrary decoration that wealthy Romans were now painting the *exedrae* in their gardens and peristyles with imitation stage sets.[124]

---

[118] Donat. *vit. Verg.* 32, cf. 27 (*Georgics*), Serv. *ecl.* 6.11 (*Eclogues*); cf. Quinn 1982, 87 and 142.

[119] See Quinn 1982, 156 (Pliny *ep.* IX 34.2) and 158 (Hor. *Sat.* I 9.23–5) on interpretative gestures.

[120] Or four: Ariadne and Aegeus could double as two of the Fates.

[121] Serv. *ecl.* 6.11, 'cum eam postea Cytheris cantasset in theatro . . .' (Cicero supposedly in the audience); Donat. *vit. Verg.* 26, 'bucolica eo successu edidit, ut in scaena quoque per cantores crebro pronuntiarentur'; Tac. *dial.* 13.2, 'auditis in theatro Vergilii versibus' (Virgil himself – and Augustus? – in the audience). Ovid *Trist.* II 519f, 'et mea sunt populo saltata poemata saepe' (Augustus in the audience); ibid. v 7.25f, 'carmina quod pleno saltari nostra theatro | versibus et plaudi scribis, amice, meis'. See Quinn 1982, 152–6, though I think his reconstruction is a little schematic, and I do not accept his assumption of a post-Catullan innovation.

[122] *Populus* mentioned in Tac. *dial.* 13.2 and Ovid *Trist.* II 519, implied in *Trist.* v 7.25; cf. also Suet. *Nero* 54, Nero's promise of *ludi* at which he would star as Turnus in the *Aeneid*.

[123] On the other hand, Cairns 1984, 150 argues that difficult and allusive poetry might well be written for public performance in the first instance.

[124] Vitr. *Arch.* VII 5.2, cf. v 6.9; see pp. 44–7 above for *ludi* at private parties.

The relationship of 'second-style' wall painting with theatrical decoration is a notoriously controversial problem; but it is worth noting that a recent discussion suggests precisely this type of after-dinner entertainment as an explanation of the ubiquitous masks. So too with luxury tableware, the decoration of which also included theatrical masks and scenes from mythological drama. Two splendid examples from close to Catullus' own time give us an idea of the social ambience: the walls of the *sala delle maschere* in the so-called 'House of Augustus' on the Palatine, with their painted architecture projected forward to enclose the interior space and turn the whole room into a stage set (Plate 3); and the superb cameo-carved sardonyx cup now in Paris, with its theatrical symbols among the rich hangings and the sideboards laden with precious plate (Plate 4).[125]

Whether or not we are right to attribute a scenic dimension to Catullus' epyllion as well, I think it is reasonable to see reflected in all three works of art the tastes of a single recognisable milieu, which valued exquisitely delicate craftsmanship and sumptuous colour, and combined luxurious self-indulgence with aesthetic sensibility of a high order.

Catullus' masterpiece, 'so full . . . of light and colour and precious substances',[126] was written in and for a world rather different from the old-fashioned frontier province where he grew up. If there is a point in it where his artistry fails,[127] it is because his moral standards obtrude upon his creative vision. Art matters, but so does decent behaviour. Perhaps he never reconciled the conflicting imperatives of the life he had chosen. 'His tragedy was that he had not fully rejected the moral standards of the Valerii of Verona when he tried to live in the world of the patrician Claudii.'[128] That shows above all in his poetry of love.

125 Wall painting: E. W. Leach in *Literary and Artistic Patronage* (n. 19 above) 141–56, esp. 153–5 on the 'ceremonies of hospitality and dining'. Luxury ware: M. Henig, *A Handbook of Roman Art* (London 1983) 142, 160f.

126 Jenkyns 1982, 150.

127 See n.99 above.

128 Wiseman 1974, 118.

CHAPTER V

'LESBIA ILLA'

Or, as true deaths, true maryages untie,
So lovers contracts, images of those,
Binde but till sleep, deaths image, them unloose?

JOHN DONNE, 'Womans Constancy', *Poems* (1633) 197

I. *FALSO NOMINE*

The name 'Lesbia' occurs sixteen times in Catullus' poems, always in the nominative or vocative case.[1] The phrase *mea puella*, or *puella* alone, occurs twelve times, and *mulier mea* once.[2] We know the name was a pseudonym, and we can guess why: 'Lesbia' was married, the affair was clandestine, the lady's real name could not be publicised. Even a generation later, Ovid did not reveal it. It may have been Ovid's friend Hyginus, an authority on modern poets, who first made public the identification referred to by the learned Apuleius in A.D. 158: 'Gaius Catullus used the name Lesbia instead of Clodia.'[3]

Even in the permissive moral climate of the fifties B.C., a formal anonymity was required to protect the reputation of a person of quality. Take Juventius, that youthful blossom on a noble family tree: like some other young aristocrats, he was prepared to make himself sexually available, but that could not be said quite openly.[4] Where Catullus names him, he does not

---

[1] Nominative: 43.7, 58.1f (three times), 79.1, 83.1, 86.5, 87.2, 92.1f (twice). Vocative: 5.1, 7.2, 72.2, 75.1, 107.4. Cf. Quinn 1972, 60, 66f.

[2] *Mea puella*: 2.1, 3.3, 3.4, 3.17, 11.15, 13.11, 36.2. *Puella*: 8.4, 8.7, 8.12, 36.9, 37.11 (3.7?). *Mulier mea*: 70.1. Also *lux mea* (68b.132 and 160), *mea vita* (104.1, 109.1).

[3] Ovid *Trist.* II 427–30, Apul. *Apol.* 10 (Appendix, nos. 19, 23); Wiseman 1969, 50–2.

[4] Cat. 24.1–3 ('flosculus Iuventiorum'), cf. Cic. *Planc.* 12, 18, 51, 67 on the *nobilitas* of the family (consular since M'. Iuventius Thalna in 163 B.C.). *Adulescentuli nobiles*: Cic. *Att.* I

name his lovers, and refers to nothing more specific than kisses; where he mentions Aurelius and his hopes of *pedicatio*, the boy remains anonymous. The subsequent juxtaposition of the poems, in a single cycle of love and jealousy, makes the identification practically inevitable, but it is still not explicit.[5]

So too with 'Lesbia'. Even under the protection of her pseudonym, she is not named with any identifiable man except Catullus himself. 'Lesbius' in poem 79 is as pseudonymous as she is, and Caelius in poem 58 is merely the addressee; otherwise, the only person named in the same poem as 'Lesbia' is Quinctia, the rival beauty of poem 86. Where her other lovers are named, 'Lesbia' is not.[6] The phrases he uses to describe her make his meaning clear enough, but the separation of her name, even in disguise, from those of identifiable individuals is formally preserved. Even in poem 100, where the man named was a loyal friend, the love of 'Lesbia' must be inferred from a periphrasis.

As in the case of Juventius, this cautious covering of tracks would be more effective with poems circulated individually than it is in the collection, where the thematic development makes it clear how the poems in which 'Lesbia' is named are related to those in which she is not. Perhaps by the time he put the collection together he cared less about her reputation. 'Lesbius est pulcher' in poem 79 certainly suggests something like that, if it is really the allusion to Clodia's family name that it seems to be.[7] But even if, in the bitterness of his anger, Catullus came so close to revealing her identity, what is important is that he didn't quite do it. However tenuously, the conventions were respected.

16.5, vi 3.9 (on which see MacMullen 1982, 487), Val. Max. IX 1.8, Gell. *NA* vi 12.4f; cf. the silver cup illustrated in C. Vermeule, *Antike Kunst* 6 (1973) plate 14, and C. Johns, *Sex or Symbol* (London 1982) 103 and plate 25.

[5] Juventius named in poems 24, 48, 81, 99 (love and kisses only), not named in 15 and 21 (Aurelius and *pedicatio*); the lover in poem 24 is identified as Furius only by cross-reference with 23.1. Cycle: Wiseman 1969, 3f.

[6] Poems 37 (Egnatius), 40 (Ravidus), 77 (Rufus), 82 (Quinctius), 91 (Gellius); no names at all at 11.17f or 68b.135f.

[7] First suggested by Muretus in 1554: 'Cum Lesbia Clodia sit, Lesbium quoque P. Clodium, fratrem ipsius, esse arbitror . . . id magis ut suspicer, facit additum "pulchri"

How free could a Roman poet be with someone else's name and reputation? Cn. Naevius had been imprisoned by the *triumviri capitales* for persistent abuse (*maledicentia*) of distinguished citizens – but that was probably slander from the public stage, which may be thought to be a special case.[8] It is possible – though the question is very controversial – that written libel came under the Sullan law *de iniuriis*, or could even count as *maiestas*.[9] Certainly Horace in his *Satires* is very conscious of the danger of offending the victims too much, in case they go to law; Lucilius, on the other hand, had been totally uninhibited about lampooning even the most powerful and aristocratic of his contemporaries.[10] The difference lies not so much in any tightening-up of the legal position as in the poets' respective status. Lucilius was a wealthy man of senatorial family,[11] Horace the son of an ex-slave, grateful for the patronage of Maecenas. Presumably the victims of Lucilius' satire regarded it as the hostility of a social equal, like the personal attacks that were given and received in the law courts without any question of an action for libel ever arising.

The same evidently applied to Catullus, whose obscene abuse of Piso, Memmius and Caesar was as unrestrained as Lucilius' attacks on Scaevola, Lentulus and Metellus, and delivered with equal impunity. Caesar knew how much damage poems 29 and 57 did to his reputation, but was content with a private apology followed by an amicable dinner with the offending poet.[12] Such

nomen: hoc enim cognomine fuisse Clodium omnes sciunt.' See Cic. *dom.* 22 ('Caesar Pulchro s.d.'), Sen. *contr.* X 1.8; Wiseman 1970, esp. 212f, on his son Pulcher Claudius.
[8] Gell. *NA* III 3.15, 'ob assiduam maledicentiam et probra in principes civitatis'; cf. ps.Asc. 215St on the offended Metelli. See pp. 186–8 below on attacks from the stage.
[9] Ulp. *Dig.* XLVII 10.5.9f (*de iniuriis*), Cic. *fam.* III 11.2 (*maiestas*). See R. E. Smith, *CQ* I (1951) 173–7; *contra* J. Crook, *Law and Life of Rome* (London 1967) 252–5.
[10] Hor. *Sat.* I 4.24f, 33, 78f, II 1.1f, 60f, 81f ('ius est iudiciumque'); see N. Rudd, *The Satires of Horace* (Cambridge 1966) 88–92 on *Sat.* I 4, ibid. 128 on libel, 133–8 on Horace's living targets, 150f on the victims' hostility. Lucilius: Cic. *ND* I 63 (Tubulus, Lupus, Carbo), Hor. *Sat.* II 1.67f (Metellus Macedonicus, Lentulus Lupus), Pers. I 114f, Juv. I 154 (Q. Scaevola), Non. 424L (C. Cassius), etc.
[11] Hor. *Sat.* II 1.74f, 'ego . . . infra Lucili censum'; Vell. II 29.2, 'stirpe senatoria' (cf. Porph. *ad Sat.* II 1.75 for the relationship with Pompey).
[12] Suet. *Jul.* 73, q.v. also for his reconciliation with Calvus.

attacks were part of the hazards of public life, the feuding of men who would not deign to use the law of libel unless their *dignitas* were hurt by a social inferior. Catullus could get away with venomous lampoons because – like Lucilius – he was wealthy and independent, and thus effectively invulnerable to retribution except in kind.[13]

So it was not through fear of the consequences that Catullus refused to name the litigious adulterer with the ginger eyebrows, or the loose-lipped girl with the ugly walk. He was teasing his audience, inviting them to guess the name, either from the clues he offers or by reference to other poems, as poem 29 reveals the identity of 'Mentula'.[14] The pretence of concealment is just part of the joke.

Normally Catullus attacked with the proper name, as Libo, Otho, Aemilius, Victius, Silo, Cominius and others had good reason to know.[15] Women were fair game too: Aufillena and Rufa are accused of sexual enormities by name, with circumstantial details to make identification absolutely certain; so too is 'Ameana', whatever name it is that lurks behind the textual corruption. ('Ipsithilla' is a different matter; her name, also corrupted in the manuscripts, is probably the working name of a professional prostitute, for whom poem 32 would be no insult but a welcome advertisement.)[16] Maecilia, whose career of adultery Catullus dates from 70 to 55 B.C., was from a family as respectable as his own: as with the Valerii Catulli, an Augustan

---

[13] It looks as if Gellius fought back (116.2f), and perhaps 'Mentula' too (105 on his poetry).

[14] 67.45–8, 42.7–9 (cf. Forsyth 1977, 448f, convincingly identifying her as 'Ameana'), 29.13 ('ista vostra diffututa mentula', cf. 94, 105, 114–15). The anonymous *scortillum* of poem 10 could be identified via Varus (10.1), and the addressee of poem 104 via Tappo (104.4).

[15] Cat. 54, 97, 98, 103, 108; also Vibennius (33), Porcius (47), Nonius (52), Gallus (78), Naso (112); the addressees of 71 and 78b are concealed by textual corruption (but see Nisbet 1978, 109f on 71). Thallus (25) and Socration (47) are Greek names; there is no need to suppose them false.

[16] Cat. 59, 110–11, 41 (cf. Cic. *Att.* VI 1.13, 'de Amiano' – a debtor of Atticus in Cilicia?). On 'Ipsithilla', see *Filologia e forme letterarie: studi offerti a Francesco Della Corte* (Rome, forthcoming), where I suggest that the name was Hypsithylla, 'High Festival of Love'.

moneyer marks its rise to senatorial status.[17] Finally there is a patrician lady 'drunker than the drunken grape'; drunkenness was traditionally second only to adultery (to which it was assumed to lead) in the catalogue of sins unforgivable in a Roman matron, yet Postumia is named, and her ancestry alluded to, in a poem which must have caused her staider relatives anger and shame.[18]

Rome, said Cicero, was a *maledica civitas*;[19] slander was a national pastime, and Catullus did his share of it. But 'Lesbia' was immune, even when he came to hate her. His use of the phrase *male dicere* is revealing. It is what 'Lesbia' does about him – to her husband, among others – but he is quite explicit that he could never do it about her. On the contrary, he claims credit for *bene dicere*, though it was wasted on her.[20] The nearest he comes to it is in poem 11, with the *non bona dicta* Furius and Aurelius have to deliver to her – and yet even there he holds back in a significant way. Poem 11 is one of three poems (the others are 37 and 58) in which Catullus visualises the sordid reality of 'Lesbia's' sexual promiscuity. In none of them does he use the obscenity which is so conspicuous a feature of his invectives. At 11.20 *ilia* is a respectable anatomical term, at 58.5 *glubit* is metaphorical, but an innocent word in itself.[21] In each case the picture Catullus summons so vividly to the reader's mind is foul, but expressed with no foulness of language. It seems that even at the bitterest moments 'Lesbia' was kept separate in his mind from the victims of his invective. And that, I think, is why he preserves her anonymity (however tenuously), while attacking them by name with total freedom.

[17] Cat. 113; M. Maecilius Tullus (Mattingly and Sydenham 1923, 79).
[18] Cat. 27, with Cairns 1975, 27f. On *matronae* and wine, see Cato *ap*. Gell. *NA* x 23.4, Pliny *NH* xiv 89f, Juv. vi 300–19 (part of *luxuria*); cf. Cic. *de rep*. iv 6 (authority to be exercised), Val. Max. ii 1.5 ('proximus gradus ad inconcessam venerem').
[19] Cic. *Cael*. 38, *Flacc*. 7.
[20] Cat. 104, 'credis me potuisse meae male dicere vitae?'. Lesbia's *male dicta*: 83.1 (husband), 92.1 (Catullus in return uses only *deprecatio*). *Bene dicta* (and *facta*): 76.7f, cf. 30.9.
[21] *Ilia*: *TLL* vii.1 325f, Adams 1982, 50f. *Glubit*: B. Arkins, *LCM* 4.5 (May 1979) 85f; H. D. Jocelyn, ibid. 87–91; O. Skutsch, *LCM* 5.1 (Jan. 1980) 21. See in general *Latin Teaching* 35.6 (1979) 11–15.

The women of Lesbos were proverbially beautiful. Every year in the precinct of Hera the Lesbian girls in their trailing robes were judged for beauty, 'and all around there rang the wondrous sound of the loud holy cry of women'.[22] The Lesbos *kallisteia* were familiar from Homer, Alcaeus and Theophrastus, and may still have been held in Catullus' own time. Lesbos was traditionally associated with refinement and sophistication, for example in music, poetry and dress.[23] Above all, it was the home of Sappho, whose poetry exemplified that refinement and celebrated that beauty. We have seen already that Sappho's work appealed to Catullus, with its emphasis on love, marriage, and the world of the emotions. It is not difficult to see why he chose to disguise his beloved as 'Lesbia'.

The comic poets of Athens interpreted the life of the women of Lesbos in the way their audiences would most appreciate, and used *lesbiazein* as a slang term for *fellare*. Alexandrian commentators preserved that interpretation, with predictably disastrous results for the reputation of Sappho; Didymus 'Chalkenteros', the record-holder in scholarly productivity, even included among his four thousand titles an essay on 'Was Sappho a whore?'.[24] Though that probably appeared a little after Catullus' time, the material it depended on was no doubt already familiar to Hellenistic scholars in late-Republican Rome. But the suggestion that Catullus alluded to it in his choice of the name 'Lesbia'[25] seems to me very unlikely, reflecting the self-conscious emancipation of late-twentieth-century scholarship rather than any helpful insight into the sensibilities of Catullus and his age. If he

22 Alcaeus 130.32–5 L–P, Hom. *Il.* IX 129f (with Schol. A), Theophrastus *ap.* Athen. XIII 610a.
23 Sappho fr. 106 L–P, Cratinus fr. 243K (bards); Sappho frr. 24, 57, 98 L–P, Anacreon fr. 13G (clothes). See in general L. Woodbury, *TAPA* 109 (1979) 281–3.
24 Attic dramatists: Aristoph. *Wasps* 1346, *Frogs* 1308, *Eccl.* 920, Pherecrates fr. 149, Theopompus fr. 35, Strattis frr. 40–1; Jocelyn 1980, 31–4, cf. 18f, 21. Cf. Plut. *Thes.* 16.3 (on Minos) for the Attic theatre's treatment of historical – or pseudo-historical – characters. The modern sense of 'lesbian' goes back to Byzantine scholiasts (A. C. Cassio, *CQ* 33 (1983) 296f), but did not become part of current usage until the nineteenth century. Didymus: Sen. *ep.* 88.37; cf. Pfeiffer 1968, 274–9.
25 J. G. Randall, *LCM* 4.2 (Feb. 1979) 28–30; E. Wirshbo, *CP* 75 (1980) 70.

didn't use obscenities in even the bitterest of his poems about her, he would hardly have introduced an obscene *double-entendre* into her very name.

The name 'Lesbia' was a graceful compliment, and he must have trusted her taste to accept it as such. Whether she did or not, whether she even understood it, are questions we cannot answer. For the brute fact is that apart from her real name we know nothing about 'Lesbia', except what we can infer through the distorting medium of Catullus' poems about her. Her real name tells us, if we allow ourselves the inference from poem 79, that she was a noblewoman, from the same family as Clodia Metelli (see chapter II) – conceivably even Clodia Metelli herself, more probably one of her sisters.[26] That is certainly something, in that it provides a social context for the affair, a background against which we may read the poems. But it is only from the poems themselves that we can hope to discover what 'Lesbia' was like.

Furthermore, we do not have *carte blanche* to read the poems any way we choose. Our body of evidence is a collection headed *Catulli Veronensis liber* and beginning with a dedication poem. In the absence of any demonstration to the contrary – and the arguments advanced so far are certainly not compelling[27] – I think we must work on the assumption that it is what it purports to be, Catullus' own collection of his poems, and not the work of some unattested compiler or 'posthumous editor'. And if that is so, then the collection as a whole is itself part of the poet's work of art, the ordering of the poems within it part of the message to the reader.[28] Catullus was a subtle poet, and we need not expect the message to be an obvious one; but we are not entitled just to take out poems irrespective of their context and arrange them in what looks like a plausible biographical sequence.

[26] Wiseman 1969, 50–60; 1974, 104–14. On the non-identity of 'Lesbia' and Clodia Metelli, see now Hillard 1981, 151–4.
[27] They are best presented in Wheeler 1934, 13–31; *contra* Quinn 1972, 9–20, whose view seems to me to be clearly right (see Endnote 2 below).
[28] For the orthodox dogma, cf. most recently M. C. J. Putnam, *TAPA* 113 (1983) 261, on Catullus and Robert Frost: 'It is unfortunate that the corpus of Catullus' poetry, as we

We cannot know how the affair between the real Catullus and the real Clodia worked out in life; all we have is what he made of it. Interpreting what he made of it is not a simple matter. There are two stages to be borne in mind: that of the first-time reader of the collection, recognising the 'Lesbia' relationship as a major theme and having his insight into it progressively developed as he proceeds; and that of the returning reader, who knows what comes afterwards, and can use his knowledge to pick up cross-references in both directions. I think it is a fair assumption that Catullus hoped for readers who would not be satisfied with going through the collection only once.[29]

2. THE INTRODUCTORY SEQUENCE

The first poem after the dedication was the most famous Catullus ever wrote.[30] It introduces the poet's mistress – indirectly, through her pet bird – but unfortunately for us, the text is not entirely certain. I print a version as close as possible to the manuscript archetype:[31]

> Passer, deliciae meae puellae,
> quicum ludere, quem in sinu tenere,
> cui primum digitum dare appetenti
> et acris solet incitare morsus,
> cum desiderio meo nitenti
> carum nescioquid lubet iocari
> et solaciolum sui doloris,
> credo, ut tum gravis acquiescat ardor;
> tecum ludere sicut ipsa possem
> et tristis animi levare curas!   10

have inherited it from antiquity, does not offer the critic the rewards that he can claim from exploring Frost through the dialogue of juxtaposed poems.'

[29] Cf. Hor. *AP* 365: 'haec placuit semel, haec deciens repetita placebit'.

[30] See Appendix nos. 25–30: from Mart. IV 14.14 it looks as if *Passer* was the title of a whole book (i.e. the 1–60 volume?).

[31] Cat. 2. The *Veronensis* evidently read 'cum acquiescet' at line 8; Goold (1983, 32) accepts that reading, and transposes lines 7 and 8, reading *sit* for *et* at 7; he also reads

O sparrow that are my sweetheart's pet, with whom she likes to play, whom to hold in her lap, to whose pecking to offer her finger-tips and provoke you to bite sharply whenever it pleases her, bright-eyed with longing for me, to engage in some endearing frolic – and as a diversion for her pain, I fancy, so that the fierce passion may subside. Could I but play with you, as does your mistress, and allay the sad cares of my heart!

Sparrows were sacred to Aphrodite (they pull her chariot in Sappho's well-known poem),[32] and this poem is about love, not birds. The sparrow's mistress is *his* girl, and he is confident that desire for him is what makes her eyes shine.[33] Or is he? The crucial word is *credo*: he thinks, but does not know, that she feels the pain of love. He certainly feels it himself, and would like Aphrodite's bird to cure his heartache as Aphrodite herself was asked to cure Sappho's.[34] The double allusion reminds the reader of what Sappho asked for in her prayer to the goddess of love: 'bring about my heart's desire'. The possessive confidence of the first half of the poem is cut away in the second; we are to see an aspiring lover, not yet a successful one.

There may have been success in the next poem, of which all that survives is a simile comparing the speaker to Atalanta, too long a virgin and now glad to loose her girdle.[35] Poem 3, on the death of the sparrow, is a *tour de force* of affectionate wit and

posse for *possem* at 9, and includes the three lines of 2b as part of this poem; so I have had to adapt his translation rather drastically.

[32] Sappho 1.10 L–P, cf. Athen. IX 391e–f, Schol. B *Iliad* II 305; Cic. *de fin.* II 75 on *passeres* and *voluptas*.

[33] Nisbet 1978, 92f. Before that, *desiderium* used to be taken in a personal sense ('whenever it pleases my bright-eyed love'), which ought to suggest that the girl is somehow unattainable, since *desiderium* is properly desire for something lost or absent; cf. Cic. *fam.* XIV 2.2 and 4, *mea desideria* used of the exiled Cicero's wife and children – but at Petr. *Sat.* 139 *meum desiderium* is used of a lover safely in the arms.

[34] Sappho 1.25f L–P (χαλέπαν δὲ λῦσον ἐκ μερίμναν); F. E. Brenk, *Latomus* 39 (1980) 713.

[35] Cat. 2b, p. 121 above. Alexander Guarinus in 1521 reported a gap in the text of 'an ancient manuscript' after *curas* in poem 2; whatever the truth of that, I would rather assume a loss like 14b and 78b than emend poem 2 to enable these lines to be part of it (n.31 above).

verbal music,[36] but does not advance our picture of the poet's relationship. For that we must wait till poem 5, where it comes with a bang.

> Vivamus, mea Lesbia, atque amemus,
> rumoresque senum severiorum
> omnes unius aestimemus assis!
> Soles occidere et redire possunt;
> nobis, cum semel occidit brevis lux,
> nox est perpetua una dormienda.

Let us live, my Lesbia, and love, and value at one penny all the talk of stern old men. Suns can set and rise again: we, when once our brief light has set, must sleep one never-ending night.

Now for the first time we have the lady's name, its significance already perhaps prepared for the alert reader by the Sapphic echoes in poem 2. And he uses it in a cry of defiance – the old men disapprove, but what the hell? It's a reasonable inference that what they disapproved of was not love as such, but illicit love. Catullus and 'Lesbia' will have to brave the conventions of society to enjoy their life together. The togetherness – we two against the world – is expressed by those conspicuously first-person-plural verbs; in the whole collection there are only two other places, to which we shall come in due course, where Catullus refers to his mistress and himself as 'we'. But the verbs are only subjunctive: this is what Catullus wants to happen, not necessarily what is the case. Did 'Lesbia' respond, and give all for love before their brief light set?

'Give me a thousand kisses, then a hundred . . .' Catullus flicks his abacus like an accounts clerk,[37] and then muddles the total deliberately to avoid bewitchment:

---

[36] Note the double *l*'s in 13 of its 18 lines. (Against the notion that *passer* is an obscene *double entendre*, see Jocelyn 1980a and Adams 1982, 32f; one of the arguments cited in its favour, Festus 410L on *struthion*, is in fact an *e silentio* argument against.)

[37] P. 104 above. (Cf. Varro *Men.* 346B 'vive meque ama mutuiter', from a satire subtitled 'On coins', though the context is totally unknown.)

dein, cum milia multa fecerimus,   10
conturbabimus illa, ne sciamus,
aut ne quis malus invidere possit,
cum tantum sciat esse basiorum.

Then, when we have made up many thousands, we will wreck the count, lest
we know it or any devil have power to cast an evil eye upon us when he
knows the total of our kisses.

The financial imagery we have looked at already, in the last
chapter; here we must think about superstition. Astrology and
magic were real, and intellectually respectable, in the Rome of
the late Republic. A man who hoped against hope for something
he had set his heart on might well be afraid of bewitchment by
the 'evil eye'.[38] Here the word he uses of it is *invidere*, and Invidia,
the companion of Nemesis, was the power who hurled men
down from the summit of felicity.[39] The usual term was *fascinatio*,
and that is what he uses at the equivalent point in the other
kiss poem, no. 7:

Quaeris quot mihi basiationes
tuae, Lesbia, sint satis superque.
Quam magnus numerus Libyssae harenae
lasarpiciferis iacet Cyrenis
oraclum Iovis inter aestuosi
et Batti veteris sacrum sepulcrum;
aut quam sidera multa, cum tacet nox,
furtivos hominum vident amores;
tam te basia multa basiare
vesano satis et super Catullo est,   10
quae nec pernumerare curiosi
possint nec mala fascinare lingua.

[38] See Liebeschuetz 1979, 120–3 (astrology), 129–33 (magic); they were part of Rome's
intellectual legacy from the Hellenistic world. On the 'evil eye', see Virg. *ecl.* 3.103,
Hor. *ep.* 1 14.37f, Pliny *NH* XXVIII 39, Gell. *NA* IX 4.8, Plut. *Symp.* 5.7 (*Mor.*
680c–683b), and a mosaic from Antioch (D. Levi, *Antioch Mosaic Pavements* (Princeton
1947) 33f and plate IV); there is an entertaining account in W. W. Story, *Roba di Roma* II
(London 1863) ch. 9, esp. 299–319.
[39] Stat. *Silv.* II 6.68–79, Aus. *Mos.* 379 (Nemesis); Lucr. V 1125–8.

You ask, Lesbia, how many kissings of you are enough and to spare for me. As great the number of the sands of Libya to be found in silphium-bearing Cyrene between Jove's torrid oracle and the sacred tomb of legendary Battus; or as many the stars which in the silence of night behold the stealthy loves of mankind: so many kisses to kiss you with would be enough and to spare for love-crazed Catullus, too many for the inquisitive to be able to count or bewitch with their evil tongues.

The mood has changed since poem 5. The two are no longer 'we', but 'you' and 'I'; the open defiance of the world's opinion has become a sense of stolen love, observed by the stars; and for the first time Catullus comments on his own state – it's madness. In its context, *vesano* suggests a quotation: 'Catullus, you're crazy – when will you be satisfied?' The very notion of *satis superque* betrays a difference in emotional commitment to the affair. She was cool and moderate; he was emotionally insatiable.

Meanwhile, something startling has happened; the first obscenity of the collection has been perpetrated. The two kiss poems are separated by an entertaining little scene set in the bedroom of a bachelor flat. Flavius is still in bed, but it's obvious that there has been someone else in it, and that they have been giving the bed a lot of exercise. It's no good pretending, Flavius – who is she? Catullus wants to know, so that he can celebrate them in elegant verse.[40] Part of the evidence is Flavius' 'fucked-out crotch';[41] the vulgar phrase comes as a shock, and probably came as a shock to Catullus' contemporaries too. Such language was acceptable in certain genres, such as satire or epigram, but in a collection of mixed short poems a warning or apology might be expected.[42]

Poem 6 offers one view of the sexual life – rumpled sheets, the smell of last night's perfume, the cheerful bawdry of young men

[40] Poem 6 is the fulfilment of its own promise (Morgan 1977, 341); cf. 37.10, 42.1–6 for self-fulfilling poems.

[41] 6.13, 'latera ecfututa'; for *latus* in this sense see Ovid *AA* II 413, Juv. VI 37, with D. W. T. C. Vessey, *LCM* I (1976) 39.

[42] E.g. Mart. I pref., I 35 (straight after the first obscenity of the book, *futui* at 34.10), III 68.7 and 69.2, X 64 (apology for *mentula* at 63.8?), XI 15.8–10 (followed by 16.5). On Catullus 14b and 27, see Wiseman 1969, 7f.

discussing 'some hot little tart' (*nescioquid febriculosi scorti*, 6.5f).
The vivid detail, and the one explicit obscenity, point the
contrast with the poems on either side. Flavius is expected to say
who the girl is and tell Catullus all about her ('Venus loves gossip
and chat'),[43] and what he has been doing with her is referred to in
realistic detail and uninhibited language. In the kiss poems, on
the other hand, 'Lesbia' is in pseudonymous disguise, Catullus is
determined to frustrate the curiosity of other people, and the
action as reported is just a hyperbole of kisses, effeminately
unerotic in view of men like Furius and Aurelius.[44] The juxtaposition makes it unmistakable that the 'Lesbia' affair was something special: very private, and much more than just sex.

That, at least, is what it was for 'crazy Catullus' (7.10).
Straight away, we see he has been fooling himself. Poem 8 is a
masterpiece of construction, of which the first ten lines run as
follows:

> Miser Catulle, desinas ineptire,
> et quod vides perisse perditum ducas.
> Fulsere quondam candidi tibi soles,
> cum ventitabas quo puella ducebat
> amata nobis quantum amabitur nulla:
> ibi illa multa cum iocosa fiebant,
> quae tu volebas nec puella nolebat,
> fulsere vere candidi tibi soles.
> Nunc iam illa non vult: tu quoque impotens noli,
> nec quae fugit sectare, nec miser vive . . .   10

Poor Catullus, you must stop being silly, and count as lost what you see is lost.
Once the sun shone bright for you, when you would go whither your
sweetheart led, she you loved as no woman will ever be loved again; when there
took place those many jolly scenes which you desired, nor did your sweetheart
not desire, truly the sun shone bright for you. Now she desires no more: do you
too, weakling, not desire; and do not chase her who flees, nor live in
unhappiness . . .

[43] 55.20, where I think Camerius is frustrating Catullus' curiosity just as Flavius does (cf.
LCM 6.6 (June 1981) 155).
[44] 16.12f; see Wiseman 1976, and pp. 123f above.

'Jolly scenes' may not be quite right for *iocosa*, but it is hard to improve on it; the oddity comes less from the translation than from the original, Catullus' 'plaintive whimsy of under-statement'.[45] In six beautifully chiastic lines Catullus offers the images of a lost happiness, and still he shrinks from physical description. What did they do? We can guess, of course, but all he mentions is the laughter.

He sees that time as bright suns shining. We have met those suns in poem 5, when he was carefree and triumphant – 'let's love while the suns still shine for us'. Now the suns have set, not in death but in the end of love. What tells us most about the affair, however, is line 4. 'Where she led, you kept on coming'; whether or not we are to think literally of visits and assignations, the frequentative verb gives us a glimpse into their relationship. The same relative position of leader and follower recurs in a signifi-cantly different form in line 10. When all was well and she wanted it too, she led and he went after; now that she doesn't want it, she flees and he pursues (frequentative verb again). Either way, the initiative is hers. Through this bitter little flashback, and the *quaeris* of poem 7, we can see for a moment how the affair looked to 'Lesbia'. She was in charge, and she had had enough.

The second half of the poem presents a psychological drama:

> . . . sed obstinata mente perfer, obdura.
> Vale, puella: iam Catullus obdurat
> nec te requiret nec rogabit invitam.
> At tu dolebis, cum rogaberis nulla.
> Scelesta, vae te! quae tibi manet vita?
> quis nunc te adibit? cui videberis bella?
> quem nunc amabis? cuius esse diceris?
> quem basiabis? cui labella mordebis?
> At tu, Catulle, destinatus obdura.

. . . but harden your heart, endure, and stand fast. Goodbye, sweetheart. Catullus now stands fast: he will not look for you or court you against your will. But you will be sorry when you are not courted at all. Wretch, pity on you!

45 Quinn 1970, 117.

What life lies in store for you! Who will come to you now? Who will think you pretty? Whom will you love now? Whose will people say you are? Whom will you kiss? Whose lips will you bite? But you, Catullus, be resolute and stand fast.

For the Catullus-figure in the poem, telling the girl she'll be sorry, those nagging questions require the answer 'no one'. But Catullus the poet, creating his work of art, allows us to see how easily she might answer 'someone else'. At the moment when that thought would become intolerable to Catullus-in-the-poem (and here we *do* have a little physical detail), the poet makes him repeat his resolve, thus closing the composition with a satisfying symmetry.[46] The art and the pathos lie in the self-deception: within the world of the poem, Catullus the lover can even say 'Whose will people say you are?', as if all that mattered to her was to be called Catullus' girl. In making the poem, and juxtaposing it with no. 7 in the collection, Catullus the poet delicately suggests that it was really the other way round.

After so much emotional intensity, the reader needs a respite. Poem 9 celebrates the scholarly Veranius, best of friends,[47] and poem 10, full of slang and racy humour, tells a good joke at Catullus' own expense.[48] Both pick up a theme introduced in poem 4. There, the boastful boat told of a trip from Bithynia up the Adriatic to north Italy; here, we meet Veranius returning from Spain and learn that Catullus himself has been in Bithynia.[49]

Poem 11 continues this theme of young men seeing the world – but it is a poem in Sapphics, which warns the reader to remember 'Lesbia'. For three leisurely stanzas Catullus plays with the idea that he might go with his faithful comrades Furius and Aurelius to the East (where Crassus' great new expedition

---

[46] Line 19 echoes line 11, the vocative *Catulle* echoes the first line (see Wiseman 1974, 62 for the 'double ring').
[47] See Endnote 3 below.
[48] Obscenity again at lines 12 and 24 – but *irrumator* and *cinaediorem* are not meant literally.
[49] For this theme, see Wiseman 1969, 12f (and bibliography cited there); cf. also *JRS* 69 (1979) 162f.

promised fabulous wealth) or to the West with Caesar.[50] Then comes an unexpected twist:

> . . . omnia haec, quaecumque feret voluntas
> caelitum, temptare simul parati,
> pauca nuntiate meae puellae
>   non bona dicta.
>
> Cum suis vivat valeatque moechis,
> quos simul complexa tenet trecentos,
> nullum amans vere, sed identidem omnium
>   ilia rumpens;   20
>
> nec meum respectet, ut ante, amorem,
> qui illius culpa cecidit velut prati
> ultimi flos, praetereunte postquam
>   tactus aratro est.

Ready as you are to face all these hazards with me, whatever the will of heaven above will bring: take back to my sweetheart a brief and not kind message. Let her live and be happy with her lovers, three hundred of whom at once she holds in her embraces, loving none truly but again and again rupturing the loins of them all; and let her not count on my love, as in the past, for through her fault it has fallen like a flower at the meadow's edge, after being lopped by the passing plough.

These first six poems of love describe a kind of parabola. In the sparrow poems (2 and 3), the beloved is seen indirectly, via her bird, and appears only in the genitive case (*meae puellae*).[51] In the kiss poems (5 and 7) she is named, and addressed in the vocative; in poem 8 she is not named, but she acts in the nominative and is addressed in the vocative (*puella*).[52] Now, in poem 11, she is again seen indirectly, via the bearers of the message, and appears only in the dative case (*meae puellae*).[53]

There are bitter allusions here to the earlier poems. In the

---

[50] Cf. 29.12 (Britain thought of as west, not north); Dio XL 12.1, App. *BC* II 18 etc. on Crassus ('glory and profit').
[51] 2.1, 3.3f, 3.17; cf. 2.9 (*ipsa*), 3.5 (*illa*) – in subordinate clauses.
[52] 5.1, 7.2; 8.4, 8.9 (*illa*), 8.12, 8.14 (*at tu*).
[53] 11.15; cf. 11.22 (*illius*) – in a subordinate clause.

triumphant poem 5 it was *vivamus atque amemus*; now it is *vivat valeatque*, no longer their life of love but her life of degradation.[54] In poem 8 she led and he followed, or ran and he pursued; now it is no use her looking back (*nec respectet*) – he won't come running any more. At 8.15 he called her *scelesta*, but did not say what her *scelus* was; now he defines her crime (*culpa*) as the killing of his love.[55]

What 'Lesbia' had done was to commit adultery. *Moechis* is explicit – not just lovers but adulterers, as if she were actually married to Catullus. Indeed, as Roland Mayer has acutely pointed out, the form of the poem is that of a divorce *per nuntium*.[56] But if Catullus conceived of his love-affair as a sort of marriage, which spouse was he? The poem is written in Sappho's metre, and the wonderfully evocative concluding image (which Catullus uses metrical licence to emphasise)[57] alludes to one of Sappho's wedding poems, in which the cut flower is the bride's virginity.[58] Implicit in the final stanza is the notion of rape, with Catullus' love as the innocent victim. Again, but in a different light, we see the balance of power in the lovers' relationship.

These poems tell us far more about Catullus than they do about 'Lesbia', but there is one thing about her that comes through clearly enough – her dominance. She acted, he reacted. His contribution was the concept of a love unparalleled (8.5), more than just sexual, involving both the responsibilities of the marriage bond and the vulnerability of a virgin bride. It would not be surprising if the real woman found such devotion something of a burden.

---

[54] 5.1, 11.17; cf. 8.15, 'quae tibi manet vita?'.

[55] For the quality of his love, contrast 8.5 and 11.19.

[56] Mayer 1983. J. C. Yardley, *Symb. Osl.* 56 (1981) 63–9, less convincingly takes *nuntiate* at 11.15 as the formal repudiation of a friendship.

[57] The final *i* of 11.22 is cut off (by a hypermetric elision) just like the flower; for a similar effect, cf. p. 117 above on the word-order in 45.1.

[58] See p. 120 above, on 62.39–47. For the application to poem 11, cf. Adler 1981, 143–5.

After the flower falls to the passing plough, the emotional tension is relaxed again. There follow three pieces of *urbanitas* on Catullus' friends, their parties, and the refinement of their taste. (One of them does indeed refer to *mea puella*, but only in a subordinate role: the main compliment is for Fabullus.[59]) The third, poem 14 to Calvus, refers back to the dedication poem; and since it is immediately followed by a fragmentary programmatic announcement about the next part of the collection, it is reasonable to infer that 1–14 form a sequence complete in itself.[60] By now the reader has all the essentials about Catullus and his world – his friends, his values, his circumstances, and the two bits of biographical data that will be needed to make sense of certain poems later in the collection, namely the trip to Bithynia and the affair with 'Lesbia'. There is no point asking whether the affair was really as parabolic as poems 2–11 suggest; that is what he gives us, and we must be content with it.

Poem 14b introduces a homosexual element, poem 27 gives a veiled announcement of bitter invectives. These themes are interspersed with occasional poems, and as the collection proceeds the tightness of its thematic organisation is inevitably relaxed, to make room for poems to be fitted in.[61] Of the 45 short poems after 14b, only five refer to 'Lesbia' or *mea puella*, and

[59] As indicated by the three vocatives (lines 1, 6, 14); the catch-words *sal, venustus* etc. show that Fabullus is getting the same in-group admiration as Pollio in poem 12 and Calvus in poem 14. As for *meae puellae*, Quinn (1972, 72f and 94) rightly distinguishes between passing references and 'Lesbia-poems' proper; at 13.11, 43.7 and 86.5 the compliment is conventional, and without reference to the quality of the poet's feeling for his mistress. Catullus in poem 13 is inviting Fabullus to see his girl, as Varus invited Catullus himself in poem 10, and Flavius failed to invite him in poem 6; see Quinn 1970, 134f and Vessey 1971, 45–8 for *unguentum* implying the girl's presence (the obscene interpretation is rightly rejected by C. Witke, *CP* 75 (1980) 325–9). For the poem's generic context, see L. Edmunds, *AJP* 103 (1982) 183–8.

[60] 1.1 / 14.8 and 12 (*novum libellum*), 1.10 / 14.23 (*saeculum*); Wiseman 1969, 7–13 on 14b and the coherence of 1–14.

[61] A necessary corollary of a collection of short poems on varied subjects (Wiseman 1969, 4; ibid. 7f on 14b and 27).

there are three others which may allude to her.[62] But even when relegated – for the moment – to the background, the affair remains vivid in the reader's mind thanks to the impact of the early sequence, and he is able to fit these poems into his mental picture without difficulty.

The first reference is in poem 36. As always, the context in the collection is important – and here in particular the group of five poems from 36 to 40.

The promise of invective announced at poem 27 is fulfilled with poems 28, 29 and 33. Variation of subject and metre is provided by the occasional poems between: Alfenus (30, pp. 122f above), the return to Sirmio (31), 'Ipsithilla' (32), the hymn to Diana (34, pp. 96f above), and the letter to Caecilius (35). The last of these brings us into the world of poetry, as Caecilius has been working on his *Lady of Dindymus*, and in particular the world of Sappho, to whom Caecilius' girl friend is compared.[63] Sappho, Lesbos, 'Lesbia' – the deft reminder leads us into a group of poems where the themes of invective, poetry and the poet's mistress are intertwined.

Poem 36 begins:

> Annales Volusi, cacata charta,
> votum solvite pro mea puella.
> Nam sanctae Veneri Cupidinique
> vovit, si sibi restitutus essem
> desissemque truces vibrare iambos,
> electissima pessimi poetae
> scripta tardipedi deo daturam
> infelicibus ustulanda lignis.
> Et hoc pessima se puella vidit
> iocose lepide vovere divis.   10

Annals of Volusius, you shitty sheets, discharge a vow in my sweetheart's name: for she vowed to holy Venus and Cupid that, if I were restored to her and ceased to launch vicious lampoons, she would give the choicest writings of the

---

[62] Cat. 36, 37, 43, 51, 58; 38, 40, 60. The *puella* of 56.5 is not relevant.
[63] 35.16f, 'Sapphica puella musa doctior'.

worst of poets to the limping deity to burn with wood from a barren tree. And
the naughty girl realised that this vow to the gods was a pretty piece of fun.

(She meant Catullus by 'the worst of poets', but he pays the vow
for her by burning Volusius' *Annals*.) The *iambi* of line 5 are not
just lampoons in general, but poems written in the traditional
metre of invective – either true iambics, like the attack on Caesar
and Pompey (29), or 'limping' iambics (scazons, *choliambi*) with a
dragging spondee in the final foot. The description of the
fire-god as *tardipes*, slow-footed, perhaps gives a hint that it is the
second category in particular that 'Lesbia' had in mind.[64]

Which poems did she mean? We soon discover,[65] as poem 37,
in scazons, opens with a devastatingly obscene attack on the
customers at the 'lechers' bar' nine columns down from the
temple of Castor.[66] They are both randy and exclusive ('you
think you're the only ones with pricks? the only ones who can
fuck the girls?'), but Catullus will brand them with infamy. The
cause of his fury appears in the second half of the poem:

> Puella nam mi, quae meo sinu fugit,
> amata tantum quantum amabitur nulla,
> pro qua mihi sunt magna bella pugnata,
> consedit istic. Hanc boni beatique
> omnes amatis, et quidem, quod indignum est,
> omnes pusilli et semitarii moechi;
> tu praeter omnes une de capillatis,
> cuniculosae Celtiberiae fili,
> Egnati, opaca quem bonum facit barba
> et dens Hibera defricatus urina.　　　　20

64 Cf. Pliny *ep.* v 10.2 (hendecasyllables represent *blanditiae*, scazons *convicium*); for
tardipes, cf. Varro *Men.* 57B = 55 Cèbe ('pedatus versuum tardor', of scazons).
65 Quinn (1970, 199) tentatively suggests that 36.5 refers to 37 (at 1972, 98 and 287 n.27 he
plays down the idea); preferable to Wiseman 1969, 40, who had not realised the
significance of *tardipedi deo* and the Pliny passage (n.64).
66 I.e. among the *tabernae veteres* in front of the Basilica Sempronia (Plaut. *Curc.* 480f,
Livy XLIV 16.10, Pliny *NH* XXXV 25); cf. Livy I 35.10 (anachronistic) for the portico in
front. Tenney Frank (see above, p. 26 n.39) thought it meant Clodia's Palatine house –
a wild conjecture unfortunately perpetuated by Quinn 1972, 135 (tentatively) and
Goold 1983, 243.

For the girl who fled my embrace, she I loved as no woman will ever be loved again, for whom mighty wars were waged by me, has set up her pitch there. All you men of rank and fortune are her lovers, and indeed, to her shame, all the petty lechers of the back streets, you above all, you prince of the long-haired, Egnatius, you son of rabbit-ridden Celtiberia, given class by your bushy beard and teeth that are brushed with Spanish piss.

It is a wonderful performance, the consciously masculine energy of the denunciation not weakened but enhanced by the painful flashback to poem 8.[67] We learn a little more about the later stages of the affair – Catullus has fought battles for 'Lesbia', but lost. Her successful lovers (the three hundred of poem 11) are not only the rich and noble of her own class, with whom Catullus might feel he could hardly compete, but even men like – ugh! – Egnatius. That's where it hurts: 'Lesbia' has let herself down, as the scene of the poem itself eloquently suggests. For taverns were frequently also brothels, and the emphatically postponed verb *consedit* implies that she has 'taken her seat' there professionally.[68]

Poem 38 is a reproachful appeal to Cornificius, a friend and a poet.[69] Catullus is in a bad way, and getting worse, yet Cornificius has not offered a *consolatio*. Please, just a little poem, but 'sadder than Simonidean tears'. The reason Catullus gives for his disappointment (*sic meos amores?*) is elliptical to the point of obscurity, but in the context of this sequence of poems it can only refer to his love affair; is that all Cornificius cares about it?[70] Like Bosinney in *The Man of Property*, Catullus has 'taken the knock'.[71] It's too late now for Sappho; what he needs is Simonides, to make his misery bearable.

With poem 39 we are back in limping iambics, against Egnatius again. No obscenity this time (though the final word is

---

[67] 8.5/37.12; 8.10/37.11 (*fugit*, present/perfect).

[68] *Sedere* (etc.): Plaut. *Poen.* 266–8, Prop. II 22.8, Ovid *Pont.* II 3.20, Mart. VI 66.2; cf. Dio LIX 28.9 (καθίζων). Taverns and prostitution: Ulp. *Dig.* III 2.4.2, XXIII 2.43.pref. and 2.43.9, cf. *CIL* IV 8442, IX 2689.

[69] Ovid *Trist.* II 436, Macr. *Sat.* VI 4.12, 5.13, Jer. *Chron.* 159H; Rawson 1978, 188f.

[70] *Amores* as in 7.8, 68b.69, Cic. *Cael.* 44 etc. (not as in 10.1 and 45.1, meaning a person); Wiseman 1969, 14f.

[71] John Galsworthy, *The Man of Property* (London 1906), part III ch. 4.

contemptuously vulgar),[72] but the malicious irony is brilliant, and devastating. Egnatius' toothpaste was still remembered in the second century A.D.,[73] and it is not hard to imagine the effect the poem had on contemporaries. If this was how Catullus dealt with the down-market end of 'Lesbia's' clientele, the warning in the next poem was something to be taken seriously:

> Quaenam te mala mens, miselle Ravide,
> agit praecipitem in meos iambos?
> Quis deus tibi non bene advocatus
> vecordem parat excitare rixam?
> An ut pervenias in ore vulgi?
> Quid vis? qualubet esse notus optas?
> Eris, quandoquidem meos amores
> cum longa voluisti amare poena.

What infatuation, lovesick Ravidus, drives you headlong into my lampoons? What god invoked by you in an evil hour makes haste to start the frantic duel? Is it because you want to be on people's lips? What are you after? Do you desire to be known, no matter how? So you shall be, since you've chosen to love my loved one and be pilloried for ever.

Despite some echoes of the Juventius sequence,[74] the placing of this poem makes it natural to identify Ravidus as another rival for the favours of 'Lesbia'. It was she who objected to Catullus' *iambi* (36.5); it was for her sake that he had fought duels (37.13) like the one with which he threatens Ravidus here; and it was her lover Egnatius who ran into the iambics that pilloried *him* for ever (37 and 39). The whole sequence from poem 36 to poem 40 explores love and hate, and what poetry can do for each.

After a casual reference in poem 43, where she marks the standard of beauty Mamurra's mistress fails to reach,[75] 'Lesbia' appears next in a famous and controversial scene:[76]

---

[72] For *mingere* (39.18) and *lotium* (39.21), see Adams 1982, 245–8.
[73] Apul. *Apol.* 6, quoting 39.19.
[74] 15.14 'mala mens furorque vecors' (cf. 40.1 and 4); 15.1, 21.4 (*meos amores*).
[75] 43.7; cf. n.59 above.
[76] Cat. 51 (Goold's translation slightly adapted at 11f, where he reads *geminae*, with *aures*). Bibliography up to 1974 in Harrauer 1979, 73f.

Ille mi par esse deo videtur,
ille, si fas est, superare divos,
qui sedens adversus identidem te
   spectat et audit

dulce ridentem, misero quod omnis
eripit sensus mihi: nam simul te,
Lesbia, aspexi, nihil est super mi

  . . . .

lingua sed torpet, tenuis sub artus
flamma demanat, sonitu suopte   10
tintinant aures, gemina teguntur
   lumina nocte.

Otium, Catulle, tibi molestum est:
otio exsultas nimiumque gestis:
otium et reges prius et beatas
   perdidit urbes.

He seems to me the equal of a god, he seems, if that may be, the gods' superior, who sits face to face with you and again and again watches and hears you

sweetly laughing, an experience which robs me, poor wretch, of all my senses; for the moment I set eyes on you, Lesbia, there remains not a whisper [of voice on my lips,]

but my tongue is paralysed, a subtle flame courses through my limbs, with sound self-caused my ears ring, and my eyes are covered in double darkness.

Idleness, Catullus, is your trouble; idleness is what delights you and moves you to passion; idleness has proved ere now the ruin of kings and prosperous cities.

The first line tells the reader that it is a translation of one of Sappho's most famous poems; the second line tells him that it is not only that, but a translation with Catullan additions; and the final stanza shows him that the translation has become an independent poem to be interpreted on its own terms. To make sense of it, those three levels of understanding must be considered in turn.

Sappho's original presents our first problem.[77] Who is the girl?. Who is the man? What is the occasion? Wilamowitz argued that they were the bride and groom at a wedding, and that interpretation long held the field.[78] But recent authorities reject it, with curiously intemperate polemic.[79] In the absence of other likely occasions, in archaic Greek society, for a man and a woman to be in such intimate converse, and in view of the fact that god-like felicity was part of the traditional *makarismos* of the bridegroom, it seems to me more likely than not that Wilamowitz was right.[80] If that were so, and if Catullus could count on his readers recognising the wedding background, then we might see an ironic contrast with the only other Sapphic poem in the collection, where the allusion is to divorce.[81] Given the uncertainties, of course, we cannot be confident about that; but there are other signs that Catullus' version looks back to, and is influenced by, the Lesbia-poems in the introductory cycle.

What does he add to Sappho's original? The whole of the second line; *identidem* in line 3, *spectat et* in line 4, *misero* in line 5, *eripit* in line 6, the vocative *Lesbia* in line 7, *suopte* in line 10, *gemina . . . nocte* in lines 11 and 12. The overall effect is to make it more rhetorically emphatic, and more explicit as a personal declaration.[82] Sappho's laughing girl was anonymous; Catullus names her – appropriately, of course – as 'Lesbia'. What we already know of 'Lesbia', and of Catullus' feelings towards her, gives the translator's additions an added significance.

The clearest and most shocking allusion comes in the third

---

[77] Bibliography in E. Robbins, *TAPA* 110 (1980) 255f; add Jenkyns 1982, 15–22 and 222–5.

[78] U. von Wilamowitz-Moellendorff, *Sappho und Simonides* (Berlin 1913) 56–61.

[79] D. Page, *Sappho and Alcaeus* (Oxford 1955) 30–3: 'there should never have been such a theory in the history of scholarship' (p. 33); Jenkyns 1982, 6f on 'Wilamowitz's preposterous theory'.

[80] See Merkelbach 1957, 6–12. Sitting opposite: cf. Hom *Il.* IX 190 (Patroclus and Achilles). Like gods: e.g. Sappho 44.34 L–P, Aristoph. *Birds* 1731–43, Cat. 61.16, Sen. *Med.* 82–9; B. Snell, *Hermes* 66 (1931) 71–6. I am grateful to Richard Seaford for help on this matter.

[81] Poem 11: n.56 above.

[82] Kidd 1963, 301–3.

line. Again and again (*identidem*) the fortunate man looks on
'Lesbia' and hears her laughter, just as in poem 11 her lovers
broke their manhood in her insatiable embrace. The repetition of
the rare adverb at the same metrical position in the stanza cannot
be an accident. Similarly, *misero . . . mihi* (i.e. *Catullo*) is an echo
of *miser Catulle* in poem 8; *miser* is a strong word in Catullus, and
this is the first occurrence of it since then.[83] After that, the
'double night' in lines 10–11, emphasised by the striking transferred epithet and the juxtaposition of *lumina* for 'eyes', has an
ominous ring when we remember the bright suns of life and love
in poems 5 and 8. For readers who remember those early poems,
what Catullus has added to Sappho's original has a cumulatively
sobering effect.[84]

That being so, the change of direction in the final stanza is not a
total surprise. The reader now sees that the version of Sappho in
the first three stanzas was, as it were, in inverted commas; the
'Catullus' who addressed them to the woman is now himself
addressed, and his malaise diagnosed. As in poem 8 (the last
Lesbia-poem to contain the vocative *Catulle*), we must distinguish the persona, Catullus the lover, from Catullus the poet.[85]
The former is allowed to masquerade as Sappho, but the latter
has the final comment, and it is a bitter one. Those physical
symptoms are the sign of a self-destructive emotional excess.[86]

It has been suggested recently that poem 51 was the concluding item in Catullus' book of short poems, and that 52–60, 'a
jumble of unrelated and curiously unfinished verses', were added
by the putative posthumous editor who appears so often like a

[83] Cf. 68.92f, 76.12 and 19, 91.2, 101.2 and 6; *misellus* (3.16, 35.14, 40.1, 45.21) has a quite
different tone.

[84] Wiseman 1969, 34. The effect of the cross-references escapes those who think poem 51
must be the first 'Lesbia-poem'; but that preconception, based ultimately on biographical reconstruction, seems to me gratuitous.

[85] P. 144 above (self-address also at 46.4, the farewell to Bithynia).

[86] Cic. *TD* v 16: 'quid? elatus ille levitate inanique laetitia exsultans et temere gestiens
nonne tanto miserior quanto sibi videtur beatior?' (cf. III 24 on *voluptas gestiens*, IV 66 on
exsultans gestiensque laetitia); Kidd 1963, 305 (cf. Lafaye 1894, 55f, who understood the
unity of the poem better than many of his successors). For *gestire*, see Don. *ad Eun.* 555,
'motu corporis monstrare quid sentias'; Festus 85L (Paulus), 'nimio corporis motu'.

deus ex machina in modern scholars' accounts of Catullus' collection.[87] That seems to me an unsatisfactory idea, based on an intuitive view of how Catullus *ought* to have closed his book.[88]

It is clearly right to take 50 and 51 together, as a comment on *otium* and the effects it has,[89] but the point is lost if we don't look at the poems that follow. With 52, 53 and 54 we are in the thick of Roman political life – *negotia*, the opposite of *otium*. Once more the ordering of the poems carries a message of its own, for I think no Roman reader could have failed to see in the final stanza of 51 a rejection of 'idleness', with its dangerous self-indulgence, and a return to the traditional Roman preoccupations of public life.[90] That is a long way from the defiance of convention in poem 5; but Catullus the lover has learned a lot since then, as Catullus the poet has allowed us to see. The impulse to give all for love was one part of his personality; another, as we saw in chapter IV, was an old-fashioned respect for traditional virtues. The two voices of poem 51 express the conflict between them.

The poems that follow are set firmly in the streets and squares of Rome – in the Forum, with Nonius in his curule chair and Vatinius on trial, in the Circus Maximus, on the Capitol and in Pompey's colonnade in the search for Camerius.[91] And it is on the streets of Rome that we meet 'Lesbia' again:[92]

87 Cf. C. P. Segal, *Latomus* 27 (1968) 307 n.1. Skinner 1981, 74–6 (quotation from p. 74), W. Clausen, *CP* 71 (1976) 40, and Goold 1983, 245f end the *libellus* with poem 50; as for Catullus' supposed omission of 51–60 from his book, 'reasons why can be invented' (Clausen), and have been (Goold).
88 Skinner (1981, 89–91) sees the final stanza of 51 as 'an urbane and witty affirmation of the *bios* of the neoteric poet'; it seems to me to be just the opposite.
89 Segal 1970; Skinner 1981, 8of (citing previous bibliography).
90 Cic. *Cael.* 42 expresses the conventional expectation: 'postremo cum paruerit voluptatibus, dederit aliquid temporis ad ludum aetatis atque ad inanis hasce adulescentiae cupiditates, revocet se aliquando ad curam rei domesticae, rei forensis reique publicae.'
91 52.2, 53.1 (*corona*, p. 69 above), 55.3–6 (on which see *PBSR* 48 (1980) 6–16); cf. *urbana* at 57.4.
92 Cat. 58. Goold translates 'our Lesbia' in the first line; I amend on the strength of 43.7. *Glubit* in line 5 is literally 'peels': see Adams 1982, 168 and the bibliography in n.21 above.

'LESBIA ILLA'

Caeli, Lesbia nostra, Lesbia illa,
illa Lesbia, quam Catullus unam
plus quam se atque suos amavit omnes,
nunc in quadriviis et angiportis
glubit magnanimos Remi nepotes.

Caelius, my Lesbia, the peerless Lesbia, the Lesbia that Catullus once loved
above all, more than himself and all his nearest and dearest put together, now
haunts the street-corners and alleys, sapping the great-souled descendants of
Remus.

Here is the conflict again; the third line implies a choice, 'Lesbia'
or his family. He chose her, and this is the result. The
promiscuous adulteress of poem 11 became the bar-room floozy
of poem 37; now she is imagined as the lowest of prostitutes,
handling her customers on the street corner or down the alley.
Where can we go from here?

The first book (1–60, the short-poem collection) is nearly
complete, but Catullus still has a surprise for his readers. Three
out of the four concluding poems (or all three, if 58b is misplaced
in the text) have structural and thematic elements in common.[93]
A five-line sentence on the degradation of 'Lesbia'; a five-line
sentence in scazons on the degradation of Rufa the *fellatrix* (59);
then another five-line sentence in scazons (60) which concludes
the whole series:

Num te leaena montibus Libystinis
aut Scylla latrans infima inguinum parte
tam mente dura procreavit ac taetra,
ut supplicis vocem in novissimo casu
contemptam haberes, a nimis fero corde?

Was it some lioness on Afric hills or a Scylla barking from her womb below that
bore you to have a mind so hard and inhuman as to treat with scorn a suppliant's
plea in his last need, ah, too cruel-hearted one?

[93] Weinreich 1959, 88–90. The relationship of 58b with 55 is an unsolved problem; the
manuscript archetype did sometimes misplace groups of lines, as at 54.1, 61.198,
64.386, 68.49, 84.10.

The reader is given no explicit information; what he needs in order to understand the poem must be inferred, from allusion and juxtaposition. The Greek word *leaena* – used here for the first time in Latin, as far as we know – gives the hint to look for a parallel in Greek literature. The lioness and Scylla come in Euripides, in Jason's complaint to the cruel Medea; and from similar passages in Virgil, Ovid, Lygdamus and Catullus himself we may perhaps guess that Hellenistic literature had made it a commonplace for a man to address a heartless woman in these terms.[94] The emphasis on Scylla's barking groin is not a commonplace, however: after poems 58 and 59, and in the metre of invective, it reminds us of sex and shamelessness.[95]

So the reader infers that the addressee is 'Lesbia', corrupt and callous as we now believe her to be. But who is the suppliant? It can only be Catullus, *in novissimo casu*: at this late stage, and in this last poem, Catullus the poet shows us Catullus the lover still obsessed, begging her to soften her heart to him.

4. ALLIUS' HOUSE

What have we learned about 'Lesbia' by the end of the first book of Catullus' collected poems? His subject is not so much the woman herself as his own reactions to her; nevertheless, we can recognise in that distorting mirror a will stronger than his, appetites more earthy than his, a beauty, an elegance and a capacity for laughter that captivated him against his better judgement,[96] and perhaps also a certain presence, a *hauteur* that made her intimacy all the more electrifying. For his first approach is diffident (*credo*, 2.8), he sees her in his infatuation as

---

[94] Eur. *Med.* 1341–3, 1358f, Virg. *Aen.* IV 366f, Ovid *Met.* VIII 120f, IX 613–15, Lygd. [Tib. III] 4.85–91, Cat. 64.154–7; cf. Hom. *Il.* XVI 33f (Patroclus to Achilles); Weinreich 1959, 79–84.

[95] Cf. Ferrero 1955, 190f (dogs were proverbially shameless). Metre: Wiseman 1969, 16 on the closure of the theme announced at 27 (59–60 is the only sequence of scazons in the collection).

[96] *Elegantia* inferred from 43.4, beauty from 43.5f, laughter from 2.6, 8.6 and 36.10, better judgement from 58.2f.

the consort of a god (51.1) – and she has very high-class lovers (37.14). The contrast between the patrician lady and the young man from the Transpadana is not just romantic biographers' cliché. It corresponds to a social reality.

An exactly contemporary document, Cicero's speech against Piso, shows how the family of a Transpadane business-man might be represented in Roman high society. Piso's mother came from the colony of Placentia, first established in 218 B.C.; Cicero alleges that her father, Calventius, was a Gaul from north of the Po who had settled in the colony as a mere trader.[97] The invective exaggeration is obvious, since Calventius came to Rome and married his daughter to a Roman aristocrat, but what is revealing is the prejudice Cicero can play on. Addressing an audience of senators, he can assume that a Transpadane centre like Mediolanum is essentially as barbaric as 'trousered Gaul' beyond the Alps.[98] The evidence shows two things equally: that wealthy families from the towns of Italy and Cisalpine Gaul could and did marry into the Roman nobility; and that the snobbery of the Roman élite could treat such parvenus – and their new in-laws – with hurtful contempt.[99]

How did Catullus stand in the eyes of the patrician Claudii? He was rich, cultured, well connected – but his family was in business, and he came from Transpadane Gaul.[100] He might well hope for a gracious reception, but he couldn't count on it. This social difference adds an extra dimension to Catullus' next, and most ambitious, poem about his mistress and himself.

Book Two of the collection does not touch on the poet's affairs

[97] Cic. *Pis.* fr. ix, xi (Asc. 4–5C): 'Insuber quidam fuit, idem mercator et praeco'. For *mercator* as a pejorative term, cf. Cic. *Verr.* v 167, with D'Arms 1981, 24f.

[98] Cic. *Pis.* 53 'bracata cognatio', 62 'Mediolanensis praeco', *red. Sen.* 15 'cognatio materna Transalpini sanguinis'; see Syme 1979, 34f = *JRS* 27 (1937) 130f.

[99] Wiseman 1971, 50–64. Cic. *Pis.* 14, 53, 67 ('Piso Placentinus') for the contempt extending to the in-laws; cf. Cic. *Att.* II 7.3 on 'Drusus Pisaurensis', possibly M. Livius Drusus Claudianus, whose wife was from a municipal family, the Alfidii (J. Linderski, *Historia* 23 (1974) 463–80).

[100] Well connected: e.g. with Memmius (*cohors praetoria*), Caesar (paternal *hospitium*), Manlius Torquatus (wedding poem). For business and aristocratic attitudes, see pp. 101–6 above. For the Transpadana as *Gallia*, cf. Cic. *Att.* I 1.2. etc.

(at least, not overtly); 'Lesbia' does not appear, and Catullus himself only as a narrator.[101] Book Three begins at poem 65, with the announcement of a new metre (elegiacs), and apparently a new theme to account for it: the 'sad songs' that follow are due to the death of the poet's beloved brother.[102] That theme reappears in 68a; some see a reference to 'Lesbia' and her lovers at lines 27–30 of that poem, but though the text is corrupt and hard to interpret, I think it refers rather to the effect of the poet's grief, shutting him up in Verona away from love affairs of any kind.[103] If that is the case, then the reader is quite unprepared for what happens next.[104] *Non possum reticere, deae . . .* An address to the Muses, in epic style;[105] and an emphatic announcement that the poet *cannot* keep quiet about what Allius has done for him. After that striking start, the exordium proceeds in a leisurely way for ten lines on Allius' immortal glory before the reader is given a hint of what his service to the narrator had been:

> Nam, mihi quam dederit duplex Amathusia curam,
>   scitis, et in quo me torruerit genere,
> cum tantum arderem quantum Trinacria rupes
>   lymphaque in Oetaeis Malia Thermopylis,
> maesta neque assiduo tabescere lumina fletu
>   cessarent tristique imbre madere genae.

For you [the Muses] know the suffering the treacherous goddess of love caused me and in what fashion she scorched me, when I burnt as much as Sicily's volcano or the Malian spring at Thermopylae beneath Oeta, and my

[101] 61.189, 209; 63.91–3; 64.24 and 116.
[102] 65.10–12; Wiseman 1969, 17f and 1979, 176; see p. 184 below for *carmina Battiadae*.
[103] Wiseman 1974, 96–100 (*contra* W. A. Camps, *AJP* 94 (1973) 134f). See pp. 111–15 above on the puritanical reputation of the Transpadani, which helps to explain line 29 (as does Petr. *Sat.* 132 'quis vetat in tepido membra calere toro' – the bed is only lukewarm until heated by love-making).
[104] On 68b as a separate poem, I have not been persuaded away from the position argued in Wiseman 1974, 77–103. To the bibliography cited there, and in Harrauer 1979, 95–8, add now: Della Corte 1976, 114–34; G. N. Sandy, *Phoenix* 32 (1978) 77–80; F. Cairns, *Tibullus* (Cambridge 1979) 162–5, 224f; G. W. Williams, *Figures of Thought in Roman Poetry* (Yale 1980) 50–61; Most 1981, 116–18, 120–5; Tuplin 1981, esp. 113–19.
[105] *Deae*: cf. Hom. *Il.* II 485, Virg. *Aen.* VII 641, Stat. *Theb.* I 3f. The classic instance (the first line of the *Iliad*) has a singular goddess; so too Call. *Hymn* 3.186, Theocr. 22.116.

poor eyes never stopped melting with constant tears or my cheeks streaming with a sorry flood.

So it has to do with Catullus' love affair – but how? Ten more lines of extended epic simile follow, laying on the colours with superb pictorial skill, and only then, in the 27th line of the poem, do we find out what Allius has done;[106]

> Is clausum lato patefecit limite campum,
>   isque domum nobis isque dedit dominae,
> ad quam communes exerceremus amores.

He opened up a broad path in a fenced field, and gave a house to me and to my mistress, beneath whose roof we might enjoy the love we shared.

Allius had provided a place of assignation. Now we see why the first line was so emphatic – 'I *cannot* keep quiet', despite what convention demands. It is a defiance like that of poem 5, and the *senes severiores* will disapprove. A mid-Victorian Fellow of Trinity certainly disapproved, of these 'unmeasured praises of a man guilty of as base an action as a gentleman could well commit, who lent his house to conceal an adulterous intrigue between a woman of high rank and a vicious youth'.[107] It is precisely because the act was so sordid in the eyes of the respectable world that Catullus takes such care to dress it up with all the magnificence of traditional poetic art.

Their love is to be mutual – for that is clearly the sense of *communis* here[108] – like that of Acme and Septimius or Vibia and Torquatus in Catullus' idealising conception (pp. 116–18 above). And yet they are not equals. She is his *domina*, 'mistress' in more

---

[106] 68b.67–9 (the traditional line-numbering includes the 40 lines of 68a as if it were all one poem). I accept Froelich's emendation *dominae* for *dominam* at line 68 (see Baker 1975), and must therefore revise Goold's translation at that point.

[107] H. A. J. Munro, *Criticisms and Elucidations of Catullus* (London 1878) 181. Cf. Tac. *Ann.* XI 4.2 on the brothers Petra, who provided a house for Mnester and Poppaea and were tried before the Senate and executed.

[108] Cf. Lucr. IV 1195–1208, 'communia gaudia . . . mutua voluptas . . . mutua gaudia . . . communis voluptas' (also Ovid *amores* II 5.31, *Her.* 16.319); cf. n.70 above on *amores*. Note that here, for the first time since poem 5, 'Lesbia' and Catullus together are 'we' in a first-person plural verb.

than just the diluted modern sense; in Catullus' time, before his successors had made it trivial, the metaphor still brought to mind the mistress of a slave.[109] More than that, she is a goddess:[110]

> Quo mea se molli candida diva pede
> intulit et trito fulgentem in limine plantam
> innixa arguta constituit solea,
> coniugis ut quondam flagrans advenit amore
> Protesilaeam Laudamia domum . . .

[then follows the long central 'panel' of the poem, on Laodamia]

> Aut nihil aut paulo cui tum concedere digna
> lux mea se nostrum contulit in gremium,
> quam circumcursans hinc illinc saepe Cupido
> fulgebat crocina candidus in tunica.

Thereto with dainty steps my shining goddess came, and checking her bright foot upon the polished threshold stepped on it with a tap of her sandal, as on a time ablaze with love for her husband came Laodamia to the house of Protesilaus . . . Yielding to her in naught or in but little was then my sweetheart when she brought herself into my arms; and oft about her, flitting hither, flitting thither, Cupid shone brightly in his saffron tunic.

The imagery is among the richest and most evocative in all Catullus' work. The coming of 'Lesbia' is an epiphany of Venus, with her son in attendance; and he wears a saffron tunic, like that of Hymen in poem 61. The bridal allusion, appropriate to the comparison of 'Lesbia' with Laodamia, gives a particular significance to the reflexive verbs *se intulit* and *se contulit* (she 'brought herself', but a bride should come escorted), and makes the sound of her sandal ominous in retrospect (for a bride should step over the threshold, not on it).[111] But the unease is so far only marginal; what predominates is the radiance of the scene, the sense of sudden brightness in the dark.[112]

---

[109] See p. 30 above on its corollary, *deservire* (Cic. *Cael.* 67, *parad.* 36).

[110] Lines 70–4, 131–4.

[111] 61.8–10 (Hymen), 159f (threshold); cf. Plaut. *Cas.* 815, and S. Baker, *CP* 55 (1960) 171–3.

[112] For *candidus* (lines 70, 134), cf. Serv. *Georg.* III 82 'quadam nitenti luce perfusum'; *lux mea* (132) occurs elsewhere in Catullus only at the end of this poem (146).

It is misleading, of course, to take the two halves of this scene so closely together. They are separated by sixty lines of complex, allusive, carefully structured mythological narrative, on which Catullus has lavished all the resources of his art.[113] Here too there is unease, for Laodamia has offended the gods and suffers for it; but what is more important is that we are borne away into the tragic and glamorous world of the age of heroes, and kept concentrating on a bewildering coruscation of flashback, digression and extended simile, before we are allowed to return to the scene of 'Lesbia's' arrival. We may see it only in the magical half-light of heroic legend.

But now the real world begins to break in:[114]

> Quae tamen etsi uno non est contenta Catullo,
>   rara verecundae furta feremus erae,
> ne nimium simus stultorum more molesti.
>   Saepe etiam Iuno, maxima caelicolum,
> coniugis in culpa flagrantem contudit iram,
>   noscens omnivoli plurima furta Iovis.   140

And though she is not content with Catullus alone, yet shall I put up with the rare lapses of my discreet mistress, lest I be a nuisance like stupid men: even Juno, greatest of goddesses, has often beaten down the anger that has flared up at her husband's guilt, when she learns the lapses of all-lustful Jove.

The goddess-bride is a real woman, with other sexual interests besides Catullus. Instead of the jealous rage and the venomous attack that we might expect after the earlier poems, he resolves to accept the situation, showing a worldly tolerance quite new in his portrait of the affair. But she is still the mistress (*era*) who wields the power,[115] and in his simile Catullus takes the female part, of Juno tolerating her husband's adulteries. The apparent realism is still based on illusion: Catullus is treating her affairs with other men as adulteries, as if she were being unfaithful to *him*.

---

[113] See Tuplin 1981, 119–31 on the allusions (esp. to Euphorion); Wiseman 1974, 70–6 on the structure (articulated round *coniugium* at 73, 84, 107).

[114] 68b.135–40; *contudit iram* is Hertzberg's conjecture for *cotidiana*.

[115] Note the use of *eri* for the gods at lines 76 and 78.

So a further stage of realistic analysis is necessary:[116]

> Nec tamen illa mihi dextra deducta paterna
> fragrantem Assyrio venit odore domum,
> sed furtiva dedit muta munuscula nocte,
> ipsius ex ipso dempta viri gremio.
> Quare illud satis est, si nobis is datur unis
> quam lapide illa diem candidiore notat.

Moreover, it was not on her father's arm that she came to a house scented with perfumes of the orient, but gave me stolen joys in the silence of the night, snatched from very embrace of very husband. Wherefore this is enough, if to me alone is given the day she distinguishes with a brighter mark.

Only now, and only for a moment, do we catch a glimpse of 'Lesbia' as she may have been in life – the adulterous noble-woman cheating her husband again for a night with an adoring lover. How much did it matter to her that he saw her in his fantasy as his bride? He should be glad she found time for him at all.

He *was* glad – and on her terms. Precariously, he could preserve his illusions. Of course we must distinguish Catullus the lover, a character in the drama, from Catullus the poet, who narrates it. But this delicate balance, of knowing her promiscuity and being able to live with it, suggests that in this poem the two are not far apart; that is, the reader may suspect (and I think there is some evidence) that when Catullus the poet wrote it, Catullus the lover still had some stages of his experience to come.[117]

The poem concludes with a passage that matches the exordium, promising Allius immortality and invoking the goddess of Justice to reward his devotion as she rewarded the men of old. We are back in the high style – the curtain has

---

[116] 68b.143–8 (after a resolve not to compare mortals with gods, and a corrupt passage apparently alluding to parental responsibility for brides: cf. 61.51, 62.58); *muta* at 145 is Heyse's conjecture for *mira* (cf. 7.7 for stolen love in the silent night).

[117] I infer from the disturbed symmetry of the Laodamia simile (in order to accommodate the passage on the brother's death at lines 91–100) that the original version of 68b was written some time before the organisation of the collection: Wiseman 1974, 73f, *contra* Della Corte 1976, 199 ('gratuita ipotesi'), Tuplin 1981, 118 ('arbitrary').

dropped again on that momentary glimpse of adulterous reality. Catullus gives his blessing – to Allius and his wife (or mistress), to their house itself, to the man who first introduced them to Catullus, and finally to 'Lesbia':[118]

> et longe ante omnes mihi quae me carior ipso est,
> lux mea, qua viva vivere dulce mihi est.

. . . and, far above all, she who is dearer to me than my very self, my shining star, whose living makes life happiness for me.

It is a superb ending to a superb poem; but *lux mea* takes us back to the dream world (line 132), not the real one.

5. THE EPIGRAMS

At poem 69 Catullus' elegiac collection suddenly contracts from the spacious sweep of mythological narrative to the concentrated economy of epigram. But though the scale changes, the sequence is held together by continuing themes as well as continuing metre. The first of the epigrams, on Rufus' armpits scaring the girls away, has recognisably the same tone and satirical intent as the 48 lines of poem 67; and the second, on what 'Lesbia' thinks about marriage, makes explicit what was implied in the sumptuously evocative description of her arrival at Allius' house in 68b. Indeed, the lampoons are themselves relevant to the themes of marriage and 'Lesbia'; for most of Catullus' Book Three – as far as poem 92, after which other preoccupations prevail – the juxtaposition of the poems creates a coherent drama featuring Catullus the lover, his mistress, and his rivals.[119]

The mistress – 'my woman' – appears first in a poem imitated from Callimachus, that master-epigrammatist whose name opens and closes Catullus' third book:[120]

[118] 68b.159f; cf. 153 on Themis (p. 107 above), 157f on the introduction, for which see *CR* 24 (1974) 6f and V. Cremona, *Aevum* 41 (1967) 258–64.
[119] Wiseman 1969, 22–8; on poems 69–92 see also O. Weinreich, *Catull, Liebesgedichte* (Hamburg 1960) 169, and Schmidt 1973, 228–33.
[120] Cat. 70; Call. 9 G–P (*Anth. Pal.* v 6). Callimachus' epigrams: Mart. IV 23.3f, Pliny *ep.* IV 3.4, Suda *s.vv. Archibios, Marianos*. Cat. 65.16, 116.2: Schmidt 1973, 233.

Nulli se dicit mulier mea nubere malle
    quam mihi, non si se Iuppiter ipse petat.
Dicit: sed mulier cupido quod dicit amanti
    in vento et rapida scribere oportet aqua.

The woman I love says there is no one she would rather wed than me, not
though Jupiter himself should apply. So she says: but what a woman says to an
eager lover should be written on the wind and running water.

The theme of marriage had dominated the second volume – two
wedding poems (61 and 62) and a mini-epic on the marriage of a
mortal to a goddess (64). It was continued in the third, with a
heroic Callimachean bride in poem 66, an adulterous Transpadane one in 67, and the grand illusion of the poet's mistress as his
bride in 68b.[121] So we are ready for the idea that Catullus might
want 'Lesbia' to divorce her husband and marry him – and in the
down-to-earth genre of epigram we are not surprised at his
reaction to her reply.

The man with the armpits returns in poem 71 – not named, but
the reader assumes it is Rufus again – and this time he has been
more successful with the girls: the poem is addressed to the man
whose mistress he has fucked. (Again, as in poem 6, the calcu-
lated obscenity comes between two Lesbia-poems, for contrast.)
Possibly the addressee was named, more probably not;[122] at this
stage the reader is still kept guessing.

The theme of poem 70 is resumed in 72. But by now some
time has passed, some things have been discovered:

Dicebas quondam solum te nosse Catullum,
    Lesbia, nec prae me velle tenere Iovem.
Dilexi tum te non tantum ut vulgus amicam,
    sed pater ut gnatos diligit et generos.
Nunc te cognovi: quare etsi impensius uror,
    multo mi tamen es vilior et levior.
Qui potis est, inquis? Quod amantem iniuria talis
    cogit amare magis, sed bene velle minus.

---

[121] See Schäfer 1966, 73–7; Wiseman 1969, 17–25 (detecting hints of the theme also in
poems 65 and 68a); cf. pp. 111–21 above on Catullus and marriage.
[122] At line 4, *a te* may conceal a vocative; more probably *apte* should be read (R. A. Kaster,
Phil. 121 (1977) 308–12, after Schoell). Cf. pp. 141f above on 6.13.

You once said, Lesbia, that you belonged to Catullus alone and wished not to possess even Jove in preference to me. I cherished you then, not just as an ordinary man a mistress, but as a father cherishes his children and their spouses. Now I know you: so, though I burn more ardently, you are much cheaper and slighter in my eyes. 'How so?' you ask. Because such hurt as you have inflicted forces a lover to love more, but to like less.

This is a new tone in Catullus' love poetry – cooler and more analytical than the outbursts of joy or fury in the first book. 'To isolate Catullus' feelings from the form in which he presented them is a mistake'; in the elegiacs he often seems to be sorting his experience out in his mind, trying to define its mutually inconsistent elements and somehow make sense of them.[123] Here, his attempt at definition results in a wonderfully revealing simile. His love for 'Lesbia' was not just sexual; it was also like a father's love for his sons and his sons-in-law. What did Aurelius and Furius (poem 16) make of *that*? We have seen in the last chapter how much the family and its continuity meant to Catullus; astonishingly, he applies its standards of non-erotic, altruistic affection to show how much 'Lesbia' meant to him, at the time when he believed her faithful to him alone.

Now, he has found her out. The real woman cannot be assimilated into his ingenuous fantasy. Sexual passion remains, but the rest is gone. How to express it? What verb could he use for 'love'? What is left, burning even more harmfully, is *amare*; what is lost is *diligere, bene velle*. Linguistic order, at least, has been made out of the emotional chaos.

The careless aristocrat pleases herself; her lover writes off his investment and thinks himself defrauded.[124] The sense of injustice extends into the next poem (73), a bitter attack on a friend who has paid back honest generosity with treachery and harm. 'Don't try and deserve well of anyone; don't expect *pietas*; there's no gratitude, and it does no good to do a kindness . . .' No name, no details; the reader must wait to see what the context may be.

[123] Commager 1965, 93–9, quotation from 105; cf. Lyne 1980, 22 and 41f.
[124] Lines 5f (*impensius, vilior*), 6 (*iniuria*); see pp. 104f, 123 above.

The explanation comes (after an apparently irrelevant squib on how Gellius cuckolded his uncle) in poems 75–77, where Catullus bitterly reflects on duty, treachery and emotional waste in a sequence of three interrelated poems addressed to 'Lesbia', to himself, and to Rufus.[125] Now we realise why the lampoons on Rufus alternated with Lesbia-poems at 69–72, and we can guess who the treacherous friend was, and what his offence, in poem 73.

In 76, the central poem of the trio, as he dwells at length on his betrayal, Catullus invokes a new and momentous idea:

> Si qua recordanti benefacta priora voluptas
> est homini, cum se cogitat esse pium,
> nec sanctam violasse fidem, nec foedere in ullo
> divum ad fallendos numine abusum homines,
> multa parata manent in longa aetate, Catulle,
> ex hoc ingrato gaudia amore tibi.

If, remembering his former kindnesses, a man can feel pleasure, when he reflects that he has done his duty, that he has not broken sacred faith or in any agreement has abused the sanction of the gods in order to deceive men, then many joys in a long life await you, Catullus, earned from this ill-requited love.

It is not just that he has acted properly and in good faith. We are to think of a *foedus* sanctioned by the gods – that is, an agreement or contract bound by oath – which he has dutifully kept, and she has broken. 'So why torture yourself any more? Harden your heart and go back to where you were: the gods don't want you to be wretched.'[126] Catullus himself has done right by the gods; it is she who has offended them[127] – and in so far as he is still obsessed with her, he too incurs their displeasure.

---

[125] Duty: 75.2 (*officium*), 76.2 and 26 (*pietas*), 76.3 (*fides*). Treachery: 75.1 (*culpa*), 76.6 (*ingrato amore*), 76.9 (*ingratae menti*), 77.6f (*crudele venenum*). Waste: 75.2 (*perdidit*), 76.9 (*perierunt credita*), 77.1 (*nequiquam credite*), 77.2 (*magno cum pretio*). Other cross-references: 75.3 / 76.24; 76.20 / 77.6; 76.21 / 77.3. At 75.3f, *bene velle* and *amare* look back to 72.8; at 77.4f, *eripuisti* looks back to 51.6 (p. 152 above).

[126] 76.10–12; cf. *Mélanges M. Renard* 1 (Brussels 1969) 782f, and p. 105 above.

[127] Cf. 8.15 (*scelesta*), 11.22 and 75.1 (*culpa*), 60.4 (rejection of suppliant), 72.7 (*iniuria*).

So when he has argued himself into a total impasse ('you must give her up even if it's impossible'), he can only pray for mercy:[128]

> O di, si vestrum est misereri, aut si quibus umquam
>   extremam iam ipsa in morte tulistis opem,
> me miserum aspicite et, si vitam puriter egi,
>   eripite hanc pestem perniciemque mihi,
> quae mihi subrepens imos ut torpor in artus
>   expulit ex omni pectore laetitias.
> Non iam illud quaero, contra ut me diligat illa,
>   aut, quod non potis est, esse pudica velit:
> ipse valere opto et taetrum hunc deponere morbum.
>   O di reddite mi hoc pro pietate mea.

Ye gods, if it is in you to have mercy, or if ever to any you have given aid at the last in the very hour of death, look on me in my misery and, if I have led a pure life, rid me of this plague and pestilence, which, creeping like a paralysis into the depths of my being, has banished happiness from every corner of my heart. I do not now seek this, that she should love me in return, or, what is not possible, that she should wish to be chaste: I yearn to be well and to get rid of this foul disease. Ye gods, grant me this as a reward for my devotion.

The fact that he cannot stop 'loving' her (in his redefined sense of *amare* as sexual passion only) is the reason he must ask for the gods' mercy on him, and he excuses himself for it by likening it to an illness.[129] On the other hand, the fact that he is conscious of rectitude in all other matters (the 'purity' of his life being unaffected by *her* adultery with *him*) is the reason he can also ask for a just reward in return for *pietas*.[130] The fault in the eyes of the gods is hers, not his.

The predictable, and necessary, relaxation of emotional intensity comes in poem 78 on Gallus, another uncle with a randy nephew (even in good humour we are not allowed to forget

---

[128] 76.17–26; line 26 refers back both to the beginning of the prayer (*o di*) and to the beginning of the whole poem (*pietate*).

[129] *Amare*: 72.8, 75.4, cf. 76.13 (*amor*). Disease: the parallels with poem 51 are revealing (Kidd 1963, 304f); cf. p. 154 above.

[130] See Liebeschuetz 1979, 45–7.

adultery). 78b is too fragmentary for us to be able to see how it contributed to the sequence. But after that we have 'Lesbia' in six out of the next nine poems, in three of them with other men ('Lesbius' in 79, Quinctius in 82, her husband in 83). Moreover, one of the three apparently unconnected items is on Gellius, as was poem 74: four consecutive attacks on Gellius and his incestuous vices follow at 88–91, in the last of which it is revealed that he too was one of Catullus' treacherous rivals. In short, the whole sequence 69–92 is devoted to 'Lesbia' and the various men in her life, with only three other poems inserted for variety:

	69	Rufus	
Lesbia	70		
	71	(Rufus)	
Lesbia	72		
	73	(Rufus?)	
	74	Gellius	
Lesbia	75		
Lesbia	76		
(Lesbia?)	77	Rufus	
	(78)		
Lesbia	79	Lesbius	
	80	Gellius	
	(81)		
(Lesbia)	82	Quinctius	
Lesbia	83	husband	
	(84)		
Lesbia	85		
Lesbia	86		Quinctia
Lesbia	87		
	88	Gellius	
	89	Gellius	
	90	Gellius	
(Lesbia)	91	Gellius	
Lesbia	92		

With one conspicuous exception – the comparison with Quinctia in poem 86, where the words and the mood recall the more carefree parts of the first book[131] – the poems on 'Lesbia' all have a characteristic shape and tone, a kind of tension between the argumentative symmetry of the elegiac form and an anarchic sense of resentment and desperation. What exercises him still is the nature of love; the dilemma expressed at length in poem 76 is reduced to its essentials in the famous couplet, poem 85:

> Odi et amo. Quare id faciam, fortasse requiris.
> Nescio, sed fieri sentio, et excrucior.

I hate and love. Perhaps you ask how I can do this? I know not, but I feel it so, and I am in agony.

What cannot be caught in English is the transition from active to passive. No use asking how Catullus *does* it; it's something that *is done* (to him), and all he can do is suffer.

The imagery of poem 76 reappears in a beautifully controlled exposition of his case against her (poem 87):

> Nulla potest mulier tantum se dicere amatam
> vere quantum a me Lesbia amata mea est.
> Nulla fides ullo fuit umquam in foedere tanta
> quanta in amore tuo ex parte reperta mea est.

No woman can truly say that she has been loved as much as my Lesbia has been loved by me. No faithfulness in any contract ever proved so great as that which was found on my side in my love for you.

The postponement of *vere* to follow *amatam*, in emphatic enjambment at the beginning of line 2, produces a rich ambiguity: is it 'no woman can truly say', or 'that she has been truly loved'? We know from poem 11 that *real* love was not what 'Lesbia' gave her men; we know from poems 8 and 37 that Catullus' love for her, on the other hand, was unique, and from poem 72 that he even tried to define it in familial terms.[132] His type of love was the real thing, faithful as if to a contract signed and sworn. But her type was *amor* as well, and he was subject to

---

[131] E.g. *candida* (86.1/13.4), *venustas* (86.3/3.2, 13.6), *sal* (86.4/12.4, 13.5), *Veneres* (86.6/3.1, 13.12).

[132] 11.19 (*nullum amans vere*); 8.5, 37.12; 72.3f (pp. 146, 166 above).

that even when all other feeling was gone, or changed to hate (*odi et amo*).

In this long fugue of love, hate and self-justification, two distasteful themes obsessively recur. They are combined in the person of the unspeakable Gellius, first introduced in a deceptively good-humoured piece on his seduction of his aunt (poem 74); the otherwise unknown Gallus features in a similar scenario in poem 78, after which three successive poems refer to *fellatio* (78b–80). Of those guilty of this vice, one is unidentified because the poem is incomplete; one is 'Lesbius', whom any Roman reader would infer from the name to be the brother of 'Lesbia' (she prefers him to Catullus, nevertheless); and the third is Gellius. In the final succession of attacks on Gellius it is the incest – not only his aunt but his sister, his mother and all the girls in the family – that draws Catullus' increasingly severe condemnation. Why should he go after 'Lesbia' as well? Because betraying an old friend appealed to his taste for gratuitous evil-doings:[133]

> . . . tantum tibi gaudium in omni
> culpa est, in quacumque est aliquid sceleris.

. . . such is the delight you take in any offence which has some portion of sheer wickedness.

'Now I have found you out', says Catullus to 'Lesbia' at the beginning of this sequence (72.5); and what he had found out was that *fellatio* and incest were two of the pastimes of her milieu. They offended two of his own most cherished values, the virtues on which he had based his appeal to the gods in poem 76: purity ('si vitam *puriter* egi') and *pietas* ('reddite mi hoc pro *pietate* mea').[134] Purity was inconsistent with oral intercourse,[135] and incest was *impietas*, an offence against the gods of the family.[136]

---

133 91.9f; see Wiseman 1974, 119–29 on Gellius – probably L. Gellius Poblicola, later consul in 36 B.C.

134 76.19 and 26. On *pietas* and *fides* (76.2f), see Henry 1950–51; for purity and the marriage ideal, cf. 66.84.

135 78b.1f; *comminxit* at line 2 (cf. 67.30 and Adams 1982, 142 for *mingere* in a sexual sense) reminds us of Egnatius, whose mouth was impure (39.14) for a different reason.

136 64.397–408 (esp. 403f), 67.29f; cf. 88.4–8 (*scelus*), 89.5 and 90.1 (*nefas*), 90.4 (*impia*).

The two recurring themes were not just random targets for Catullus' invective, but expressions of a moral revulsion inseparable from his own dilemma of simultaneous abhorrence and desire.

What did the liberated lady herself think of her puritanical admirer? As usual, 'Lesbia' is a shadowy figure. But we see her as an arrogant aristocrat in the poem on 'Lesbius' (79), where she and her brother dismiss Catullus 'and all his kin', and Catullus in return boldly puns on the name of their noble house (p. 131 above). Then, in poem 83, we see her with her husband, delighting him by speaking ill of Catullus. Fool! It just shows Catullus is on her mind: better to be the object of her anger than simply forgotten.

A similar poem closes this lengthy sequence. After the culminating attack on Gellius, with its reference to Catullus' 'doomed and wretched love' and the mistress whose love was 'eating him away' like a cancer,[137] poem 92 seems to offer a change for the better:

> Lesbia mi dicit semper male nec tacet umquam
> de me: Lesbia me dispeream nisi amat.
> Quo signo? Quia sunt totidem mea: deprecor illam
> assidue, verum dispeream nisi amo.

Lesbia is for ever criticising me and never shuts up about me: I'm damned if she's not in love with me. How do I know? Because I've the same symptoms: I curse her all the time, but I'm damned if I'm not in love with her.

After all that has gone before, that seems extraordinary. But not when we remember the redefinition of *amor*. All the 'real love' has gone, but what is left – *amare*, not *diligere* or *bene velle* – is more compulsive than ever. Poem 72 spelt it out at the start: now that he knows her, he has no liking or respect for her, but desires her more no matter what she does.[138] The symmetry shows that he has accepted love on her terms – physical desire based on mutual dislike and defamation. Since the meaning of *deprecari* in

---

[137] 91.2, cf. 8.1f, 51.5, 75.2; 91.6 ('cuius me magnus *edebat* amor'), cf. 76.21, 77.3.
[138] 72.7f (p. 166 above); 75.4, 'nec desistere amare, omnia si facias'.

line 3 is to beg to be rid of something, we are entitled to expand
'I'm damned if I don't love her' with the reflection that if he does
love her he's damned as well.[139]

The second half of the epigram collection (poems 93–116) is
introduced by a dismissive couplet on Caesar and has one
recurring theme, Caesar's henchman Mamurra in his guise as
The Prick ('Mentula': p. 105 above).[140] The proportions are
reversed from the first half: out of 24 poems, 'Lesbia' is mentioned in only four, and in two of those not as the main subject.

In poem 100 Caelius of Verona is praised for his loyalty when
the 'mad flame' was burning Catullus' marrow, and in poem 104
an unnamed person is rebuked for supposing Catullus could
speak ill of his love (*mea vita*), who is dearer to him than his two
eyes.[141] Then come two poems addressed to 'Lesbia' herself,
separated by a vitriolic attack on a certain Cominius and his
impuri mores.[142] They are the last love poems in the entire
three-volume collection, and they are unlike anything we have
met so far:[143]

> Si quicquam cupidoque optantique obtigit umquam
>   insperanti, hoc est gratum animo proprie.
> Quare hoc est gratum nobisque est carius auro,
>   quod te restituis, Lesbia, mi cupido,
> restituis cupido atque insperanti, ipsa refers te
>   nobis. O lucem candidiore nota!
> Quis me uno vivit felicior, aut magis hac res
>   optandas vita dicere quis poterit?

[139] *Deprecari*: pointed out by A. Gellius (*NA* VII 16, Appendix no. 37) with explicit reference to this poem. *Dispeream*: cf. 8.2 for the association of *perire* and *perditus* (91.2).

[140] It is possible that several of the persons attacked in this sequence were Caesarian partisans (Wiseman 1969, 28f).

[141] 100.7, 'cum vesana meas torreret flamma medullas'; 7.10 (p. 141 above) for *vesanus*. 104.1f (p. 134 above); cf. 82.3f for the simile.

[142] 108.2, *'spurcata* [cf. 78b.2, 99.10] impuris moribus'. Again (cf. poems 5–7, 70–2), the juxtaposition seems to be for the sake of contrast.

[143] Cat. 107, 109. The text is uncertain at 107.3 and 7f, where (without much confidence) I follow Goold in printing the emendations of Haupt and Lachmann respectively.

If aught was ever granted to anyone who desired and prayed and never hoped,
that is truly welcome to the soul. So is this welcome and dearer to me than gold,
that you restore yourself, Lesbia, to me who desired, restore to me who desired
and never hoped, that you return yourself to me. O day distinguished with a
brighter mark! Who lives happier than I in all the world? Or who can tell of
anything more desirable than the life that is mine?

> Iucundum, mea vita, mihi proponis amorem
>   hunc nostrum inter nos perpetuumque fore.
> Di magni, facite ut vere promittere possit,
>   atque id sincere dicat et ex animo,
> ut liceat nobis tota perducere vita
>   aeternum hoc sanctae foedus amicitiae.

You assure me, my darling, that this mutual love of ours will be happy and last
for ever. Ye gods, grant that she may be capable of promising truly and say this
sincerely and from the bottom of her heart, so that we may our whole life long
maintain this eternal compact of hallowed friendship.

There are several unobtrusive cross-references to earlier
poems,[144] but both the tone and the subject matter are quite
different from what has gone before. 'Lesbia', it seems, is
offering love on Catullus' terms – a love which is also a
friendship, and for ever, and bound by a bond. In both poems the
idea of *life* predominates, even to the extent of appearing (here
and nowhere else) as a vocative for 'Lesbia' herself.[145] In 109 the
emphatic repetition *nostrum . . . nos . . . nobis* brings us back to
those rare moments of felicity when he and she are combined as
'we'.[146] But it is not quite the mood of 'vivamus, mea Lesbia,
atque amemus'. He needs the help of the gods to make her mean
it, to bring those first-person-plural pronouns out of the subordinate clauses of her proposal and his prayer into the indicative
mood of actual experience.

Whether they heard his prayer, we are not to know. Catullus

---

[144] 107.1 and 4f (*cupido*)/72.3; 107.5 (*refers te*)/68b.70f and 132 (p. 161 above);
107.6/68b.148; 107.7 (*vivit*)/8.10; 109.6 (*foedus*)/87.3.

[145] 107.7 (*vivit*), 107.9 (*vita*), 109.1 (*mea vita*), 109.5 (*tota vita*). For the *foedus*, cf. Lyne
1980, 36.

[146] 5.1f, 68b.69 (see above, p. 139 and n.108).

the poet leaves Catullus the lover in a precarious balance of sudden happiness and sober, unconfident hope. And his readers take their leave of 'Lesbia' on a grave and moving line; what lives on, despite everything, is the poet's stubbornly old-fashioned view of the responsibilities of love.

6. REFLECTIONS IN MYTH

Who knows the human heart so well as to think it incapable of an uneasy and hopeful return to its beloved after a desperate refusal?

Eckart Schäfer's wise warning against attempts to put the 'Lesbia' poems into a chronological order should be heeded especially by those who believe that Catullus had nothing more to say to his mistress after poem 11.[147] The temptation to identify 'the end of the affair' leads only to biographical fantasy. We may reasonably assume that the real affair with his Clodia was an emotionally devastating experience for C. Valerius Catullus. But he was not wholly devastated. As a poet, he was in control of his material, able to present it as a drama, with himself and his infatuated illusions among the *personae*. And since he chose to leave it open-ended, we have no right to impose an ending to suit ourselves. All we have is what he gives us. 'Lesbia' lives only in his collected poems.

But there may be a way, still within the collection, of seeing her from a different angle. It has often been thought that the choice and treatment of Catullus' mythological themes were influenced by his own experience in love.[148] It is dangerously easy to slip into mere intuitive speculation, but I think there are some parallels for which objective arguments may be advanced.

In poem 68b, for example, the long passage on Laodamia has a significance more complex than its ostensible function as a simile

---

[147] Schäfer 1966, 49: 'Wer kennt das menschliche Herz so gut, dass er ihm nicht nach der verzweifelten Absage an die Geliebte eine bangende, hoffende Rückkehr zutraute?'
[148] See Forsyth 1976 and Della Corte 1976, 317–47 (both citing previous bibliography).

comparing the heroine with 'Lesbia'. It begins at line 73 (following the passage quoted at p. 161 above):

> . . . coniugis ut quondam flagrans advenit amore
>   Protesilaeam Laudamia domum
> inceptam frustra, nondum cum sanguine sacro
>   hostia caelestis pacificasset eros.
> Nil mihi tam valde placeat, Ramnusia virgo,
>   quod temere invitis suscipiatur eris.

. . . as on a time ablaze with love for her husband came Laodamia to the house of Protesilaus, a house begun in vain, before a victim's sacrificial blood had appeased the lords of heaven. May nothing please me so mightily, Rhamnusian maid, as to be rashly ventured against heaven's will!

Implicit in the prayer to Nemesis (a goddess he took seriously)[149] is a comparison of Laodamia with Catullus himself. We have seen elsewhere that it came naturally to him to compare himself with a woman; this example adds two further dimensions, marriage and the approval of the gods. Laodamia offended them, and lost her husband; is Catullus' quasi-marriage doomed as well? Like him, Laodamia is insatiable in love.[150] And her love, like his, is deeper than physical passion, fully expressible only in terms of familial devotion between the generations.[151] It is hard to avoid the inference that the development of her story reflects his own emotional preoccupations – and not just in the way the narrative of his poem requires.

More elusive, in that the narrative is wholly mythological, is the question of personal relevance in poem 64. Here the signal is not by first-person comment but by imagery and phraseology which remind the reader of the love poems, and the comparison is again with a tragic heroine.

The description of the coverlet on the marriage-bed of Peleus and Thetis begins with Ariadne on the shore, watching Theseus sail away and unable to believe her eyes (64.56–9):

---

[149] 50.20f, cf. p. 140 above on Invidia.
[150] 68b.81–83, cf. 7.2 and 10 (p. 141 above).
[151] 68b.119–24, cf. 72.3f (p. 166 above). The simile of the doves (68b.125–8) emphasises unique fidelity; normally, women are *multivolae*.

> . . . utpote fallaci quae tum primum excita somno
> desertam in sola miseram se cernit harena.
> Immemor at iuvenis fugiens pellit vada remis,
> irrita ventosae linquens promissa procellae.

. . . no wonder, since then first she woke from treacherous sleep and saw
herself, poor thing, abandoned on a lonely strand. But the youth fleeing
unmindful of her beats the waters with his oars, leaving his vain vows to the
blustering gale.

In much the same words she begins her bitter speech of complaint (64.132-5):

> Sicine me patriis avectam, perfide, ab aris,
> perfide, deserto liquisti in litore, Theseu?
> Sicine discedens neglecto numine divum
> immemor ah devota domum periuria portas?

'Thus, faithless one, having lured me from my ancestral altar, faithless
Theseus, have you left me on a desolate shore? Thus indifferent to the will of
heaven, do you depart and ah, unmindful, carry home the curse upon your
broken oath?'

With *fallax*, *immemor*, *perfidus*, the promise blown to the empty
breezes, and other verbal echoes as well, the reader cannot help
but remember poem 30 (pp. 122f above). Moreover, as Ariadne's
speech proceeds, he will recognise two Lesbia-poems. First at
64.139-42:

> At non haec quondam blanda promissa dedisti
> voce mihi, non haec miserae sperare iubebas,
> sed conubia laeta, sed optatos hymenaeos,
> quae cuncta aerii discerpunt irrita venti.

'But not such were the promises you gave me once with winning words, not
such the hopes you bade me, poor fool, conceive, but happy wedlock and the
nuptials I longed for; all which the winds of the air have shredded into
nothingness.'

When 'Lesbia' said she would marry Catullus, it was words
written on the wind – and the emphatic *dicit* fell at the beginning
of the hexameter just as *voce* does here (p. 165 above). These four

lines have just the same message as the four lines of poem 70, with Ariadne playing the Catullus part. Twelve lines later (64.154–7):

> Quaenam te genuit sola sub rupe leaena,
> quod mare conceptum spumantibus exspuit undis,
> quae Syrtis, quae Scylla rapax, quae vasta Charybdis,
> talia qui reddis pro dulci praemia vita?

'What lioness bore you beneath some solitary rock, what sea conceived and vomited you from its foaming waters, what Syrtis, what ravening Scylla, what monstrous Charybdis, you who for precious life have given me such return?'

The parallel with poem 60 (p. 156 above) is unmistakable. And when at last Ariadne makes her prayer to the gods, with a desperate trust in the rightness of her cause, it is in phraseology reminiscent of poem 76.[152]

There are equally significant allusions to the wedding songs; in the flashback to the moment when she falls in love with Theseus, the reader has seen Ariadne as a virgin bride.[153] If he sees her now also as Catullus the lover, that recalls the comparison of Catullus himself with Atalanta and Laodamia, and of his love with the fragile flower of virginity.[154] The theme of brides and marriage (or the promise of marriage) is central to both narratives of Catullus' epic, in conspicuous contrast with the tales of incestuous passion and metamorphosis that seem to have attracted his contemporaries.[155] In the Peleus and Thetis story too there is an echo of the Lesbia-poems at a critical moment: when the Fates sing the wedding hymn, the structure of their song emphasises the happiness of a marriage expressed as a *foedus*.[156]

---

[152] 64.191 (*postrema hora*), 76.18 (p. 168 above). See Henry 1950–51, 52–4; on Ariadne in general, Putnam 1961, 168–80 and Adler 1981, 111–14.

[153] 64.86–90/61.21–5 and 56–9, 62.21–3 and 39–41; Klingner 1956, 82f.

[154] See above, pp. 121 (2b), 176 (68b.73–8), 146 (11.21–4).

[155] Cinna's *Zmyrna*, Calvus' *Io*, Cornificius' *Glaucus*, etc.; see Wiseman 1974, 54–6 (on the influence of Parthenius).

[156] 64.335 (cf. 87.3) and 373; for the ring-construction see Wiseman 1974, 69f, the wedding night and the morning after enclosing the story of the son conceived between. The good omens (64.329) recall those at 45.19, 61.19f and 159 (p. 118 above).

There are stylistic differences between the 'main' narrative on Peleus and Thetis and parts of the 'inserted' narrative on Ariadne and Theseus; the latter shows some Lucretian influence, and it may be that it was written later (Lucretius died in 54 or 53 with his great work unfinished, though it is possible that Catullus had heard some of it before its posthumous publication).[157] It is tempting to guess that the theme of a mortal marrying a goddess in blissful felicity and that of an innocent betrayed by false promises and heartless cruelty suggested themselves to Catullus in that order. If we do guess at such a sequence, we are going behind what the poet wants to tell us, and trying to analyse the compositional history of a work which he presents to us as an integral whole.[158] There is nothing wrong with that, but we must realise that we are dealing with a different sort of evidence.

To revert to the safer territory of the text as it is (presumably the poet's final version), it is worth considering the way he presents the Ariadne and Theseus story as an *ekphrasis*, the description of a work of visual art. What the wedding guests are imagined as looking at on the tapestry, Catullus' readers probably had in their minds already as a familiar composition in Hellenistic painting or relief.[159] On one side, the sea, with Theseus' ship in the distance; in the centre, the shore, with distraught Ariadne gazing out after him; on the other side, the land behind her, with Iacchus and his rout of satyrs and bacchantes.[160] In the work of art, both sides of the composition are equally important: Theseus abandons Ariadne, the god finds her and makes her his heavenly consort. Her anguish will be followed by unparalleled felicity; amid all the variants in the details

---

[157] There are as many spondaic endings in the sixty lines 67–119 and 252–8 as in the whole of the rest of the poem (368 lines); and out of 18 possible Lucretian echoes in the poem, 15 come between lines 125 and 250 (C. Bailey, *Titi Lucreti Cari de rerum natura libri sex* (Oxford 1947) III 1753f). On the evidence for Lucretius' death, see Wiseman 1974, 40–3.

[158] Cf. n.117 above for a similar analysis of the Laodamia passage in 68b.

[159] T. B. L. Webster, *Hellenistic Poetry and Art* (London 1964) 308, and *GR* 13 (1966) 29f.

[160] 64.52–70, 249–64 ('parte ex alia', 251). Everything between is marked as digression: see lines 76, 116f, 124, 212 for variants of 'they say . . .'.

of the story, those two poles are fixed. Catullus may not rewrite
the happy ending, but he can overshadow it by lavishing all his
attention on the anguish, and leaving the felicity wholly unem-
phasised.[161] What he does choose to emphasise in the Iacchus
scene is something the reader of the previous poem in the
collection associates with madness and barbarism:

What we are shown is not the meeting of Ariadne and the god, not the
joy and glory he brings her, but only his outlandish and barbarous
company. We leave the Ariadne story to the wild strains of the
Bacchantes, beside themselves in the same hysterical and potentially
destructive frenzy that Catullus evokes in that disturbing *tour de force*, the
Attis. This terrifying scene and the picture of the betrayed Ariadne are
what linger in the mind, not her deliverance.

This final echo in the Ariadne story directs us to Catullus' greatest
poem.[162]

Book Two consists of the two wedding poems (61 and 62), the
epic tale with its double narrative (64) – and between them, *Attis*
(63). What exactly poem 63 is, is a question we shall have to face in
the next chapter. For the moment it is enough to point out that the
poem ends with a prayer in the first person (like that in 68b: p. 176
above), and so may reasonably be brought into the question of
Catullus' experience and the reflection of it in his narrative poems.

There were many versions of the story of Cybele, the Great
Mother of the Gods, and her consort Attis; the only element
common to them all was castration, to account for the Mother's
eunuch priests.[163] The one Catullus tells is unlike any of the
others, and may have been composed in conscious opposition to
them.[164] His Attis, like his Ariadne, leaves the security of home

---

[161] Forsyth 1980, 101 and 104f; 64.253 for the one reference to the god's love, echoing that
of Peleus in the 'main' narrative (64.19).

[162] Curran 1969, 180: cross-references between 64.254–64 and 63.21–5. See especially
lines 254 ('lymphata mente') and 264 ('barbaraque horribili . . .').

[163] Summarised in Vermaseren 1977, 90–2 and 111f: Paus. VII 17, Arnob. *adv. nat.* V 5–7,
Diod. Sic. III 58f, Ovid *Fasti* IV 221–44; cf. Neanthes of Cyzicus *FGrH* 84F37,
Alexander 'Polyhistor' *FGrH* 273F74.

[164] Contrast 63.76–90 (Attis and the lion) with Dioscorides 16 G–P (*Anth. Pal.* VI 220); cf.
also *Anth. Pal.* VI 217–19, 237 and Varro *Men.* 364B (Nonius 775L) for the orthodox
version of the incident.

and family; she was led by a false lover to expect marriage, he was led by madness to expect communion with a goddess. Both find themselves on an alien and deserted shore, looking desperately for a safety they will not find – she deserted, he self-castrated. In each case, Catullus has altered the emphasis – or even the data – of the received story. Ariadne's communion with the god is played down, and the Bacchic rout behind her is made to seem dangerous and sinister. Attis' marriage with the goddess is replaced by madness and slavery, and Cybele's home in the forests of Ida behind him is made to seem a place of savagery, the lair of wild beasts.[165]

Madness and slavery were two of the metaphors Catullus used for his own love ('Lesbia' was a *domina*, like Cybele);[166] his mistress was a goddess manifest, and to follow her meant in some sense to deny his kin.[167] The world she inhabited was a moral wilderness, where the values he had been brought up with did not apply: *fides* and *pietas* were treated with contempt, and the responsibilities of marriage and the family were corrupted into incest and sexual perversion.[168]

Like most of the poems in the collection, poem 63 probably had a life of its own before the collection was put together. But in its setting next to the wedding-songs and the epic tale, in the central position between the two blocks of personal and occasional poetry, it acquires an extra resonance, echoing in another genre the preoccupations of the poet–lover. The collection is in itself a work of art. What Catullus did within the confines of a single poem in the Laodamia digression in 68b, he has done on a bigger scale with the long poems of his second book. By placing

165 63.50–73; 64.86–90, 117–20, 178–87 (home, shore, desperation); verbal cross-references between 63.47–56 and 64.124–30 (*aestus, vastos, maesta, aciem*). Madness: 63.4, 38, 44, 57, 79, 89. Slavery: 63.68, 80, 90. Beasts: 63.53f, 70–2; cf. 63.13, 33, 77, with Sandy 1968, 390–5.

166 7.10 (*vesano*), 100.7 (*vesana flamma*), cf. 76. 20–5; 68b.68 and 156, 63.13 and 91 (*domina*); 68b.136, 63.18 (*era*); pp. 160f above.

167 68b.70 (*candida diva*), cf. 51.1f, 70.2, 72.2; 58.3 ('plus quam se atque *suos* amavit omnes'), 79.2–3 ('cum tota gente tua').

168 Wiseman 1974, 117f; on 64.397–408, see D. Konstan, *Catullus' Indictment of Rome: the Meaning of Poem 64* (Amsterdam 1977) 83; on incest, Rankin 1976, 120f.

them there he has set his personal experience – or such of it as he allows us to see – in suggestive juxtaposition with the grand and tragic themes of Greek mythology.

Catullus wrote for people who took poetry seriously – for re-readers, who would come back to Attis, Peleus and Ariadne with the whole cycle of Lesbia-poems in their minds. For such readers, the collection is more than the sum of its parts. From the bright seascape where Peleus fell in love, in the 'too happy time' when mortals and goddesses were on earth together, to the shores of Ariadne's island and the dark woods of Attis' insanity, the experience of Catullus the lover is acted out on the opera-stage of myth and legend. And his mistress, in the process, is invested with an epic grandeur – beautiful as Thetis, heartless as Theseus, implacable as Cybele.

CHAPTER VI

THE UNKNOWN CATULLUS

At last he rose, and twitch'd his Mantle blew:
To morrow to fresh Woods, and Pastures new.

JOHN MILTON, 'Lycidas', *Poems* (1645) 65

1. POEM 116

Catullus was a learned and allusive poet, but the loss of so much of the poetry of the Hellenistic age has made it impossible to judge the full extent of his technique. It is characteristic of the state of our knowledge that a hexameter from an unknown Greek poet, casually quoted in one of Cicero's letters, should be the original of a line in Catullus' miniature epic.[1] However, papyri are steadily increasing our stock of Hellenistic literature, if only in fragments; in particular, one seminal Alexandrian work – the *Aetia* of Callimachus – is now understood in a way the great Catullan scholars of the nineteenth century could not have dreamed of.

We can now see, as they could not, how Catullus exploited his readers' knowledge of the *Aetia* at the beginning of all three books of his collection. In poem 1 he asks of the Muse what Callimachus asked of the Graces in *Aetia* I, and describes his book, via a bilingual pun, as Apollo describes Callimachus' work in the *Aetia* prologue.[2] At the beginning of poem 61, where Hymen is summoned to the wedding of Manlius Torquatus, his home on Helicon and his descent from the Muse Urania can now

---

[1] Cat. 64.111; Cic. *Att.* VIII 5.1 (?Callimachus fr. 732 Pf).
[2] Cat. 1.9f, *Aetia* I 7.14; Zicàri 1965, 239, Cairns 1969, 156, Carilli 1975, 927, Wiseman 1979, 174. Cat. 1.1, *Aetia* I 1.24; for *lepidus* and λεπτός, see Latta 1972, 204 and 210–13, Wiseman 1979, 169f.

be recognised as an allusion to the *Aetia*.[3] And poem 65 to Hortensius both announces the translation of a work included in *Aetia* IV (the *Lock of Berenice*, poem 66), and perhaps alludes in its final simile to a story told at length in *Aetia* III (*Acontius and Cydippe*).[4]

We might expect the concluding poem in the collection to continue this play of allusions; and sure enough, there is Callimachus in the second line. The repeated phrase *carmina Battiadae* has been rightly seen as a cross-reference to 65.14, tying together the beginning and end of Catullus' third book.[5] But the poem as a whole is not quite what one would expect as an epilogue:

> Saepe tibi studioso animo venante requirens
>   carmina uti possem mittere Battiadae,
> qui te lenirem nobis, neu conarere
>   tela infesta ⟨meum⟩ mittere in usque caput,
> hunc video mihi nunc frustra sumptum esse laborem,
>   Gelli, nec nostras hic valuisse preces.
> Contra nos tela ista tua evitabimus acta
>   et fixus nostris tu dabis supplicium.

Often with mind earnestly hunting have I sought how I might possibly send you poems of the Battiad,[6] that I might win you over, and that you might not try to land deadly shafts upon my head. But now I see that this has been toil vainly undertaken, Gellius, and that herein my prayers have not availed. Those shafts of yours launched against me I shall evade; but you shall be pierced by mine and pay the penalty.

Gellius is familiar as the chief target of Catullus' attacks on his rivals in love in the first half of the epigram collection (p. 169 above); but since then we have been concerned with other matters, in particular the cycle of satirical poems against

---

[3] Cat. 61.1f, *Aetia* I 2a.42f (p. 113 n.71 above). The Muses appear in the introductions to all three books: 1.9, 61.2, 65.3.

[4] Cat. 65.16, *Aetia* IV 110; Cat. 65.19–24, *Aetia* III 67–75, cf. Daly 1952, 98f.

[5] Schmidt 1973, 223; P. Y. Forsyth, *CQ* 27 (1977) 352f.

[6] From this point the translation is Goold's; he reads *verba ante* for *venante* and *vertere* for *mittere*, so I am reluctantly compelled to offer my own much clumsier version of the first two lines. (At the end of line 7, *acta* is Baehrens' emendation for *amitha* or *amicta* in the MSS.)

'Mentula', which ends superbly in the last line of the previous poem: 'non homo, sed vero mentula magna minax'.[7] Why is Gellius suddenly reintroduced?

More important, how are we to explain the metrical peculiarities of the poem? The hexameter in line 3 is wholly spondaic, a Homeric licence no Roman poet had allowed himself since Ennius, whose work we know Catullus' poetic friends despised.[8] And in the final line – the very last phrase of a consciously avant-garde collection – we have an example of elided *s*, which we know the 'new poets' of Catullus' time avoided as artistically unacceptable.[9] What *is* he playing at?

A proper understanding of the poem was first made possible by Colin Macleod in 1973. He pointed out the juxtaposition of phraseology appropriate to two different types of poetic activity, the laborious erudition of the followers of Callimachus, and the violent crudeness of invective: 'Catullus is here distinguishing two styles of his own, the vituperative and the Callimachean', and the programmatic nature of the poem is as appropriate for the end of the collection as it would be for the beginning. Béla Németh made a further advance with the observation that Catullus' 'single-combat' imagery in lines 4 and 7–8 is reminiscent of the way he speaks of his iambics in poems 36 and 40 (pp. 148–51 above).[10]

But there are still some puzzles. Why those conspicuous future tenses in the last two lines? It seems that the erudite Calli-

---

[7] 'A line any lampoonist would be glad to leave in his reader's mind' (Wiseman 1969, 29 – but the supposed corollary, that it was the last line of the whole collection, should be abandoned; I had not understood poem 116). Cf. Ross 1969, 103f – an echo from Ennius alluding to Mamurra's literary style?

[8] Cic. *TD* III 45 (45 B.C.): 'o poetam egregium! quamquam ab his cantoribus Euphorionis contemnitur.' For the *cantores Euphorionis* see Tuplin 1977.

[9] Cic. *orator* 161 (46 B.C.): 'quod iam subrusticum videtur . . . ea offensio quam nunc fugiunt poetae novi' (cf. also Quint. IX 4.83 and Endnote 3). The *first* line of Catullus' collection, 'lepidum *novum* hunc libellum', makes it clear where he stands; cf. Wiseman 1979, 156f and 169 (q.v. for earlier bibliography).

[10] Macleod 1973, esp. 304f on 'Callimachean' terms (for *laborem* cf. 1.7), 307 on uncouth archaisms as 'harshness designed to convey strong feeling', 308f on the poem as an 'inverted dedication'. Németh 1977, 28–30: Cat. 36.5, 40.2, Appendix no. 52; cf. Cic. *Cat.* I 15, *div. Caec.* 14, *de or.* II 316, *orator* 228.

macheanism is being put behind him ('now I see it was wasted labour'), and the aggressive invective is to be the *next* stage.[11] Here we must remember the *Aetia* again. At the end of that work Callimachus too had dropped into the future tense:

αὐτὰρ ἐγὼ Μουσέων πεζὸν ἔπειμι νομόν.

As for me, I shall pass on to the Muses' prosaic pasture.

It looks as if Catullus, like Callimachus, was announcing a change of genre.

At first sight, the parallel seems to work exactly, since it is generally supposed that Callimachus' phrase referred to his *Iambics*. But Catullus has already given us iambics in the Callimachean style (especially scazons in the manner of Hipponax)[12] in the collection to which he is now saying farewell. They were as finely polished as the rest of his poems, so Catullus can hardly be announcing *that* genre with the breaking of 'Callimachean' artistic norms which lines 3 and 8 so conspicuously represent. What other vehicle for personal attack was there, which differed from those Catullus had already used in admitting a style that was the opposite of polished, artistic and finely wrought? There is, I think, only one answer, and it is a surprising one.

Look again at the six consecutive spondees of line 3; in an elegiac poem they must be read as a dactylic hexameter without the defining fifth-foot dactyl. But in a different context they could be read as an iambic senarius without the defining sixth-foot iamb. Either way the line is defective; but its particular type of defectiveness allows Catullus to hint, in elegiacs, at a forthcoming genre which uses iambic senarii (and which admits the colloquial elided *s*). It must be a theatrical genre.[13]

It is generally thought that the Roman stage did not permit

---

[11] *Contra* (adversative) marks the change from past to future. (I owe this point, and others on poem 116, to David West.)

[12] Call. *Iamb.* 1.1, announcing himself as Hipponax (whose metre he uses in the first five poems).

[13] *Dare supplicium* is a phrase common in comedy (e.g. Plaut. *Asin.* 481f, *Miles* 502–11), and was probably equally common in mime (e.g. Publilius 601R = 660 Duff); for what it referred to, see pp. 6f above.

personal attacks of the kind Aristophanes and the Athenian Old
Comedy poets allowed themselves. But the main evidence for
that view is a passage in Cicero's *de re publica* with a dramatic date
of 129 B.C. – and even there Scipio is referring back to the
customs of the men of old.[14] The Naevius case (p. 132 above)
shows why such attacks were dangerous to playwrights who
were of comparatively humble station; but by the first century
B.C. men of equestrian and even senatorial rank were writing for
the stage.[15] Like Lucilius in his satirical genre, they would not be
afraid of attacking their equals by name if it suited them to do so.
We know that in the late Republic the *ludi scaenici* were an
important index of political feeling, not only because of the
applause or barracking that greeted individual senators as they
took their seats, but also because of the audience's reaction to
lines in the play which seemed to apply to topical issues.[16] Actors
certainly made the most of such lines,[17] and with the advent of
playwrights who were socially less vulnerable it was natural that
the plays themselves would be written with this topical and
political effect in mind.

The clearest evidence comes from the mimes of D. Laberius,
whose position in society was much the same as that of Catullus
himself – municipal origin, equestrian rank, relatives in business
in the provinces.[18] Laberius attacked an avaricious provincial
governor (name unfortunately not preserved in our fragments),
and named one play after C. Antius Restio, the author of a

14 Cic. *de rep.* IV 10–12 (*ap.* Aug. *CD* II 9, 13).
15 E.g. in tragedy, C. Caesar Strabo (Val. Max. III 7.11 for the ambiguities of social and
professional status) and the *eques* C. Titius (Cic. *Brut.* 167); in comedy, L. Sulla (Athen.
VI 261c, σατυρικαὶ κωμῳδίαι τῇ πατρίῳ φωνῇ); in both, Q. Cicero (Cic. *QF* II 16.3 on
Q. performing his own version of a Sophoclean satyr play, III 1.13, 4.4, 5.7 on his
tragedies, which Cicero says were good).
16 The *locus classicus* is Cic. *Sest.* 115–23; also *Att.* II 19.3, IV 15.6, XIV 2.1, 3.2, XVI 2.3, *Phil.*
I 36f.
17 Cic. *Att.* II 19.3 (Diphilus), *Sest.* 118, 120–2 (Aesopus), Suet. *Nero* 39.3 (Datus); cf.
Diod. Sic. XXXVII 12.1, ἀγανακτοῦντα.
18 Details in Nicolet 1974, 919–21, suggesting Puteoli (where he died) as Laberius' *origo*; I
prefer Lanuvium, on the strength of the Maecia tribe of a senatorial Laberius (Sherk
1969, 66), a Lanuvine local magistrate M. Laberius (*ILLRP* 263), and the theatrical
tradition attested by the playwright Luscius and the actor Roscius, both Lanuvine.

sumptuary law, whose son was now living a life of conspicuous extravagance.[19] He mocked Caesar's new aediles, and when the dictator made him lose status by performing in one of his own plays, repaid him with an open attack on the loss of Roman liberty.[20] Since these are the very themes that appear in Catullus' few overtly political invectives ('socer generque, perdidistis omnia'),[21] it would not be wholly surprising if the new and aggressive genre to which he turned in his feud with Gellius were to be Laberian mime.

The latest date assignable to any of the poems in Catullus' collection is August 54 B.C., for Calvus' prosecution of Vatinius.[22] Five or six months later, Cicero was writing to his friend C. Trebatius, a young lawyer serving with Caesar's staff in Gaul (and the previous year in Britain), suggesting that it was time to come back to Rome:[23]

Denique, si cito te rettuleris, sermo nullus erit; si diutius frustra afueris, non modo Laberium sed etiam sodalem nostrum Valerium pertimesco. Mira enim persona induci potest Britannici iurisconsulti.

Furthermore, if you come back soon, there won't be any talk; whereas if you are away for a long while to no purpose, I am afraid of Laberius, even of our friend Valerius. A Britannic counsellor would be a marvellous figure of fun!

A figure of fun on the stage, that is.[24] And which satirical playwrights might produce him? Laberius, of course, the accepted master of the art – but also 'our friend Valerius'. We know of a Catullus who wrote mimes – one of them was being

---

[19] Laberius fr. 38f Ribbeck = 51f Bonaria ('cum provincias dispoliavit columnas monolithas, labella . . .'); Gell. NA x 17.3 (fr. 72–9R = 90–7B), cf. Syme 1979, 563 = JRS 53 (1963) 59, who acutely refers to Cat. 44.11f. Cf. Hor. Sat. 1 10.5f on Laberius as a satirist comparable with Lucilius.

[20] Gell. NA xvi 7.12 (fr. 63–4R = 79–80B), from the Necyomantia; Cicero called Caesar's Senate a νέκυια (Att. ix 10.7, 11.2, 18.2). Macr. Sat. ii 7.2–5, Sen. de ira ii 11.3 (frr. 98–130R = 139–72B).

[21] Cat. 29, cf. p. 105 above for his attitude to Mamurra's plunder and extravagance.

[22] Cat. 53, Cic. QF ii 16.3; E. S. Gruen, HSCP 71 (1966) 217–21.

[23] Cic. fam. vii 11.3 (Shackleton Bailey's translation); Reynolds 1943, 38, q.v. for the question of stage invective in general.

[24] For inducere, cf. Hor. Sat. 1 2.20–2 etc.

shown the day the emperor Gaius was murdered[25] – and Shackleton Bailey has very plausibly suggested that he might be identical with the Valerius mentioned by Cicero. 'But the theory that he was the poet C. Valerius Catullus can hardly be taken seriously.'[26] Why not? If we have read poem 116 right, it is exactly what we should expect.

2. EXTERNAL EVIDENCE

It is tantalising to reflect that an ancient biography of Catullus may have survived as late as the fifteenth century. In March 1460, Giovanni Pontano completed his copy of a codex containing Tacitus' *Germania* and *dialogus* and the *de grammaticis et rhetoribus* of Suetonius. The latter work was headed *de viris illustribus*, the title Suetonius gave to his whole collection of lives, of which the *de grammaticis et rhetoribus* formed only a part. Commenting on this, Pontano alleged that the codex had once contained also the *de poetis* and *de oratoribus*, but that these had been detached. Going to Padua in search of them, he was told that they had been acquired and then burnt by the Paduan humanist Sicco Polentonus, himself the author of an eighteen-volume work on famous Latin authors (the implication being, presumably, that Sicco had plagiarised the Suetonius for his own book and then destroyed the evidence).

Since Sicco's work shows no sign at all of any otherwise unknown source of information on Latin poets and orators, the accusation was evidently a slander. But it does not therefore follow that the whole story is untrue. The codex had been brought from Germany only very recently (by Enoch of Ascoli on behalf of Pope Nicolas V), so Pontano was well placed to know whether or not it had once contained more than it did

---

[25] Suet. *Gaius* 57.4, Jos. *AJ* XIX 94; cf. Mart. *spect.* 7.3f, Juv. VIII 187, Tert. *Adv. Val.* 14 (Appendix nos. 97–9).

[26] Shackleton Bailey 1977a, I 338 and *Two Studies in Roman Nomenclature* (American Classical Studies 3, New York 1976) 71. W. S. Watt (*Hermes* 83 (1955) 498) had already suggested that 'Catullus the mimographer' might be late-Republican, but discounted the identification with Cicero's Valerius.

when he saw it; the fact that he thought it worth while trying to track down the missing part is itself evidence to be taken seriously. Sicco evidently wasn't guilty, but someone else may have been. In which case Suetonius' life of Catullus was lost between 1455 and 1460.[27]

Versions of the Terence, Horace and Lucan biographies survive independently; otherwise, the only fragments of Suetonius' *Lives of the Poets* that we have are the notes St Jerome added to his translation of Eusebius' *Chronicle*.[28] There are two items on Catullus: under the year 87 B.C., 'Gaius Valerius Catullus, lyric writer, born at Verona'; and under 58 B.C., 'death of Catullus at Rome in his 30th year'.[29] The dates are self-consistent but demonstrably wrong, since several Catullan poems are internally dateable to 55 B.C. or later.[30] To judge by the surviving life of Terence, it is quite possible that Suetonius gave Catullus' age when he died, but not the dates of either birth or death; in that case, Jerome will probably have put the death notice at what seemed to him an appropriate place, and counted back for the date of birth.[31]

[27] Leiden Periz. Q21, f. 47v: text, photograph and discussion in B. L. Ullman, *Italia medioevale e umanistica* 2 (1959) 309–11. Sicco Polentonus' book *Scriptorum illustrium Latinae linguae libri XVIII* was edited by Ullman in 1928 (Papers and Monographs of the American Academy in Rome 6); Catullus is at p. 63. It is disputed whether Pontano's codex was the Hersfeldensis, brought to Rome in 1455: cf. D. Schaps, *CP* 74 (1979) 31f, with bibliography cited there, and M. Winterbottom in L. D. Reynolds (ed.), *Texts and Transmission* (Oxford 1983) 405 and 410 n.5. Pontano's account implies that the Suetonius became available (in its truncated state?) shortly after the death of Bartolomeo Fazio in November 1457 (cf. Ullman pp. 322f).

[28] Jer. *Chron.* 6–7H: 'admixta sunt plurima, quae de Tranquillo et ceteris inlustribus historicis curiosissime excerpsi.'

[29] Jer. *Chron.* 150H, 154H (Appendix nos. 11–12). One group of MSS puts the items under 88 and 57 B.C. respectively (Helm 1929, 37f).

[30] 11.10–12, 29.11f, 45.22, 55.6, 113.2. Cf. n.22 above for 53.2f (54 B.C.?).

[31] For Suetonius and dates of birth and death, see E. Paratore, *Una nuova ricostruzione del 'de poetis' di Suetonio* (Rome 1946) 27–30; for Jerome's placing of undated items, see F. Ritschl, *Parerga zu Plautus und Terenz* I (Leipzig 1845) 623–8. Cf. Helm 1929, 38f (following B. Schmidt, *Rh. Mus.* 69 (1914) 269) for the suggestion that Suetonius' notice of Catullus' death immediately followed that of his reconciliation with Caesar in Gaul (Suet. *Jul.* 73), and that Jerome therefore chose the first year of Caesar's Gallic command as the peg on which to hang Catullus' dates. The reconciliation took place in the winter of 55–54, 54–53 or 53–52 B.C. (Wiseman 1969, 36).

The modern consensus, that Catullus' dates were 'probably' 84–54 B.C., is based on the following premisses: that Suetonius dated his birth to the fourth consulship of L. Cinna (84 B.C.) and Jerome misread it as the first (87 B.C.); that by 'in his thirtieth year' Suetonius meant 'at the age of thirty'; and that Catullus died before publishing his collected poems, so the latest dateable poems in the collection belong in the last year of his life.[32] It seems to me that none of these assumptions is at all likely, and that a theory dependent on a combination of them is not worth very much. Accepting the age at death as accurate, we should be prepared to admit 82–53, 81–52, 80–51, or even a later thirty-year span, as the dates of Catullus' life.[33]

Unfortunately, casual acceptance of the *communis opinio* has diverted attention away from an important source of information, the quotations from and references to Catullus which are preserved in other authors.[34] If Catullus did *not* die pen in hand, but lived to publish his three-volume collection and then went on to a new literary career, writing for the stage, then we might expect to find, in what later authors say of him, some indication, and perhaps even some fragments, of his later work. And that is exactly what we have.

Listed in the Appendix are 109 passages where Catullus is mentioned, more than half of which include quotations from his work. Out of that total, 78 evidently refer to the collection that has come down to us – 56 to the first volume (poems 1–60),[35] 11 to

---

[32] Another premiss, usually unadmitted, is the identification of 'Lesbia' as Clodia Metelli: the later the dates of birth and death, the greater the age difference between them.

[33] Ovid (Appendix no. 14) implies that he died young, which encourages belief in the age at death reported by Jerome; and Nepos (Appendix no. 1) provides a formal but not very helpful *terminus ante quem* of 32 B.C. See now Granarolo 1982, 19–30, who goes against current convention and proposes 82–52 as Catullus' dates.

[34] See the Appendix, the first list (to the best of my knowledge) since Schwabe 1886, vii–xvi. Goold (1983, 240) even goes so far as to say 'there is not the slightest probability that any of these pieces [i.e. 'poems 18–20' in Muretus' edition, which include the Priapean fragment, Appendix nos. 89–91] or any of the other fragments occasionally attributed by editors to Catullus is authentic'.

[35] Appendix nos. 13–31, 48–81, 83, 105, 108. I include no. 52 not only as a *testimonium* for iambic invectives, but also because the hendecasyllable quoted may have been lost from our collection by textual corruption (cf. no. 44); see above, pp. 138 n. 35 and 156 n. 93 for corruptions in the archetype.

the second (poems 61–64),[36] and 11 to the third (poems
65–116).[37] But there is also an irreducible minimum of 17 which
evidently refer to works that have *not* come down to us.[38]

Seven of these (Appendix nos. 93–9) are references to 'Catullus
the mimographer', author of the mimes *Phasma* and *Laureolus*,
who has always been regarded as a character quite separate from,
and later than, Catullus the love poet.[39] But as Shackleton Bailey
points out, the fact that his plays happen not to be mentioned in
any context earlier than the death of Caligula (A.D. 41) does not
necessarily mean that they were not written earlier than that; and
since Cicero refers to a Valerius who wrote mimes, he could well
be late-Republican.[40] Moreover, it is striking that no author
bothers to distinguish between Catullus the mimographer and
Catullus the love poet;[41] Martial in particular refers to both
without distinction, and the one author who does specify that
'this Catullus was a mimographer' is the wretched scholiast on
Juvenal, who was demonstrably unaware of Catullus the love
poet in any case.[42] The simplest hypothesis is that they were
identical. It is quite credible *a priori* that the author of poem 10 and
poem 55 wrote lively dramatic sketches;[43] it is consistent with

---

[36] Appendix nos. 42–6, 82, 84–8. I take it that nos. 86 and 88 are textually corrupt
references to Catullus' Galliambics in poem 63.

[37] Appendix nos. 32–41, 104.

[38] Appendix nos. 89–103, 107, 109. I assume that no. 47 is a misattributed quotation from
Cinna, and omit no. 106 because of the possibility that Servius was thinking of poem
63 and the Galli.

[39] See M. Bonaria, *Romani mimi* (PLR VI.2, Rome 1965) 80, 133–5; ibid. 79, 132f for the
Phormio of 'Valerius' (Prisc. VI 7, 73).

[40] See n. 26 above, and Appendix no. 64 ('Asinius in Valerium . . . idem Catullus') for
the use of the *nomen gentilicium*. (Cf. also p. 260 no. i, Schwabe's reading.)

[41] I thought at one time (*CR* 29 (1979) 180, reviewing Shackleton Bailey) that the use of
'Catullus *Veronensis*' by some authors might count as a distinguishing device; but it
seems to be random (Appendix nos. 47, 53, 70, 71, 78, 80).

[42] Appendix no. 96 (merely an inference from the text of Juvenal). Cf. the scholiast's
comment on Juv. VI 7f ('nec tibi, cuius | turbavit nitidos extinctus passer ocellos'):
'matrona quaedam passerem plangens caeca facta est'!

[43] See Kroll 1923, 20 for the influence of mime on poem 10, and Lyne 1980, 42–52 on the
'dramatic' nature of Catullus' short poems in general. The end of poem 22 is a *sententia*
worthy of Publilius Syrus; it is taken from Aesop, but cf. Giancotti 1967, 323f and 413
on the common ground of mime and fable.

poem 116, as interpreted above; and above all, it helps to make sense of some of the remaining unattributed fragments.

Early in the 28th book of his *Natural History*, the elder Pliny addresses himself to the question whether words and incantations have any power.[44] After discussing prayers and ritual formulae, he gets on to bewitchment and spells: everyone, he says, is frightened of them, just as everyone breaks the shells after eating eggs or snails. 'Hence the erotic imitation of spells in Theocritus among the Greeks, in Catullus and most recently in Virgil among the Romans.'[45] Theocritus' second poem (*Pharmakeutria*) was a dramatic monologue in which a girl used magic and spells to try to restore her lover to her; Alphesiboeus' song in Virgil's eighth *Eclogue* was a similar scene, based on Theocritus but differing in details; Catullus' poem is lost, but was evidently closer to the Theocritean original than Virgil's if Ellis was right in identifying the fragments.[46]

We happen to know that one of the characters in the *Pharmakeutria* was borrowed from a mime by Sophron, and Virgil's *Eclogues*, as we saw in chapter IV, were performed in the theatre by Cytheris the mime-actress. Were all three poems written in some sense for the stage? Virgil's more complex piece was a sophisticated extension of the genre – a performance within a performance, for Alphesiboeus is a sort of rustic mime, here impersonating a lovesick woman.[47] The *Pharmakeutria*, whether in Theocritus' Greek or Catullus' Latin, would be more straightforward, providing a splendid vehicle for melodramatic soliloquy.

[44] Pliny *NH* xxviii 10, 'polleantne aliquid verba et incantamenta carminum?'; sections 10–21 deal with this, 22–9 with superstitions, 30ff with witchcraft and the evil eye (p. 140 above).
[45] Ibid. 19 (Appendix no. 100), cf. 10 for the secret fears even of sceptics.
[46] Ellis 1878, 356f, on Charisius *GL* I 87K (Tibullus?) and Serv. *Aen.* vii 378 (Appendix nos. 100, 107): cf. Theocr. 2.140 and 2.17 etc. (ἴυγξ).
[47] Schol. Theocr. 269f Wendel; for Sophron mimes involving magic, cf. Athen. xi 480b, *Select Literary Papyri* (ed. Page) 328–31; Serv. *ecl.* 6.11, see above, p. 128 and n.121; cf. Cairns 1984, 150 on Theocritus and Sophron writing for performance. Virg. *ecl.* 5.73, 'saltantes satyros imitabitur Alphesiboeus'; cf. Hor. *ep.* II 2.124f, Athen. vi 261c (n.15 above) on Roman 'satyric comedy'.

Then there are the lines cited by the grammarians to illustrate the Priapean metre (Appendix nos. 89–91). They are from a hymn or prayer to Priapus, dedicating to him a grove at his native city of Lampsacus on the Hellespontine coast. From what sort of work are they taken? Nonius Marcellus tells us, in the item in his dictionary on *ligurrire*, to lick or taste, where he cites 'Catullus in *Priapus*'. That looks like the name of a play, and the phrase *de meo*, which occurs in the quotation, is an idiom common in comedy. In fact, we know of an Athenian comedy called *Priapus*, and the god appeared in the prologue of a *fabula togata* by Afranius.[48] Not surprisingly, Priapus often featured in mimes (as did other gods), and the hymn in appropriately Priapean metre could be a *canticum* to be sung on stage.[49]

Ovid, whose material had much in common with contemporary mime, has two versions in the *Fasti* of a story of Priapus' frustration (the victim of his attempt at rape is woken by a braying ass) which might well come from such a source.[50] Indeed, since they serve as *aitia* for the sacrifice of asses to Priapus at Lampsacus in particular, the parallel with the Catullan fragments is significantly close.

It is reasonable to suppose, then, that Catullus the author of *Pharmakeutria* and *Priapus* is identical with Catullus the author of *Laureolus* and *Phasma*, and with Valerius the author of *Phormio*.[51] And it seems that he was not only a practitioner but a theorist as well. A learned commentator on Lucan tells us that he had come

---

[48] Non. 195L (Appendix no. 92); Ellis 1889, 504. Athen. XI 473f (Xenarchus, Middle Comedy); Macr. *Sat.* VI 5.6; also the title of a poem by Sotades (Suda *s.v.*). However, Herter (1932, 53f, cf. 28) does not accept the MS reading here, assuming instead that Catullus wrote a series of *Priapea*.

[49] Aug. *CD* VI 7 (Priapus); Arn. *adv. nat.* IV 35, VII 33, Tert. *Apol.* 15 (gods in general). For *cantica* in mime, see Petr. *Sat.* 35.6; song is implied also by Macr. *Sat.* III 14.7 (quoting Scipio Aemilianus), Plut. *Sulla* 2.3 (μιμῳδοί), Hor. *Sat.* I 2.1–3 (with Porph. *ad loc.*), Jer. *Chron.* 165H (Suetonius on Pylades).

[50] Ovid *Fasti* I 391–440 (Lotis), VI 319–48 (Vesta); see Herter 1932, 81f and McKeown 1979, esp. 76. Lampsacus: VI 345, cf. I 440. See Herter 1932, 88 on Priapus' pursuit of Flora and Pomona (Mart. X 92.11f, Ovid *Met.* XIV 640); that would be a theme very suitable for the Floralia.

[51] See n.39 above.

across a book by Catullus evidently entitled 'An Essay on Mimes';[52] the Greek title is entirely appropriate for the discussion by a bi-cultural Roman of a genre that was always associated with the Hellenistic world.[53] In it he offered a rationalised version of the Atreus legend: the story that the sun refused to look on the banquet of Thyestes really referred to an eclipse, and the succession of Thyestes by Atreus was really because the latter won over the citizens by explaining the astronomical facts to them.

It is not immediately clear what that had to do with mimes (my guess is that Catullus was extending the idea of mimic 'imitation of reality' to include supposedly historical events),[54] but it offers a possible context for an otherwise mysterious Catullan quotation in Varro. Suggesting a derivation of *nox* (night) from *nocere* (to harm), Varro cites Catullus as saying 'Unless the sun appears, everything will be stiff with frost.'[55]

Scaliger in 1564 boldly attributed this to the tragedian Pacuvius, attaching it to a quotation from his *Antiopa* preserved by Varro and Festus; and that is where it will be found to this day, in the standard works of Diehl, Warmington and Klotz.[56] But though the context is plausible, the combination is not convincing. It requires substantial emendation, to get the Catullus

---

[52] Appendix no. 101, accepting Ussani's reading 'qui inscribitur περὶ μίμων λογάριον'; Müller's περὶ μιμολογιῶν is also possible.

[53] See pp. 34f above on the *Graeca scaena*. Cf. Charisius I 189 Keil (Varro's περὶ χαρακτήρων), Suet. *gramm.* 9.2 (L. Orbilius' περὶ ἄλγεος?); also L. Accius' *Pragmatika*, Q. Valerius' *Epoptides*, L. Cincius' *Mystagogika*, M. Tiro's *Pandektai*, Cornelius Balbus' *Exegetika* (Funaioli 1907, 27, 77, 375, 401, 541); and of course Cornelius Nepos' *Chronika* (n.61 below).

[54] The scholiast's conclusion ('later tragedians turned it into a prodigy') may have been Catullus' point, that tragedy did not deal with 'real' events. On the other hand, the idea of Atreus as an astronomer probably went back to Sophocles and Euripides: Schol. Arat. 28f Maass (Soph. fr. 672N, Eur. fr. 861N).

[55] Varro *LL* VI 6 (Appendix no. 103).

[56] E. Diehl, *Poetarum Romanorum veterum reliquiae* (1911) 50; E. H. Warmington, *Remains of Old Latin* II (1936) 170f; A. Klotz, *Scaenicorum Romanorum fragmenta* I (1953) 114f. Varro *RR* I 2.5, 'verum est illud Pacuvi sol si perpetuum sit aut nox, flammeo vapore aut frigore fructos omnis interire'; Fest. 482L, 'ut est apud Pacuvium in Antiopa, "flammeo vapore torrens terrae fetum exusserit"'.

quotation into the required trochaic metre; it offers no explanation why Varro, or a later scribe, should turn Pacuvius into Catullus at this point but cite him correctly six lines below; and it does not even provide an effective reconstruction of Pacuvius' supposed text (the change of subject ruins the antithesis). The only reason to doubt Varro's attribution of the quotation is the unexamined dogma that Catullus didn't write prose (or drama, if one wants to emend it into verse). Baehrens insisted that Catullus did write prose, on the strength of a quotation in Servius about the poor quality of Raetic wine;[57] subsequent scholars have not been prepared to follow him, but the evidence is clearly on his side. So why should Varro not be quoting Catullus in prose?

Though the suggestion must inevitably be tentative, I wonder whether the 'harmful night' might not be another part of Catullus' version of the Atreus story, explaining the crop failure that followed Thyestes' banishment as due to the eclipse cutting off the sunlight. (That was one of the effects of a later legendary eclipse, the one that supposedly marked the death of Caesar.)[58]

What is important about the rationalisation of Atreus and Thyestes, whether or not the quotation in Varro belongs to it, is that it reveals Catullus distinguishing *fabula* and *veritas* (so-called) in a way wholly characteristic of the hellenised intellectual world of the late Republic.[59] 'By eliminating the excessively fabulous one reduces it, by reasoning, to a natural meaning'; that formulation by Dicaearchus, who was read with enthusiasm by Atticus and Cicero, sums up the attitude of the

---

[57] Baehrens 1885, 613f; Serv. *Georg.* II 95 (Appendix no. 102), context unknown.

[58] Hyg. *Fab.* 88.5, 'sterilitas Mycenis frugum ac penuria oritur ob Atrei scelus'; cf. Plut. *Caes.* 69.4 (crop failure), Pliny *NH* II 98 ('longior solis defectus'), Virg. *Georg.* II 467f (fear of *aeterna nox*); Lucan (I 544) explicitly compares the Caesarian and Thyestean portents.

[59] Cf. Serv. *Aen.* I 568, Hyg. *Fab.* 258 ('sed veritatis hoc est'), corresponding to the scholiast's 'hoc fabulosum inveni'. See Varro *de vita p.R.* as quoted in Aug. *CD* XIII 12 and 16: *historica veritas* as against *vanitas fabularum*, *fabulosum mendacium* as against *historica attestatio*.

time towards ancient history.[60] And Catullus' observance of it places him in a recognisable literary context – one rather more heterogeneous than his single-minded love poetry might lead us to imagine, but entirely consistent with the known interests of his friends and contemporaries.

It was neither accident nor irony that made Catullus dedicate the first volume of his collected poems to the author of a historical work in a Greek genre, with a Greek title, and full of characteristically Greek learning;[61] besides that, Cornelius Nepos wrote biography, moralising essays, and even erotic poetry.[62] Catullus' dear friend Calvus had more talent than Nepos, but just as wide a range – a great orator, a learned theoretician, and a poet whose themes (epic, erotic, invective) closely parallel Catullus' own, he also wrote an essay 'On the Use of Cold Water' (Calvus was very fussy about his health).[63] Young Pollio, whose precocious gifts are celebrated in poem 12, became famous later as orator, tragedian, historian and critic of historians;[64] but already as a young man he was writing on grammatical subjects, one controversial work being even directed against Catullus himself.[65] Another friend, mentioned not in the poems but in a letter of Cicero's, was C. Trebatius the legal expert, who not only wrote on civil law but published at

[60] Dicaearchus *bios Hellados* fr. 49 Wehrli (cf. Cic. *Att.* II 2.2, 12.4, XIII 30.2): a classic example is Dion. Hal. I 39.1 and 41.1 on Herakles in Italy. See Walbank 1960, 225–8; Wiseman 1979, 49 and 158f (ibid. 143–66 on the intellectual background).

[61] Nepos' *Chronika*: after Apollodorus (*FGrH* 244), characterised by 'portentosa Graeciae mendacia' (Pliny *NH* v 4); examples, including a rationalised version of the reign of Saturn, in Wiseman 1979, 157f and 161f.

[62] Gell. *NA* xv 28.2 (*Life of Cicero*, in several books), XI 8.5 etc (*de viris illustribus*), VI 18.11 etc. (*exempla*); Pliny *ep.* v 3.6 on *versiculi severi parum*.

[63] Cic. *Brut.* 283 etc. (oratory), *fam.* xv 21.4 ('multae et reconditae litterae'), Tac. *dial.* 23 (*commentarii*), Charisius GL I 77K (*ad amicos*); poetic fragments in Morel *FPL* 84–7. *De aquae frigidae usu*: Mart. XIV 196, cf. Pliny *NH* XXXIV 166 on his use of lead plates as an antaphrodisiac.

[64] Hor. *Odes* II 1, Tac. *dial.* 21; Quint. X 1.113 etc. (oratory); Virg. *ecl.* 8.10, Hor. *Sat.* I 10.42f (tragedies); Sen. *suas.* 6.25, Val. Max. VII 13 ext.4 etc. (history); Suet. *gramm.* 10, Gell. *NA* x 26.1 (on Sallust), Quint. VIII 1.3 (on Livy), IX 3.13 (on Labienus).

[65] Funaioli 1907, 499f (frr. 5–11). *In Valerium*: Charis. 124B, GL I 97K (Appendix no. 64), on *pugillares/pugillaria*.

least ten volumes on religious terminology, and was 'well known among poets' as well.[66] Similarly wide-ranging literary interests can probably be inferred (though the evidence is less clear) for two other friends – Veranius and Cornificius – and also for an enemy, if Mamurra is rightly identified with Vitruvius the author of *de architectura*.[67]

Poet, playwright, learned essayist – one wonders what else Catullus might have turned his hand to in middle and old age, if he had lived on with Pollio, Trebatius and Vitruvius into the days of Augustus Caesar.

3. ATTIS AT THE MEGALESIA

No great writer was ever reconstructed out of fragmentary quotations alone. Inevitably, it is on the collected poems that Catullus' reputation rests. But the pursuit of the unknown Catullus will have a more than merely historical interest if we can read something back from it into the poems that survive.

In both love and hate, a certain continuity may be detected between the different parts of Catullus' *oeuvre*. For instance, we can guess why he chose to imitate Theocritus' *Pharmakeutria*, several passages of which seem already to have influenced his extant work; he took bewitchment seriously, and knew what it was to lose a lover.[68] As for Gellius, and the punishment Catullus threatened to inflict on him by moving into mime ('tu dabis supplicium'), perhaps the horror-comic plot of the *Laureolus* was composed with him in mind: a runaway slave becomes a bandit

---

[66] Cic. *fam.* VII 11.3 (p. 188 above), Porph. *Sat.* II 1.11. Funaioli 1907, 437f for the fragments of the *de religionibus* (Macr. *Sat.* III 3.5 for vol. x); Pomp. *Dig.* 12.2.45 and 47, Just. *Inst.* II 25 pref. on the legal works.

[67] Veranius: see Endnote 3. Cornificius: see Rawson 1978. Mamurra: Cat. 58.7 (*eruditulus*), 105 (poetry); P. Thielscher, *RE* IXA (1961) 420–2, 431–60 (*CIL* VIII 18913, X 6143, 6169, 6190f, *NS* 1908 391); *contra* R. E. A. Palmer, *Athenaeum* 61 (1983) 343–55. See now N. Purcell, *PBSR* 51 (1983) 155f on Vitruvius' career.

[68] See p. 140 above on poems 5 and 7. Possible influence: Cat. 34.15 / Theocr. 2.33–6 (Diana, Hecate, Trivia); 64.52ff / 2.45f (Theseus, Ariadne, Dia); 68b.71 / 2.104 (foot on threshold); 51.9–12 / 2.106–8 (though closer to the Sapphic original); and Attis at 63.64f is reminiscent of Delphis in Theocr. 2.51, 80, 125, 153.

chief, is captured and crucified; the play ends with him hurling himself down (from the cross?), vomiting blood in his death agony. The vicarious sadism is not too surprising when we look at some of Catullus' invective epigrams.[69]

Moreover, once the idea is accepted that Catullus might be writing for performance (in however broad a sense), some very familiar poems may perhaps be looked at in a new light. We have already seen that poem 34 may well be a real choral ode, composed to be sung at a festival of Delian Artemis (p. 99 above). There is another, and much longer, poem in the same metre – the wedding song for Manlius and Aurunculeia. Was that meant to be read in private from a papyrus *volumen*? or to be recited, for example at the wedding banquet, by a reader acting out the various stages of the *deductio* of the bride? Or is it what it purports to be, an actual choral ode to be sung simultaneously with, and as a part of, the ceremonies it describes? We must remember that wedding processions in the Roman aristocracy were a public performance, with stands for spectators set up along the route;[70] and that according to the conventions of the choric ode, as illuminated by recent work on Pindar, the apparent distinction in poem 61 between the girls' and boys' choirs and the 'narrator' who gives them their instructions is no hindrance at all to the idea that the whole work could be intended for choral performance.[71]

Perhaps we may go a step further. Poem 62 is certainly a choric poem; if 61 is as well, what about 63? It would certainly give Catullus' second volume a generic coherence if the poems it contains were three choral hymns (61–63) and a miniature epic

[69] Cf. poem 108, and p. 5 above. *Laureolus*: n.25 above, and Schmidt 1983 on 'proripiens se ruina'.

[70] Juv. VI 78, 'longa per angustos figamus pulpita vicos'.

[71] W. J. Slater, *CQ* 19 (1969) 89f, whence Cairns 1984, 139f: 'the so-called ἐγώ-figure . . . blends the personalities of the poet, the chorus and the *choregus* in such a way that any element can be dominant at any moment'. Cf. Cairns 1972, 192 and 1984, 151 for a brief identification of Cat. 61 as a choric ode, though without necessarily implying anything about performance in real life; for the latter question, see the important discussion of Propertius IV 6 in Cairns 1984, 149–51. I am very grateful for help on this matter from Francis Cairns and the members of the Liverpool Latin Seminar at a meeting in October 1982.

(64), combining two Callimachean forms in one book as the third volume combines elegy and epigram.

In fact, the *Attis* has precisely the form we might expect for a hymn – lengthy narrative followed by a short prayer at the end, just as in the 'Homeric' hymns – and the companions of Attis do describe themselves as a *chorus*.[72] Even more significant is the metre. It is not enough merely to say that 'the galliambic metre owed its name to its connection with the cult of Cybele'; our sources are explicit that it was the metre used for hymns *to* Cybele sung by her eunuch priests, the Galli.[73] So we are faced with three possibilities: first (if the poem is purely literary) that the reader or reciter of it takes on the *persona* of a Gallus hymning his goddess-mistress;[74] second (on the analogy of the hymn to Priapus) that it was meant for performance on stage by an actor representing a Gallus, or a number of actors representing a chorus of Galli;[75] third (on the tentative analogy of poem 61) that it presents not the imitation of a ritual but the ritual itself, a real hymn to be sung at a real festival.[76]

One apparently puzzling feature of the poem, the disappearance of Attis' companions after line 38, is more easily explicable if the poem was written for performance: the chorus could retire to the periphery and leave the 'centre stage' to the chorus leader (protagonist or archigallus), which would be obvious to an audience as it is not to a reader.[77]

But the main difficulty, and one which applies to all three

[72] 63.30, cf. 28 *thiasus* (Suda, θίασος ἱερὸς χορός); Kroll 1923, 140 on *Hymnenstil*.

[73] Hephaestion 12.3 (p. 39 Westphal), εἰς τὴν μητέρα τῶν θεῶν, with Choeroboscus' comment (ἀπὸ τοῦ τοὺς Γάλλους ... ὑμνεῖν τὴν Ῥέαν); Terentianus 2889–91 (*GL* VI 410K), imitating the speech of the Galli; Mart. II 86. 4f, dictated by Attis. Quotation from Fordyce 1961, 263.

[74] See Dion. Thrax *ars gramm.* 2, Don. *vita Verg.* 29 (pp. 124f above) for the importance of *hypocrisis*, impersonation.

[75] See p. 194 above for the hymn to Priapus (Appendix nos. 89–91). For Galli on stage, see Nonius 205L and Gell. *NA* VII 9.3 (Laberius' *Galli*), Suet. *Aug.* 68; Vermaseren 1977, 66 and plate 47 for the Attis drama pictured in the house of Pinarius Cerealis at Pompeii.

[76] See Vermaseren 1977, 86 on the *hymnologi* of Cybele and Attis: late and syncretistic examples in Hippolytus *Refut.* V 4 (note the theatrical context) and Julian *Or.* 5.

[77] Bongi 1944, 33 and 49 rightly compares the *comites* to the κωφὰ πρόσωπα of tragic drama.

varieties of the 'hymn' hypothesis, is much more fundamental. Whether in the form of literary imitation, dramatic representation or script for ritual performance, surely this terrible and tragic drama of madness and vain repentance cannot be a hymn to Cybele by the priests of Cybele? The goddess' power is indeed acknowledged; but it is merciless, and Attis' self-castration in her honour – the very *aition* of her priesthood – is presented as an act of insane delusion, the denial of freedom, civilisation and even humanity.[78] So the form and metre show that it must be a hymn, the content suggests that it cannot be. Is there an escape from the dilemma? I think there is; and it must be sought in the realities of Catullus' world, the place of the Great Mother and her retinue in the society and rituals of late-Republican Rome.

The Great Idaean Mother of the Gods, best known by one of her many names, Cybele, was brought to Rome from Phrygia in solemn state in 204 B.C.; a temple was built for her in the precinct of Victory on the Palatine, immediately above the Lupercal and the Clivus Victoriae, and dedicated on 10 April 191; thereafter the Megalesia, or *ludi Megalenses*, were held annually in her honour, with stage performances for six days (4–9 April) and chariot-racing or beast-hunts in the Circus on the anniversary day itself.[79] The Megalesia were celebrated with traditional Roman decorum,[80] as was appropriate for a divinity who had been domesticated in the very heart of the city, and even associated with its foundation legend.[81] But the Megalesia were part of

---

[78] See Sandy 1968 on the beast-imagery of poem 63.

[79] Livy XXIX 10.4–11.8, 14.5–14, XXXIV 54.3, XXXVI 36.3–4, *Inscr. It.* XIII 2.435–8; Fasce 1978, 12–19, Scullard 1981, 97–100. For the topography, see *AJ* 61 (1981) 35–52, esp. 46f; for the *ludi scaenici*, Wiseman 1974, 159–69 on Cic. *har. resp.* 22–6 (for the two theatres, add Plut. *Cato min.* 46.4).

[80] Cic. *har. resp.* 24, 'more institutisque maxime casti, sollemnes, religiosi'; Gell. *NA* II 24.2, Cic. *de sen.* 45 (old-fashioned frugality of *sodalitates*).

[81] The mother of Romulus became *Rhea* Silvia (Castor of Rhodes *FGrH* 250F5, Varro *LL* v 144; Rosenberg, *RE* IA (1920) 343); and the hut used by the Galli was probably identified as that of Romulus, Remus or Faustulus (Philodemus 26.3 G–P, Jos. *AJ* XIX 75 and 90; cf. Plut. *Rom.* 20.5f, Prop. IV 1.9, Solinus 1.18, with *LCM* 5.10 (Dec. 1980) 231–8 and *CQ* 32 (1982) 475f). See Fasce 1978, 14 n.22: the temple on the Palatine

the Roman state cult, and represented only a very expurgated version of the Great Mother's worship.

Many foreign religious practices were deliberately excluded by the Romans from their public ceremonies:[82]

One will see among them, even though their manners are now corrupted, no ecstatic transports, no Corybantic frenzies, no begging under the colour of religion, no bacchanals or secret mysteries, no all-night vigils of men and women together in the temples, nor any other mummery of this kind . . .

Dionysius, who offers us this list, goes on to cite the worship of 'the Phrygian goddess' as an example: the magistrates' public games in her honour were according to Roman custom, and participation in her native Phrygian rites was forbidden to Roman citizens. He also points out that the Romans did not admit 'unseemly myths' about the gods, and since the castration of Uranus is one of his examples, we may reasonably infer that the castration of Attis was equally unacceptable.[83]

In fact, Attis was central to the Great Mother's worship in precisely those aspects which were excluded from the Roman public cult – in particular, 'bacchanals and secret mysteries'. Who or what Attis was, was itself a mystery, revealed only to initiates in rites which had much in common with those of Dionysus.[84] A sentence from the liturgy happens to survive: 'I have eaten from the tambourine; I have drunk from the cymbal; I have become an initiate of Attis.'[85] Tambourine and cymbal were borne by the emasculated Galli, for whose condition Attis provided the legendary explanation and example. Only on certain specified days were the Galli allowed to process through the streets of Rome to their raucous music ('Corybantic frenzies, begging

implies that the Great Mother was considered as in some sense a national deity,
presumably because of the Trojan connection.
[82] Dion. Hal. II 19.2 (trans. E. Cary, after Spelman's 1758 version).
[83] Dion. Hal. II 19.3–5; 18.3–19.1.
[84] Identity ἀπόρρητον: Paus. VII 17.5, Jul. Or. 5.159A. Dionysiac syncretism: Eur.
Bacch. 55–61, 120–34, Dem. cor. 260 (ὑῆς Ἄττης) etc.; Vermaseren 1977, 118f.
[85] Firm. Mat. de err. 18.1, cf. Clem. Alex. protr. II 15; Vermaseren 1977, 116f.

under the colour of religion'), brandishing as they went the knives that symbolised the act of Attis and put them beyond the pale of Roman citizenship.[86]

But Rome was a very cosmopolitan place, and the austere standards of official religion did not inhibit the Great Mother's devotees from practising the Phrygian rites in a private capacity. Excavation of Cybele's temple on the Palatine revealed that right from the beginning, in the early second century B.C., her worshippers were dedicating votive statuettes of Attis, unmistakable in his Phrygian cap and effeminately plump physique.[87] As for the Galli, they no doubt found in the increasingly hellenised Roman élite the same uneasy mixture of contemptuous acceptance and eccentric privilege that applied to them in the Hellenistic world. In a recently discovered fragment of a Greek 'novel' – in prose and verse, like the *Satyricon* – a lover hopes to gain admission to his lady's house by posing as a Gallus; he will learn the necessary mysteries from a friend, who is about to be initiated. Evidently the Galli were an accepted part of Hellenistic society, enjoying in particular free access to the private quarters of women of fashion. We know from Catullus that at Rome in his time such women were interested in foreign cults; no doubt they too would enjoy the company of a Gallus, perhaps all the more so if their husbands disapproved.[88]

Two judgements from widely contrasting viewpoints give an idea of the range of attitudes to the Galli in late-Republican Rome. The first comes from Mamercus Aemilius Lepidus, a patrician, a conservative, and a man of weight and authority in

---

[86] Lucr. II 618–21, Cic. *de leg.* II 22, 40; of the other un-Roman features mentioned by Dionysius, 'all-night vigils' and 'ecstatic transports' are attested by Thyillus (for whom see Wiseman 1974, 145f) *Anth. Pal.* VII 223. Fasce (1978, 95–9, cf. 21, 25, 83f) argues convincingly that the more orgiastic rites of 15–27 March, which were accepted into the Roman religious calendar in the time of Claudius, were what the faithful had continuously practised in honour of Attis without the approval of the Roman state.

[87] P. Romanelli, *Hommages à Jean Bayet* (Coll. Latomus 70, 1964) 619–26 = *In Africa e a Roma, scripta minora selecta* (Rome 1981) 737–46. Romanelli's dating of the material (619f = 737f) is corrected by F. Coarelli, *PBSR* 45 (1977) 10–13.

[88] *Ox. Pap.* XLII 3010; Cat. 10.26 (Serapis); cf. Mart. III 81 (a Gallus as *cunnilingus*).

the state.[89] As consul in 77 he reversed, on appeal, the judgement of the urban praetor that a certain Genucius, a Gallus, could legally inherit as the heir of a Roman citizen; Genucius, he said, having voluntarily amputated his genitals, could be considered as neither man nor woman. Valerius Maximus, always a supporter of old-fashioned morality, reports the judgement with enthusiasm:[90]

A decision worthy of Mamercus, worthy of the leader of the Senate, which prevented the tribunals of the magistrates from being polluted by Genucius' obscene presence and contaminated voice . . .

The second comes from Philodemus of Gadara, poet, critic and philosopher, the archetypal *Graeculus* in the eyes of Cicero's senatorial audience.[91] He wrote an epitaph for Trygonion ('Little Dove'), leading light of the club-house on the Palatine where the Galli met to enjoy their gossip:[92]

. . . who alone among the effeminates adored the Cyprian's rites and took to the seductions of a Lais. Holy earth, put forth against this orgy-lover's headstone not brambles but the delicate buds of white-violets.

Between these extremes of stern contempt and tolerant affection, the view of a thoroughly hellenised Roman may be inferred from one of the Menippean satires of M. Terentius Varro, who was both a Roman senator like Mamercus and an intellectual in the Greek style like Philodemus.[93] The protagonist of his *Eumenides*, convinced that the whole world is mad, sets out to discover whether true sanity can be found in any religious or philosophi-

[89] Asc. 60C, 79C, with G. V. Sumner, *JRS* 54 (1964) 41–8; he was probably named as *princeps senatus* by the censors of 70–69.

[90] Val. Max. VII 7.5, 'obscaena Genucii praesentia inquinataque voce'.

[91] Cic. *Pis.* 68–71; see R. G. M. Nisbet, *Cicero in L. Calpurnium Pisonem oratio* (Oxford 1961) 183–6, and G. M. A. Grube, *The Greek and Roman Critics* (London 1965) 193–206.

[92] Philodemus 26 G–P (*Anth. Pal.* VII 222), D. L. Page's translation; see *CQ* 32 (1982) 475f for the club-house (χαλύβη).

[93] Plut. *Rom.* 12.3, Βάρρωνα τὸν φιλόσοφον . . . ἄνδρα Ῥωμαίων ἐν ἱστορίᾳ βιβλιακώτατον; App. *BC* IV 47, Οὐάρρων . . . φιλόσοφός τε καὶ ἱστορίας συγγραφεύς; Cic. *Acad. Post.* I 9f, Quint. I 1.95, etc.

cal sect. Passing the temple of the Great Mother, he hears the sound of cymbals. He disguises himself in women's clothes to get in, and finds a ceremony in progress: the aedile is replacing on the goddess' statue the crown that has represented her godhead in the theatre during the Megalesia, while the Galli, in their characteristically delirious enthusiasm, chant their hymn to the goddess over and over again. He admires their youth and beauty, the naiad-like simplicity of their dresses, and the gorgeous apparel of the archigallus in his golden crown and his purple cope with the flashing jewels. Having listened to the galliambic hymn, he undergoes instruction from a hierophant, who begins by pointing out the moral excellence of the Galli. But their rejection of the sins of the flesh is achieved by self-castration, which is the essential feature of initiation into their mysteries. With a curse against such madness, he takes refuge on the altar. The Galli try to move him by chanting spells, and when that fails begin to pull him down by force. Somehow he escapes, and we next see him trying his luck with the mysteries of Serapis.[94]

So there was a double ambivalence about the cult of the Great Mother in Catullus' Rome: the bowdlerised public worship organised by the aediles at the Megalesia contrasted with what went on behind the scenes in the temple and its precinct, just as the exotic attraction of the Galli and their mysteries for unprejudiced philhellenes contrasted with the total rejection of all they stood for by Romans who clung to the austere standards of ancestral tradition. In Varro, the attraction is admitted but the Roman ethos prevails. What we know of Catullus' attitudes suggests that he would have taken the same view; in fact the prayer at the end of poem 63 is very like the imprecation of Varro's character against the madness of the Galli.[95]

In the light of these ambivalent late-Republican attitudes, I think we are a little nearer to understanding the form and purpose of poem 63. It would make sense to see it as indeed a

---

[94] Varro *Men*. 132–43 Cèbe (see Endnote 4 for text and translation); the reconstruction is inevitably tentative.

[95] Cèbe 1977, 654–8 on Cat. 63.92 and Varro *Men*. 133B = 142 Cèbe.

hymn, as its form and metre require, but a hymn for the Megalesia, where the Romanised ritual could accommodate its message. For the state cult, a hymn that celebrated the terrible power of the goddess herself and at the same time portrayed as tragic delusion the un-Roman excesses of her acolytes would be a very acceptable combination of religion and traditional morality. The great goddess is honoured, fanaticism and *furor* are deplored, the mystic god of the Galli is portrayed as a Greek youth afflicted with a madness he cannot control. The performers can hardly be real Galli, but they hymn Cybele as if they were; and at the end they speak in a sense for the Roman people:[96]

> Dea, magna dea, Cybebe, dea domina Dindymi,
> procul a mea tuus sit furor omnis, era, domo:
> alios age incitatos, alios age rabidos.

Goddess, great goddess, Cybele, goddess, lady of Dindymus, far from my house be all your fury, queen: others to that frenzy summon, others to that madness drive!

Was the hymn commissioned by an aedile, as Clodius in 56 tried to commission a play by Laberius?[97] It is quite possible: we know from poem 52 that Catullus took a great interest in the question of who was to sit in the aedile's chair of state. But if so, we may guess that he had his own reasons for accepting the commission (pp. 180–1 above). Like the *Laureolus* and *Pharmakeutria* later, the *Attis* brought to the stage a drama whose origins lay deep in its author's psychological experience.

4. FAREWELL CATULLUS

Catullus died young, probably in the late fifties B.C. at the age of twenty-nine. His work had made him famous, and he long remained so: his plays were still read after two hundred years, his

---

[96] Cat. 63.91–3; n.71 above for the 'choric *ego*'. For the contrast between the 'Roman' Megalesia and the rites of Attis, see Fasce 1978, esp. 12–15, 95–9.

[97] Macr. *Sat.* II 6.6 (p. 38 above).

love poems after five hundred.[98] But from the sixth century A.D. to the fourteenth, he was practically unknown. It was about 1305 that a manuscript of the collected poems was discovered – the lost *Veronensis*, from which all our knowledge of the collection ultimately derives.[99] The first printed edition appeared in Venice in 1472, prefaced by the following biographical sketch:[100]

Valerius Catullus, scriptor lyricus, Veronae nascitur olympiade CLXIII anno ante natum Sallustium Crispum diris Marii Syllaeque temporibus, quo die Plotinus Latinam rhetoricam primus Romae docere coepit. Amavit hic puellam primariam Clodiam, quam Lesbiam suo appellat in carmine. Lasciviusculus fuit et sua tempestate pares paucos in dicendo frenata oratione, superiorem habuit neminem. In iocis apprime lepidus, in seriis vero gravissimus extitit. Erotica scripsit et epithalamium in Manlium. Anno vero aetatis suae XXX Romae moritur elatus moerore publico.

Valerius Catullus, lyric writer, born in the 163rd Olympiad the year before the birth of Sallustius Crispus, in the dreadful times of Marius and Sulla, on the day Plotinus [*sic*] first began to teach Latin rhetoric at Rome. He loved Clodia, a girl of high rank, whom he calls Lesbia in his poetry. He was somewhat lascivious, and in his time had few equals, and no superior, in verse expression. He was particularly elegant in jests, but a man of great gravity on serious matters. He wrote erotic pieces, and a marriage-song to Manlius. He died at Rome in the thirtieth year of his age, with public mourning at his funeral.

It is clearly a compilation by a learned humanist, but where did the anonymous author get his information from? The first sentence consists of material straight out of Jerome, improved with a couple of flourishes by the author;[101] and no doubt the

---

[98] See the Appendix, nos. 11–12, 14 (age at death, pp. 190f above); 1, 4, 5, 13, 18 etc. (fame): 99 (plays still read); 24, 78 etc. (poems still read).

[99] Except for poem 62 (independently preserved in a ninth-century anthology) and the fragments collected in the Appendix. For the details, see Ullman 1960, Thomson 1978, 3–63 (esp. 9–12), and R. J. Tarrant in L. D. Reynolds (ed.), *Texts and Transmission* (Oxford 1983) 43–5.

[100] Ellis 1878, lxv–vi, Schwabe 1886, xxiii. The life appeared also in the Rome edition (*c.* 1475): Ellis 1878, lix–x, Mynors 1958, xi.

[101] Namely *diris temporibus* (cf. Juv. IV 80) and *quo die* (cf. Don. *vita Verg.* 6). Jer. *Chron.* 150–1H: the item before the notice of Catullus' birth is 'Plotius Gallus primus Romae

first half of the final sentence comes from the same source. Much of the rest may be inference from the poems, but we must remember that according to a contemporary scholar a manuscript of Suetonius' *de poetis* and *de oratoribus* had been in existence until only recently in nearby Padua; it is not inconceivable that some of the items he produces do come ultimately from an ancient source now lost to us.[102]

For instance, though the real name of 'Lesbia' is given by Apuleius, the phrase *puella primaria* is not Apuleian; nor does it sound like the author's own contribution, for the Ciceronian adjective is in conspicuous contrast with such non-classical usages as *lasciviusculus* and *frenata oratio*.[103] In the third sentence, the judgement on Catullus' poetic ability could have been imitated from those in the ancient *Lives* of Terence and Tibullus – or it could be genuine, reflecting Suetonius' interest in placing poets in order of merit.[104] Similarly, the last three words of the final sentence may be taken either as plausible imitation or as a sign of authenticity; for Suetonius was certainly interested in the funerals of his subjects, whether poets or statesmen.[105]

Our degree of belief in what this curious hotch-potch offers is inevitably conditioned by what we know, or think we know, about Catullus from more reliable sources. For instance, is it really credible that his funeral was marked by 'public mourning'?[106] Not if we believe that he was a coterie poet interested

---

Latinam rhetoricam docuit . . .', and the one after is 'Sallustius Crispus scriptor historicus in Sabinis Amiterni nascitur'.

[102] Cf. Baehrens 1885, 22 (footnote), suggesting a Suetonian excerpt like the *Life* of Tibullus. See pp. 189f above; none of the items adduced in the following paragraph appears in Sicco Polentonus' life of Catullus (n. 27 above).

[103] *Primarius*: a favourite adjective of Cicero's in the *Verrines*, where he uses it (II 24) of a patrician lady, Servilia. *Frenata oratio*: on the analogy of *oratio soluta*, prose (*TLL* IX.2 884.26–48), of which the opposite in classical idiom would be *vincta* (Cic. *orator* 64, Quint. IX 4.19 and 77).

[104] Cf. Velleius' judgement on Catullus (Appendix no. 5).

[105] Suet. *ap*. Jer. *Chron*. 148H (Lucilius), 157H (Ser. Sulpicius Rufus, P. Servilius Isauricus), Gell. *NA* xv 4.4 (P. Ventidius Bassus), on those who were *publico funere elati*.

[106] The phrase could be a garbled report of a *funus publicum* (not inconceivable, since Octavian's freedman tutor was so honoured only a decade or so later: Dio XLVIII 33.1),

only in pleasing a learned élite. But Catullus was more than that, as I hope the last three chapters have shown. The Roman populace had reason to feel affection for him, and sadness at his loss.

The popular impact of his shorter poems – particularly the ones at the beginning of the collection – is shown by the sincerest of compliments, imitation.[107] Twenty years later, Horace was irritated that the poems of Catullus and Calvus were on everyone's lips.[108] Calvus, of course, as an orator, was a well-known personality in any case; but perhaps Catullus too, with the plays he wrote for the great popular festivals, became something of a national figure for a year or two in that ill-documented period from 54 to 51 B.C.[109] I imagine that in Roman eyes his greatest virtue was to have mastered every refinement of the new Greek literary culture without compromising a moral standpoint that was reassuringly old-fashioned. As we have seen in the hymn to Diana, in the two epithalamia, in the Sappho ode, and above all in his greatest work, the *Attis*, Catullus used his Hellenistic learning to express traditional Roman values in Greek generic forms.[110] *In iocis lepidus, in seriis gravissimus* is not a bad description of his work.

The learned humanist's summary is a credible one, though whether it was good sources or good guessing that led him to it we shall probably never know. At any rate, there is a finite chance that the item on the funeral is authentic, and that Catullus was indeed borne to his tomb amid the mourning of his fellow-

but more probably refers to spontaneous grief, as at the funeral of Atticus (Nep. *Att.* 22.4).

107 E.g. *CIL* XIII 488.4, XIV 3565.11, 14, 49 (poems 3, 42, 2b), *Priapea* 52.12 (poem 5), 64.1 (poem 25), *Catalepton* 6 (poem 29), 10 (poem 4); cf. Appendix nos. 20, 28 (poems 5 and 7), 25–30 (poems 2 and 3).

108 Hor. *Sat.* I 10.18f (Appendix nos. 2–3), cf. 72–91 for Hermogenes and Demetrius representing popular taste.

109 Ill-documented: no letters from Cicero to Quintus or Atticus between December 54 and May 51; the *ad fam.* collection adds about 20 letters for that period, of which only those to Trebatius and Curio are of more than private interest.

110 See above, pp. 98f (34.22–4), 112f (61.61–75, 204–23), 111 (62.59–65), 122 (64.384–408). 155 (51.13–16), 206 (63.91–3).

citizens. There will certainly have been a funeral oration, at the tomb if not in the Forum.[111] Was it his friend Licinius Calvus who spoke the last farewell to the young man from the Transpadana?

[111] Suet. *Jul.* 6.1 (*pro rostris* for a public funeral, n.106 above); W. Kierdorf, *Laudatio Funebris* (Beiträge zur klassischen Philologie 106, Meisenheim am Glan 1980), 111–21.

CHAPTER VII

THE AFTERLIFE OF LESBIA

It's strange to think of Catullus as having my feelings
without my background. He'd hardly read anything,
not a line of the Romantic poets or Shakespeare,

didn't even know English, which is almost a prerequisite
for a poet whose subject is me. Somehow he managed,
in spite of these classical failings, to blunder into

our song.

G. T. WRIGHT, 'On translating Catullus',
Centennial Review 19 (1975) 174

I. BEFORE SCHWABE

From the Renaissance to the nineteenth century, Catullus' influence on modern literature is a familiar story.[1] This final chapter brings it partly up to date, in an attempt to trace the origins of the twentieth century's image of Catullus and his world by concentrating in particular on the figure of 'Lesbia'.

The story begins with Petrarch. It is very likely that he owned one of the first copies made from the lost Verona manuscript; that copy in its turn has disappeared, but the surviving manuscripts *G* and *R* were transcribed from it about 1375. At the end of it, possibly surviving from the *Veronensis* itself, was the note 'Lesbia damnose bibens interpretatur' – '"Lesbia" means "one

---

[1] See Harrington 1923, and bibliography in Harrauer 1979, 141–5. English only: E. S. Duckett, *Catullus in English Poetry* (Smith College Classical Studies 6, Northampton Mass. 1925), an anthology; J. B. Emperor, *The Catullan Influence in English Lyric Poetry, c.1600–1650* (University of Missouri Studies 3.3, 1928); J. A. S. McPeek, *Catullus in Strange and Distant Britain* (Harvard Studies in Comparative Literature 15, 1939), up to the eighteenth century.

who drinks at great expense".'[2] The gloss – garbled, perhaps, from a line of Horace and a Martial epigram – is taken from the eleventh-century dictionary of Papias.[3] From that piece of medieval nonsense to the scholarly identification of 'Lesbia' as Clodia, *puella primaria*, in the 1472 biography, is a measure of the achievement of Petrarch and his humanist successors in the rediscovery of the classical world.

Knowledge of the real name of 'Lesbia' soon led to her being identified as a sister of P. Clodius Pulcher,[4] but that did not prompt any biographical speculation. The kiss poems and the sparrow poems had an enormous influence on Italian, French and English poetry in the sixteenth and seventeenth centuries, but the woman Catullus addressed them to was just a name, and not even an attractive one. Among the classical-sounding names that English poets now bestowed on the objects of their own love-lyrics, 'Lesbia' is a long way down the list, put quite in the shade by Phyllis, Chloris, Celia and the rest. (As Charles Sackville put it, at a time when this Catullan tradition was about played out, 'Methinks the poor town has been troubled too long | With Phillis and Chloris in every song.')[5] The anonymous author of *The Adventures of Catullus and History of his Amours with Lesbia* (London 1707) was untypical of his time in showing some interest in the 'real' love affair behind the poetry.

Sirmione sometimes inspired a thought of Catullus' mistress, as in Marcantonio Flaminio's address to the Catullan Muse in 1539;[6] but Sirmione was long neglected by literary Europe, and

---

[2] Ullman 1960, 1043–9, cf. Thomson 1978, 28f.

[3] Ullman 1960, 1049f. Cf. Hor. *Sat.* II 8.34 ('nisi damnose bibimus'), Mart. II 50 (Lesbia drinking water)?

[4] Muretus in 1552 (above, p. 131 n.7).

[5] A convenient sample is provided by A. H. Bullen's three anthologies: *Lyrics from the Song-Books of the Elizabethan Age* (London 1891), *Speculum amantis: Love-Poems from Rare Song-Books and Miscellanies of the Seventeenth Century* (London 1902), and *Musa proterva: Love-Poems of the Restoration* (London 1902), q.v. (p. 35) for the Sackville quotation. The count is: Phyllis 21, Chloris 16, Celia 11, Silvia 8, Chloe 6, Amaryllis 4, Corinna 3, Lesbia and six others two each (and one of the Lesbias is in fact Campion's translation of Catullus 5).

[6] *Carmina* IV I (first published 1548), introducing a pastoral romance in Latin verse.

it is not until 1801 – at a wonderfully absurd lunch party given on the peninsula by a French general after the retreat of the Austrians – that we find Lesbia's name again invoked at the site of Catullus' beloved home.[7] After that, Chateaubriand in 1822 and Carducci in 1881 both thought of her at Sirmione, and the combination of ideas still has some power in our own day.[8] But in this tradition she is still just the object of love, with no life or identity of her own.

For the mainstream of Catullan influence, what made the difference was a combination of Romanticism and the more scientifically philological scholarship of the nineteenth century. Both factors are crucial: the Romantic movement alone certainly revived enthusiasm for Catullus, but it was not at first the imperious mistress on whom attention was concentrated.

As a characteristic example, take the *Poems of Walter Savage Landor*, published six years after the French Revolution, when the author was only nineteen (he was a slightly older contemporary of Keats and Shelley). The collection includes some 'imitations of Catullus' – poems 2 and 3, 5 and 7, parts of poem 61, all old favourites that had appealed to Jonson, Campion, Waller, Herrick and the rest – and a series of Latin poems called 'Hendecasyllabi' (though including other metres) which begins with an address to Catullus himself. In it Landor weighs the good fortune of Rome in having Catullus as a poet against the misfortune of her *civilia bella Caesaresque*.[9] The reference to the Caesars is an early hint of the rebellious republicanism that was to mark Landor's later career, and it may well have been the attacks on Caesar no less than the love poems which made Catullus Landor's favourite author throughout his long life.

Fifty years later he published an essay on the poems of Catullus

---

[7] See Wiseman 1986, ch. 1; for La Combe St Michel and the sisters of the poet Anelli ('Sur cette rive cherie | Je vois plus d'une Lesbie'), see also Granarolo 1982, 225–30.

[8] See Granarolo 1982, 212–20 (Carducci, *Odi barbare* 15) and 223f (Chateaubriand, *Les Alpes ou l'Italie*); John Cotton, 'Catullus at Sirmio', *Ambit* 89 (1982) 54f, where Catullus' shade contemplates the summer tourists, German girls in tight shorts, and remembers taking 'Lesbia' from behind.

[9] *The Poems of Walter Savage Landor* (London 1795) 134–43, 167–98.

– a chaotic rag-bag, containing some good translations and imitations, but memorable mainly for the portentous rhetoric of its closing paragraph:

> They who have listened, patiently and supinely, to the catarrhal songsters of the goose-grazed commons will be loth and ill-fitted to mount up with Catullus to the highest steeps in the forests of Ida, and will shudder at the music of the Corybantes in the temple of the Great Mother of the Gods.

Catullus is valued now not just for pretty lyrics, but for a post-Romantic sublimity. The *Attis* has become the crucial text.[10]

In March 1864, shortly before he died, the 88-year-old Landor was visited in Florence by Algernon Charles Swinburne, then aged 26. Swinburne was a hero-worshipper full of revolutionary enthusiasms, one of which was for Landor's beloved Catullus;[11] two years later, in his scandalous *Poems and Ballads*, he showed how he could use him in a totally unprecedented and subversive way. The 55 stanzas of 'Dolores' celebrate a sinister *nôtre dame des sept douleurs*, the daughter of Priapus and Libitina, Sex and Death; under her rule, our sensibilities are not those of the vigorous phallic god, but of the castrated acolytes of Cybele. In stanza 41, Priapus is first addressed:

> What broke off the garlands that girt you?
>   What sundered you spirit and clay?
> Weak sins yet alive are as virtue
>   To the strength of the sins of that day.
> For dried is the blood of thy lover,

[10] W. S. Landor, 'The Poems of Catullus', *Foreign Quarterly Review* (July 1842) 329–69, reprinted in *The Last Fruit off an Old Tree* (London 1853) 237–80. The older Landor was much exercised by Catullus' obscenities: see 'On Catullus' (*Last Fruit* 366), invoking Thalia, the muse of comedy, and 'Written in a Catullus' (*Heroic Idyls, with additional poems* (London 1863) 178), where they are ascribed to 'uncleanly wit'.
[11] Cf. his *Poems and Ballads, second series* (1878), where the Latin iambics *ad Catullum* (237f) are really a celebration of Landor himself.

Ipsithilla, contracted the vein,
Cry aloud 'Will he rise and recover,
    Our Lady of Pain?'

Cry aloud; for the old world is broken:
    Cry aloud; for the Phrygian is priest,
And rears not the bountiful token
    And spreads not the fatherly feast.
From the midmost of Ida, from shady
    Recesses that murmur at morn,
They have brought and baptized her, Our Lady,
    A goddess new-born.

And the chaplets of old are above us,
    And the oyster-bed teems out of reach,
Old poets outsing and outlove us,
    And Catullus makes mouths at our speech.
Who shall kiss, in thy father's own city,
    With such lips as he sang with, again?
Intercede for us all of thy pity,
    Our Lady of Pain.

For this intoxicating chant of studied impropriety, Swinburne
could deploy a profound knowledge of the whole text of Catullus. But he was very selective: what he needed for his contrast
was masterful priapic vigour, so the allusions (*Attis* apart) are to
poem 32 ('Ipsithilla') and the hymn to Priapus (Lampsacus
oyster-beds), which in Swinburne's pre-Lachmann text was
poem 18.[12] 'Lesbia' had no place in that world. Nor had she for
the later Swinburne, even after the febrile excesses of the *enfant
terrible* had been abandoned: as with Tennyson, what mattered to
him then was the poet's brother, and *ave atque vale* in poem 101.[13]

[12] *Poems and Ballads* (London 1866) 178–96; cf. Appendix, nos. 89–91.
[13] *Poems and Ballads, second series* (1878) 71–83, 235f; *A Century of Roundels* (London 1883)
    89; in all three poems, for Gautier, Baudelaire and Catullus himself, 'brother' means
    'brother-poet'. *Frater Ave atque Vale* was the title (and poem 101 part of the inspiration)
    of the famous poem Tennyson wrote at Sirmione in the summer of 1880, soon after the
    death of his own brother: H. Tennyson, *Alfred Lord Tennyson: a Memoir* (London 1897)
    II 247.

The year after 'Dolores' had scandalised the literary world, a translation of Catullus was published in Edinburgh by James Cranstoun, Rector of Kirkcudbright Grammar School. It was a complete translation, with no poems omitted (though inevitably some had to be paraphrased):

The plan of reproducing all the poems may appear objectionable to some; but to the translator it seemed preferable to that of mutilating the poet, and presenting him in a totally different aspect from that in which he has revealed himself in his writings . . . His expressions, it is true, are often intensely sensuous, sometimes even grossly licentious, but to obliterate these and to clothe him in the garb of purity would be to misrepresent him entirely. He would be Atys, not Catullus.

That is a striking image, which reminds us of Landor and Swinburne. Like them, authors so different from himself, the Scottish schoolmaster picks on *Attis* as the essential Catullus text. And he praises it in terms that could hardly be more characteristic of the nineteenth century's love of the sublime: 'it is like the live thunder leaping from crag to crag over mountains wrapt in the impenetrable gloom of chaos and of night'.[14]

But Cranstoun was more than a child of the Romantic age. He was a serious scholar, whose learning was matched by sound sense and an independent mind. He deserves to be better known, not least for his treatment of the Lesbia affair. Rightly arguing that poem 43, like poem 11, must date to the time of Caesar's Gallic command, he puts the affair after 58 B.C.; consequently 'Lesbia' cannot be Clodia Metelli, 'as we learn from Catullus himself that her husband was living during their intimacy, while we know that Metellus Celer died in 59 B.C.'.[15] Cranstoun acknowledged a debt to Rossbach's edition (1854), Haupt's *Observationes criticae* (1837) and Schwabe's *Quaestiones Catullianae*

[14] Cranstoun 1867, v–vi (preface), 240f (on poem 63). For a sketch of classical education in Scotland in Cranstoun's time, by one who had benefited from it, see J. W. Mackail, *Studies in Humanism* (London 1938) 45f.

[15] Cranstoun 1867, 11f. He is also sensible on Piso in Spain (11, 191) and the date of the poet's death (13, cf. 15); on the other hand, he dates the poet's birth to 76 B.C. (8, 227 – after Lachmann and Haupt?), and supposes that the lady of poem 68b was not 'Lesbia' (14).

(1862). The revolution in classical studies achieved in Germany by Lachmann and his followers meant much more than the scientific establishment of texts; systematic collation of the historical evidence made it possible to reconstruct periods like the late Republic with a degree of sophistication hitherto unattempted. From now on, Catullus and his world could be studied together; and 'Lesbia', perhaps, could become a historical character.

It was Ludwig Schwabe who tackled the question most thoroughly. In a long, learned and eloquent dissertation, he reconstructed Catullus' biography on the assumption that 'Lesbia' was Clodia Metelli, and that the poet's affair with her therefore began in the late sixties; by combining the evidence of the poems with what Cicero tells us about Clodia and Caelius Rufus, he was able to draw up a detailed chronological table of Catullus' life and work.[16] It is a plausible and attractive scheme, if the necessary premises are admitted,[17] and it has the great advantage of offering a coherent and dramatic story of love and jealousy.

Cranstoun was not persuaded, fortified perhaps by a healthy Scots tradition of empirical scepticism. But Cranstoun was soon forgotten, and the men who are remembered – Baehrens and Ellis, whose magnificent commentaries are the foundation of all modern work on Catullus – were prepared to accept the essentials, if not every detail, of Schwabe's reconstruction.[18] As a result, scepticism about the theory could be presented as an attack on the great nineteenth-century commentators themselves,[19] and scholars over a century later could rely on their

---

[16] Schwabe 1862, esp. 53–135 on 'Lesbia' (see 67f for his methodology), 358–61 (chronological table).

[17] E.g. that the undateable love poems should be put several years earlier than the dateable ones; and that what the *pro Caelio* tells us about Clodia Metelli is all there ever was to know about the three sisters of Clodius.

[18] Baehrens 1885, 31–6, Ellis 1889, xii and lxiii–xx; cf. also Schmidt 1887, xvi–xxv.

[19] E.g. R. J. M. Lindsay, *CP* 43 (1948) 43; for the context, cf. Wiseman 1974, 105f.

authority as a substitute for evidence or argument.[20] Thanks to Schwabe, 'Lesbia' had taken on a whole new lease of afterlife.

2. MORALISERS

The new orthodoxy quickly found a wider public, in school editions and works for the general reader.[21] Indeed, it became a favourite exhibit in the late Victorians' gallery of scenes from classical life. Their sentimental view of the ancient world, which valued the classical authors in direct proportion to the applicability of their experience and attitudes to those of contemporary England,[22] lasted well into the first half of the twentieth century (and incidentally did the study of Greece and Rome a great deal of harm in English educational circles, from which it is only now beginning to recover). In 1897, J. H. A. Tremenheere of the Indian Civil Service published *The Lesbia of Catullus*, a translation of the love poems in 'chronological order' with a connecting biographical commentary ('It is here sought to trace the course of that ill-fated passion which wrecked the happiness of the tenderest of Roman poets . . .'); three decades later, F. A. Wright was still playing the same game in an essay on 'Lesbia and Catullus' in the *Fortnightly Review*:[23]

---

[20] Many examples could be cited; I choose two, from arguments that actually *depend* on the identification of 'Lesbia' as Clodia Metelli: J. W. Zarker, *CJ* 68 (1972–3) 107 ('for the purposes of this paper the traditional identification . . . will be assumed'), and H. D. Rankin, *Latomus* 35 (1976) 8 ('if we follow the commonsense identification . . .').

[21] E.g. J. Davies, *Catullus, Tibullus, and Propertius* ('Ancient Classics for English Readers', Edinburgh & London 1876) 13–32; F. P. Simpson, *Select Poems of Catullus* (London 1879) xli; H. V. Macnaghten and A. B. Ramsay, *Poems of Catullus* (London 1899) 1–5.

[22] See for instance R. R. Bolgar in *Classical Influences on Western Thought A.D. 1650–1870* (Cambridge 1979) 337f, on the Arnolds; cf. J. Seznec, ibid. 355f for an analogous continental view (Welcker, against the sounder instincts of Renan). The same love of the recognisable applied in art: see R. Jenkyns, *The Victorians and Ancient Greece* (Oxford 1980) 312–18.

[23] J. H. A. Tremenheere, *The Lesbia of Catullus* (London 1897, repr. New York 1962); for the author, see S. G. Tremenheere (his brother), *The Tremenheeres* (privately printed

Love stories in themselves have a perennial charm for the young and old of both sexes, appealing, as they do, to the strongest and most universal of all emotions. But if one of the lovers is the most brilliant figure of her day, a woman whose influence both in politics and in society was as great as it was disastrous, then the affair takes on a wider importance . . . These are the excuses, if excuses be needed, for telling their tale once again.

And again, and again.[24]

Three examples of this soft-centred romanticism, so characteristic of the age, are worth looking at in detail – all professional educators, one English, one American, one South African.

Hugh Vibart Macnaghten (1862–1929), whose memorial is the Macnaghten Library at Eton, was a schoolmaster of genius. In the end, his life was tragic – he killed himself soon after the death of his beloved sister – but his inspiration and sympathy earned him the affection, and indeed the love, of generations of his pupils.[25] His two books of verse reveal the ingenuousness of his view of the classics – tales of British imperial heroism are juxtaposed with Simonides and Horace – and a quite astonishingly romanticised view of women. A poem entitled 'To a Girl' runs as follows:

> Be gay and gallant, dream not of surrender,
>   Unfurl the flag, and clasp the maiden shield.
> Gallant and gay will never prove untender,
>   And with war's honours at the last will yield.

1925) 91. F. A. Wright, *Fortnightly Review* 123 (1925) 635–46 – later adapted for the introduction to his translation (see next note) at pp. 25–52.

[24] Apart from the standard editions and histories of Latin literature, whose treatment of Catullus and 'Lesbia' was devastatingly exposed by R. G. C. Levens in *Fifty Years of Classical Scholarship* (Oxford 1955) 362f (Harrington 1923, 3–44 is a beautiful example he happened to miss), popular translations often arranged the love poems in 'biographical' sequence: see for instance L. R. Levett, *Valerius Catullus B.C. 87: Selected Poems rendered into English rhymed verse* (Cambridge & London 1905); R. K. Davis, *Translations from Catullus* (London 1913); F. A. Wright, *Catullus: the Complete Poems* (Broadway Translations, London & New York 1926).

[25] He became Assistant Master at Eton in 1886, was House-master from 1899 to 1920, and thereafter Vice-Provost. See *In Memoriam Hugh Macnaghten 1862–1929*, and *Hugh*

Today's reader has to make a real effort to think himself back into a world where that could be said in all seriousness.[26] For an understanding of the world of 'Lesbia', such attitudes certainly seem to be unpromising equipment, yet Macnaghten loved Catullus, and came back to him again and again.

In 1899 he published *The Story of Catullus*. After a characteristically tender-minded preface,[27] he tells the Schwabe tale pleasantly enough, with his own translations at the appropriate points; but what makes his treatment of it interesting, as a document for the sensibilities of his time, is the way his own feelings are engaged in it:[28]

It is difficult not to feel a sense of almost personal disappointment at the thought of what might have been, if Catullus had found, before meeting Clodia, a woman who could have saved him. That there were such women at Rome, even in that age of profligacy, who can doubt? [Cicero's daughter Tullia, for example.] . . . If only Cicero had chosen Catullus for his son-in-law, we should have lost Lesbia's sparrow and Lesbia's kisses, but we should have gained nobler poems inspired by a good woman's love, and Catullus might have risen to Virgil's height instead of sinking at times to the level of Ovid and Propertius.

It seems we should also have lost Acme and Septimius. Here is Macnaghten's reaction to poem 45:

Macnaghten's House Record, Eton 1899–1920, both compiled by E. Millington Drake (Eton 1931).

[26] *Verse Ancient and Modern* (London 1911) 91; ibid. 5, 41f for brave and graceful girls, 100f for classical education as the source of their bravery and grace; 54–9 for Horace's Regulus between two stories of imperial self-sacrifice, 68f for Simonides' epitaph on the Athenians who died at Plataea and Macnaghten's on the Etonians who died in South Africa. Cf. also *Ave Regina and other poems* (London 1904) 44 and 92 on 'the golden birthright of our youth'.

[27] Macnaghten 1899, vii: 'Who will read this book? . . . Perhaps even an Eton boy who has read Catullus at school, and is a little ashamed at having cared so much for any part of his work, or the sister of an Eton boy, if I may speak out all my dreams, who has read in Tennyson of the "tenderest of Roman poets" and would learn something which her brother refuses to tell her of that Catullus "whose dead songster never dies".'

[28] Macnaghten 1899, 65f, 73. Catullus translations also in *Ave Regina* 76f, *Verse Ancient and Modern* 86–90 (n.26 above); for his *Poems of Catullus* (1925), which resulted from readers' reactions to the 1899 book, see n.43 below.

Is this all? Has the tenderest of Roman poets no other, no higher message to give than this? Is the mission of woman only to delight, and never to raise and ennoble the man she loves, so that he shall be capable of devotion and self-sacrifice? It is clear that Catullus no longer dreams of such possibilities, and the reason is not far to seek. Could Clodia teach him self-denial? Could she inspire a chivalrous love? Some woman might have saved him and shown him the truth: there were such wives in Rome. But married happiness was not destined for Catullus, and so the poet of love died, and left us no record of any woman whom we can reverence.

It would be too easy just to dismiss this with a laugh. However naively, Macnaghten expresses something not wholly foreign to Catullus' values.[29] But with the best will in the world, one cannot pretend that he ever made sense of 'Lesbia'. In the first scene of his playlet *Clodia* (published in 1927), Metellus Celer and his wife are portrayed choosing the guest list for their forthcoming dinner party. Then follows a stage direction:

Clodia rushes out into the great hall, and dances a pas seul with abandon: then she comes back to the study and says 'I feel better now'. Her husband looks at her with distrust and involuntary admiration.

And as a later scene with Caelius reveals, for Macnaghten's Clodia love-making is hide and seek and running races on the lawn.[30]

Meanwhile, readers on the other side of the Atlantic had been offered a less excruciating scenario in a book of short stories entitled *Roads from Rome*, by Anne C. Emery (1871–1932), daughter of the Chief Justice of the State of Maine. A prize-winning graduate of Bryn Mawr (her fellow-students called her 'the paragon') and talented both as a classicist and as an administrator, she held responsible positions at Bryn Mawr and Wisconsin before moving to Providence, R.I., in 1900 to be Dean of the Women's College at Brown University. There in 1905 she married the Professor of Greek Literature and History,

---

[29] See above, p. 118.

[30] *Virgil's Secret and other Plays* (London 1927) 10, 17–22; cf. 33, where Clodia tells Caesar in 47 B.C. that she wants a son by him, and the Dictator replies 'My God, no: not that.'

Francis G. Allinson, and retired to preside over a home which 'for over three decades . . . was the meeting place of professors and students, journalists, writers and artists, ministers, bankers, and simple people'. Together they wrote *Greek Lands and Letters* (the Allinsons were at the American School in Athens in 1910–11); *Roads from Rome* was her first book as sole author, and inaugurated a twenty-year career as a popular essayist.[31]

The first story, 'The Estranger',[32] opens on Catullus in Verona, grief-stricken for his brother Valerius, a soldier, dead from a fever on active service. Valerius had been the keeper of his conscience when they were young, and on his last leave had asked him anxiously about Clodia. Catullus had defended her passionately as the innocent victim of slander; all men loved her, but she loved him alone. Valerius was reassured: 'I know this hot heart of yours is as pure as the snow we see on the Alps in midsummer.' The second scene finds Clodia in Rome, socially ostracised, remembering Catullus with contempt ('how the thought of that boy sickened her!') and setting about the easy seduction of Caelius Rufus. In the third scene, Catullus returns to Rome to see his 'Lesbia', but sees something else instead:

A woman and a man walked to the fountain and sat down upon the carved balustrade. The woman unfastened her white cloak. The man laughed low and bent and kissed her white throat where it rose above soft silken folds. Clodia loosened the folds. Caelius laughed again.

Catullus rushes off to drown his sorrows in the Subura ('haunts . . . which later became familiar enough to him'), falls ill with a fever and recovers to find 'a sneering desire for Lesbia's beauty divorced from a regard for her purity'. When she sends for him, he goes. And the story ends:

---

[31] *Dictionary of American Biography* XXI (Supplement 1, 1944) 23–5. The Union Library catalogue reveals that her Bryn Mawr Ph.D. thesis, *The Historical Present in Early Latin*, was published by a local firm in her home town of Ellsworth, Maine.
[32] A. C. E. Allinson, *Roads from Rome* (New York 1913) 1–36: quotations from pp. 17, 30, 33, 34, 36, vii.

He had blamed death for his separation from Valerius. But what death had been powerless to accomplish his own choice of evil had brought about. Between him and his brother there now walked the Estranger – Life.

As the author makes clear in the Preface, her purpose was an exemplary one: 'the men and women of ancient Rome were like ourselves', and in recognising our human nature in theirs, the reader would find in Rome's literature 'an intimate rather than a formal inspiration, and in its history either comfort or warning'.

Mrs Allinson does not quote the poems, though many phrases from them are woven into her prose; the form she chose was fictional narrative. Macnaghten, on the other hand, was supposedly writing non-fiction (at least before his disastrous attempt at drama), with frequent translations of the poems to illustrate it. The third of our trio – T. J. Haarhoff (1892–1972), Professor of Classics at the University of the Witwatersrand – offered 'The Life of Catullus' in yet another genre, and in another language, Afrikaans.[33] 'Since classical forms have hitherto had little effect on our literature, a simple narrative form is used' – but it was verse narrative, in 56 consecutive poems, of which 22 were translations or imitations of Catullus.[34]

The sequence begins at Sirmio, with Catullus as a child, sailing toy boats on the lake. It is a northern, Celtic Catullus, and the author of *The Stranger at the Gate* is recognisable in the early poems: 'from the rich mixture of races a nation grows'.[35] From his northern country home he comes to the great city,

[33] *Die Liefde van Catullus*, deur T. J. Haarhoff (Nasionale Pers Berperk, Bloemfontein en Kaapstad 1933). I am very grateful to Professor B. X. De Wet of the University of Natal for translating Haarhoff's work for me while he was Honorary Research Fellow at Exeter in 1979–80.

[34] The poems concerned, 'in the order of the poet's emotional development as the writer sees it', are 51, 2, 5, 43, 3, 70, 8, 109, 38, 104, 82, 85, 72, 58, 76, 73, 11, 46, 101, 31, 4 (cf. n. 55 below).

[35] T. J. Haarhoff, *The Stranger at the Gate: Aspects of Exclusiveness and Co-operation in Ancient Greece and Rome, with some reference to modern times* (London 1938), esp. 294–308, 'Romans, Boers and Britons'. The book is dedicated 'To the Spirit of Racial Co-operation'.

where wealth and the pursuit of knowledge are equally inimical to the simple moral standards of his youth. A long glance from between the curtains of a luxurious litter sets off a blaze of Sappho in his head. 'Be careful,' whispers Calvus in his ear, 'it's Clodia.' Too late! Her husband Metellus is cold and proud and preoccupied with politics;[36] as for her, her great dark eyes are full of secret fires, her body lives for love alone. She becomes his 'Lesbia', and as he pours out his poems of love, 'half amused she turns her eyes to him like daybreak on a silver beach'. But *surgit amari aliquid*: the Lucretian tag marks the turning point to doubt and pain and bitterness. After 'the last message' (poem 11), Catullus goes with Memmius to Bithynia; his spirit revives a little, his brother's memory inspires him to better things, he returns at last to Sirmio (a quotation from Tennyson here) and reflects on how the wind and waves have driven off course the toy boat of his life. The sun goes down; his fire is almost out.[37]

What all three presentations have in common is a determined concern with their own time, with the moral preoccupations of Eton, Providence or Johannesburg. Central to them all is the conflict of moral innocence and corrupt sophistication, a theme with some historical justification (as I hope chapter IV has shown), but distorted out of all recognition by anachronistic romanticising.

It is, moreover, a theme quite independent of the Schwabe story in which they set it. It could be just as well expressed without bringing in Caelius Rufus and Metellus Celer, as is shown by a refreshingly sober statement of the moralisers' case, by J. C. Squire (1884–1958). His poem 'To a Roman'[38] addresses

---

[36] A nice topical touch: he is afraid of the effect of farmers migrating to the city, of bread and circuses for the 'poor whites' weakening the farmers' backbone (*boere-ruggegraat*).

[37] Quotations from pp. 15 (race mixture), 20 (northern morals and the city), 30 (litter), 33 (Calvus), 27 (Metellus), 35 (Clodia), 41 (*Soos dagbreek op 'n silwerstrand*), 50 (Lucretius), 68 (last message), 72f (brother), 76 (*Dan kom jy waar die purperblomme bloei | By ou ruïnes van Romeinse tyd*), 80 (sunset).

[38] First published in *The Living Age*, 28 April 1923, whence J. C. Squire, *American Poems and Others* (London 1923) 57–62.

a Catullus who is at least recognisable as the author of obscene
invectives as well as love poems – 'With certain supercilious
gross companions | Talking their filth more cleverly than they'
(though inwardly contemptuous of them). The last two sections
begin with an allusion to poem 16:

III

'The poet should be chaste, his verses – ' Well,
    It wasn't Lesbia's view, she did her best,
Tempting and spurning, to weary and degrade you,
    To callous you and make you like the rest.

Disliking, piqued by, that strange difference in you,
    Contemptuous and curious, she would dare
And then deny, provoke, and then repel you,
    Yet could not make you other than you were.

The soft-pressed foot, the glance that hinted heat,
    The scanty favours always auguring more,
The haughty, cold indifference, mingling twin
    Frigidities of the vestal and the whore

Still could not even more than wound, cloud over,
    The eager boy in you she so despised,
The love of fineness, sweetness, loyalty, candour,
    The innocent country memories you prized.

IV

A flower in a garden grew, Catullus,
    Sometime you saw it, and the memory stayed.
One flower of all the flowers you ever glanced at,
    A perfect thing of dew and radiance made:

Emblem of youth, plucked, carried away and drooping,
    Out of the garden; emblem of your lot,
Perplexed, bewildered, languishing, an alien
    Who was born to cherish all his world forgot.

3. CYNICS

But there are two sides to every story. Though the tender-hearted might sigh for the blighted innocence of the eager boy, there were also those who preferred to take the part of the worldly lady.

It might be done tongue in cheek, as in Maurice Baring's skit 'Lesbia Illa'; this was one of a sequence of imaginary letters giving a new slant on historical events, written for the *Morning Post* while Baring was its correspondent in St Petersburg.[39] Clytemnestra, Guinevere, Goneril and Lady Macbeth are all recognisable as Edwardian ladies, anxious about servants, dinner parties, social niceties – and of course they are all innocent, grossly misrepresented. So too his Clodia, who had been foolishly kind to Catullus and regrets it now that he is making himself a nuisance. He gate-crashes her dinner party, gets drunk, insults Caesar ('he asked Lavinia in a loud whisper, which we all heard, who the gentleman sitting opposite might be who was slightly bald'), and finally in a jealous rage announces he is going to recite:

> Then, looking me straight in the face, he recited a poem which was *quite*, *quite* impossible, with a *horrible* word in it (at least Lalage said it was horrible). Pollio came to the rescue, and said that Catullus was ill, and dragged him out of the room. And in a way it was true, for he was quite tipsy, and tears were rolling down his cheeks; and I do hate drunken men, but, above all, I hate coarseness.

Far away in Russia, Baring depended on 'the hazy memories of a distant education indolently received'; evidently his reading at Eton and Trinity had included poem 58.

Or it might be done more seriously, as by Arthur Symons, the friend of Verlaine and Mallarmé, Beardsley and Yeats. His collection *Knave of Hearts* included a sequence of translations 'From Catullus: chiefly concerning Lesbia', and a poem 'Lesbia in Old Age' which deserves to live beyond its time:[40]

[39] M. Baring (1874–1945), *Dead Letters* (London 1910) 29–38.

[40] A. Symons, *The Knave of Hearts: 1894–1908* (New York & London 1913) 16f; cf. 42, 44 (poems 48 and 96), 132–63.

You see these shrunken arms, this chin,
A sharp bone wrapped about with rags
Of scrawled and wrinkled parchment skin;
This neck now puckered into bags
Was seamless satin at the first;
And this dry broken mouth a cup
Filled up with wine for all men's thirst;
This sodden hair was lifted up
About a brow that once was low,
As any woman's in the world;
And these two eyes of smouldering tow
That scarcely light me to this hearth
Were as two torches shaken out
To be a flame upon the earth.
What is it that he said about
Beauty I stole, to be my own,
All beauty's beauty? Look at this:
Finger by finger, to the bone,
His lips and teeth would bite and kiss
These joints of these abhorred hands,
These cheeks that were not always thus;
What was it that he said of sands
And stars that could not count for us
Our kisses? Let us live and love,
My Lesbia: yes, and I shall live,
A hungering, thirsting shadow of
That love I gave and could not give.
I gave him pleasure, and I sold
To him and all men; he is dead,
And I am infamous and old,
And yet I am not quieted.
Take off your curses from my soul:
Can not Catullus pity me
Although my name upon his scroll
Has brought him immortality?

This was the time when Yeats and Pound were reading
Catullus, and protesting at the treatment he was receiving from
their contemporaries. Yeats's famous poem 'The Scholars'

('Lord, what would they say | Did their Catullus walk that way?') was published in 1919; three years earlier, Pound had reacted violently to an elegant little volume entitled *The Lesbiad of Catullus* which he had been sent for review:[41]

LESBIAD. NO. HELL NO.

I began reading it carefully, pleased that someone should try the impossible, knowing the immense difficulty . . . Even Landor turned back from an attempt to translate Catullus. I have failed forty times myself so I do know the matter. *But* there are *decent* and *dignified* ways of failing, and this female has not failed in any respectable way.

The most hard-edged and intense of the Latin poets should *not* be cluttered with wedding-cake cupids and clichés like 'dregs of pain', etc, etc, ad inf. Pink blue baby ribbon.

Meanwhile, what had happened to the Catullus of Swinburne's *Dolores*? Another rebel against Victorian convention, Swinburne's friend Sir Richard Burton, had written a complete and determinedly unexpurgated translation; but he died before seeing it through the press, and the version that appeared in 1894 had been doctored by Lady Burton, who burnt the original manuscript. Even so, it was 'for private subscribers only'.[42] For the general public, the censorship Cranstoun had so deplored in

[41] W. B. Yeats, 'The Scholars', *The Wild Swans at Coole* (Dundrum 1919) 161, on which see W. H. Auden, *The Dyer's Hand and other essays* (London 1963) 42f; *The Letters of Ezra Pound* (ed. D. D. Paige, London 1951) 116f, to Harriet Monroe, editor of *Poetry* (Chicago), on Ruth S. Dement, *The Lesbiad of Catullus and Pervigilium Veneris (Mood Transcriptions) and Songs of a Wayfarer* (Chicago 1915); cf. also p. 138 (to Iris Berry, 1916) on Catullus. Pound's 'Lesbia Illa' and 'To Formianus' Young Lady Friend' were first published in *Lustra* (London 1916).

[42] *The Carmina of Caius Valerius Catullus now first completely Englished into Verse and Prose, the Metrical Part by Capt. Sir Richard F. Burton, K.C.M.G., F.R.G.S., etc, etc, etc, and the Prose Portion, Introduction and Notes Explanatory and Illustrative by Leonard C. Smithers* (London 1894, printed for the translators); as Smithers pointedly remarked (xv), 'Sir Richard laid great stress on the necessity of thoroughly annotating each translation from an erotic (and especially a paederastic) point of view', but Lady Burton insisted that the asterisks in her typescript copy – which was all Smithers had to work on – were Burton's own; they replaced two whole couplets (67.21f, 80.7f), and various obscene verbs (particularly *irrumare*) in fourteen other places. See F. M. Brodie, *The Devil Drives: a Life of Sir Richard Burton* (London 1967) 320f.

1867 was now seen as inevitable. As late as 1925, Macnaghten's *The Poems of Catullus* gives the reader no hint in either the title or preface that only 75 out of the 116 poems have been translated. (I suspect Macnaghten simply never admitted the obscene poems into his picture of Catullus, and so felt no need to explain their omission.) It ends with an 'Envoy' to his readers, surely the most egregious tripe the Cambridge University Press has ever printed:[43]

> Dear men and women, girls and boys,
> Who have your own, your special joys,
> No right have I to ask of you
> That you should read Catullus through:
> I only ask you just to look
> One moment at this little book,
> To open it, and just to glance,
> Whate'er the page on which you chance,
> At any lyric gay or sad, –
> Catullus is a starry lad,
> And if you bring him to the test,
> Believe me, he will do the rest.

'Whate'er the page', because every page is equally innocuous. The obscenities are out of sight and out of mind.

The reaction was not long in coming. In 1929 two complete translations appeared, both beautifully produced by small presses and with illustrations in the manner of the time. One, by F. C. W. Hiley, had few scholarly pretensions, but was introduced by a coy little address to Catullus in Latin hendecasyllables, apologising for the prudishness of English readers; the other, by Jack Lindsay, was a substantial historical commentary on Catullus and his times, incorporating, among much else, a

---

[43] H. Macnaghten, *The Poems of Catullus Done into English Verse* (Cambridge 1925) 148. Cf. viii: 'in three cases, to preserve a poem, I have altered one objectionable word of the original'; I can only find one (*captat* for *glubit* at 58. 5), but at least six poems (10, 24, 25, 28, 29, 39) have been tacitly shortened by anything from one to sixteen lines.

complete translation of the *pro Caelio*.[44] With Lindsay, a young Australian poet and very consciously a modernist, Catullus enters a new world, the world of Marx and Freud. But the rebels of the past are elegantly honoured: his *Attis* is translated into the stanza form of Swinburne's *Dolores*.

As for the starry lad, he is treated with a faintly contemptuous tolerance. Deliberately cynical, Lindsay ranges himself alongside the successful rivals:[45]

> And you, Catullus, welcome! here
> take Clodia to bed again.
> If I had lived next door to you
> you'd not have found my love more true
> than that which Caelius had to feign
> or than Alfenus. Others' pain
> cannot but be grotesque and queer.
> Still, take my love for what it's worth.
> I would have given you my jeer;
> I give you sympathy instead . . .
> I am not jealous now you're dead:
> between the pair of you I stand
> and stretch to each a various hand.
> The rage is gone, the tears are shed.
> Past patient doors of death and birth
> I take her to my callous bed
> and laugh with you at all the earth.

We have come a long way from Macnaghten's wish for a woman whom we can reverence.

Here too there is a transatlantic parallel. In America, the first modernist Catullus was that of Horace Gregory in 1931, likewise complete, illustrated, from a small press. 'I was convinced that

---

[44] F. C. W. Hiley, *Carmina Catulli: the Poems of Catullus* (ill. Vera Willoughby, Piazza Press, London 1929). Jack Lindsay, *The Complete Poetry of Gaius Catullus* (ill. Lionel Ellis, Fanfrolico Press, London 1929); cf. Lindsay's autobiography *Fanfrolico and After* (London 1962).

[45] In the dedication poem to his brother Philip Lindsay.

however far short of perfection some of my versions fell . . . my Catullus would not be mistaken as the author of verses published in popular magazines.'[46] That barbed comment was provoked, perhaps, by a pseudonymous sonnet in the *Saturday Review* the year before:[47]

To Gaius Valerius Catullus, 84–54 B.C.

Veronian wizard, thou! who couldst replace
A cup of Latian bronze by gleaming gold;
Fashion a filigree of haunting grace
The very wine of thy caress to hold!
We strive in vain to lift the veil of years –
to catch the glint of thy white, homing, sail;
To soothe the sadness of thy Troad tears;
Or joyous birth of thy first book, to hail.
Rest on, O human heart, whose pulses beat
So fiercely through thy slender span of days;
Though Clodia hear no more thine eager feet
Above the clamour of the Forum ways –
Yet may thine ashes gild the dust of Rome,
And thy dear song claim wider worlds thy home!

The spectacular over-punctuation even includes an exclamation mark after the vocative, in true nineteenth-century style.

That, at any rate, was an outdated mannerism that could be cast off completely. Here is an American Catullus of ten years later, wholly unpunctuated in the style satirised by Don Marquis as that of archy the cockroach:[48]

---

[46] H. Gregory, *The Poems of Catullus* (ill. Zhenya Gay, New York 1931); see the Introduction to the second edition (London 1956), esp. v–xi, xxii–iv (quotation from p. xi) – 'it was my belief that Catullus lacked a twentieth-century interpreter'.

[47] 'Anak Sungei', *Saturday Review* 5 July 1930, p. 6.

[48] William D. Hull II, 'In Memoriam I: Catullus', *Sewanee Review* 48 (1940) 32; Don Marquis, *archy and mehitabel* (London 1931).

flower of evil
rooted in a rotting rome

pure lyricist
vituperative ranter

possessor of something fine
haunter of the gutters

impetuous swallow
with wings
clipped

you wrote
odi et amo
to lesbia
and lesbia got more
elsewhere

There were real poets in the thirties, in both Britain and America, for whom Catullus was an inspiration and a challenge.[49] But my concern here is with 'Lesbia', and her interpretation by those who rejected the pieties of the moralising school. A pleasantly ironical version – Maurice Baring brought up to date, as it were – was provided by Dorothy Parker, in her extract 'From a Letter from Lesbia':[50]

That thing he wrote, the time the sparrow died –
    (Oh, most unpleasant – gloomy, tedious words!)
I called it sweet, and made believe I cried;
    The stupid fool! I've always hated birds . . .

---

[49] See for instance Basil Bunting, 'Attis: or, something missing' (1931) and 'Once, so they say, pinetrees . . .' (1933), *Collected Poems* (London 1968) 19–24, 139; E. E. Cummings, 'o pr' (1935), *Complete Poems* (London 1968) II 392; Keith Douglas, 'Distraction' (1936?), *Complete Poems* (Oxford 1978) 11; R. P. Blackmur, 'Phaselus ille' (1937), *Poems of R. P. Blackmur* (Princeton 1977) 43; Rex Warner, 'Contradictions (1937–40)', *Poems and Contradictions* (London 1945) no. xviii; W. H. Auden, *New Year Letter* (London 1941) 23f. Cf. also Havelock 1939 – perhaps the last Catullan volume to contain scholarship and poetry between the same covers for the general reader.

[50] *Not so Deep as a Well: Collected Poems* (New York 1936) 181, first published in *Death and Taxes* (New York 1931): last of three stanzas.

232

4. WILDER'S CLODIA

In 1890, when the Schwabe hypothesis was already a generation old, R. Y. Tyrrell observed that

it is strange that none of our novelists or imaginative writers have taken as their subject this brilliant circle, and given body and substance to . . . the life in Clodia's mansion and gardens on the Palatine and by the shore and on the waters at Baiae.

Forty years later – for Mrs Allinson's short story hardly counts – the opportunity had still not been grasped.[51] It was Jack Lindsay who first put Clodia and Catullus into English novels, with *Rome for Sale* (1934), *Despoiling Venus* (1935) and *Brief Light* (1939); it has to be admitted that they are disappointing, too full of Lindsay's own emotional life, and his 'obsession with points of social explosion, with the causes of mass-movements, the relation of individual aims to the larger whole', to be satisfyingly alive as historical reconstructions.[52] Not that his successors did any better, though some of them sold well in post-war paperback: W. G. Hardy, *Turn Back the River* (1938) and *The City of Libertines* (1957); Pierson Dixon, *Farewell Catullus* (1953); Robert De Maria, *Clodia* (1965); and Kenneth Benton, *Death on the Appian Way* (1974).[53] Even the best of these authors (De Maria, in my view) doesn't succeed in establishing the Schwabe reconstruction at any very exalted artistic level – perhaps because it was too novelettish to start with.

It may be that the story does not lend itself to treatment in the straight narrative mode, and that continental authors have been more astute in realising the fact. For example, Marcel Schwob's 'imaginary life' of Clodia (1895) was one of a series of bio-

---

[51] R. Y. Tyrrell and L. C. Purser, *The Correspondence of M. Tullius Cicero* III (Dublin & London 1890) xliii; Wiseman 1975, 96f. Novels on classical subjects are listed in W. B. Thompson's pamphlet *Classical Novels*, published by the Association for the Reform of Latin Teaching in 1966 (addenda 1975).

[52] Quotation from *Fanfrolico and After* (n.44 above) 213, cf. 261 on the autobiographical motivation; in general, see Wiseman 1975, 97–100.

[53] On all these, see Wiseman 1975, 100–4.

graphies in which the author deliberately avoided historical data
as much as he could; Schwob's previous book, *Mimes*, had been a
pastiche of Herodas' dramatic sketches, and his Clodia belongs
more to that milieu than to the world of the realistic novel.[54] In
Freud's Vienna in 1932, the pseudonymous 'R. W. Trune' produced his psychological study *Catullus und Clodia* in dramatic
form, the scenes interspersed with 'documents' (i.e. translated
poems).[55] Five years later, *Il bacio di Lesbia*, by the veteran
novelist and critic Alfredo Panzini, was subtitled 'romanzo' but
made no attempt at realistic illusion, the author being constantly
presented in his own person; one of his reminiscences is a
beautiful vignette of Giosue Carducci declaiming poem 61 to a
class of schoolchildren in Bologna, presumably some time in the
1870s.[56] Finally, the work that has brought Catullus and 'Lesbia'
to the widest modern audience, Carl Orff's *Carmina Catulli*
(1943), was created by a man with an obsession for theatre; the
love story is presented as *ludi scaenici*, a performance within a
performance, with the poems not as mere punctuation but as the
essence of the drama itself.[57]

In English, there has been only one full-scale interpretation of
Catullus and his mistress with any real distinction as a work of

[54] M. Schwob (1867–1905), 'Clodia, matrone impudique', *Le journal* (11 Nov. 1895) 1,
Vies imaginaires (Paris 1896); Wiseman 1975, 108–10. On Schwob, see now P.
Fawcett, *TLS* 4149 (8 Oct. 1982) 1096.
[55] 'R. W. Trune', *Catullus und Clodia: Mysterium einer Liebe* (Vienna & Leipzig 1932);
see esp. p. 3, where the author anticipates hostility from 'the numerous opponents
of the new psychology'. The poems he translates (cf. n.34 above for Haarhoff's
version at just this time) are 85, 51, 3, 5, 39, 36, 69, 60, 37, 58, 41, 43, 29 and 31, in
that order. The note on sources at the end names as *Hauptquelle* Rudolf Westphal's
Catulls Gedichte in ihrem geschichtlichem Zusammenhange (Breslau 1870), an early
elaboration of Schwabe 'the extravagance of which at times reaches romance' (Ellis
1889, x).
[56] A. Panzini (1863–1939), *Il bacio di Lesbia, romanzo* (Milan 1937) – pp. 177–9 for
Carducci.
[57] C. Orff (b.1895), *Carmina Catulli: ludi scaenici* (Mainz 1943); it consists of a *praelusio*,
then the 'play' (Act I, poems 85, 5, 51, 58, 70; Act II, poems 109, 73; Act III, poems 85,
32, 41, 8, 87), and finally an *exodium*. See A. Liess, *Carl Orff, his Life and his Music* (Eng.
tr. London 1966) 98–104; cf. 125–30 on the Catullan *Trionfo di Afrodite: concerto scenico*
(1953), and 63–74 on Orff and the theatre.

art: Thornton Wilder's 'fantasia' *The Ides of March*.[58] I think it is
no accident that his treatment is practically independent of the
Schwabe reconstruction (Caelius Rufus and Metellus Celer have
no role to play, and the chronology of the affair is brought down
to the forties B.C.), and that the playwright author has totally
avoided narrative. 'I had long deliberations before I launched on
my novel', he wrote:[59]

I had long felt that the historical drama 'works' and the historical novel
doesn't. Shakespeare's *Caesar* and *Antony*, the history plays; Goethe's
Egmont and Schiller's *Don Carlos*, Büchner's *Dantons Tod* and a few
others (several of Lope de Vega's) work splendidly: but the historical
novel, with the exception of *War and Peace* and *I promessi sposi*, breaks
down – certainly Scott's novels are no longer readable. The concept of
the omniscient author cannot extend to [the] fiction of 'knowing' the
thoughts and motivations of historical persons.

So – inspired by some insights during wonderful conversations with
Gertrude Stein – I decided to write my Caesar book as a collection of
documents (assumed to be authentic). Historical drama succeeds
because it *apparently* eliminates the intervening narrator ('on the stage it
is always *now*'). In a novel of documents, similarly, where is the
story-teller?

The documents are arranged in four books, in a progressively
expanding chronology: Book One, in which Clodia is the central
character, covers a single month, September 45 B.C.; Book Two,
which introduces Cleopatra, runs from 17 August to the end of
October, Book Three, 'mainly occupied with religion', from 9
August to 13 December, and Book Four, with Brutus as protagonist, from 8 August to the Ides of March 44 B.C. Each book
ends with a dramatic climax: Clodia's dinner party, interrupted
by an attempt on the Dictator's life; Cleopatra's reception, at
which Antony compromises the queen; the profanation by
Clodius of the rites of the Bona Dea;[60] and finally the assassi-

[58] New York 1948; best known to English readers in the Penguin Modern Classics
paperback edition (1961).
[59] In a letter to the author, 17 October 1975.
[60] A deliberate liberty, of course, as Wilder explains in his Foreword: the event
actually took place 17 years earlier.

nation itself. As historical reconstruction it is nonsense; as a meditation on love, poetry, political responsibility and man's place in the universe it is a rich and subtle work.

The first book is organised round Clodia, about to return to respectable society after a year of depravity and fashionable slumming in the gladiators' bars. She and her brother arrange a dinner party, to be conducted 'in the old mode', for Caesar and his wife, his aunt Julia (Marius' widow), Cicero, Pollio, and Catullus.[61] All the guests have their reasons for accepting: Julia, to warn Clodia that her behaviour may get her disbarred from the rites of the Bona Dea; Pollio, to try to reconcile his friend Catullus to his master Caesar; Cicero, to make clear the seductive dangers of poetry like Catullus' ('if we are to be condemned to a poetry based on buried trains of thought, my dear Pomponius, we shall soon be at the mercy of the unintelligible parading about among us as a superior mode of sensibility').[62] Catullus himself goes because he is obsessed with Clodia, to the astonishment of all who know her; and Caesar finally decides to accept in order to remind Clodia that it was not he who made her what she is.[63] It is that question, of Clodia's nature and who was responsible for it, that echoes throughout the book.

We see her first through Caesar's eyes, as 'one of those innumerable persons who trail behind them a shipwrecked life':

I see them sitting on the throne of their own minds, excused, acquitted, and hurling indictments against the mysterious Destiny which has wronged them and exhibiting themselves as pure victim. Such a one is Clodia . . . I am, I think, the only person living who knows of a certain circumstance of which she was perhaps a victim and on which she has for over twenty-five years based her claim to being, each day, a fresh victim.

---

[61] I 2, 3, 5, 6, II 26 (references by book and document number). Wilder calls Clodia 'Clodia Pulcher' and Julia 'Julia Marcia' throughout, and is in general very careless about Roman nomenclature; Julia is another deliberate anachronism (she died about 70 B.C.).

[62] I 4, III 44 (Julia); I 14 (Pollio); I 17 (Cicero).

[63] Astonishment: I 8 (Caesar), I 12 (Nepos), I 14 (Pollio). Caesar's motive: I 10A (cf. IV 62A for a political reason later revealed, to talk to Catullus about seditious letters).

With beauty, wealth and high intelligence, she had some greatness in her; but she has chosen to take her revenge on the world, and lives only 'to impress the chaos of her soul on all that surrounds her'.[64] Staying at Capua on her way from Baiae to Rome, she insults her host and mocks his piety; she invites Catullus to join her, only to teach him brutally that he has no claim on her by locking him out and taking another man to bed. But this havoc gives her no satisfaction. Even Catullus can see she is desperate ('cruelty is the only cry that is left to you to utter') and in her reply to his letter she reveals her trauma – at the age of twelve she was violated by her uncle. 'On what, on whom, can I avenge that?'[65]

But Caesar is to blame too: 'In order not to importune you with this thing they call love I have done what I have done: I have brutified myself.' It was he who had told her that the world had no meaning – but yet he lives, and works. Why? What does he know that she does not? This outpouring (the day after the scene at Capua), which decides Caesar to go to her dinner, brings Clodia into the main theme of the novel: is there a mind behind the universe?

Caesar ponders the question constantly; he sees four possible pieces of evidence, namely, love, great poetry, the insights that accompany his epilepsy, and perhaps his work for Rome.[66] The last is important, in more ways than one: do the Gods protect Rome, and are the ancient rituals meaningful? A significantly repeated quotation from Marius, spokesman for old Roman traditions, describes the rites of the Good Goddess as being 'like a column upholding Rome'. Caesar comments:

I could wish that it be said of them and of the body of our Roman ceremonies what Pindar said of the Eleusinian mysteries: *that they held the world together from falling into chaos.*

[64] I 3, 8; cf. I 14 (Pollio: 'She hates the air she breathes and everything and everyone about her').

[65] I 9 for the scene at Capua; at II 26 we discover that Clodia had already made it clear to Catullus what to expect. His letter and her reply: I 13 (II 28 for his first drafts: 'a monster and an assassin, to kill all that lives and loves').

[66] Clodia's blame: I 10. Caesar's enquiries: I 8, cf. III 42B, 46, IV 61, 67.

The 'old Roman way' is something to be taken seriously: Clodia has consciously rejected it, Catullus tries to inculcate it into his own generation, Caesar treats it with respect in public and wonders in private how it can change without being lost.[67]

On the wider question, another significant quotation is attributed both to Caesar and to his wise friend Turrinus: 'the universe does not know that men are living in it'. That is what haunts Clodia.[68] Of Caesar's four possible pointers to the contrary, none can give her any hope. The epilepsy is Caesar's alone; on the Roman tradition, and on love (as offered by Catullus)[69] she has deliberately turned her back. As for poetry, her view of that is delivered in a formal speech; at the *ad hoc* symposium organised by the wounded Caesar after the fiasco of her dinner party, he sets as the subject for debate 'whether great poetry is the work of men's minds only, or whether it is, as many have claimed, the prompting of the Gods'. Clodia argues that poetry is dangerous illusion, weakening the resolve of men to face the world as it really is, 'for discord is at the heart of the world and is present in each of its parts'.

I say that if the Gods exist I can imagine them to be cruel or indifferent or incomprehensible . . . but I cannot imagine them to be occupied with the childish game of deluding men as to their state through the agency of poets.

Catullus is in the process of answering her bleak vision with a mythological parable when Caesar is convulsed by an epileptic fit, and the debate ends with the question left unresolved.[70]

In Book Two, Caesar 'suggests' that Clodia should retire to the country. He has Catullus' welfare in mind, but Catullus, in love with her all over again, is horrified at the idea. Clodia writes

[67] Marius: I 5, III 42 (Wilder's italics); cf. I 4, Marius on Caesar and his friend Turrinus as boys – 'saplings of our great Roman oak'. Old Roman way: I 3 (Clodia), I 5 (Caesar in public), I 12 (Catullus).
[68] I 10, IV 67; cf. III 49A on Turrinus as Caesar's instructor in this ('the universe goes on its mighty way and there is very little we can do to modify it').
[69] II 28A: 'Insane one, do you know what you have thrown away?'
[70] I 21 – Pollio's narrative for Virgil and Horace, c.30 B.C.

238

with kindness and sympathy: he must not be jealous, her only companion will be Sosigenes, with whom she studies astronomy; Catullus must look after his health – and why not write something for her, a tragedy, a *Helen*? But old habits of havoc are still active; at the same time she is setting up Antony to achieve 'the greatest feat of daring ever seen in Rome' – the seduction of Cleopatra at the queen's reception. That goes disastrously wrong. Cleopatra's midnight note to Caesar, explaining why she was caught in Antony's arms, finds the Dictator at Catullus' sickbed.[71]

The third book, retracing the same period (September and October, 45), explains how that had come about. Catullus is portrayed as physically very strong, but with a recurrent internal disorder aggravated by the psychological strains of his relationship with Clodia.[72] Prostrated by her withdrawal, he suffers a terminal attack on the night of Cleopatra's reception. Caesar leaves the party early to be at his bedside.[73]

Apparently at one point, Gaius, the tears streaming down his face, almost flung himself out of bed crying that he had wasted his life and his song for the favours of a harlot. I would not have known how to answer that, but it seems that the Dictator could.

What the lady of the house doesn't hear, Caesar himself reports to his confidential friend:

Clodia! Every moment as I watch this I understand more clearly her ruined greatness.[74]

Oh, there are laws operating in the world whose import we can scarcely guess. How often have we seen a lofty greatness set off a train of evil, and virtue engendered by wickedness. Clodia is no ordinary woman and colliding with her Catullus has struck off poems which are

[71] III 35, 37, 39, 41a.
[72] I 12, II 29, 37.
[73] III 49; cf. IV 63 (Caesar thus escapes a plot on his life by Cassius).
[74] Cf. I 8 (Caesar): 'Does [Catullus] see the greatness that undoubtedly was in her before she wrought on herself the havoc which now arouses detestation and laughter throughout the city?' I 14 (Pollio): 'Valerius tells my brother of her wisdom . . . her greatness of soul'. II 28A (Catullus to Clodia): 'Some great intention for the world's enlightenment stirred in you and was poisoned at the source.'

not ordinary. At the closer range we say *good* and *evil*, but what the world profits by is intensity.

And he consoles the dying man with what Clodia had asked for in vain – his own conviction, drawn from Sophocles, that though the Gods are unknowable one must live as though they exist.[75] From Clodia, Catullus had learned that the world is a place of night and horror; now he dies to a choral ode from *Oedipus at Colonus*.[76]

As for Clodia herself, she has one more act of chaos to promote. The study of astronomy has given her dangerous ideas about infinity. There are no limits for her; she burns her mathematical notebooks and plans an act 'to darken the sun' – the profanation of the mysteries of the Bona Dea.[77] Only in the final book, with its reflections on freedom and responsibility, is Clodia's malaise (tacitly) defined.[78] 'The central movement of the mind', Caesar writes, 'is the desire for unrestricted liberty . . . accompanied by its opposite, a dread of the consequences of liberty.' (Clodia did not dread them, she embraced them.)

No bounds have been conceived for crime and folly. In this also I rejoice and call it a mystery. This also prevents me from reaching any summary conclusion concerning our human condition. Where there is an unknowable there is a promise.

Clodia appears only once in Book Four. She comes to Caesar, veiled and in secret, to warn him of the conspirators. 'I was on the point of telling my visitor that I knew all this already, but I held my tongue. I saw her as an old woman sitting by the fire and remembering that she had saved the state.'[79] He takes no extra

[75] III 49A; cf. I 10 for Clodia's desperate question.
[76] III 49, cf. I 13.
[77] III 54: 'The worst of being charged with crimes . . . is that it makes one restless to deserve all that censure. But, of course, only something enormous would do.' For the impact of the sacrilege, see III 56, IV 65.
[78] IV 61, 69, both to Turrinus; cf. III 53 (Cytheris quoting Turrinus), 'Wickedness may be the exploration of one's liberty . . . it can be the search for a limit that one can respect.' Clodia is not mentioned in any of these passages, but the juxtaposition of III 53 and 54 is eloquent in itself.
[79] IV 67.

precautions, and is killed. But at least this time Clodia has defied the temptations of discord and destruction.

As with any historical novel, readers who happen to be well informed about the period must decide for themselves whether or not disbelief can be suspended. But I think Wilder's deliberate anachronisms are irrelevant to that decision. We must remember that the only certain evidence for Catullus' love for his Clodia, whoever she was, is a sequence of poems of which none is demonstrably earlier than 56 B.C. or demonstrably later than 54 B.C. To bring the affair down to 45, in order to include imperial Caesar, seems to me no more (and no less) gratuitous than to put it back to 60 or before, in order to include Metellus Celer.

5. SOME POST-WAR VERSIONS

At the time of the Suez crisis in 1956, the first Lord of the Admiralty found it comforting to translate Catullus. His versions of poems 8 and 101 were printed soon afterwards in the *Spectator*, and appeared along with nos. 5 and 85 in the author's collected poems in 1968. For Lord Hailsham, as for Tennyson, poem 101 had a personal significance; and perhaps in a way the Lesbia-poems did too: 'all the time I was seeking to establish for myself the continuity of thought and emotion between the ancient and the modern worlds'.[80] Two days after 'Frater, Ave atque Vale' had appeared in the *Spectator*, Harold Nicolson wrote in his diary:[81]

In bed I read Catullus. It passes my comprehension why Tennyson could have called him 'tender'. He is vindictive, venomous, and full of obscene malice. He is only tender about his brother and Lesbia, and in the end she gets it hot as well.

[80] Viscount Hailsham, *PCA* 58 (1961) 10; *Spectator* 4 Jan. 1957 p. 11, 29 March 1957 p. 400; Quintin Hogg, *The Devil's Own Song and other verses* (London 1968) 15f, 24, 29, quotation from p. 3 of the Introduction (see n.13 above for Tennyson).
[81] Harold Nicolson, *Diaries and Letters 1945–1962* (London 1968) 305.

No emotional continuity there – but his reaction shows how Catullus was being read in the post-war world.

Even for a man of Nicolson's generation (he was seventy at the time), 'Catullus' evidently means the whole collection, obscenities included. There was much adverse criticism when Fordyce's commentary appeared in 1961 with 'a few poems which do not lend themselves to comment in English' – in fact, 32 out of 116 – entirely omitted; 'Tropic of Cancer has been published in vain. Lady Chatterley has tiptoed naked through the bluebells to no avail.'[82] The verse translations of the fifties, sixties and seventies are all complete and unexpurgated, sometimes defiantly, sometimes gloatingly, but no longer hiding behind the subscription-list of a private press.[83]

Several of the translators are poets in their own right; as the best of them, C. H. Sisson, puts it, 'I had had my eye on Catullus for years – as what poet would not who could make out even a little of the Latin?'[84] One can even identify a whole genre – going back to Landor and beyond – of poems on (or to) Catullus by poets who have translated him: Sisson himself, Peter Whigham, Humphrey Clucas, and the American G. T. Wright, from whose 'On Translating Catullus' I have taken the epigraph for this chapter.[85]

---

[82] 'Asinius Pollio', *Glasgow University Magazine* 74 (1962–3) 250; I am grateful to Professor P. G. Walsh for the information that the pseudonymous review was written by a student in Fordyce's own department.

[83] F. O. Copley, *Gaius Valerius Catullus, the Complete Poetry* (Ann Arbor 1957); R. A. Swanson, *Odi et Amo: the Complete Poetry of Catullus* (New York 1959); C. H. Sisson, *Catullus* (London 1966); Peter Whigham, *The Poems of Catullus* (Penguin Classics 1966); James Michie, *The Poems of Catullus* (London 1969); R. Myers and R. J. Ormsby, *Catullus, the complete poems for modern readers* (London 1972); Frederic Raphael and Kenneth McLeish, *The Poems of Catullus* (London 1978). First in the post-war field was Lindsay's new translation, *Catullus: the Complete Poems* (London 1948), but that was from a small press and with the order of the poems rearranged, a style that soon went out of fashion.

[84] C. H. Sisson, *In the Trojan Ditch* (Manchester 1974) 161; cf. 159 and 160f on Catullus' 'plainness'.

[85] C. H. Sisson, *Catullus* 9 and 94 = *In the Trojan Ditch* 102; Peter Whigham, *The Poems of Catullus* 11; Humphrey Clucas, 'Living On', *Agenda* 16.3–4 (1978–9) 79 – for his translations, see *Agenda* 14.4/15.1 (1977) 10–14, 16.3–4 (1978–9) 22–38; G. T. Wright,

Another index of his continuing fascination for contemporary poets is the use of Catullan lines as titles or even as integral parts of poems. It can be done straight, as in Basil Bunting's love-poem 'Ille mi par esse deo videtur', based on poem 51 (though not the last stanza); or as a travesty, like Allen Ginsberg's 'Malest Cornifici tuo Catullo', celebrating a homosexual pick-up in San Francisco (with Jack Kerouac as his Cornificius); or as an ironic counterpoint, as in D. M. Thomas' interweaving of lines from poem 5 into a poem about two less successful modern lovers.[86] Poem 5 is also quoted by Carol Rumens, promising 'the gaze of an enchanting young man, | a poet they called Catullus', as the payoff for a schoolgirl's struggles with Latin grammar.[87] The schoolroom Catullus can be used ironically, too; in a collection that broods on mass suffering and the effects of war, James Hamilton-Paterson ends his poem 'latin lesson' with Catullus and Caesar:

> hard to believe that any
> red blooded boy would rather
> wander with lesbia through
> lemon groves than
> run with cohorts[88]

As for 'Lesbia' herself, she re-enacts her Catullan role (under a different pseudonym) for James K. Baxter in his 'Words to Lay a Strong Ghost' – a fourteen-poem sequence that dates from

Centennial Review 19 (1975) 174, cf. 172–3 for his translations. See above, nn.9–10 (Landor), 11 and 13 (Swinburne), 43–5 (Macnaghten, Hiley, Lindsay); also Havelock 1939, vii. The first of all was probably stanza 7 of Robert Herrick's 'To live merrily, and to trust to good verses' (*Hesperides*, 1648).

86 Basil Bunting, *Collected Poems* (London 1968) 131; Allen Ginsberg, *Reality Sandwiches 1953–60* (San Francisco 1966) 47; D. M. Thomas, *Logan Stone* (London 1971), 'Computer 70: Dreams and Lovepoems, 16'. For a different type of homage, cf. D. M. Thomas, *The Honeymoon Voyage* (London 1978) 39 and 44f, based on poems 5 and 62 in the manner of Celia and Louis Zukofsky's *Catullus* (London 1969), 'translating' the sound of Catullus' text.

87 Carol Rumens, 'A Latin Primer: for Kelsey', *Ambit* 80 (1979) 26.

88 James Hamilton-Paterson, *Option Three* (London 1974) 16.

Baxter's collaboration with Kenneth Quinn at Otago in 1966.[89] So Lesbia's afterlife continues. She has survived the moralisers; echoes of Macnaghten's generation could still be heard twenty years ago,[90] but not any more. David Vessey offers a Lesbia for our own time:

> Reading Catullus on the Northern Line
> in Fordyce's edition (which omits the obscene),
> I wondered if Lesbia would have got out at Hampstead
> or come on with me to Golders Green . . .
>
> Who? Lesbia? I know her: she went to Leicester Square
> and hurried through to Soho in the evening rain,
> where she helps the sons of Romulus
> drink Japanese champagne.[91]

The danger now, to judge from some recent translations, is a too self-consciously permissive obscenity which will no doubt seem as absurd to future generations as Macnaghten's see-no-evil innocence does to ours.[92]

We owe it to the dead not to use their world just as a mirror for our own preoccupations. Of all the modern interpreters of 'Lesbia', Alfredo Panzini seems to me to take the soundest line:[93]

Nel parlare di questa dama noi procederemo con prudenza e non con indifferenza, perchè abbiamo paura dei morti. Se essi ascoltano, si possono vendicare.

---

[89] James K. Baxter, *Collected Poems* (Wellington 1979) 356–64, first published in *Runes* (1973); I am very grateful to John Barsby for directing me to Baxter, and for sending me a review of *Runes* (by 'H.D.McN.' in the *Christchurch Press*) which gives the Dunedin background.

[90] Adrian Bury (born 1891), 'Campagna Reverie', *The Immortal Ship* (London 1965) 21f, reflections on Tivoli and poem 44 which contrast sharply with those of John Cotton (born 1925) on Catullus and Sirmione (n.8 above).

[91] David Vessey, 'Lesbia in Orco', *The Ice Age and other Poems* (Scrinium Press, London 1973) 29: I quote the first and last of seven stanzas.

[92] See for instance Raphael and McLeish's version of the fifth stanza of poem 11, totally false to the vocabulary of the original.

[93] A. Panzini, *Il bacio di Lesbia* (Milan 1937) 74. 'In speaking of this lady we shall proceed with prudence, for we are afraid of the dead. If they hear, they can take vengeance.'

They were real people, and we should do our best to understand them in their own terms. It has been the purpose of this book to investigate the world of Catullus and his mistress with as few anachronistic preconceptions as possible. It is hard to make out what there is in the darkness beyond the window, but at least we can try not to be distracted by our own reflections.

APPENDIX

REFERENCES TO CATULLUS IN ANCIENT AUTHORS

I GENERAL REFERENCES

1. Nepos *Atticus* 12.4:
Idem L. Iulium Calidum, quem post Lucreti Catullique mortem multo
elegantissimum poetam nostram tulisse aetatem vere videor posse contendere, neque minus virum bonum optimisque artibus eruditum . . .

2. Horace *Satires* I 10.17–19 (on Old Comedy authors):
> . . . quos neque pulcher
> Hermogenes umquam legit nec simius iste
> nil praeter Calvum et doctus cantare Catullum.

3. Porphyrion on Hor. *Sat.* I 10.19:
Hos autem duos Hermogenem et Demetrium negat antiquas comoedias
legere neque alios quam Licinii Calvi et Valerii Catulli versus modulari.

cf. ps. Acro on the same passage:
Ad nullam rem doctus Demetrius nisi Catulli et Calvi versus cantare et imitari, qui dramatopoeos erat h.l. amatorias cantiones scripserat.

4. Ovid *amores* III 15.7–8:
>Mantua Vergilio gaudet, Verona Catullo;
>Paelignae dicar gloria gentis ego.

5. Velleius Paterculus II 36.2:
Quis enim ignorat diremptos gradibus aetatis floruisse hoc tempore Ciceronem Hortensium †sanequet† Crassum Catonem Sulpicium, moxque Brutum Calidium Caelium Calvum et proximum Ciceroni Caesarem, eorumque velut alumnos Corvinum ac Pollionem Asinium, aemulumque Thucydidis Sallustium, auctoresque carminum Varronem et Lucretium neque ullo in †suspecti operis sui carmine† minorem Catullum.

6. Martial I 61.1–2:
>Verona docti syllabas amat vatis,
>Marone felix Mantua est . . .

7. Martial X 78.14–16 (to Macer):
>Sic inter veteres legar poetas,
>nec multos mihi praeferas priores,
>uno sed tibi sum minor Catullo.

8. Martial XIV 100 (panaca):
>Si non ignota est docti tibi terra Catulli,
>potasti testa Raetica vina mea.

9. Martial XIV 152 (gausapum quadratum):
>Lodices mittet docti tibi terra Catulli:
>nos Helicaonia de regione sumus.

10. Martial XIV 195 (Catullus):
>Tantum magna suo debet Verona Catullo
>quantum parva suo Mantua Vergilio.

11. Jerome *Chronica* 150H (Ol. 173.2):
Gaius Valerius Catullus scriptor lyricus Veronae nascitur.

12. Jerome *Chronica* 154H (Ol. 180.3):
Catullus XXX aetatis anno Romae moritur.

II   LOVE POETRY, LESBIA AND THE *PASSER*

13. Propertius II 25.3–4:
>Ista [sc. Cynthiae] meis fiet notissima forma libellis,
>Calve, tua venia, pace, Catulle, tua.

14. Ovid *amores* III 9.62 (on Tibullus):
> Obvius huic venies hedera iuvenalia cinctus
> tempora cum Calvo, docte Catulle, tuo.

15. Pliny *epistulae* I 16.5 (on Pompeius Saturninus):
Praeterea facit versus qualis Catullus aut Calvus, re vera qualis Catullus aut
Calvus. Quantum illis leporis, dulcedinis, amaritudinis, amoris! Inserit sane,
sed data opera, mollibus levibusque duriusculos quosdam, et hoc quasi Catullus
aut Calvus.

16. Sentius Augurinus, quoted in Pliny *epistulae* IV 27.4:
> Canto carmina versibus minutis
> his olim quibus et meus Catullus
> et Calvus veteresque. Sed quid ad me?
> Unus Plinius est mihi priores:
> mavult versiculos foro relicto
> et quaerit quod amet putatque amari.
> Ille o Plinius, ille quot Catones!
> I nunc, quisquis amas, amare noli!

17. Gellius *noctes Atticae* XIX 9.7 (on Greeks' disdain for Latin love poets):
'Nisi Catullus' inquiunt 'forte pauca et Calvus itidem pauca. Nam Laevius
inplicata et Hortensius invenusta et Cinna inlepida et Memmius dura ac
deinceps omnes rudia fecerunt atque absona.'

18. Propertius II 34.87–8:
> Haec quoque lascivi cantarunt scripta Catulli
> Lesbia quis ipsa notior est Helena.

19. Ovid *tristia* II 427–30:
> Sic sua lascivo cantata est saepe Catullo
> femina cui falsum Lesbia nomen erat;
> nec contentus ea, multos vulgavit amores
> in quibus ipse suum fassus adulterium est.

20. Martial VI 34.7–8 (on kisses):
> Nolo quot arguto dedit exorata Catullo
> Lesbia: pauca cupit qui numerare potest.

21. Martial VIII 73.5–10:
> Cynthia te vatem fecit, lascive Properti;
> ingenium Galli pulchra Lycoris erat;
> fama est arguti Nemesis formosa Tibulli;
> Lesbia dictavit, docte Catulle, tibi;
> non me Paeligni nec spernet Mantua vatem
> si qua Corinna mihi, si quis Alexis erit.

22. Martial XII 44.5–6 (to a poet):
> Lesbia cum lepido te posset amare Catullo,
> te post Nasonem blanda Corinna sequi.

23. Apuleius *apologia* 10:
Eadem igitur opera accusent C. Catullum quod Lesbiam pro Clodia nominarit, et Ticidam similiter quod quae Metella erat Perillam scripserit, et Propertium, qui Cunthiam dicat Hostiam dissimulet, et Tibullum, quod ei sit Plania in animo, Delia in versu.

24. Sidonius Apollinaris *epistulae* II 10.6:
Certe si praeter ‹artem› oratoriam contubernio feminarum poeticum ingenium et oris tui limam frequentium studiorum cotibus expolitam quereris obtundi, reminiscere quod saepe versum Corinna cum suo Nasone complevit, Lesbia cum Catullo, Caesennia cum Gaetulico, Argentaria cum Lucano, Cynthia cum Propertio, Delia cum Tibullo.

25. Martial I 7:
> Stellae delicium mei Columba,
> Verona licet audiente dicam,
> vicit, Maxime, passerem Catulli.
> Tanto Stella meus tuo Catullo
> quanto passere maior est columba.

26 Martial I 109.1 (on a pet dog):
> Issa est passere nequior Catulli . . .

27. Martial IV 14.11–14 (to Silius Italicus):
> . . . nec torva lege fronte sed remissa
> lascivis madidos iocis libellos.
> Sic forsan·tener ausus est Catullus
> magno mittere passerem Maroni.

28. Martial XI 6.14–16 (on poetry and wine, to a cup-bearer):
> Da nunc basia, sed Catulliana:
> quae si tot fuerint quot ille dixit,
> donabo tibi passerem Catulli.

29. Martial VII 14.1–6:
> Accidit infandum nostrae scelus, Aule, puellae:
> amisit lusus deliciasque suas:
> non quales teneri ploravit amica Catulli
> Lesbia, nequitiis passeris orba sui,
> vel Stellae cantata meo quas flevit Ianthis,
> cuius in Elysio nigra columba volat . . .

30. Martial XIV 77 (cavea eborea):
> Si tibi talis erit qualem dilecta Catullo
> Lesbia plorabat, hic habitare potest.

Cf. Juvenal VI 5–10 (on the chaste age of Saturn):
> Silvestrem montana torum cum sterneret uxor
> frondibus et culmo vicinarumque ferarum
> pellibus, haut similis tibi, Cynthia, nec tibi, cuius
> turbavit nitidos extinctus passer ocellos,
> sed potanda ferens infantibus ubera magnis
> et saepe horridior glandem ructante marito.

31. *Grammatici Latini* VI 260f Keil (Caesius Bassus):
Nam et hendecasyllabus, quem phalaecium vocamus, apud antiquos auctores eodem modo solebat incipere alias a spondeo, alias ab iambo, alias a trochaeo, ut apud Catullum a spondeo 'passer deliciae meae puellae', a trochaeo 'arido modo pumice expolitum', ab iambo 'meas esse aliquid putare nugas'. Quae omnia genera hendecasyllabi Catullus et Sappho et Anacreonta et alios auctores secutus non tamquam vitiosa vitavit, sed tamquam legitima inseruit.

Cf. ibid. VI 293 Keil (Atilius Fortunatianus):
Ecce et phalaecium metrum partem primam de antispastico metro habet, sequentem de iambico, ut 'passer deliciae meae puellae'.

Cf. ibid. VI 614 Keil (Censorinus):
Undecim syllabarum phalaecius 'passer deliciae meae puellae'.

III EPIGRAMS

32. Martial I preface:
Lascivam verborum veritatem, id est epigrammaton linguam, excusarem, si meum esset exemplum: sic scribit Catullus, sic Marsus, sic Pedo, sic Gaetulicus, sic quicumque perlegitur.

33. Martial II 71.1–5:
> Candidius nihil est te, Caeciliane. Notavi,
> si quando ex nostris disticha pauca lego,
> protinus aut Marsi recitas aut scripta Catulli.
> Hoc mihi das, tamquam deteriora legas,
> ut conlata magis placeant mea?

34. Martial VII 99.5–9 (to a friend of Domitian):
> Dicere de nobis ut lector candidus aude
> 'Temporibus praestat non nihil iste tuis,
> Nec Marso nimium minor est doctoque Catullo.'
> Hoc satis est: ipsi cetera mando deo.

35. Quintilian I 5.8 (on aspiration):
Erupit brevi tempore nimius usus, ut 'choronae', 'chenturiones', 'praechones'
adhuc quibusdam in inscriptionibus maneant, qua de re Catulli nobile epigramma est.

36. Quintilian VI 3.18:
Nam et Cicero omne quod salsum sit ait esse Atticorum, non quia sunt maxime
ad risum compositi, et Catullus, cum dicit 'nulla est in corpore mica salis', non
hoc dicit, nihil in corpore eius esse ridiculum.

37. Gellius *noctes Atticae* VII 16.2 (on an ignorant person):
Nam cum esset verbum 'deprecor' doctiuscule positum in Catulli carmine, quia
id ignorabat, frigidissimos versus esse dicebat omnium quidem iudicio venus-
tissimos, quos subscripsi:
        Lesbia mi dicit semper male nec tacet umquam
            de me: Lesbia me dispeream nisi amat.
        Quo signo? Quia sunt totidem mea: deprecor illam
            assidue, verum dispeream nisi amo.

38–39. Festus 260L:
Ploxinum appellari ait Catullum capsum in cisio capsa‹m›ve cum dixit 'gingivas
vero ploxini habet veteris'.

38–39. Quintilian I 5.8 (on barbarisms):
. . . sicut Catullus 'ploxenum' circa Padum invenit.

40. Donatus on Terence *Andria* 718:
Amicus animi est, amator corporis. Non enim continuo amator et bene vult, ut
Dido amavit quidem Acneam, sed non ut amica fuit, quae ait [*Aen.* IV 600f]
'non potui a. d. c. e. v. s.' et item Catullus 'cogit amare magis, sed bene velle
minus'. Et est hoc officium et blandimentum.

41. Philargyrius on Virg. *ecl.* 9.35:
Cinna Smyrnam scripsit, quam nonum post annum, ut Catullus ait, edidit, id
quod et Quintilianus ait [x 4.4].

IV   MYTHOLOGICAL EPIC

42. Lygdamus [Tib. III] 6.39–42:
            Gnosia, Theseae quondam periuria linguae
                flevisti ignoto sola relicta mari:
            sic cecinit pro te doctus, Minoi, Catullus
                ingrati referens impia facta viri.

43. Nonius 154L:
Externavit, ut consternavit, id est dementem fecit. Catullus: 'a misera! adsiduis
quam luctibus externavit | spinosas Erycina serens in pectore curas.'

44. Schol. Veronensis on Virg. *Aen.* v 80:
Salve sancta parens: Catullus 'Salvete, deum gens, o bona matrum progenies, salvete iter‹um . . .›.'

45. Servius on Virg. *Aen.* v 591 ('frangeret indeprensus et irremeabilis error'):
Est autem versus Catulli.

46. Macrobius *Saturnalia* vi 1.41–2:
'Talia saecla, suis dixerunt, currite, fusis.' Catullus 'currite ducenti subtemine, currite fusi.' 'Felix, heu nimium felix, si littora tantum | numquam Dardaniae tetigissent nostra carinae.' Catullus 'Iuppiter omnipotens, utinam ne tempore primo | Gnosia Cecropiae tetigissent litore puppes.'

47. Nonius 876L (charcesia):
Alias summa pars mali, id est foramina quae summo mali funes recipiunt . . .
Catullus Veronensis: 'lucida quae splendent ‹. . .› carchesia mali.'
[Attributed to Cinna by Isid. *Orig.* xix 2.10 and Schol. Lucan v 418.]

V IAMBICS AND INVECTIVE

48. Quintilian x 1.96:
Iambus non sane a Romanis celebratus est ut proprium opus ‹sed aliis› quibusdam interpositus; cuius acerbitas in Catullo, Bibaculo, Horatio, quamquam illi epodos interveniat, reperietur.

49. Tacitus *Annals* iv 34.8 (speech of Cremutius Cordus):
Carmina Bibaculi et Catulli referta contumeliis Caesarum leguntur; sed ipse divus Iulius, ipse divus Augustus et tulere ista et reliquere, haud facile dixerim moderatione magis an sapientia.

50. Suetonius *Julius* 73:
Valerium Catullum, a quo sibi versiculis de Mamurra perpetua stigmata imposita non dissimulaverat, satis facientem eadem die adhibuit cenae hospitioque patris eius, sicut consuerat, uti perseveravit.

51. *Grammatici Latini* i 495 Keil (Diomedes):
Cuius carminis [sc. iambi] praecipui scriptores apud Graecos Archilochus et Hipponax, apud Romanos Lucilius et Catullus et Horatius et Bibaculus.

52. Porphyrion on Hor. *Odes* i 16.24:
Iambi autem versus aptissimi habentur ad maledicendum. Denique et Catullus, cum maledicta minaretur, sic ait: 'at non effugies meos iambos'.

53. Pliny *Natural History* xxxvi 48:
Primum Romae parietes crusta marmoris operuisse totos domus suae in Caelio monte Cornelius Nepos tradit Mamurram, Formiis natum equitem R., praefectum fabrum C. Caesaris in Gallia, ne quid indignitati desit, tali auctore inventa

re. Hic namque est Mamurra Catulli Veroniensis carminibus proscissus, quem, ut res est, domus ipsius clarius quam Catullus dixit habere quidquid habuisset Comata Gallia.

54. ibid. XXXVII 81 (on opals):
Magnitudo abellanam nucem aequat, insignis etiam apud nos historia, siquidem exstat hodieque huius generis gemma, propter quam ab Antonio proscriptus est Nonius senator, filius Strumae Nonii eius quem Catullus poeta in sella curuli visum indigne tulit avusque Servili Noniani quem consulem vidimus.

55. Boethius *de consolatione* III 4 (on *dignitates*):
Quo fit, ut indignemur eas saepe nequissimis hominibus contigisse; unde Catullus licet in curuli Nonium sedentem strumam tamen appellat.
Cf. *Grammatici Latini* VI 257 Keil (Caesius Bassus):
Cuius exemplum 'sella in curuli struma Nonius sedet' fac pro sedet sedit, erit scazon.
Cf. ibid. VI 136 (Marius Victorinus):
Erit in exemplo versus hic 'sella in curuli struma Nonius sedet'.

56. Apuleius *apologia* 6:
Nisi forte in eo reprendendus sum, quod Calpurniano pulvisculum ex Arabicis frugibus miserim, quem multo aequius erat spurcissimo ritu Hiberorum, ut ait Catullus, sua sibi urina 'dentem atque russam pumicare gingivam'.

57. Porphyrion on Hor. *Sat.* II 3.299:
Hoc Catullus meminit: '⟨sed non⟩ videmus manticae quod in tergo est'.

58–60. *Grammitici Latini* I 252 Keil (Charisius 330B):
Senesco autem nunc in usu est frequens, apud antiquos tamen et seneo dicebatur; unde et Catullus sic rettulit, 'nunc recondita | senet quiete seque dedicat tibi, | gemelle Castoris'.

58–60. ibid. I 344 (Diomedes):
Nam senesco et seneo apud antiquos dicebatur, unde et Catullus 'nunc recondita | senet quiete seque dicebat tibi, | gemelle Castor et gemelle Castoris'.

58–60. ibid. II 484 (Priscian):
Catullus: 'sed haec fuere; nunc recondita senet quiete'; senesco enim inchoativum est.

61–62. ibid. II 188 (Priscian):
'Unus', quia de vocativo quidam dubitant, Caper, doctissimus antiquitatis perscrutator, ostendit hoc usum Catullum et Plautum. Catullus: 'tu praeter omnes une de capillatis, | Celtiberosae Celtiberiae fili'.

61–62. ibid. II 305 (Priscian, on the vocative of *filius*):

Catullus autem: 'tu praeter omnes une de capillatis | Celtiberosae Celtiberiae fili'.

63. *Glossaria Latina* I 443 Lindsay = *Corp. Gloss. Lat.* V 233 Goetz:
Pinguis: grassus. Nam obesus plus est quam pinguis. Catullus ait: 'aut pinguis ubera aut obesus et grossus'.

VI HENDECASYLLABLES

64. *Grammatici Latini* I 97 Keil (Charisius 124B):
Hos pugillares et masculino genere et semper pluraliter dicas, sicut Asinius in Valer‹ium›, quia pugillus est qui plures tabellas continet in seriem sutas. At tamen haec pugillaria saepius neutraliter dicit idem Catullus in hendecasyllabis.

65. Seneca *controversiae* VII 4.7 (on Calvus):
Idem postea, cum videret a clientibus Catonis, rei sui, Pollionem Asinium circumventum in foro caedi, imponi se supra cippum iussit – erat enim parvolus statura, propter quod etiam Catullus in hendecasyllabis vocat illum 'salaputium disertum' – et iuravit, si quam iniuriam Cato Pollioni Asinio accusatori suo fecisset, se in eum iuraturum calumniam.

66–73. Pliny *Natural History* preface 1:
Libros naturalis historiae, novicium Camenis Quiritium tuorum opus, natos apud me proxima fetura licentiore epistula narrare constitui tibi, iucundissime imperator – sit enim haec tui praefatio, verissima, dum maximi consenescit in patre – namque tu solebas nugas esse aliquid meas putare, ut obiter emolliam Catullum conterraneum meum (agnoscis et hoc castrense verbum). Ille enim, ut scis, permutatis prioribus syllabis duriusculum se fecit quam volebat existimari a Veranolis suis et Fabullis.

66–73. *Grammatici Latini* VI 401 Keil (Terentianus Maurus):
> exemplis tribus hoc statim probabis
> docti carmine quae legis Catulli,
> 'cui dono lepidum novum libellum
> arido modo pumice expolitum',
> 'meas esse aliquid putare nugas'.

66–73. Ibid. VI 148 (Marius Victorinus):
Nam quidam et trochaeum et iambum in ea sede collocasse reperiuntur, inter quos et Catullus est sub exemplis huius modi, 'cui dono lepidum novum libellum | arido modo pumice expolitum', 'meas esse aliquid putare nugas'.

66–73. Ibid. VI 298 (Atilius Fortunatianus):
Talis est pars ex Catulliano hendecasyllabo detracta priore parte, 'pumice expolitum'.

66–73. Schol. Veronensis on Virg. *ecl.* 6.1:
'Dignata est' adroganter dictum, quasi potuerit maiora scribere ‹quam Bucolica› quod ex facili compositione ‹paratur. 'Ludere' autem, ut Horatius› 'nec
sicut olim lusit Anacreon', vel Veronensis Catullus: '‹cui dono lepidum novum
libellum› | arido modo pumice expolitum? | Corneli tibi: namque tu solebas |
meas esse aliquid putare nugas.'

66–73. Ausonius *opuscula* XIII pref. 1:
    'Cui dono lepidum novum libellum?'
    Veronensis ait poeta quondam
    inventoque dedit statim Nepoti.

66–73. Ausonius *opuscula* XVIII preface.
Dein cogitans mecum, non illud Catullianum 'cui dono lepidum novum
libellum' sed ἀμουσότερον et verius 'cui dono inlepidum rudem libellum',
non diu quaesivi.

66–73. Isidore *origines* VI 12.3:
Circumcidi libros Siciliae primum increbuit. Nam initio pumicebantur. Unde
et Catullus ait: 'cui dono lepidum novum libellum | arido modo pumice
expolitum.'

74–75. Pliny *epistulae* IV 14.5 (on his hendecasyllables):
Scimus alioqui huius opusculi illam esse verissimam legem, quam Catullus
expressit: 'nam castum esse decet pium poetam | ipsum, versiculos nihil necesse
est, | qui tunc denique habent salem et leporem | si sunt molliculi et parum
pudici.'

74–75. Apuleius *apologia* 11:
Catullum ita respondentem malivolis non legistis: 'nam castum esse decet pium
poetam | ipsum, versiculos nihil necesse est'.

76. Gellius *noctes Atticae* VI 20.6 (on euphony of vowels):
Catullus quoque elegantissimus poetarum in hisce versibus 'minister vetuli
puer Falerni, | inger mi calices amariores, | ut lex Postumiae iubet magistrae |
ebria acina ebriosioris', cum dicere 'ebrio' posset et, quod erat usitatius,
'acinum' in neutro genere appellare, amans tamen hiatus illius Homerici
suavitatem, 'ebriam' dixit propter insequentis a litterae concentum. Qui
'ebriosa' autem Catullum dixisse putant aut 'ebrioso', nam id quoque temere
scriptum invenitur, in libros scilicet de corruptis exemplaribus factos
inciderunt.

77. *Grammatici Latini* I 133–4 Keil (Charisius 170B):
Inpotente Catullus: 'deperit inpotente amore'.

78. Macrobius *Saturnalia* II 1.8:

Excepit Symmachus: 'Quia Saturnalibus optimo dierum, ut ait Veronensis poeta, nec voluptas nobis ut Stoicis tamquam hostis repudianda est . . .'

79. Martianus Capella III 229:
Itaque assertor nostri [sc. Litteraturae] nunc litteratus dicitur, litterator antea vocabatur. Hoc etiam Catullus quidem, non insuavis poeta, commemorat dicens 'munus dat tibi Sylla litterator'.

80. *Grammatici Latini* II 16 Keil (Priscian):
Similiter Catullus Veronensis 'quod zonam soluit diu ligatam' inter hendeca-syllabos phalaecios posuit, ergo nisi 'soluit' trisyllabum accipias, versus stare non possit.

VII LYRIC METRES

81. Jerome *epistulae* 53.8.17:
David, Simonides noster, Pindarus et Alcaeus, Flaccus quoque, Catullus et Serenus, Christum lyra personat et in decacordo psalterio ab inferis excitat resurgentem.

82. Quintilian IX 3.16:
Catullus in epithalamio: 'dum innupta manet, dum cara suis est', cum prius 'dum' significat 'quoad', sequens 'usque eo'.

83. Festus 396L (suppernati):
Et Catu‹l›lus . . . 'in› fossa Liguri ia‹cet suppernata se›curi'.

84. *Grammatici Latini* VI 411–12 Keil (Terentianus Maurus, on Galliambics):
          . . . servasse quae Catullus probat ipse tibi liber,
          'super alta vectus Attis celeri rate maria'.
    Cf. ibid. VI 154 (Marius Victorinus):
Hoc genus metri maxime desiderat separari in duas clausulas, tamquam 'super alta vectus Attis', dehinc 'celeri rate maria'.

85. Ibid. VI 262 (Caesius Bassus):
Sed quo magis hic versus, quod matri sacer est Idaeae, vibrare videatur, proximum ab ultimo pedem brachysyllabon fecerunt et Graeci et hic ipse Maecenas iis quos modo rettuli proximum sic, 'latus horreat flagello, comitum chorus ululet', et Catullus 'Phrygium nemus citato cupide ‹pede› tetigit'.

86. Ibid. (Caesius Bassus, immediately following):
Catullus in anacreonteo ‹. . .› 'ades inquit o Cybebe'.
    [Keil marks a lacuna (concealing the first half of Cat. 63.91?).]

87. Festus 338L:
Ra‹bidus a rabie dictus, qui morbus caninus est.› Catullu‹s . . . 'abit in quiete mol›li rabidus ‹furor animi›'.

88. Nonius Marcellinus 517L:
Properiter. Catullus 'animula miserula properiter abiit'.
[Attributed to Serenus by Diomedes *Gramm. Lat.* I 513K.]

89–91. *Grammatici Latini* VI 260 Keil (Caesius Bassus):
De priapeo metro. Ex hac divisione et priapeus nascitur versus, cuius exemplum apud Catullum 'hunc lucum tibi dedico consecroque, Priape' . . . Non ignoro autem variari primas et secundas syllabas utriusque in priapeo commatis, ut modo ab iambo incipiat, modo a trochaeo, tamquam 'hunc locum tibi dedico consecroque, Priape, | libens hoc tibi dedico, libens, sancte Priape.'

89–91. Ibid. VI 406 (Terentianus Maurus):
     Ipse enim sonus indicat esse hoc lusibus aptum,
     et ferme modus hic datur a plerisque Priapo.
     Inter quos cecinit quoque carmen tale Catullus,
     'hunc lucum tibi dedico consecroque, Priape,
     qua domus tua Lampsaci est ‹usque› quaque, Priape:
     nam te praecipue in suis urbibus colit ora
     Hellespontia ceteris ostriosior oris.'
     Et plures similes sic conscripsisse Catullum
     scimus.

89–91. Ibid. VI 151 (Marius Victorinus):
Nam divisio huius in secundo commate infracta paululum ac mollior receptis in versu primo et quarto spondeis efficitur, ut apud Catullum 'hunc lucum tibi dedico consecroque, Priape', quos distinctio occultat auribus . . . Igitur quod hoc versu Priapi laudes plerique canendo prosecuti sunt, priapeum metrum nuncuparunt, quod genus hexametri adeo abhorret ab heroi lege, ut utraque pars [commatis] non numquam trochaeis et iambis aut pro spondeo anapaestis inchoetur aut etiam cretico prius comma pro dactylo terminetur, ut est apud Catullum 'nam te praecipue in suis', dehinc 'Hellespontia ceteris', quia bina sunt cola mora distinctionis intercedente.
    Cf. ibid. VI 615 (Censorinus):
Priapeum 'hunc lucum tibi dedico consecroque, Priape'.
    Cf. ibid. VI 292 (Atilius Fortunatianus):
Est alius priapeus, qui et bucolicus vocatur, ut 'hunc lucum tibi dedico consecroque, Priape'.
    Cf. ibid. VI 119 (Marius Victorinus, on trimeters):
Huius exemplum . . . 'hunc lucum tibi dedico', dehinc 'consecroque Priape'.

92. Nonius Marcellinus 195L:
Ligurrire, degustare, unde abligurrire, multa avide consumere . . . Catullus †priopo† 'de meo ligurrire libido est'.

VIII SCAENICA

93. Martial V 30. 1–4:

> Varro, Sophocleo non infitiande coturno
> nec minus in Calabra suspiciende lyra,
> differ opus nec te facundi scaena Catulli
> detineat cultis aut elegia comis.

94. Martial XII 83:

> Derisor Fabianus hirnearum,
> omnes quem modo colei timebant
> dicentem tumidas in hydrocelas
> quantum nec duo dicerent Catulli,
> in thermis subito Neronianis
> vidit se miser et tacere coepit.

95. Juvenal XIII 110f (on perjurers):

> . . . mimum agit ille
> urbani qualem fugitivus scurra Catulli.

96. Scholiast on Juv. XIII 109f (p. 205 Wessner):
Nam cum, inquit, hominis, qui malam causam habet, id est qui denegat alienum, visa fuerit improba contentio, audacia creditur innocens, ut mimum urbani scurrae agere hac inrisionis audacia videatur. Talis est enim mimus, ubi servus fugitivus dominum suum trahit. Catullus mimographus fuit.

97. Juvenal VIII 185–8:

> Consumptis opibus vocem, Damasippe, locasti
> sipario, clamosum ageres ut Phasma Catulli.
> Laureolum velox etiam bene Lentulus egit,
> iudice me dignus vera cruce.

98. Scholiast on Juv. VIII 185–7 (p. 147 Wessner):
Id est, praeco fuisti in mimo. Velum, sub quo latent paradoxi, cum in scaenam prodeunt, (2) aut ostium mimi, (3) aut quod appellant comicum. Ut Phasma Catulli: nomen est mimographi, et Phasma nomen est fabulae. Hoc ideo, quia in ipso mimo Laureolo figitur crux. Unde vera cruce dignus est Lentulus, qui tanto detestabilior est quanto melius gestum imitatus est scaenicum. (2) Hic Lentulus nobilis fuit et suscepit servi personam in agendo mimo et deprehensus in falso cruci fixus est.

99. Tertullian *adversus Valentinianos* 14:
Inde invenitur Iao in scripturis. Ita depulsa, quominus pergeret, nec habens supervolare Crucem, id est Horon, quia nullum Catulli Laureolum fuerit exercitata, ut destituta, ut passioni illi suae intricata multiplici atque perplexae, omni genere eius coepit adfligi . . .

> Cf. Martial *de spectaculis* 7.1–4, 11–12:

Qualiter in Scythica religatus rupe Prometheus
   adsiduam nimio pectore pavit avem,
nuda Caledonio sic viscera praebuit urso
   non falsa pendens in cruce Laureolus . . .
Vicerat antiquae sceleratus crimina famae,
   in quod quae fuerat fabula poena fuit.

IX OTHER GENRES?

100. Pliny *Natural History* XXVIII 19:
Defigi quidem diris deprecationibus nemo non metuit. Hoc pertinet ovorum quae exorbuerit quisque calices coclearumque protinus frangi aut isdem cocleariibus perforari. Hinc Theocriti apud Graecos, Catulli apud nos proximeque Vergilii incantamentorum amatoria imitatio.
   Cf. *Gramm. Lat.* I 87 Keil (Charisius 109B):
Hoc femur huius femoris. Sed frequenter huius feminis huic femini dictum ‹est, et› pluraliter tam femina quam femora; ideoq‹ue . . .›ullus hoc ipsum erudite custodit, cum dicit 'inplicuitque femur femini'.
   [Attributed to Tibullus by Charisius 166B; but Tib. I 8.26 is 'femori conseruisse femur'. Cf. Theocr. 2.140: καὶ ταχὺ χρὼς ἐπὶ χρωτὶ πεπαίνετο.]

101. Schol. Bernensis on Lucan I 544 (pp. 35f Usener):
Atreus Thyestis fratris sui filios ob adulterium Aeropae uxoris suae ad aram mactavit simulato sacrificio. Vinum sanguine mixtum visceraque filiorum eius pro epulis Thyesti adposuisse dicitur. Quod nefas ne sol aspiceret, nubibus se abscondit, hoc est eclipsin passus est, Mycenisque nox fuit. Sed hoc fabulosum inveni in libro Catulli †quis cribitur permimologiãrum†. Qui ait ‹Atreum› primum civibus suis solis cursus veros et ante inauditos ostendisse ac persuasisse illum contrarium signis omnibus ascendere et quod ceterae vagae stellae facere dicuntur: et ob hanc scientiam inclitum summoto fratre regnum accepisse. Quod in prodigium minores tragoedi converterunt.

102. Servius on Virg. *Georgics* II 55 ('quo te carmine dicam Raetica'):
Hanc uvam Cato praecipue laudat in libris quos scripsit ad filium; contra Catullus eam vituperat et dicit nulli rei esse aptam, miraturque cur eam laudaverit Cato. Sciens ergo utrumque Vergilius medium tenuit . . .

103. Varro *de lingua Latina* VI 6:
Nox, quod, ut Catullus ait, 'omnia nisi interveniat sol pruina obriguerint', quod nocet, nox, nisi quod Graece νύξ nox.

X UNSPECIFIED

104. Nonius Marcellinus 291L:
Cinis masculino Vergilius in bucolicis . . . Feminino aput Caesarem et Catullum et Calvum lectum est, quorum vaccillat auctoritas.

105. Servius on Virgil *Aeneid* IV 409 (on *fervere*):
Sed dicimus a tertia esse coniugatione imperativum, ut 'cavo cavis'; hinc etiam Catullus 'cavere' dixit.

106. Servius on Virgil *Aeneid* V 610:
Notandum sane etiam de Iride arcum genere masculino dicere Vergilium. Catullus et alii genere feminino ponunt, referentes ad originem, sicut 'haec cattus' et 'haec gallus' legimus.

107. Servius on Virgil *Aeneid* VII 378 (on *turbo*):
Catullus 'hoc turben' dicit, ut 'hoc carmen, fulmen'. Est autem 'hic turbo', unde 'turbinis' facit: nam si 'turbonis' sit, erit a proprio nomine genetivus.

108. Servius on Virgil *Aeneid* XII 587:
'In pumice' autem masculino genere posuit, et hunc sequimur; nam et Plautus ita dixit, licet Catullus dixerit feminino.

109. Schol. Veronensis on Virgil *Aeneid* VIII 34 (cf. Baehrens 1885, 126):
Carbasus et masculino et feminino genere dictus est. Catullus 'cannubiae ‹. . .› carbasus ‹. . .›ros'.

UNATTRIBUTED QUOTATIONS

i. Varro *de lingua Latina* VII 50:
Vesperugo stella quae vespere oritur, a quo eam Opillus scribit vesperum: itaque †dicitur alterum† 'vesper adest', quem Graeci dicunt †di† ἑσπέριον.
   [Schwabe 1886, 47 reads DICITVALERIVS for DICITVRALTERVM.]

ii. Seneca *apocolocyntosis* 11.6:
Pedibus in hanc sententiam itum est. Nec mora, Cyllenius illum collo obtorto trahit ad inferos, a caelo 'unde negant redire quemquam'.

iii. Quintilian IX 4.141:
Aspera vero et maledica, ut dixi, etiam in carmine iambis grassantur: 'quis hoc potest videre, quis potest pati | nisi impudicus et vorax et aleo?'

iv. Quintilian XI 1.38:
Negat se magni facere aliquis poetarum, utrum Caesar ater an albus homo sit, insania.

v. *Grammatici Latin* VI 125 Keil (Marius Victorinus):
In suprema autem parte versus, id est ante ultimum spondaeum, quo herous clauditur, et post quintum pedem, interponimus dactylum, quo pes septimus anapaestus efficiatur superfluente semipede, veluti 'Peliaco quondam prognatae vertice pinus': adicio versui primam syllabam longam 'ex', item ante ultimum pono pedem 'per freta', fiet talis, 'ex Peliaco quondam prognatae vertice per freta pinus'.

vi. Ibid. vi 293 (Atilius Fortunatianus):
In iambico metro si paenultimam longam feceris, scazon vocatur, quem et choliambon et hipponaction vocant, ut 'salax taberna vosque contubernales'.

vii. Ibid. vi 612 (Censorinus):
Trimetrus iambicus Latine senarius dicitur, cuius exemplum 'phaselus iste quem videtis hospites'.
    Ibid. vi 134 (Marius Victorinus):
Exemplum ergo trimetri iambici erit 'phaselus ille quem videtis hospites'.
    Ibid. vi 393 (Terentianus Maurus):
        Sed hic trimetrus quando duplicem pedem
        a capite sumet, tunc quadratus dicitur,
        idemque dictus est et octonarius.
        Ante ergo versum collocabo iambicum,
        'phaselus ille quem videtis hospites':
        quadratus iste talis effici potest,
        'adest celer phaselus ille quem videtis hospites'.
    Schol. Bernensis on Virgil Georg. iv 289:
Phaselis: genus navium pictarum, sicut 'phaselus ille', quem †agiunt auctorem† esse navium †calcaetarum†, quem habuit hospes Serenus.
    Scholiast on Lucan v 518:
Phaselus genus navis, ut ait Plautus, 'phaselus ille quem videtis hospites', et Vergilius, 'et circum pictis vehitur sua rura phaselis'.
    Augustine de musica v 5, 11, 16:
Nam neque quisquam umquam, sive doctissimorum hominum sive mediocriter, vel etiam tenuiter eruditorum, versum esse dubitavit 'phaselus ille quem videtis hospites' . . . Quapropter, omni iam dubitatione sublata, etiam istum versum metire, si placet, et mihi de membris eius pedibusque responde, 'phaselus ille quem videtis hospites' . . . Et 'phaselus ille quem videtis hospites' primum membrum habet 'phaselus ille' in semipedibus quinque, secundum in septem, 'quem videtis hospites'.

viii. Isidorus origines xix 33.3:
Strophium et cingulum aureum cum gemmis. De quo ait Cinna 'strophio lactantes cincta papillas'.

INDEX TO APPENDIX (by item number)

34, 37, 42, 67; *dulcedo* 15; *duritas* 15, 66; *elegantia* 1, 76; *facundia* 93; *lascivia* 18, 19, 32; *lepor* 15, 22; *levitas* 15; *mollitia* 15; *nobilitas* 35; *suavitas* 76, 79; *teneritas* 27, 29; *urbanitas* 95; *venustas* 37

Poets compared or associated with Catullus:

Alcaeus 81; Anacreon 31; Archilochus 51; Bibaculus 48, 49, 51; Calvus 2, 3, 13, 14, 15, 16, 17; Cinna 17; Gaetulicus 25, 32; Gallus 21; Hipponax 51; Horace 48, 51, 81; Hortensius 17; Iulius Calidus 1; Laevius 17; Lucan 24; Lucilius 51; Lucretius 1, 5; Marsus 32, 33, 34; Martial 7, 21, 27, 32, 33, 34; Memmius 17; Ovid 4, 14, 19, 21, 22, 24; Pedo 32; Pindar 81; Propertius 13, 18, 23, 24 (cf. 30); Sappho 31; Serenus 81 (cf. 88); Simonides 81; Stella 25, 29; Tibullus 21, 23, 24; Ticida 23; Varro 5; Virgil 4, 6, 10, 21

ENDNOTES

1. MURENA DANCING

Defending L. Murena on a charge of *ambitus* late in 63 B.C., Cicero begins with a refutation of the prosecution's attack on Murena's private life.[1] He selects two apparently unconnected jibes: that Murena had been in the province of Asia ('obiecta est enim Asia'), and that Murena was a dancer.[2] In fact, the two *are* connected, in that Asia was regarded as synonymous with luxury and self-indulgence, and luxury and self-indulgence – in the shape of drunken and licentious parties – provided the only reason for a sane man to get up and dance. The key words are *voluptas, luxuria, deliciae*, and they are applied by Cicero in both contexts.[3]

Cicero presents these allegations as if they were merely gratuitous slander, and the structure of his speech separates them wholly from the main burden of the charge against Murena. We may suspect, however, that the prosecution's case had more coherence than Cicero gives it credit for, and that he deliberately dealt with it piecemeal in order to minimise its impact. For the key words turn up again much later in the speech, on the question of Murena's bribery. He was alleged to have issued invitations to dinner not just to his fellow-*tribules*, which was legally acceptable, but indiscriminately (*volgo*). Cato, for the

---

[1] Cic. *Mur.* 11–13, announced in the *divisio* at the beginning of §11 as *reprehensio vitae.*

[2] *Mur.* 13: 'Saltatorem appellat L. Murenam Cato. Maledictum est, si vere obicitur, vehementis accusatoris, sin falso, maledici conviciatoris.'

[3] 'Asia . . . non ad *voluptatem* et *luxuriam* expetita est' (11); 'si habet Asia suspicionem *luxuriae* quandam' (12); '*deliciarum* comes est extrema saltatio' (13); 'cum ea non reperiantur quae *voluptatis* nomen habent . . ., in quo ipsam *luxuriam* reperire non potes, in eo te umbram luxuriae reperturum putas?' (13); 'Asiam istam . . . *delicatam* sic obiit ut in ea neque avaritiae neque *luxuriae* vestigium reliquerit' (20). For Asia and its temptations see Cic. *QF* 1 1.7f and 19 ('tam corruptrice provincia'), *Flacc.* 5.

prosecution, had been indignant at the idea of enticing goodwill with food and corrupting the voters with *voluptates*:[4]

> Quippe, inquit, tu mihi summum imperium, tu summam auctoritatem, tu gubernacula rei publicae petas fovendis hominum sensibus et deleniendis animis et adhibendis voluptatibus? Utrum lenocinium, inquit, a grege delicatae iuventutis, an orbis terrarum imperium a populo Romano petebas?

> 'Shall you', says he, 'seek to obtain supreme power, supreme authority, and the helm of the republic, by encouraging men's sensual appetites, by soothing their minds, by tendering luxuries to them? Are you asking employment as a pimp from a band of luxurious youths, or the sovereignty of the world from the Roman people?'

Cicero can afford to reproduce this *horribilis oratio* because he has already softened up his audience with a long and very funny account of Cato as a rigid Stoic, unable to distinguish venial faults from serious ones, followed immediately by a passage on service and obligation between high and low, making out that what Murena did for his *amici tenuiores* was no more than time-honoured generosity.[5] That was to cancel out the effect on the jury's minds of Cato's speech for the prosecution, which evidently presented Murena as a wealthy playboy devoted to extravagance and self-indulgence in food, drink and sex, who not only bribed the electorate with money and lavish shows,[6] but won over influential voters by inviting them to dinner-parties at which there was plenty to drink, entertaining cabaret featuring the host himself as well as the professional *saltatores*, and no doubt a certain amount of 'what comes after' as well (pp. 44f above), justifying Cato's denunciation of him as a pimp.

From what we know of their respective attitudes to moral depravity

---

[4] *Mur.* 74 (quotation from C. D. Yonge's 1851 Bohn translation); *voluptas* occurs three times in §74, *voluptas* and *luxuria* once each in §76.

[5] *Mur.* 61–6 (note 'austere et Stoice' at the beginning of §74); 68–73, honorific escort-duty rewarded by seats at the games (chariots in the Circus, gladiators in the Forum) and invitations to dinner.

[6] *Mur.* 40 (addressing Ser. Sulpicius) on 'huius istam ipsam quam inrides argenteam scaenam'; the whole passage 38–40 is important for the significance of *ludi* in Roman life (pp. 2f above).

and political expediency,[7] we may reasonably guess that Cato's version was closer to the reality of things than Cicero's.

2. CATULLUS' COLLECTION

The orthodox view is that the collection of Catullus' poems that has come down to us was first compiled after the poet's death, and does not represent (or represents only in part) the order in which Catullus intended the poems to be read. I have argued elsewhere that this is an unnecessary hypothesis, and that the ordering of the poems can and should be read as Catullus' own.[8] Without going into the details again, it may be worth looking briefly at the methodological issue.

One might expect, *a priori*, that a collection entitled *Catulli Veronensis liber* and beginning with a dedication poem ought to be Catullus' own arrangement. Three main arguments are adduced to defeat this expectation, and to make necessary the hypothesis of an unattested 'post-humous editor': first, that the collection is about 2,300 lines long, much too big to fit into a single *volumen*; second, that the dedication poem refers to *nugae*, 'trivialities', and cannot therefore serve to introduce a collection containing poem 64 and the other long poems; and third, that the ordering of the poems makes no sense, chronological or thematic, and therefore cannot have been designed by the poet himself.

The third argument, which usually resolves itself into the supposed impossibility of poem 11 coming before poem 51,[9] is naturally the weakest, since it depends on subjective judgement. (I think it also depends on a misreading of poem 51.) Chapter V offers an interpretation, for what it is worth, that assumes the order is Catullus' own; the reader must judge for himself whether that assumption is plausible or not. At any rate, the view that the poems are in a meaningful order is not, I think, self-evidently absurd.

The other two arguments seem more formidable. But already in 1885

[7] Cf. Cic. *Att.* II 1.8. For the political necessity of Murena's acquittal (a major part of Cicero's argument), see *Mur.* 3–6, 49–53, 78–86.

[8] Wiseman 1969, 1–31 and 1979, 175–82; polemical observations also in *JRS* 69 (1979) 166f.

[9] E.g. (most recently) Goold 1983, 238 and 246: poem 11 'designedly composed in the metre of his first poem to her (51, which we are presumed to recognise . . .)'; poem 51 'was the earlier of Catullus' two Sapphic odes . . . That the poem should be placed so late in Catullus' collected works (especially later than 11, which was written in repudiation of it) is misleading and inappropriate.'

Emil Baehrens suggested that the collection was composed of three volumes, comprising poems 1–60 (about 900 lines, allowing for some losses in our manuscript tradition), 61–64 (about 840 lines, same proviso), and 65–116 (about 660 lines); and that the dedication poem referred to the first only.[10] Baehrens made things unnecessarily complicated with his view that Catullus published only one of these volumes, the second and third being posthumous, but that does not invalidate his main point. The natural breaks in the collection, where the long poems begin and where the elegiac poems begin, divide it into lengths entirely appropriate for three papyrus rolls. That a literary work might consist of several *volumina* in one box (*capsa*, τεῦχος) is both attested in the ancient sources[11] and inferred by textual critics to account for dislocations of order when the rolls were transcribed into a single *codex*.[12]

In 1972, Kenneth Quinn argued the case for a three-volume collection, pointing out that *tribus chartis* at 1.6 (referring to Cornelius Nepos' *Chronika*) might count as evidence for it. Recent interpretations of poem 1 had emphasised the programmatic nature of the virtues Catullus ascribed to Nepos' work (*doctrina* and *labor*); so, as Quinn pointed out, 'size is in that case one of the things that Cornelius' History and Catullus' Collected Poems have in common – both three volumes'.[13] Since each of the three putative volumes opens with a reference to one of the Muses (1.9, 61.2) or all of them (65.2f),[14] the Baehrens–Quinn hypothesis seems more likely to be right than not.

The onus of proof has always been with those who believe that the collection as we have it cannot be Catullus' own work; since their arguments are not, after all, compelling, we may gratefully accept the order of the poems in our collection as evidence for how Catullus wanted them read.

3. VERANIUS

Catullus' friend, with the inseparable Fabullus, had been in Spain on the

---

[10] Baehrens 1885, 57–61.

[11] E.g. Crinagoras 7 G–P = *Anth. Pal.* IX 239 (5 books of Anacreon), Phot. *Bibl.* 77 = I 159f Henry (2 books of Eunapius), Porph. *Sat.* I 4.21.

[12] See M. W. Haslam, *LCM* I (1976) 9f, using Demosthenes as an example.

[13] Quinn 1972, 9–20 (quotation from p. 19); for the programmatic interpretation of poem I, see Cairns 1969 and the bibliography cited at Wiseman 1979, 171 nn.33–4.

[14] See also pp. 183f above, on the Callimachean allusions at 1.9f, 61.1f and 65.16.

staff of an unknown Piso.[15] He was a young man of scholarly habits
(9.6–8, 'ut mos est tuus'), and three sets of references to an author (or
authors) on various learned subjects may perhaps be combined as
evidence for his work.

First, a Veranius who wrote on religious antiquities.[16] Festus cites a
work on electoral auspices, Macrobius one (or two) on the *pontifices* and
their formulae.[17]

Second, Veranius Flaccus, one of the authors cited by Octavian in an
argument with Antony about literary style:[18]

> Tuque dubitas, Cimberne Annius ac Veranius Flaccus imitandi sint
> tibi, ita ut verbis quae Crispus Sallustius excerpsit ex Originibus
> Catonis uteris, an potius Asiaticorum oratorum inanibus sententiis
> verborum volubilitas in nostrum sermonem transferenda?

> Can't you decide whether to imitate Annius Cimber and Veranius
> Flaccus, and use words Sallustius Crispus borrowed from Cato's
> *Origins*, or to translate into Latin the meaningless wordiness of the
> Asiatic orators?

Annius Cimber (a friend of Antony) was an Atticist and an archaiser;
the logic of the sentence requires that Veranius Flaccus was too.[19]

Third, an author cited by Quintilian on the question of the elided *s*.
Servius Sulpicius Rufus thought final *s* should be dropped before a
word beginning with another consonant, a practice objected to by
'Luranius' but defended by Messalla.[20] For LVRANIVS, an unattested
name, Bergk read VERANIVS, which is very attractive (perhaps L.
V‹E›RANIVS?). The younger Sulpicius Rufus was a literary scholar as well
as a great orator.[21] So too was Messalla Corvinus, who wrote a whole

[15] Cat. 9; 12.14–17; 28; 47. Not Macedonia: Wiseman 1969, 38–40 and *JRS* 69 (1979)
162f.

[16] Funaioli 1907, 429–33.

[17] Festus 366L, 'Veranius in eo qui est auspiciorum de comitiis'; Macr. *Sat.* III 20.2,
'Veranius de verbis pontificalibus'; ibid. III 5.6, 'Veranius in pontificalibus quaestioni-
bus'. Untitled fragments at Fest. 148L, 152L, 221L (Paulus), 222L, 296L, 298L, Macr.
Sat. III 2.3.

[18] Suet. *Aug.* 86.3; in the first line, *ac* is Bentley's emendation for *an* in the MSS.

[19] J. Fairweather, *Seneca the Elder* (Cambridge 1981) 243f and 302. For Annius, see
Catalepton 2 with Quint. VIII 3.28.

[20] Quint. IX 4.83.

[21] Cic. *Brut.* 153, 'litterarum scientia et loquendi elegantia'; R. Syme, *CQ* 31 (1981)
421–7.

book about the letter *s*; he was a stylistic purist, a translator of the Attic orators and author of Attic poetry.[22] The two men were respectively brother-in-law and half-brother of Catullus' friend (and later enemy) Gellius.[23] It was in a poem addressed to Gellius that Catullus pointedly admitted an elided *s* (116.8, p. 185 above), alluding perhaps to a literary dispute of which the details escape us.

Are all three items to be combined into a single character, called perhaps L. Veranius Flaccus, with linguistic interests ranging into religious and constitutional antiquarianism at one end and the controversies of oratorical style at the other? A very similar question of identity applies to another of Catullus' friends, the poet Q. Cornificius, later well known as an Atticising orator with a taste for Stoic philosophy: was he also the Cornificius who wrote on religious etymology? Elizabeth Rawson argues very plausibly that he was.[24] For both Veranius and Cornificius, the better-attested cases of Cornelius Nepos, Trebatius, Pollio, Calvus and Catullus himself (pp. 196–8 above) encourage belief in a single author with wide-ranging literary interests.

Like the Rubellii of Tibur, the Caecinae of Volaterrae and the Valerii Catulli of Verona, the Veranii (Sabine or Umbrian, perhaps) rose from literary distinction in the first century B.C. to political influence at a high level under the Julio-Claudians.[25] There would have been an empress Verania if Galba's chosen heir had been able to succeed him.[26] As it turned out, the most distinguished lady of the family was Verania the Vestal Virgin, supposedly one of the original pair appointed to their holy office by Numa himself (Plut. *Numa* 10.1). It looks as if Veranius, like Rubellius Blandus and A. Caecina, turned his attention

---

[22] Quint. 1 7.23; Suet. *Tib.* 70.1, Sen. *contr.* II 4.8, cf. Hor. *Sat.* I 10.85 etc.; Quint. x 5.2 (orators), *Catalepton* 9.14 ('carmina cum lingua tum sale Cecropio'). He was 'in verbis magis elaboratus' than Cicero (Tac. *dial.* 18.2), so not an Atticist proper.

[23] See Wiseman 1974, 128 for the stemma.

[24] Rawson 1978, esp. 192–4; Funaioli 1907, 473–80. One fragment (Serv. *Aen.* III 332) attributes to him the *cognomen* Longus.

[25] On *domi nobiles* moving from literary to political prominence (the Passieni, origin unknown, are another example), see Syme 1982, 78f; Syme 1983, 107–15 (q.v. for the Q. Veranius who was tutor to the elder Drusus); Wiseman 1983, 306. Rubellii: Syme 1982, passim. Caecinae: E. Rawson, *JRS* 68 (1978) 137f (cf. above p. 95 n.12). Veranii: Syme 1979, 333–5 = *CQ* 7 (1957) 123–5.

[26] *CIL* VI 31723, Tac. *Hist.* I 14f (wife of L. Piso); *AE* 1953 251 for the *cos.* A.D. 49, adlected into the patricians by Claudius and legate of Britain under Nero.

to legendary history.[27] His disquisition on the peoples of Spain was expected to be historical as well as geographical – 'loca, *facta*, nationes' (Cat. 9.7).

4. VARRO ON CYBELE

Of all Varro's Menippean satires, only the *Eumenides*, with 49 surviving fragments, offers us the hope of being able to reconstruct the plot. In fact, the hope is delusive, as is shown by the wide variety of reconstructions different scholars have offered.[28] The detailed commentary of Jean-Pierre Cèbe has now opened a new era in the study of the Menippeans;[29] unfortunately, however, I think his account of the *Eumenides* is mistaken in one fundamental respect.

Cèbe believes that the action of the satire takes place in Greece. Some of his arguments simply underestimate the degree of cultural hellenisation in late-Republican Rome,[30] or take too literally what may be mere allusions.[31] His strongest point is the reference to the Dionysia at fragment 130 (142B); but Varro puts that into the mouth of a certain Scantius, who could easily be a pretentiously over-hellenised Roman like Albucius (mentioned at fragment 151 = 127B).[32] The Roman names are a problem for Cèbe – not only Scantius and Albucius, but Flora the high-class prostitute (ex-mistress of the young Pompey), and

[27] Cf. Serv. *Georg.* 1 103 (Rubellius Blandus *historicus*), Schol. Ver. *Aen.* x 200 (Caecina on the foundation of Mantua).
[28] See Cèbe 1977, 748–54, conveniently summarising ten reconstructions from Vahlen in 1858 to Marzullo in 1958; ibid. 548–55 for those of Bolisani (1936), Mosca (1937) and Cèbe himself. Cf. also F. Della Corte, *La poesia di Varrone reatino ricostruita* (Turin 1938) 46–8; O. Weinreich, *Römische Satiren* (Zurich 1962) 43–50; M. Coffey, *Roman Satire* (London 1976) 156f; W. Krenkel, *Römische Satiren* (Darmstadt 1976) 68–72; D. Romano, *Atti del congresso internazionale di studi varroniani* II (Rieti 1976) 497–9. Unfortunately the *Eumenides* did not attract Mommsen in his long footnote on the Menippean satires: *Römische Geschichte* (ed. 8, Berlin 1889) III 609–11.
[29] Cèbe 1977, the fourth volume of a series begun in 1972 and still in progress.
[30] E.g. Cèbe 1977, 559–61 on philosophical clubs, hunting, and the cult of Serapis; it is quite arbitrary to declare that the temple of Serapis mentioned by Catullus (10.26) must have been an innovation of the early fifties, inappropriate to Rome ten or twenty years earlier.
[31] E.g. Cèbe 1977, 558 on refuge at the altar (inevitable in a satire called *Eumenides*?); 684f on Diogenes' jar next to the Stoa (surely metonymic for the two sects rather than the actual vessel and the actual building) – where in any case the context may be realistic, not philosophical at all (Macr. *Sat.* III 16.15 for street-corner pots).
[32] Cèbe 1977, 558; cf. 690f on Albucius (Cic. *Brut.* 131, *de fin.* I 9).

Naples as the centre for luxury fish-ponds. These have to be explained away, as does the item which is surely fatal to Cèbe's thesis – the aedile at fragment 134 (150B).[33]

As Mommsen long ago pointed out, '*aedilis* is nowhere attested in the sense of *aedituus*, least of all in the seriously corrupt Varro fragment'. Cèbe has to rely on two late glosses, which are probably mere etymological guesswork; the inscriptions he cites refer to priesthoods in Italian towns, derived from the Roman magistracy and certainly no evidence for sacristans in Greek temples.[34] The *Thesaurus* offers no parallel in any Latin author for *aedilis* in the sense Cèbe's theory requires.[35] So the emendation and interpretation of the fragment must depend on the presence of the aedile, and not vice versa; in particular, the meaningless *essena hora nam* of the Nonius manuscripts should be corrected not to *messem hornam* (Lachmann), but to *e scena coronam* (Scaliger),[36] a brilliant emendation which gives the aedile, who was in charge of the *ludi scaenici*, an intelligible role in the ceremony of the Galli.[37]

The action of the satire should therefore be set in Rome, and the Cybele episode at the temple on the Palatine at the time of the Megalesia. The twelve fragments of the episode are given below, in the order convincingly argued by Cèbe;[38] in several places, however, my text and interpretation differ substantially from his.

– 132 (149B, 138 Bolisani, 117 Della Corte): Nonius 849L; prose.

iens domum praeter matris deum aedem exaudio cymbalorum sonitum.

iens *Buecheler*: en *MSS*   matris *Iunius*: matrem *MSS*

Going home past the temple of the Mother of the Gods, I distinctly hear the sound of cymbals.

[33] Cèbe 1977, 564; cf. 593 (Flora), 626 (aedile), 728 (*infamia*), 745 (*forenses*).
[34] T. Mommsen, *Römische Staatsrecht* II.1 (ed. 3, Leipzig 1887) 479 n.1; Cèbe 1977, 626 (*CGL* v 619, III 238).
[35] *TLL* I 932f; for Varro on *aedituus* and *aeditumus* (not, of course, *aedilis*), see *RR* I 2.1.
[36] Usually attributed to Buecheler, but wrongly: see H. Nettleship, *JPh* 21 (1893) 225.
[37] See Wiseman 1974, 159f on *exuviae* at the theatre.
[38] Fragments numbered according to his edition; I also give the Buecheler, Bolisani and Della Corte numbers (E. Bolisani, *Varrone menippeo* (Padua 1936) 74–94; F. Della Corte, *Varronis Menippearum fragmenta* (Genoa 1953) 25–35, 175–83).

– 133 (155B, 152 Bolisani, 155 Della Corte): Nonius 383L; prose.

stolam calceosque muliebris propter positos capio.
positos *Iunius*: positas *MSS*
I take a dress and some women's slippers that had been put down
nearby.

– 134 (150B, 140 Bolisani, 118 Della Corte): Nonius 171L; prose.

cum illoc venio, video gallorum frequentiam in templo, qui dum e
scena coronam adlatam imponeret aedilis signo deae, eam gallantes
vario recinebant studio.
e scena coronam *Scaliger*: essena hora nam *MSS*   signo deae eam *Madvig*: signosiae et
deam *MSS*   recinebant *Mueller*: retinebant *MSS*
When I get there, I see a crowd of Galli in the temple, raving about and
hymning the goddess in enthusiastic confusion, while the aedile placed
on her statue the crown brought from the theatre.

– 135 (119B, 139 Bolisani, 123 Della Corte): Nonius 171L, 408L, 618L;
iambic senarii.

> nam quae venustas his adest gallantibus!
> quae casta vestis aetasque adulescentium!
> quae teneris species!
> > his *Salmasius*: hic *MSS*
> What grace these holy ravers have!
> How chaste their costume and their youth!
> How delicate their beauty!

– 136 (120B, 146 Bolisani, 124 Della Corte): Nonius 862L; iambic
senarius.

> partim venusta muliebri ornati stola.
> > ornati *Ribbeck*: ornat *MSS*
> Some decked out in elegant ladies' dresses.

– 137 (130B, 141 Bolisani, 134 Della Corte): Nonius 377L; dactylic
pentameter?

> ut Naides undicolae.
> Like Naiads that inhabit the waves.

– 138 (121B, 147 Bolisani, 125 Della Corte): Nonius 836L, 867L, 881L;
iambic senarii, dactylic pentameter?

271

aurorat ostrinum hic indutus supparum,
coronam ex auro et gemmis fulgentem gerit,
luce locum afficiens.
He shines like the dawn in his long purple robe,
he wears a crown of gold that gleams with jewels,
filling the place with light.

– 139 (131B, 142 Bolisani, 135 Della Corte): Nonius 347L, 526L;
galliambic.

Phrygius per ossa cornus liquida canit anima.
The Phrygian horn sings through the bones with its liquid breath.

– 140 (132B, 143 Bolisani, 136 Della Corte): Nonius 70L, 515L;
galliambics.

tibi typana non inanis sonitus matri' deum
tonimus ‹chorus› tibi nos; tibi nunc semiviri
teretem comam volantem iactant tibi famuli.
typana *Hermann*: tympana *MSS*   chorus *add. Buecheler*   famili *Buecheler*: galli *MSS*
For you we thunder the tambourines (no empty sound),
we the chorus of the Mother of the Gods, for you; for you the
half-male servants toss their smooth hair flying, for you.

– 141 (140B, 145 Bolisani, 144 Della Corte): Nonius 783L; prose.

pruditatem ac pudorem gallum, coepit, mihi vide sis.
vide sis *Riese*: videri *MSS*
'Please', he began, 'see the good sense and good morals of the Galli.'

– 142 (133B, 151 Bolisani, 137 Della Corte): Nonius 70L, 177L; iambic
septenarius.

apage in dierectum a domo nostra istam insanitatem.
Away! to hell with it, far from my home, that madness!

– 143 (151B, 150 Bolisani, 119 Della Corte): Nonius 145L; prose.

ubi vident se cantando ex ara excantare non posse, deripere incipiunt.
When they see they can't exorcise me from the altar by chanting, they
start to pull me down.

BIBLIOGRAPHY

ADAMS, J. N. (1982)   *The Latin Sexual Vocabulary*, London (Duckworth)

ADLER, E. (1981)   *Catullan Self-Revelation*, New York (Arno Press)

AUSTIN, R. G. (1952)   *M. Tulli Ciceronis pro M. Caelio oratio*, Oxford (Clarendon Press), 2nd ed.

BADIAN, E. (1964)   *Studies in Greek and Roman History*, Oxford (Blackwell)

(1965)   'M. Porcius Cato and the annexation and early administration of Cyprus', *Journal of Roman Studies* 55:110–21

(1967)   'The testament of Ptolemy Alexander', *Rheinisches Museum* 110:178–92

(1968)   *Roman Imperialism in the Late Republic*, Oxford (Blackwell), 2nd ed.

BAEHRENS, A. (1885)   *Catulli Veronensis liber*, Leipzig (Teubner), vol. II

BAKER, R. J. (1975)   'Domina at Catullus 68.68: mistress or châtelaine?', *Rheinisches Museum* 118:124–9

BONGI, V. (1944)   *Catullo, Attis (Carme 63)*, Florence (le Monnier)

BOWRA, C. M. (1961)   *Greek Lyric Poetry*, Oxford (Clarendon Press), 2nd ed.

BRAUND, D. (1983)   'Royal wills and Rome', *Papers of the British School at Rome* 51:16–57

(1984)   *Rome and the Friendly King: the Character of Client Kingship*, London (Croom Helm)

BRUNT, P. A. (1971)   *Italian Manpower 225 B.C.–A.D. 14*, Oxford (Clarendon Press)

CAIRNS, F. (1969)   'Catullus 1', *Mnemosyne* 22:153–8

(1972)   *Generic Composition in Greek and Roman Poetry*, Edinburgh (University Press)

(1975)   'Catullus 27', *Mnemosyne* 28:24–9

(1984)   'Propertius and the Battle of Actium (4.6)', *Poetry and*

Politics in the Age of Augustus (ed. T. Woodman and D. West, Cambridge), 129–68

CAMERON, A. (1976) *Circus Factions: Blues and Greens at Rome and Byzantium*, Oxford (Clarendon Press)

CARILLI, M. (1975) 'Le nugae di Catullo e l'epigramma greco', *Annali della Scuola normale di Pisa* 5:925–53

CÈBE, J.-P. (1977) *Varron, Satires Ménippées*, Rome (École française), vol. 4

CIACERI, E. (1929–30) 'Il processo di M. Celio Rufo e l'arringa di Cicerone', *Atti della reale Accademia di archeologia, lettere e belle arti di Napoli* 11:3–24

CLASSEN, C. J. (1973) 'Ciceros Rede für Caelius', *Aufstieg und Niedergang der römischen Welt* I 3 (ed. H. Temporini, Berlin & New York) 60–94

COARELLI, F. (1965–7) 'Il tempio di Bellona', *Bullettino della Commissione archeologica comunale in Roma* 80:37–72

COARELLI, F. et al. (1982) *Delo e l'Italia*, Rome (Bardi)

COMMAGER, S. (1965) 'Notes on some poems of Catullus', *Harvard Studies in Classical Philology* 70:83–110

CRANSTOUN, J. (1867) *The Poems of Valerius Catullus translated into English Verse*, Edinburgh (W. P. Nimmo)

CRAWFORD, M. (1974) *Roman Republican Coinage*, Cambridge (University Press)

    (1977) 'Rome and the Greek world: economic relationships', *Economic History Review* 30:42–52

DALY, L. W. (1952) 'Callimachus and Catullus', *Classical Philology* 47:97–9

D'ARMS, J. (1970) *Romans on the Bay of Naples*, Cambridge, Mass. (Harvard University Press)

    (1981) *Commerce and Social Standing in Ancient Rome*, Cambridge, Mass. (Harvard University Press)

DELLA CORTE, F. (1976) *Personaggi Catulliani*, Florence (La nuova Italia), 2nd ed.

DREXLER, H. (1944) 'Zu Ciceros Rede pro Caelio', *Nachrichten der Akademie der Wissenschaften in Göttingen* (1944) 1–32

ELLIS, R. (1878) *Catulli Veronensis liber*, Oxford (Clarendon Press), 2nd ed.

    (1889) *A Commentary on Catullus*, Oxford (Clarendon Press), 2nd ed.

FASCE, S. (1978) *Attis e il culto metroaco a Roma*, Genoa (Tilgher)

FERRERO, L. (1955) *Interpretazione di Catullo*, Turin (Rosenberg & Sellier)

FORDYCE, C. J. (1961) *Catullus, a Commentary*, Oxford (Clarendon Press)

FORSYTH, P. Y. (1976) 'Catullus, the mythic persona', *Latomus* 35:555–66

(1977) 'The Ameana cycle of Catullus', *Classical World* 70:445–50

(1980) 'Catullus 64: Dionysus reconsidered', *Studies in Latin Literature and Roman History* II (ed. C. Deroux, Brussels) 98–105

FRASER, P. M. (1972) *Ptolemaic Alexandria*, Oxford (Clarendon Press)

FRIEDRICH, G. (1908) *Catulli Veronensis liber*, Leipzig & Berlin (Teubner)

FUNAIOLI, H. (1907) *Grammaticae Romanae Fragmenta*, Leipzig (Teubner)

GIANCOTTI, F. (1967) *Mimo e gnome: studio su Decimo Laberio e Publilio Siro*, Messina & Florence (G. D'Anna)

GOOLD, G. P. (1983) *Catullus*, London (Duckworth)

GRANAROLO, J. (1982) *Catulle, ce vivant*, Paris (Les belles lettres)

GRIFFIN, J. (1976) 'Augustan poetry and the life of luxury', *Journal of Roman Studies* 66:87–105

GRUEN, E. S. (1973) 'The trial of C. Antonius', *Latomus* 32:301–10

(1974) *The Last Generation of the Roman Republic*, Berkeley (University of California Press)

HÄGG, T. (1983) *The Novel in Antiquity*, Oxford (Blackwell)

HARDIE, A. (1983) *Statius and the Silvae: Poets, Patrons and Epideixis in the Graeco-Roman World*, Liverpool (Francis Cairns)

HARRAUER, H. (1979) *A Bibliography to Catullus*, Hildesheim (Gerstenberg)

HARRINGTON, K. P. (1923) *Catullus and his Influence*, London (Harrap)

HAVELOCK, E. A. (1939) *The Lyric Genius of Catullus*, Oxford (Blackwell)

HEINZE, R. (1925) 'Ciceros Rede pro Caelio', *Hermes* 60:193–258

HELLY, B. (1983) 'Les italiens en Thessalie au IIe et au Ier s. av. J.-C.', *Les 'bourgeoisies' municipales italiennes aux IIe et Ier siècles av. J.-C.* (ed. M. Cébeillac-Gervasoni, Paris & Naples) 355–80

HELM, R. (1929) *Hieronymus' Zusätze in Eusebius' Chronik und ihr Wert für die Literaturgeschichte*, Leipzig (Dieterich)

275

HENRY, R. M. (1950–51) 'Pietas and fides in Catullus', Hermathena 75:63–8 and 76:48–57

HERTER, H. (1932) De Priapo, Giessen (Töpelmann)

HILLARD, T. W. (1981) 'In triclinio Coam, in cubiculo Nolam: Lesbia and the other Clodia', Liverpool Classical Monthly 6.6 (June 1981) 149–54

HOPKINS, K. (1983) Death and Renewal, Cambridge (University Press)

HORSFALL, N. (1979) 'Doctus sermones utriusque linguae?', Echos du monde classique/Classical News and Views 23:79–95

HOUSMAN, A. E. (1931) 'Praefanda', Hermes 66:402–12

JENKYNS, R. (1982) Three Classical Poets: Sappho, Catullus and Juvenal, London (Duckworth)

JOCELYN, H. D. (1980) 'A Greek indecency and its students', Proceedings of the Cambridge Philological Society 206:12–66

(1980a) 'On some unnecessarily indecent interpretations of Catullus 2 and 3', American Journal of Philology 101:421–41

KELLY, J. M. (1966) Roman Litigation, Oxford (Clarendon Press)

KIDD, D. A. (1963) 'The unity of Catullus 51', Aumla 20:298–308

KLINGNER, F. (1956) Catulls Peleus-Epos, Munich (Bayerische Akademie der Wissenschaften)

KROLL, W. (1923) C. Valerius Catullus, Leipzig (Teubner)

LAFAYE, G. (1894) Catulle et ses modèles, Paris (Imprimerie nationale)

LATTA, B. (1972) 'Zu Catulls Carmen 1', Museum Helveticum 29:201–13

LIEBESCHUETZ, J. H. W. G. (1979) Continuity and Change in Roman Religion, Oxford (Clarendon Press)

LINTOTT, A. W. (1968) Violence in Republican Rome, Oxford (Clarendon Press)

LYNE, R. O. A. M. (1979) 'Servitium amoris', Classical Quarterly 29:117–30

(1980) The Latin Love Poets from Catullus to Horace, Oxford (Clarendon Press)

MACLEOD, C. W. (1973) 'Catullus 116', Classical Quarterly 23:304–9

MACMULLEN, R. (1982) 'Roman attitudes to Greek love', Historia 31:484–502

MACNAGHTEN, H. (1899) The Story of Catullus, London (Duckworth)

MATTINGLY, H. and SYDENHAM, E. (1923) The Roman Imperial Coinage, London (Spink & Son), vol. I

MAYER, R. (1983) 'Catullus' divorce', Classical Quarterly 33:297–8

MCKEOWN, J. C. (1979) 'Augustan elegy and mime', *Proceedings of the Cambridge Philological Society* 205:71–84

MERKELBACH, R. (1957) 'Sappho und ihr Kreis', *Philologus* 101:1–29

MERRILL, E. T. (1893) *Catullus*, Boston (Ginn)

MORGAN, M. G. (1977) '*Nescioquid febriculosi scorti*: a note on Catullus 6', *Classical Quarterly* 27:338–41

MOST, G. W. (1981) 'On the arrangement of Catullus' carmina maiora', *Philologus* 125:109–25

MUELLER, L. (1869) 'Der Mimograph Catullus', *Rheinisches Museum* 24:621–2

MÜNZER, F. (1909) 'Aus dem Leben des M. Caelius Rufus', *Hermes* 44:135–42

(1920) *Römische Adelsparteien und Adelsfamilien*, Stuttgart (J. B. Metzler)

MYNORS, R. A. B. (1958) *C. Valerii Catulli carmina*, Oxford (Clarendon Press)

NÉMETH, B. (1977) 'To the evaluation of Catullus 116', *Acta Classica* (Debrecen) 13:23–31

NICOLET, C. (1974) *L'ordre équestre à l'époque républicaine (312–43 av. J.-C.)*, Paris (De Boccard), vol. 2

NICOLET, C. et al. (1980) *Insula Sacra: la loi Gabinia-Calpurnia de Délos (58 av. J.-C.)*, Rome (École française)

NISBET, R. G. M. (1978) 'Notes on the text of Catullus', *Proceedings of the Cambridge Philological Society* 204:92–115

PFEIFFER, R. (1968) *History of Classical Scholarship from the Beginnings to the End of the Hellenistic Age*, Oxford (Clarendon Press)

PUTNAM, M. C. J. (1961) 'The art of Catullus 64', *Harvard Studies in Classical Philology* 65:165–205

QUINN, K. (1970) *Catullus, the Poems*, London (Macmillan)

(1972) *Catullus: an Interpretation*, London (Batsford)

(1982) 'The poet and his audience in the Augustan age', *Aufstieg und Niedergang der römischen Welt* II 30.1 (ed. W. Haase, Berlin & New York) 75–180

RANKIN, H. D. (1976) 'Catullus and incest', *Eranos* 74:113–21

RAWSON, E. (1973) 'The eastern clientelae of Claudius and the Claudii', *Historia* 22:219–39

(1977) 'More on the clientelae of the patrician Claudii', *Historia* 26:340–57

(1978) 'The identity problems of Q. Cornificius', *Classical Quarterly* 28:188–201

REITZENSTEIN, R. (1925) 'Zu Ciceros Rede für Caelius', *Nachrichten von der Gesellschaft der Wissenschaften zu Göttingen* (1925) 25–32

REYNOLDS, R. W. (1943) 'Criticism of individuals in Roman popular comedy', *Classical Quarterly* 37:37–45
(1946) 'The adultery mime', *Classical Quarterly* 40:77–84

RICKMAN, G. (1980) *The Corn Supply of Ancient Rome*, Oxford (Clarendon Press)

ROSS, JR, D. O. (1969) *Style and Tradition in Catullus*, Cambridge, Mass. (Harvard University Press)

RUNDELL, W. M. F. (1979) 'Cicero and Clodius: the question of credibility', *Historia* 28:301–28

SANDY, G. N. (1968) 'The imagery of Catullus 63', *Transactions of the American Philological Association* 9:389–99

SCHÄFER, E. (1966) *Das Verhältnis von Erlebnis und Kunstgestalt bei Catull*, Wiesbaden (Franz Steiner)

SCHMIDT, B. (1887) *C. Valerii Catulli Veronensis carmina*, Leipzig (Tauchnitz)

SCHMIDT, E. A. (1973) 'Catulls Anordnung seiner Gedichte', *Philologus* 117:215–42

SCHMIDT, V. (1983) 'La *ruina* du mime Mnester: à propos de Suetone, *Cal.*, 57,4', *Latomus* 42:156–60

SCHWABE, L. (1862) *Quaestiones Catullianae*, Giessen (I. Ricker)
(1886) *Catulli Veronensis liber*, Berlin (Weidmann)

SCULLARD, H. H. (1981) *Festivals and Ceremonies of the Roman Republic*, London (Thames & Hudson)

SEGAL, C. P. (1970) 'Catullan otiosi: the lover and the poet', *Greece & Rome* 17:25–31

SHACKLETON BAILEY, D. R. (1965–68) *Cicero's Letters to Atticus*, Cambridge (University Press)
(1977) 'Brothers or cousins?', *American Journal of Ancient History* 2:148–50
(1977a) *Cicero: epistulae ad familiares*, Cambridge (University Press)

SHATZMAN, I. (1971) 'The Egyptian Question in Roman politics (59–54 B.C.)', *Latomus* 30:363–9

SHERK, R. K. (1969) *Roman Documents from the Greek East*, Baltimore (Johns Hopkins Press)

SKINNER, M. (1981)   *Catullus' Passer: the Arrangement of the Book of Polymetric Poems*, New York (Arno Press)

SUMNER, G. V. (1971)   'The Lex Annalis under Caesar', *Phoenix* 25:246–71, 357–71

(1973)   *The Orators in Cicero's Brutus: Prosopography and Chronology*, Toronto (University Press)

SYME, R. (1939)   *The Roman Revolution*, Oxford (Clarendon Press)

(1979)   *Roman Papers*, Oxford (Clarendon Press)

(1982)   'The marriage of Rubellius Blandus', *American Journal of Philology* 103:62–85

(1983)   'Eight consuls from Patavium', *Papers of the British School at Rome* 51:102–24

THOMSON, D. F. S. (1978)   *Catullus: a Critical Edition*, Chapel Hill (University of North Carolina Press)

TREGGIARI, S. (1969)   *Roman Freedmen during the Late Republic*, Oxford (Clarendon Press)

TUPLIN, C. J. (1977)   'Cantores Euphorionis', *Papers of the Liverpool Latin Seminar* (ed. Francis Cairns, Liverpool) 1–23

(1979)   'Cantores Euphorionis again', *Classical Quarterly* 29:358–60

(1981)   'Catullus 68', *Classical Quarterly* 31:113–39

ULLMAN, B. L. (1960)   'The transmission of the text of Catullus', *Studi in onore di Luigi Castiglioni* (Florence, Sansoni) 1027–57

USSANI, V. (1902–3)   'Catullo mimografo e uno scolio lucaneo', *Bollettino di filologia classica* 9:63–4

VERMASEREN, M. J. (1977)   *Cybele and Attis: the Myth and the Cult*, London (Thames & Hudson)

VESSEY, D. W. T. C. (1971)   'Thoughts on two poems of Catullus: 13 and 30', *Latomus* 30:45–55

WALBANK, F. W. (1960)   'History and tragedy', *Historia* 9.216–34

WEINREICH, O. (1959)   'Catull c. 60', *Hermes* 87:75–90

WHEELER, A. L. (1934)   *Catullus and the Traditions of Ancient Poetry*, Berkeley (University of California Press)

WISEMAN, T. P. (1969)   *Catullan Questions*, Leicester (University Press)

(1970)   'Pulcher Claudius', *Harvard Studies in Classical Philology* 74:207–21

(1971)   *New Men in the Roman Senate 139 B.C.–A.D. 14*, Oxford (University Press)

(1974)   *Cinna the Poet and other Roman Essays*, Leicester (University Press)

(1975) 'Clodia: some imaginary lives', *Arion* n.s. 2/1:96–115

(1976) 'Catullus 16', *Liverpool Classical Monthly* 1:14–17

(1979) *Clio's Cosmetics: Three Studies in Greco-Roman Literature*, Leicester (University Press)

(1982) '*Pete nobiles amicos*: poets and patrons in late-Republican Rome', *Literary and Artistic Patronage in Ancient Rome* (ed. B. K. Gold, Austin, Texas) 28–49

(1983) '*Domi nobiles* and the Roman cultural elite', *Les 'bourgeoisies' municipales italiennes aux IIe et Ier siècles av. J.-C.* (ed. M. Cébeillac-Gervasoni, Paris & Naples) 299–307

(1986) 'The masters of Sirmio', to appear in *Roman Studies, Literary and Historical*, Liverpool (Francis Cairns)

ZICÀRI, M. (1965) 'Sul primo carme di Catullo', *Maia* 17:232–40

INDEX OF PASSAGES

INDEX OF PASSAGES

GENERAL INDEX

Aemilius Lepidus, Mam. (*cos.* 77)   203f
Albucius, T., overhellenised
  Roman   269
Alexandria   54–60;   mimes from   35
Alfenus, in Catullus   122f, 148
Allinson, Mrs Anne C. (née
  Emery)   221–3, 233
Allius, in Catullus   159f, 163f
Annius Cimber, archaic stylist   267
Annius Milo, T. (*pr.* 55)   33, 37
Antiodemis, dancing girl   35
Antonius, C. (*cos.* 63), trial of   42, 64
Antonius, M. (*cos.* 44) extravagance
  of   102
Aquinus, bad poet and business man   95
Archias, *see* Licinius
argumenta   70, 81
Asia, reputation of   263
Asicius, P., assassin   62, 73, 81
Asinius Pollio, C. (*cos.* 40)   197, 268
astrology   140
Atratinus, *see* Sempronius
Atticus, *see* Pomponius
Attis, myth of   202f, 206
Aufillena, in Catullus   105, 122, 133
Augustus, marriage legislation of   113f
Aurelius, in Catullus   5, 123f, 134, 142,
  144f, 166
Aurunculeia, wedding of   112–16
Avillii of Lanuvium   93

Baring, Maurice   226, 232
Baxter, James K.   243f
Bellona, temple of   21, 26
Benton, Kenneth   233
Bestia, *see* Calpurnius
Bunting, Basil   243
Burton, Sir Richard   228

Caecilia Metella, daughter of Clodia   51,
  53
Caecilius, in Catullus   148

Caecilius Metellus Celer, Q. (*cos.*
  60)   19, 24, 49–51;   death of   24f, 42,
  89, 216
Caecinae of Volaterrae   95, 100, 268
Caelius, in Catullus   173
Caelius Rufus, M. (*pr.* 48)   42, 62–8, 90f;
  character of   65f, 71f, 75;   Palatine
  apartment   25, 64;   trial of   24f, 28f,
  68–90
Caesar, *see* Iulius
Callimachus, poet of Alexandria   183f,
  186
Calpurnius Bestia, L., father of
  Atratinus   67f, 73, 79
Calpurnius Piso Caesoninus, L. (*cos.*
  58)   2, 158
Calpurnius Piso Frugi, L., proconsul in
  Spain?   2
Calventius of Placentia   158
Calvus, *see* Licinius
Carducci, Giosue   213, 234
carnifices   7f
Cato, *see* Porcius
Catullus, *see* Valerius
Chateaubriand, François René de   213
children, invisibility of   23
Cicero, *see* Tullius
Cimbri, invasion by   107f
Claudia, Q., as example of excellence   36
Claudii, patrician *gens*: clients of   36,
  40f; connections of   18–20;   *potentia*
  of   38f, 81
Claudius, Ap. (*cos.* 495)   17f, 21
Claudius Caecus, Ap. (*cos.* 307)   15, 20f,
  84
Claudius Pulcher, Ap. (*cos.* 79)   21f, 23f
Claudius Pulcher, Ap. (*cos.* 54)   22f
Claudius Pulcher, C. (*cos.* 92)   18, 36
Claudius Pulcher, C. (*pr.* 56)   22, 36
Clodia Luculli   2, 19, 22
Clodia Metelli   2, 15–53, 136;   character
  of   39, 52, 76, 83–7;   as dancer   27f,

284

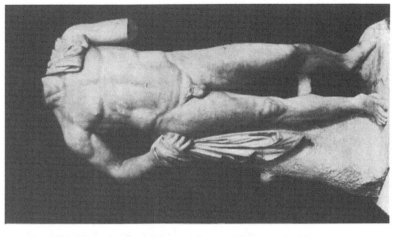

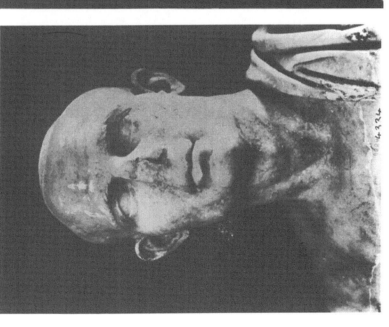

1 Delos: portrait head and heroic body. (Now National Museum, Athens.)

2 Delos: a Roman business man. (In situ.)

3 Rome: the *sala delle maschere* in the 'House of Augustus' on the
Palatine. (In situ.)

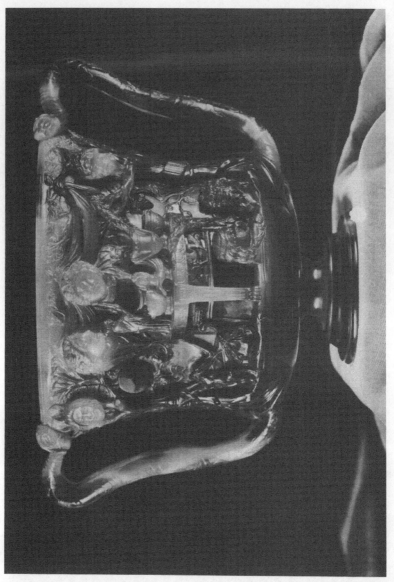

4 The 'tasse des Ptolémées', cameo carved sardonyx. (Bibliothèque Nationale, Paris.)

1093659R0

Printed in Great Britain by
Amazon.co.uk, Ltd.,
Marston Gate.